Personal Reminiscences
of General Robert E. Lee

Personal Reminiscences
of General Robert E. Lee

Rev. J. William Jones, D. D.

A TOM DOHERTY ASSOCIATES BOOK
NEW YORK

PERSONAL REMINISCENCES OF GENERAL ROBERT E. LEE

A Forge Book
Published by Tom Doherty Associates, LLC
175 Fifth Avenue
New York, NY 10010

www.tor.com

Forge® is a registered trademark of Tom Doherty Associates, LLC.

Library of Congress Cataloging-in-Publication Data

Jones, J. William (John William), 1836–1909.
    Personal reminiscences of General Robert E. Lee / J. William Jones.
        p. cm.
    Originally published: New York : D. Appleton, 1875.
    "A Forge book"—T.p. verso.
    ISBN 0-765-30584-4 (hc)
    ISBN 0-765-30604-2 (pbk)
    EAN 978-0-765-30604-3
    1. Lee, Robert E. (Robert Edward), 1807–1870. 2. Generals—Confederate States of
America—Biography. 3. Generals—United States—Biography. 4. Confederate States
of America. Army—Biography. I. Title.

E467.1.L4 J78   2003
973.7'3'092—dc21

                                                                                    2002035424

Printed in the United States of America

D 0 9 8 7 6 5 4 3

TO

<small>THE BELOVED MEMORY</small>

<small>OF</small>

MRS. MARY CUSTIS LEE,

<small>BY WHOSE KIND ENCOURAGEMENT THIS WORK WAS UNDERTAKEN, AND WHOSE</small>

<small>VALUABLE AID HAS ENRICHED ITS PAGES,</small>

THIS BOOK

<small>IS AFFECTIONATELY DEDICATED</small>

<small>BY</small>

THE AUTHOR

Preface

The author does not propose to add another "Life of Lee" to the several that have been given to the public.

Mine is a humbler but scarcely less important work.

It was my proud privilege to have known General Lee intimately. I saw him on that day in April 1861, on which he came to offer his stainless sword to the land that gave him birth. I followed his standard from Harper's Ferry, in 1861, to Appomattox Courthouse, in 1865, coming into somewhat frequent contact with him, rejoicing with him at his long series of brilliant victories, and weeping with him when "compelled to yield to overwhelming numbers and resources."

It was my still higher privilege to have been intimately associated with him during the last five years of his career, to have been one of the regular chaplains of his college, to have visited him frequently at his office and in his home, and to have had him sometimes under my own humble roof; to have mingled with him in the freest social intercourse, and to have been the daily witness of those beautiful traits of character which made him seem even grander in peace than in war.

I was one of that band of loving hearts whose sad privilege it was to bear him to the tomb, when two continents mourned his death. And I have enjoyed some peculiar facilities for knowing the events of his life, and studying his private character.

It has been for me, therefore, a "labor of love," and one which, I trust, will not seem presumptuous or prove wholly unacceptable to the public, to recall a few personal reminiscences, cull a few anecdotes, and give a few of his private letters, which may present a picture of ROBERT E. LEE, THE MAN, as he lived and moved, and was loved, among us.

A large part of this book was originally prepared for the "Lee memorial volume," which the faculty of Washington and Lee University designed publishing, and which I had the honor of assisting in preparing; and Mrs.

Lee did me the kindness to read carefully, and very warmly approve, my manuscript.

When the publication of that volume was abandoned, and I proposed, with the consent of the faculty, to use the material in a book of my own, Mrs. Lee wrote me a kind letter in which she said: ". . . Whatever the Faculty decide upon will, I know, meet with my approbation, and to no one would I more confidently trust the completion of the work, in the way you propose, than to yourself." Mrs. Lee was very much interested in the proposed publication, and I feel that, in giving this volume to the public, I am but carrying out her earnest wishes.

I was especially indebted to Mrs. Lee, and have been placed under high obligations to General G. W. Custis Lee, and General W. H. F. Lee, for the letters which form so interesting and valuable a part of this volume. My thanks are also due to the faculty of Washington and Lee University, not only for kind encouragement, but for invaluable assistance in the preparation of the work.

Everything of doubtful authenticity has been excluded from these pages, and the reader will, therefore, miss a number of popular anecdotes which he would expect to find.

This first attempt at authorship is sent forth with a sincere desire that it may prove acceptable to the countless admirers of the great Confederate chieftain, that it may serve to give to all a higher appreciation of his noble character, and that it may prove a blessing to the young men of the country (more especially to those who wore the gray), by inducing them to study, in order that they may imitate, his shining virtues.

J. W. J.
RICHMOND, VA., *August* 1, 1874.

Note

A t the death of General Lee a memorial volume was announced, and this committee was appointed to superintend the publication. Circumstances, for which neither the committee nor the publishers were responsible, delayed and finally prevented the publication of that work. In the mean time, Rev. John William Jones had prepared this book to aid in the completion of Valentine's beautiful sepulchral monument to General Lee. Mr. Jones was a faithful chaplain in the army of General Lee, and, subsequently, while minister of the Baptist Church in Lexington, enjoyed in an unusual degree his favor and regard. During this period, and while acting at times as chaplain of Washington College, Mr. Jones had special opportunities to observe the character of General Lee, for whom he entertained an enthusiastic devotion. The committee, knowing the peculiar qualifications which the author brings to this work, have afforded him the fullest access to the materials in their possession, and are happy now to commend to the public the completed volume as a valuable contribution toward a biography of Robert E. Lee.

Signed: COMMITTEE OF THE FACULTY
OF WASHINGTON AND LEE UNIVERSITY.

Contents

Chapter IV

HIS MODEST HUMILITY, SIMPLICITY, AND GENTLENESS

SIMPLICITY OF HIS DRESS—LACK OF DISPLAY AT HIS HEADQUAR-
TERS—INCIDENTS ILLUSTRATING HIS MODESTY—COLONEL
CHARLES MARSHALL'S INCIDENTS OF CHANCELLORSVILLE AND
GETTYSBURG—INCIDENTS ILLUSTRATING THE WARM FRIENDSHIP
BETWEEN LEE AND JACKSON—LETTERS—HIS CONDUCT TOWARD
HIS OTHER OFFICERS—THE ACCOUNT OF LEE AT GETTYSBURG
GIVEN BY COLONEL FREEMANTLE, OF THE ENGLISH ARMY—
ORDERS TO HIS TROOPS ISSUED AT HAGERSTOWN ON HIS RETREAT
FROM GETTYSBURG—INCIDENTS—EXTRACTS FROM PAPERS
FOUND IN HIS ARMY SATCHEL—INCIDENTS ILLUSTRATING HIS TEN-
DERNESS FOR BIRDS AND ANIMALS—LETTERS TO PARTIES DESIR-
ING TO WRITE HIS BIOGRAPHY.

Chapter V

HIS SPIRIT OF SELF-DENIAL FOR THE GOOD OF OTHERS

INCIDENT RELATED BY HON. A. H. STEPHENS—ABOUT TO GO INTO
THE RANKS AS A PRIVATE SOLDIER—EX-PRESIDENT DAVIS'S IN-
CIDENT—SELF-DENIAL OF HIS LIVING—NEVER USED TOBACCO OR
INTOXICATING LIQUORS—INCIDENTS—LETTER TO A COLLEGE
TEMPERANCE SOCIETY—STONEWALL JACKSON'S TEMPERANCE
PRINCIPLES—INCIDENT RELATED BY GENERAL EWELL—GENERAL
LEE'S "TREAT"—AN ENGLISH OFFICER'S ACCOUNT OF HIS VISIT
TO GENERAL LEE'S HEADQUARTERS—INCIDENTS ILLUSTRATING
HIS DEEP INTEREST IN HIS MEN—LETTER TO THE CITY COUNCIL
OF RICHMOND DECLINING THE GIFT OF A RESIDENCE—REFUSAL OF
GIFTS AT THE CLOSE OF THE WAR—SPECIMENS OF HIS LETTERS
DECLINING PECUNIARY ASSISTANCE—HIS REFUSAL TO ACCEPT A
LARGE SALARY, OR ANY GRATUITY FROM THE COLLEGE—HIS LET-
TERS ON THE SUBJECT—HIS OBJECT IN WRITING A HISTORY OF HIS
CAMPAIGNS TO VINDICATE OTHERS RATHER THAN HIMSELF—CIR-
CULAR LETTER—HIS WANT OF NEPOTISM—INCIDENTS ILLUSTRAT-
ING HIS REFUSAL TO PROMOTE HIS SONS—DR. MOORE'S INCIDENT
OF HIS REFUSAL TO APPLY FOR A SPECIAL EXCHANGE FOR HIS SON
WHEN IN PRISON.

Chapter VI

HIS WANT OF BITTERNESS TOWARD THE NORTH, BUT DEVOTION
TO THE INTERESTS OF THE SOUTH

INCIDENTS—HIS GENERAL ORDERS IN PENNSYLVANIA, AND
THE CONDUCT OF HIS TROOPS—INCIDENTS—TREATMENT OF

PRISONERS—HIS TESTIMONY BEFORE THE CONGRESSIONAL RE-
CONSTRUCTION COMMITTEE—PRIVATE LETTER TO DR. CARTER,
OF PHILADELPHIA—THE REAL FACTS IN REFERENCE TO THE
TREATMENT OF PRISONERS—INCIDENTS ILLUSTRATING HIS WANT
OF BITTERNESS—SPLENDID CONDUCT OF LEE'S VETERANS SINCE
THE CLOSE OF THE WAR, AND HIS INFLUENCE IN BRINGING IT
ABOUT—LETTERS TO GENERAL GRANT—HIS APPLICATION TO
PRESIDENT JOHNSON FOR "AMNESTY"—LETTERS TO COLONEL R.
L. MAURY, EX-GOVERNOR JOHN LETCHER, HON. A. M. KEILEY,
COUNT JOANNES, COMMODORE TATNALL, COMMODORE MAURY,
GENERAL BEAUREGARD, GENERAL WILCOX, CHAUNCEY BURR,
ESQ., HON. REVERDY JOHNSON, MRS. JEFFERSON DAVIS, REV. G.
W. LEYBURN, GENERAL EARLY, CAPTAIN JAMES MAY, JUDGE
ROBERT OULD, GENERAL D. H. MAURY, GENERAL JAMES LONG-
STREET, HON. J. S. BLACK, HON. THOMAS LAWRENCE JONES, COL-
ONEL BLANTON DUNCAN, HON. JAMES M. MASON, AND OTHERS—
HIS REFUSAL TO ATTEND MEETINGS HAVING ANY REFERENCE TO
THE WAR.

Chapter VII

SIMPLICITY OF HIS DRESS—"GIVEN TO HOSPITALITY"—UNIFORM
COURTESY—RETENTIVE MEMORY OF NAMES AND FACES—INCI-
DENTS—LETTERS TO FEDERAL OFFICERS—REPLY TO SPIRIT-
RAPPERS—INCIDENTS ILLUSTRATING HIS QUIET HUMOR—A
NUMBER OF HIS PRIVATE LETTERS.

Chapter VIII

INCIDENTS—HIS DEVOTION TO THE SOUTHERN CAUSE, AND FIRM
ADHERENCE TO ITS FORTUNES—THE TRUE STORY OF APPOMATTOX
COURTHOUSE—GENERAL LEE'S OWN ACCOUNT—POPULAR ER-
RORS REFUTED—THE CORRESPONDENCE—LEE'S APPEARANCE—
HIS FAREWELL ADDRESS—TOUCHING SCENE—TWO OF GENERAL
LEE'S LETTERS TO PRESIDENT DAVIS.

Chapter IX

INCIDENTS—"GENERAL LEE TO THE REAR"—A SOLDIER'S SHORT
ARGUMENT AGAINST ATHEISM—INCIDENTS AND LETTERS—THE

Personal Reminiscences
of General Robert E. Lee

Chapter I

THE SOLDIER

General Lee was in the highest, truest sense of the term, A SOLDIER; and, while a detailed narrative of his military achievements is not proposed, our portraiture would be incomplete without a chapter on his character and career in his chosen profession.

With ample materials at hand, I prefer that the picture should be drawn by abler pens than my own, and shall, therefore, freely cull from what has been said by some of the ablest military critics of this and other countries.

And I am fortunate in being able to present the estimate of Lee's generalship given by Lieutenant General J. A. Early, in his address before Washington and Lee University, January 19, 1872, on the occasion of the second anniversary celebration of General Lee's birthday.

Omitting only a few of the opening and concluding paragraphs, I give in full this splendid tribute of an able soldier to the chieftain whom he followed so faithfully during the war, and whose memory and fame it seems his proudest ambition to perpetuate:

"The commencement of hostilities in Charleston harbor, the proclamation of Lincoln, calling for troops to make an unconstitutional war on the seceded states, and the consequent secession of Virginia, found General Lee a colonel in the United States Army, with a character and reputation which would have insured him the highest military honors within the gift of the United States government. In fact, it has been said that the command of the army intended for the invasion of the South was tendered him. However, rejecting all overtures made to him, as soon as he learned the action of his native state, in a dignified manner, and without parade or show, he tendered his resignation, with the determination to share the fate of his state, his friends, and kindred. The then governor at once, with the unanimous consent of the Convention of Virginia, tendered him the command of all the forces of the state. This he accepted, and promptly repaired to Richmond, to enter upon the discharge of his duties, knowing that this act must be attended with a very heavy pecuniary loss to himself on account of the locality of his estates. Those who witnessed his appearance before the convention, saw his manly bearing, and heard the few grave, dignified, and impressive words with which he consecrated himself and his sword to the cause of his native state, can never forget that scene. All felt at once that we had a leader worthy of the state and the cause.

"As a member of the military committee of the convention, and afterward as a subordinate under him, I was in a condition to witness and know the active energy and utter abnegation of all personal considerations with which he devoted himself to the work of organizing and equipping the Virginia troops for the field. While he bore no active part in the first military operations of the war, yet I can safely say that, but for the capacity and energy displayed by General Lee in organizing and equipping troops to be sent to the front, our army would not have been in a condition to gain the first victory at Manassas. I do not, however, intend, by this statement, to detract from the merit of others. The Confederate government, then recently removed to Richmond, did well its part in bringing troops from the South; and I take pleasure in bearing testimony to the fidelity and ability with which the then governor of Virginia cooperated with General Lee in his efforts to furnish men as well as the munitions of war.

"His first appearance in the field, as a commander, was in western Virginia, after the reverses in that quarter. The expectations formed in regard to his operations there were not realized, and, though he met with no disaster or defeat to his troops, the campaign was regarded as a failure. The public never thought of inquiring into the causes of that failure, and it is not to be denied that an impression prevailed among those who did not know him well, that General Lee was not suited to be a commander in an active campaign. There were some editors who, while safely entrenched behind the impregnable columns of their newspapers, proved themselves to be as fierce in war as they had been wise in peace, and no bad representatives of the snarling Thersites, and these hurled their criticisms and taunts, with no sparing hand, at the head of the unsuccessful commander. It would be profitless, now, to inquire into the causes of the failures in western Virginia. It is sufficient to say that they were not attributable to the want of capacity or energy in the commanding general.

"He was, subsequently, sent to the Southern seaboard, for the purpose of supervising the measures for its defense, and he proved himself a most accomplished engineer, and rendered most valuable services in connection with the seaboard defenses in that quarter.

"In March 1862, he was called to Richmond, and charged with the conduct of military operations in the armies of the Confederacy, under the direction of the president. Just before that time, the evacuation of Manassas took place; and, subsequently, the transfer of the bulk of the opposing armies in Virginia to the Peninsula, the evacuation of Yorktown and the line of Warwick River, the battle of Williamsburg, and the transfer of the seat of war to the Chickahominy, in the vicinity of Richmond, occurred.

"On the 31st of May and 1st of June, the battle of Seven Pines was fought, and General Johnston was so severely wounded as to be disabled for duty in the field for some time. Fortunately, the eminent and patriotic statesman who was at the head of the government well knew the merits of General Lee, and at once assigned him to the vacant command; and then, in fact, began that career to which I invite your attention.

"When General Lee assumed command of the army, which before that time had borne the name of the 'Army of the Potomac,' but was soon rechristened by the name of the 'Army of Northern Virginia,' he found the Confederate capital beleaguered by an army of over one hundred thousand men, with a very large train of field and siege guns, while his own force was very little more than half that of the enemy. Nevertheless, he conceived the idea of relieving the capital of the threatening presence of the besieging army, by one of those bold strategic movements of which only great minds are capable. General Jackson, by his rapid movements and brilliant operations in the Valley, had prevented the march of a column of about forty thousand men, under McDowell, from Fredericksburg on Richmond, to unite with the besieging army; and a part of McDowell's force, and Fremont's army from northwestern Virginia, had been sent to the Valley, for the purpose of crushing Jackson. It was very apparent that Jackson's force, then consisting of his own command proper, Johnson's command from Alleghany Mountain, and Ewell's division, could not long withstand the heavy forces concentrating against it; and that, when it was overwhelmed, the enemy's troops operating in the Valley and covering Washington would be at liberty to move on Richmond; while the detachment, from the army defending that city, of a force large enough to enable Jackson to contend successfully, in a protracted campaign, with the forces accumulating against him, would probably insure the fall of the Confederate capital. Preparations were, therefore, made to attack the besieging army, with the forces covering Richmond and in the Valley, by a combined movement. Some reinforcements were brought from the South, and three brigades were sent to the Valley, for the purpose of deceiving the enemy, and facilitating the withdrawal of General Jackson. Fortunately, that able and energetic commander had been enabled to prevent the junction of Fremont's army with the troops sent from McDowell's command, and, taking advantage of their separation and the swollen condition of the water courses, had defeated both forces in succession, and so bewildered their commanders by the rapidity of his movements, that they retreated down the Valley, under the apprehension that Washington was in danger. Leaving all of his cavalry but one regiment to watch the enemy and mask his own movement, General Jackson, on the 17th of June, commenced his march toward the enemy's lines near Richmond, in compliance with the plan and orders of General Lee; and on the 26th of June, less than four weeks after General Lee had been assigned to the command of the army, his attacking columns swung around McClellan's right flank, and fell like an avalanche on the besieging army. Next day, Jackson was up, and then ensued that succession of brilliant engagements which so much accelerated McClellan's famous 'change of base,' and sent his shattered army to Harrison's Landing, under cover of the gunboats on the James.

"To give you some idea of the boldness and daring of this movement, and the impression it made on the enemy, I will call your attention to some facts and figures.

"In his report, dated in August 1863, and printed in 1864, McClellan gives the strength of the troops under his command at Washington, on the Potomac, and within reach, on the 1st of March, 1862, as—

" 'Present for duty, one hundred and ninety-three thousand, one hundred and forty-two.'

"A portion of this force had been left to operate in the Valley, another to cover Washington; and he puts the strength of the 'Army of the Potomac,' which designation his army bore, on the 20th day of June, 1862, just six days before the battles began, at—

" 'Present for duty, one hundred and five thousand, eight hundred and twenty-five.'

"He further says that he had sixty batteries with his army, aggregating three hundred and forty field pieces. Besides these he had a large train of siege guns.

"General Lee's whole force, of all arms, including the troops of Magruder, Huger, Holmes, and Jackson, when the latter arrived, did not reach eighty thousand effective men, and of these, Holmes's command, over six thousand strong, did not actively engage in any of the battles. There were thirty-nine brigades of infantry in all engaged on our side in the battles around Richmond, inclusive of Holmes's command. The strength of twenty-three of them is given in the official reports, and was forty-seven thousand and thirty-four, including the batteries attached to a number of them. In these were embraced the very largest brigades in the army, as, for instance, Lawton's. The sixteen brigades, whose strength is not given, were four of A. P. Hill's, two of Longstreet's, two of Huger's, and eight of Jackson's. Taking the average of those whose strength is given for the eight brigades of A. P. Hill, Longstreet, and Huger, and an average of fifteen hundred for Jackson's eight brigades—which would be a very liberal estimate for the latter, considering the heavy fighting and long and rapid marches they had gone through—and it will give about seventy-five thousand men, including a number of batteries attached to the brigades. The cavalry with the army was less than two brigades, and that, with the artillery not included in the reports of brigades, could not have reached five thousand men. The field guns with our army, which were all that were used, were not near half as many as those of the enemy, and many of them were of inferior metal and pattern. We had not, then, had an opportunity of supplying ourselves with the improved guns of the enemy. Much the largest portion of our small arms consisted of the smooth-bore musket, while the enemy was well supplied with improved rifle muskets.

"From the data I have given, you will perceive that I have not underestimated the strength of the forces at General Lee's command; and this was the largest army he ever commanded. The idea of relieving Richmond, by an attack on McClellan's flank and rear, was a masterly conception, and the boldness, not to say audacity, of it will appear when we take into consideration the relative strength of the two armies, and the fact that, in swinging around the enemy's flank, General Lee left very little over twenty-five thousand men between the capital and the besieging army. Timid minds might regard this as rashness, but it was the very perfection of a profound and daring strategy. Had McClellan advanced to the assault of the city, through the open plains around it, his destruction would have been insured. As it was, his only chance for escape was in a retreat through the swamps and forests, which concealed and sheltered his columns on their flight to the banks of the James. Notwithstanding the favorable nature of the country for his escape, McClellan's army would have been annihilated, had General Lee's orders been promptly and rigidly carried out by his subordinates. The bloody battle of Malvern Hill would not have been fought; and, when it was fought, a crushing defeat would have been inflicted on the enemy, had the plans of the commanding general been carried into execution, as I could demonstrate to you, if it were profitable to enter into such a disquisition. McClellan was glad enough to escape from that field with his shattered forces, though he pretended to claim a victory; and the pious Lincoln gave 'ten thousand thanks for it.'

"McClellan always insisted that we had overwhelming numbers against him, and this hallucination seems to have haunted him until the close of his career, if he is yet rid of it. On the night of the 25th of June, he telegraphed to Stanton as follows:

" 'I incline to think that Jackson will attack my right and rear. The rebel *force* is stated at two hundred thousand, including Jackson and Beauregard. I shall have to contend against vastly superior odds if these reports be true. But this army will do all in the power of men to hold their position, and repulse any attack.'

"In his report he says:

" 'The report of the chief of the "secret-service corps," herewith forwarded, and dated the 26th of June [1862], shows the estimated strength of the enemy, at the time of the evacuation of Yorktown, to have been from one hundred thousand to one hundred and twenty thousand. The same report puts his numbers, on the 26th of June, at about one hundred and eighty thousand, and the specific information obtained regarding their organization warrants the belief that this estimate did not exceed his actual strength.'

"He missed it by only one hundred thousand, and his statement shows the impression made on him by the fighting of our army under General Lee, and which he never got over. All the time he was at his 'new base,' he was afflicted with this dread phantom of overwhelming numbers against him, which, according to his account, were being constantly increased, and he begged most earnestly for reinforcements. Halleck, then lately appointed commander-in-chief at Washington, visited Harrison's Landing about the last of July, and after he got back, he reported, in writing, to the secretary of war, that McClellan and his officers represented our forces, then, at not less than two hundred thousand, and his own force at about ninety thousand.

"A new commander had now appeared in Virginia, on the north of the Rapidan, in the person of Major General John Pope, whose headquarters were in the saddle; who had never seen any thing of the 'rebels' but their backs; and who felt no concern whatever about strength of positions, bases of supplies, or lines of retreat. All he wanted to know was where the 'rebels' were, so that he might 'go at them;' and he left the lines of retreat to take care of themselves, while the 'enemy's country' was to be the base of his supplies. His army, according to his own statement, amounted to over forty-three thousand men. General Jackson had been quietly sent up to Gordonsville, with his own and Ewell's divisions, which were soon followed by that of A. P. Hill. While McClellan was trembling at the idea of vastly superior numbers accumulating against him, Pope telegraphed to Halleck:

" 'The enemy is reported to be evacuating Richmond, and falling back on Danville and Lynchburg.'

"General Jackson soon began to show Pope some things that were entirely new to him. The battle of Cedar Run, or Slaughter's Mountain, was fought on the 9th of August, and a 'change came over the spirit' of Pope's dream. In fact, he began to see some remarkable sights, with which he was destined to soon become familiar. About this time, McClellan sent a dispatch to Halleck, in which is this striking passage:

" 'I don't like Jackson's movements; he will suddenly appear when least expected.'

"There were not many, on that side, who did like General Jackson's ways. The authorities at Washington were completely bewildered by his new eccentricities, and the evacuation of the 'new base,' which had been assumed with so much ability and celerity, was peremptorily ordered.

"Burnside soon arrived at Fredericksburg with thirteen thousand men, brought from North and South Carolina, eight thousand of whom, under Reno, were sent to Pope. In the meantime, General Lee had been watching McClellan's force, and, having become convinced that there was no immediate danger to Richmond, he determined to move against Pope, for the purpose of crushing him before he could be reinforced, and entirely relieving Richmond, by forcing McClellan to go to the defense of Washington. Leaving D. H. Hill's and McLaws's divisions, two brigades under J. G. Walker, a brigade of cavalry under Hampton, and some other troops, at Drury's and Chaffin's Bluffs, to watch McClellan, General Lee moved with the remainder of his army to the Rapidan. Getting wind of the intended movement against him, by the accidental capture of a dispatch to Stuart, Pope fell back behind the Rappahannock, and the two armies soon confronted each other on its banks. A raid by Stuart to Pope's rear resulted in the capture of the latter's headquarters and his correspondence, which latter showed that McClellan's army was hastening to Pope's assistance. D. H. Hill, McLaws, Walker, and Hampton, were ordered forward at once, and while Pope was looking steadily to the front for the 'rebels,' without thought for his base of supplies, and in utter oblivion of any possible line of retreat, General Jackson was sent on that remarkably bold and dashing expedition to the enemy's rear, for the purpose of destroying Pope's communications, and preventing the advance of McClellan's army to his assistance. Pope now found it necessary to look out for his supplies and his line of retreat, and then ensued that series of engagements called 'the second battle of Manassas.' Pope had already been joined by two corps of McClellan's army, Porter's and Heintzolman's, the one by the way of Fredericksburg, and the other over the railroad; and Jackson's three divisions, numbering less than twenty thousand men, after cutting the railroad, and destroying several trains of cars and immense stores at Manassas, which could not be removed for want of transportation, withstood for two days, beginning on the 28th of August, Pope's entire army, reinforced by Reno's eight thousand men, and McClellan's two corps, while General Lee was moving up with Longstreet's and Anderson's commands. Never did General Jackson display his leading characteristics more conspicuously than on this occasion, and he fully justified the confidence of the commanding general, in entrusting him with the execution of one of the most brilliant and daring strategic movements on record. Every attack by Pope's immense army was repulsed with heavy slaughter, and during the 29th all the fighting on our side was done by Jackson's corps, except an affair about dusk between a part of McDowell's corps and the advance of Longstreet's command, which began to arrive between eleven and twelve in the day, but did not become engaged until at the close, when an advance was made along the Warrenton Pike, by one of McDowell's divisions, under the very great delusion that Jackson was retreating. On the morning of the 30th the attacks on Jackson's position, on the line of an unfinished railroad track, were renewed, and continued until the afternoon, with the same result as the day before. Longstreet did not become engaged until late in the afternoon, when, by a combined attack, Pope's army was driven across Bull Run in great disorder and with immense loss.

"Pope's report and telegraphic correspondence afford a rich fund of amusement for those acquainted with the facts of his brief campaign in Virginia, but this I must pass over.

"He claimed to have entirely defeated and routed Jackson on the 29th, and he actually had one corps commander cashiered for not cutting off the retreat and capturing the whole force, which he claims to have routed. In a dispatch to Halleck, dated 5:30 A.M., on the 30th, he says:

" 'We have lost not less than eight thousand men, killed and wounded; but, from the appearance of the field, the enemy lost at least two to one. He stood strictly on the defensive, and every assault was made by ourselves. The battle was fought on the identical field of Bull Run, which greatly increased the enthusiasm of the men. The news just reaches me from the front that the enemy is retiring toward the mountains. I go forward at once to see. We have made great captures, but I am not able, yet, to form an idea of their extent.'

"He went forward, and saw more than was agreeable to him, and found that he had captured a 'Tartar.'

"In a dispatch dated 9:45 P.M., on the 30th, after the great battle of that day was over, he said:

" 'The battle was most furious for hours without cessation, and the losses on both sides were very heavy. The enemy is badly whipped, and we shall do well enough. Do not be uneasy. We will hold our own here.'

"To this Halleck replied on the morning of the 31st:

" 'You have done nobly. Don't yield another inch if you can avoid it. All reserves are being sent forward.'

"Yet, after all of McClellan's troops, except one division left at Yorktown, had arrived, and before another gun had been fired, Pope telegraphed to Halleck, at 10:45 A.M., on the 31st:

" 'I should like to know whether you feel secure about Washington, should this army be destroyed. I shall fight it as long as a man will stand up to the work.'

"The army that had been so badly whipped on the 30th, was soon advancing against Pope again. Jackson, by another flank movement, struck the retreating army at Chantilly or Ox Hill, and the shattered remains of it, now reinforced by two fresh corps and a division of McClellan's army, were hurled into the fortifications around Washington.

"Major General John Pope had now seen as much of the 'rebels' as he cared to look upon, and he disappeared from the scene of action, in many respects 'a wiser if not a better man.' To get him as far as possible from the dangerous proximity, he was sent to the extreme Northwest to loot after the redmen of the plains. When we recollect the bombastic procla-

mations and orders of Pope at the beginning of his brief campaign, and
the rapidity with which he was brought to grief, there appears so much of
the ludicrous in the whole, that we are almost tempted to overlook the
fiendish malignity which characterized some of his orders and acts.

"In his report, after saying—

" 'Every indication, during the night of the 29th, and up to ten o'clock
on the morning of the 30th, pointed to the retreat of the enemy from our
front'—

"He further says:

" 'During the whole night of the 29th and the morning of the 30th, the
advance, of the main army, under Lee, was arriving on the field to reinforce Jackson, so that by twelve or one o'clock in the day we were confronted by forces greatly superior to our own; and these forces were being,
every moment, largely increased by fresh arrivals of the enemy in the
direction of Thoroughfare Gap.' So that this was another case of overwhelming numbers on our side.

"Pope's army was originally, according to his statement, forty-three
thousand and, according to Halleck, forty thousand. He had been reinforced by eight thousand men under Reno; a body of troops from the
Kanawha Valley, under Cox; another from Washington, under Sturgis, and
all of McClellan's army, except one division, say eighty-five thousand
men. General Lee had then between one hundred and thirty-five thousand
and one hundred and forty thousand men to deal with on this occasion.
The whole of McClellan's force was not up at the battle of the 30th, but
all of it, except the one division of Keyes's corps left at Yorktown, was
up by the time of the affair at Ox Hill, on the 1st of September. General
Lee's whole force, at second Manassas, did not exceed fifty thousand men.
Neither D. H. Hill's, nor McLaws's, nor Walker's division of infantry, nor
Hampton's brigade of cavalry, had arrived, and neither of them got up
until after the affair at Ox Hill. We had only twenty-nine brigades of
infantry and two of cavalry present at second Manassas, one of the latter
being very weak. One of the infantry brigades, Starke's Louisiana brigade,
had been formed of regiments attached to other brigades at the battles
around Richmond, and another had arrived from the South during July.
This latter brigade constituted all the reinforcements, except men returned
from convalescence, received after these battles, and was twenty-two hundred strong the last of July. The whole force in the department of Northern
Virginia, on the 31st of July, 1862, was sixty-nine thousand, five hundred

and fifty-nine for duty. Deduct, ratably, for the twelve infantry brigades, with their proportion of artillery, and the one cavalry brigade absent, besides troops on detached duty at various points, and you will see how General Lee's army must have been under fifty thousand at second Manassas. Yet it had sent the combined armies of Pope and McClellan into the defenses of Washington, in a very crippled condition, and thrown the government there into a great panic in regard to the safety of that city. Fredericksburg had been evacuated, and the remainder of Burnside's corps brought to Washington, while a call had been made for three hundred thousand new troops.

"Notwithstanding the exhaustion of his troops from the heavy tax on all their energies, the heavy losses in battle, and the want of commissary stores, General Lee now undertook the bold scheme of crossing the Potomac into Maryland, with his army reinforced by the eleven brigades of infantry, under D. H. Hill, McLaws, and Walker, and Hampton's cavalry, which were coming up. On the 3d of September our army was put in motion, and, passing through Leesburg, it crossed over and concentrated at and near Frederick City, by the 7th of the month. This movement threw the authorities at Washington into great consternation and dismay. McClellan had been assigned to the command of all the troops in and around Washington, and the correspondence between himself and Halleck, conducted mostly by telegraph, shows how utterly bewildered they were. Both of them were firmly impressed with the conviction that our numbers were overwhelming, and they did not know where to look for the impending blow. McClellan moved out of the city with great caution, feeling his way gradually toward Frederick, while a considerable force, which was constantly augmented by the arrival of new troops, was retained at Washington, for fear that city should be captured by a sudden *coup* from the south side. A considerable force had been isolated at Harper's Ferry, and General Lee sent Jackson's corps, McLaws's, Anderson's, and Walker's divisions, in all twenty-six brigades of infantry, with the accompanying artillery, to invest and capture that place, retaining with himself only fourteen brigades of infantry, with the accompanying and reserve artillery, and the main body of the cavalry, with which he crossed to the west side of the South Mountain. The order directing these movements, by some accident, fell into McClellan's hands on the 13th, and he hurried his troops forward to attack the small force with General Lee, and relieve Harper's Ferry if possible. A sanguinary engagement occurred at Boonsboro Gap, on the

14th, between D. H. Hill's division, constituting the rear guard of the column with General Lee, and the bulk of McClellan's army; and Hill, after maintaining his position for many hours, was compelled to retire at night with heavy loss, the troops sent to his assistance not having arrived in time to repulse the enemy. That night, Longstreet's and Hill's commands crossed the Antietam to Sharpsburg, where they took position on the morning of the 15th. In the meantime, Harper's Ferry had been invested, and surrendered on the morning of the 15th—our victory being almost a bloodless one, so far as the resistance of the garrison was concerned; but McLaws and Anderson had had very heavy fighting, on the Maryland side, with a part of McClellan's army. As soon as General Lee heard of the success at Harper's Ferry, he ordered all the troops operating against that place to move to Sharpsburg as soon as practicable. Leaving A. P. Hill, with his division, to dispose of the prisoners and property captured at Harper's Ferry, General Jackson, late in the afternoon of the 15th, ordered his own division and Ewell's, the latter now under Lawton, to Sharpsburg, where they arrived early on the morning of the 16th. Walker's two brigades came up later in the day. The ten brigades brought by Jackson and Walker made twenty-four brigades of infantry, with the fourteen already on the ground, which General Lee had with him when the battle of Sharpsburg opened on the morning of the 17th of September. Jackson's division was placed on the left flank, and Hood's two brigades, which were next to it on the right, were relieved by two brigades of Ewell's division during the night of the 16th, and these were reinforced by another very early the next morning. General Jackson's whole force on the field consisted of five thousand infantry and a very few batteries of his own division. One brigade, my own, numbering about one thousand men and officers, was detached, at light, toward the Potomac on our left, to support some artillery with which Stuart was operating; so that General Jackson had only four thousand infantry in line, and D. H. Hill was immediately on his right, holding the center and left center with his division, then three thousand strong. General Lee's whole infantry force on the field, at the beginning of the battle, did not exceed fifteen thousand men, including Jackson's and Walker's commands. On the left and left center McClellan hurled, in succession, the four corps of Hooker, Mansfield, Sumner, and Franklin, numbering, in the aggregate, fifty-six thousand and ninety-five men, according to his report; and a sanguinary battle raged for several hours, during which, Hood's two brigades, my brigade, Walker's two brigades, Anderson's brigade of D. R. Jones's division, and McLaws's and Anderson's divisions, successively went to the support of the part of the line assailed, at different points, the last two divisions having arrived late in the morning, during the progress of the battle. And all the troops engaged, from first to last, with the enemy's fifty-six thousand and ninety-five men, on that wing, did not exceed eighteen thousand men. At the close of the fighting there, our left was advanced beyond where it rested in the morning, while the center had been forced back some two hundred yards.

"In the afternoon, Burnside's corps, over thirteen thousand strong, attacked our right, and, after gaining some advantage, was driven back with the aid of three of A. P. Hill's brigades, which had just arrived from Harper's Ferry. At the close of the battle, we held our position firmly, with the center slightly forced back, as I have stated. We continued to hold the position during the 18th, and McClellan did not venture to renew the attack. In the mean time, heavy reinforcements were moving to his assistance, two divisions of which, Couch's and Humphrey's, fourteen thousand strong, arrived on the 18th, while General Lee had no possibility of being reinforced except by the stragglers who might come up, and they constituted a poor dependence. The Potomac was immediately in his rear, and, as it would have been folly for him to have waited until an overpowering force was accumulated against him, he very properly and judiciously retired on the night of the 18th, and recrossed the river early on the morning of the 19th. A very feeble effort at pursuit by one corps was most severely punished by A. P. Hill's division on the 20th.

"This was one of the most remarkable battles of the war, and has been but little understood. You will, therefore, pardon me for going somewhat into detail in regard to it. When General Lee took his position on the morning of the 15th, he had with him but fourteen brigades of infantry, besides the artillery and cavalry. The official reports show that D. H. Hill's five brigades numbered then only three thousand men for duty, and six brigades under D. R. Jones only twenty-four hundred and thirty men. The strength of three brigades is not given, but they were not more than of an average size—and, estimating their strength in that way, it would give less than seven thousand, five hundred infantry with which, and the artillery and cavalry with him, General Lee confronted McClellan's army during the whole of the 15th and part of the 16th. The arrival of Jackson's and Walker's commands did not increase the infantry to more than fifteen thousand men, and they brought very little artillery with them. During the day, McLaws, Anderson, and A. P. Hill, came up with thirteen brigades, making thirty-seven brigades which participated in the battle. The official reports give the strength of twenty-seven of these, amounting in the aggregate to sixteen thousand, nine hundred and twenty-three men. Taking the average for the other ten—and they were not more than average brigades, if that—and it would give about twenty-three thousand infantry engaged on our side from first to last. The cavalry, consisting of three brigades, which were not strong, was not engaged and merely watched the flanks. A very large portion of our artillery, which had been used against Harper's Ferry, had not arrived, and did not get up until after nightfall, when the battle was over. We had, in fact, comparatively few guns engaged, and the enemy's guns were not only very numerous, but of heavier metal and longer range. Taking the whole force, including the cavalry and the artillery, when all of the latter had arrived, and we had less than thirty thousand men of all arms at this battle, from first to last. General Lee, in his report, says that he had less than forty thousand men; but, for reasons that can be well understood, he never did disclose his own weakness at any time, even to his own officers.

"When our army started for Maryland, after the affair at Ox Hill, it was out of rations, badly clothed, and worse shod. At the time of the battle of Sharpsburg, it had been marching and fighting for near six weeks, and the straggling from exhaustion, sore feet, and in search of food, had been terrible, before we crossed the Potomac. When it is recollected that the entire force at the end of July, in all the Department of Northern Virginia, was only a very little over sixty-nine thousand men, of which sixty thousand, including D. H. Hill's, McLaws's, and Walker's divisions, would be a liberal estimate for all that were carried into the field, you will see that a loss of thirty thousand in battle, from Cedar Run to South Mountain, inclusive, and from the other causes named, it is not an unreasonable estimate. In fact, at the end of September, when the stragglers had been gathered up, and many of the sick and wounded had returned to duty, with the additions from the conscripts, the official returns show only fifty-two thousand, six hundred and nine for duty in the whole Department of Northern Virginia.

"McClellan, in his report, gives his own force at eighty-seven thousand, one hundred and sixty-four in action, and he gives an estimate of General Lee's army, in detail, in which he places our strength at ninety-seven thousand, four hundred and forty-five men and four hundred guns at this battle. Truly, our boys in gray had a wonderful faculty of magnifying and multiplying themselves in battle; and McClellan could not have paid a higher compliment to their valor, and the ability of our commander, than he has done by this estimate of our strength, as it appeared to him.

"In giving his reasons for not renewing the battle on the 18th, he says:

" 'One division of Sumner's corps, and all of Hooker's corps on the right, had, after fighting most valiantly for several hours, been overpowered by numbers, driven in great disorder and much scattered, so that they were for the time somewhat demoralized.'

"I have shown how they were outnumbered.

"Burnside, in his testimony before the committee on the conduct of the war, said:

" 'I was told at General McClellan's headquarters, that our right had been so badly broken that they could not be got together for an attack, and they would have to wait for reinforcements; and that General Sumner advised General McClellan not to renew the attack, because of the condition of his corps; and it was also stated that very little of General Hooker's corps was left.'

"This was on the night of the 17th, after the battle was over. On the 27th, McClellan wrote to Halleck as follows:

" 'In the last battles the enemy was undoubtedly greatly superior to us in numbers, and it was only by hard fighting that we gained the advantage we did. As it was, the result was at one time very doubtful, and we had all we could do to win the day.'

"Win the day, indeed! He had not dared to renew the attack on the 18th, and he did not venture to claim a victory until the 19th, when he found General Lee had recrossed the Potomac, and then he began to breathe freely and to crow, at first feebly, and then more loudly. Whoever heard of a victory by an attacking army in an open field, and yet the victor was unable to advance against his antagonist who stood his ground?

"To give you some idea of the immense difficulties General Lee had to encounter in this campaign, and the wonderful facility the enemy had for raising men, and reinforcing his armies after defeat, through the agencies of the telegraph, railroads, and steam power, let me tell you that a certified statement compiled from McClellan's morning report of the 20th of September, 1862, contained in the report of the committee on the conduct of the war, shows a grand total present for duty in the Army of the Potomac, on that day, of one hundred and sixty-four thousand, three hundred and fifty-nine, of which seventy-one thousand, two hundred and ten were in the defenses of Washington under Banks, leaving ninety-three thousand, one hundred and forty-nine with McClellan in the field on that day. A very large portion of this force had been accumulated by means of the railroads, after the defeat of Pope. You may understand now how it was that our victories could never be pressed to more decisive results. It was genius, and nerve, and valor, on the one side, against numbers and mechanical power on the other; even the lightning of the heavens being made subservient to the latter.

"You may also form some conception of the boldness of General Lee's movement across the Potomac, the daring of the expedition against Harper's Ferry in the face of so large a force, and the audacity with which he confronted and defied McClellan's army on the 15th and 16th, and then fought it on the 17th with the small force he had.

"Sharpsburg was no defeat to our arms, though our army was retired to the south bank of the Potomac from prudential considerations.

"Some persons have been disposed to regard this campaign into Maryland as a failure, but such was not the case. It is true that we had failed to raise Maryland, but it was from no disaster to our arms.

"In a military point of view, however, the whole campaign, of which the movement into Maryland was an integral part, had been a grand success, though all was not accomplished which our fond hopes caused us to expect. When General Lee assumed command of the army at Richmond, a besieging army of immense size and resources was in sight of the spires of the Confederate capital—all northern Virginia was in possession of the enemy—the Valley overrun, except when Jackson's vigorous and rapid blows sent the marauders staggering to the banks of the Potomac for a brief interval; and northwestern Virginia, including the Kanawha Valley, was subjugated and in the firm grasp of the enemy. By General Lee's bold strategy and rapid and heavy blows, the capital had been relieved; the besieging army driven out of the state; the enemy's capital threatened; his country invaded; northern Virginia and the Valley cleared of the enemy; the enemy's troops from northwestern Virginia and the Kanawha Valley had been drawn thence for the defense of his own capital; a Confederate force had penetrated to Charleston, Kanawha; our whole army was supplied with the improved firearm in the place of the old smooth-bore musket; much of our inferior field artillery replaced by the enemy's improved guns; and, in addition to our very large captures of prisoners and the munitions of war elsewhere, the direct result of the march across the Potomac was the capture of eleven thousand prisoners, seventy-three pieces of artillery, and thirteen thousand stand of excellent small arms, and immense stores at Harper's Ferry. And, at the close of the campaign, the Confederate commander stood proudly defiant on the extreme northern border of the Confederacy, while his opponent had had 'his base' removed to the northern bank of the Potomac, at a point more than one hundred and seventy-five miles from the Confederate capital, in a straight line. In addition, the immense army of McClellan had been so crippled, that it was not able to resume the offensive for six weeks. Such had been the moral effect upon the enemy, that the Confederate capital was never again seriously endangered, until the power of the Confederacy had been so broken in other quarters, and its available territory so reduced in dimensions, that the enemy could concentrate his immense resources against the capital.

"All this had been the result of that plan of operations, of which the invasion of Maryland formed an important part. Look at the means placed at the command of General Lee, and the immense numbers and resources brought against him, and then say if the results accomplished by him were not marvelous? If his government had been able to furnish him with men and means, at all commensurate with his achievements and his conceptions, he would, in September 1862, have dictated the terms of peace in the capital of the enemy. But all the wonderful powers of the mechanic arts and physical science, backed by unlimited resources of men and money, still continued to operate against him.

"A certified statement from McClellan's morning report of the 30th of September, contained in the document from which I have already quoted, showed, in the Army of the Potomac, a grand total of one hundred and seventy-three thousand, seven hundred and forty-five present for duty on that day, of which seventy-three thousand, six hundred and one were in the defenses of Washington, and one hundred thousand, one hundred and forty-four with him in the field; and a similar statement showed, on the 20th of October, a grand total of two hundred and seven thousand and thirty-six present for duty on that day, of which seventy-three thousand, five hundred and ninety-three were in the defenses of Washington, and one hundred and thirty-three thousand, four hundred and forty-three with McClellan in the field.

"At the close of October, according to the official returns now on file at the 'Archive Office' in Washington, the whole Confederate force for duty in the department of northern Virginia amounted to sixty-seven thousand, eight hundred and five. A considerable portion of this force was not with General Lee in the field.

"At the close of October, McClellan commenced a new movement with his immense army, across the Potomac, east of the Blue Ridge, while General Lee was yet in the Valley. As this movement was developed, Longstreet's corps and the cavalry under Stuart were promptly moved to intercept it, Jackson's corps being left in the Valley. McClellan was soon superseded in the command by Burnside, and, when the latter turned his steps toward the heights opposite Fredericksburg, Jackson was ordered to rejoin the rest of the army. In the meantime, Burnside's attempt to approach Richmond on the new line had been checkmated, and he soon found himself confronted on the Rappahannock by the whole of General Lee's army. That army had to be stretched out, for some thirty miles, up and down the river, to watch the different crossings. The enemy began his movement to cross at and near Fredericksburg, on the morning of the 11th of December, and the crossing was resisted and delayed for many hours, but, owing to the peculiar character of the country immediately on the south bank, and the advantage the enemy had in his commanding position on the north bank, whence the wide plains on the south bank, and the town of Fredericksburg, were completely commanded and swept by an immense armament of heavy artillery, that crossing could not be prevented. Our army was rapidly concentrated, and took its position on the heights and range of hills in rear of the town and the plains below; and, when the heavy columns of the enemy advanced to the assault on the 13th, first on our right, near Hamilton's crossing, and then on our left, in rear of Fredericksburg, they were hurled back with immense slaughter, to the cover of the artillery on the opposite heights, and every renewal of the assault met the same fate. In this battle, we stood entirely on the defensive, except once, when the enemy penetrated an interval in our line near the right flank, and three of my brigades advanced, driving and pursuing the enemy into the plains below, until he reached the protection of his artillery and the main line. Burnside's loss was so heavy, and his troops were so worsted in the assaults which had been made, that his principal officers protested against a renewal of the attack, and on the night of the 15th he recrossed to the north bank.

"In this battle, he had all of McClellan's army, except the Twelfth Corps, which was eight or ten thousand strong, and had been left at Harper's Ferry, and in lieu of that he had a much larger corps, the Third, from the defenses of Washington. In his testimony before the committee on the conduct of the war, he says he had one hundred thousand men across the river, and he was doubtful which had the superiority of numbers. In reply to a question as to the causes of the failure of the attack, he frankly said:

" 'It was found to be impossible to get the men up to the works. The enemy's fire was too hot for them.'

"Our whole force present was not much more than half that of the enemy, which crossed over to the south side of the river. This signal victory, in which the enemy's loss was very heavy, and ours comparatively light, closed the operations for the year 1862.

"Some newspaper critics and fireside generals were not satisfied with the results of this victory, and thought Burnside's army ought to have been destroyed before it went back; and there were some absurd stories about propositions alleged to have been made by General Jackson, for driving the enemy into the river. That great soldier did begin a forward movement, about sunset, which I was to have led, but, just as my men were moving off, he countermanded the movement, because the enemy opened such a terrific artillery fire from the Stafford Heights and from behind the heavy embankments on the road leading through the bottoms on the south side of the river, that it was apparent that nothing could have lived in the passage across the plain of about a mile in width, over which we would have had to advance, to reach the enemy massed in that road. According to the statements of himself and officers, before the committee on the conduct of the war, Franklin, who commanded the enemy's left, had, confronting our right, from fifty-five to sixty thousand men, of whom only about twenty thousand had been under fire. The bulk of that force was along the Bowling Green road, running parallel to the river through the middle of the bottoms, and behind the very compact and thick embankments on each side of that road. He had taken over with him one hundred and sixteen pieces of artillery, and there were sixty-one pieces on the north bank, some of which were of very large caliber, so posted as to cover the bridges on that flank, and sweep the plain in his front. Some of these were also crossed over to him, and General Hunt, Burnside's chief of artillery, says fifty or sixty more pieces could have been spared from their right, if necessary. The attempt to drive this force into the river would have, therefore, insured our destruction.

"Franklin had eight divisions with him, while at Fredericksburg, confronting our left, were ten divisions, fully as strong, certainly, as Franklin's eight, and there were quite as many guns on that flank. It is true the enemy's loss there had been double that in front of our right, but he still had a large number of troops on that flank which had not been engaged. The character of the ground in front of our position, on that flank, was such that our troops could not be moved down the rugged slopes of the hills in any order of battle, and any attempt to advance them must have been attended with disastrous consequences. Burnside's troops were not so demoralized as to prevent him from being anxious to renew the attack on the 14th, and the objection of his officers was not on account of the condition of their troops, but on account of the strength of our position. Nothing could have gratified him and his officers more, than for us to have surrendered our advantage and taken the offensive. General Lee, ever ready to strike when an opportunity offered, knew better than all others when it was best to attack and when not to attack.

"It is a notable fact about all those people who favored such bloodthirsty and desperate measures, that they were never in the army, to share the dangers into which they were so anxious to rush others.

"About the close of the winter or beginning of the spring of 1863, two of Longstreet's divisions, one-fourth of our army, were sent to the south side of James River; and, during their absence, Hooker, who had succeeded Burnside in the command, commenced the movement which resulted in the battle of Chancellorsville, in the first days of May. Throwing a portion of his troops across the river just below Fredericksburg, on the 29th of April, and making an ostentatious demonstration with three corps on the north bank, he proceeded to cross four others above our left flank to Chancellorsville. Having accomplished this, Hooker issued a gasconading order to his troops, in which he claimed to have General Lee's army in his power, and declared his purpose of crushing it. Leaving my division, one brigade of another, and a portion of the reserve artillery, in all less than nine thousand men, to confront the three corps opposite and near Fredericksburg, General Lee moved with five divisions of infantry and a portion of the artillery to meet Hooker, the cavalry being employed to watch the flanks. As soon as General Lee reached Hooker's front, he determined to take the offensive, and, by one of his bold strategic movements, he sent Jackson around Hooker's right flank, and that boastful commander, who was successively reinforced by two of the corps left opposite Fredericksburg, was so vigorously assailed that he was put on the defensive, and soon compelled to provide for the safety of his own defeated army.

"In the meantime, Sedgwick, whose corps numbered about twenty-four thousand men, and who had a division of another corps with him, making his whole force about thirty thousand, had crossed the river, at and below Fredericksburg, with the portion of his troops not already over, and, by concentrating three of his divisions on one point of the long line, of five or six miles, held by my forces, had on the 3d of May, after repeated repulses, broken through immediately in the rear of Fredericksburg, where the stone wall was held by one regiment and four companies of another, the whole not exceeding five hundred men. General Lee was preparing to renew the attack on Hooker, whose force at Chancellorsville had been driven back to an interior line, when he was informed that Sedgwick was moving up in his rear. He was then compelled to provide against this new danger, and he moved troops down to arrest Sedgwick's progress. This was successfully done, and, on the next day (the 4th), three of the brigades of my division, all of which had been concentrated, and had severed Sedgwick's connection with Fredericksburg and the north bank, fell upon his left flank, and drove it toward the river in confusion, while other troops of ours, which had come from above, closed in on him and forced his whole command into the bend of the river. His whole command would now have been destroyed or captured, but night came on and arrested our progress. During the night he made his escape over a bridge which was laid down for him. General Lee then turned his attention again to Hooker, but he also made his escape, the next night, under cover of a storm. Thus another brilliant victory was achieved, by the genius and boldness of our commander, against immense odds.

"It is a little remarkable that Hooker did not claim, on this occasion, that we had the odds against him; but, when he went back, under compulsion, he issued an order, in which he stated that his army had retired for reasons best known to itself, that it was the custodian of its own honor and advanced when it pleased, fought when it pleased, and retired when it pleased.

"In his testimony before the committee on the conduct of the war, he made this curious statement:

" 'Our artillery had always been superior to that of the rebels, as was also our infantry, except in discipline; and that, for reasons not necessary to mention, never did equal Lee's army. With a rank and file vastly inferior to our own, intellectually and physically, that army has, by discipline alone, acquired a character for steadiness and efficiency unsurpassed, in my judgment, in ancient or modern times. We have not been able to rival it, nor has there been any near approximation to it in the other rebel armies.'

"This was the impression made by that army, under the inspiration of its great leader, on 'Fighting Joe,' as he was called. The impression made on Lincoln, at that time, may be gathered from a telegram sent to Butterfield, Hooker's chief of staff, who was on the north of the river. The telegram was sent, when Hooker had taken refuge in his new works in rear of Chancellorsville, and Sedgwick was cut off in the bend of the river, and is as follows, in full:

" 'Where is General Hooker? Where is Sedgwick? Where is Stoneman?

A. LINCOLN.'

"Hooker had with him what was left of the army of Burnside, except the Ninth Corps, which had been sent off; but two other corps, the Eleventh and Twelfth, had been added, besides recruits; and his whole force was largely over one hundred thousand men. General Lee's army, weakened by the absence of Longstreet's two divisions, was very little if any over fifty thousand men, inclusive of my force at Fredericksburg.

"As glorious as was this victory, it nevertheless shed a gloom over the whole army and country, for in it had fallen the great lieutenant to whom General Lee had always entrusted the execution of his most daring plans, and who had proved himself so worthy of the confidence reposed in him. It is not necessary for me to stop here, to delineate the character and talents of General Jackson. As long as unselfish patriotism, Christian devotion and purity of character, and deeds of heroism shall command the admiration of men, Stonewall Jackson's name and fame will be reverenced. Of all who mourned his death, none felt more acutely the loss the country and the army had sustained than General Lee. General Jackson had always appreciated, and sympathized with, the bold conceptions of the commanding general and entered upon their execution with the most cheerful alacrity and zeal. General Lee never found it necessary to accompany him, to see that his plans were carried out, but could always trust him alone; and well might he say, when Jackson fell, that *he* himself had lost his 'right arm.'

"After General Jackson's death, the army was divided into three corps of three divisions each, instead of two corps of four divisions each, the Ninth Division being formed by taking two brigades from the division of A. P. Hill and uniting them with two others which were brought from the South. These two brigades constituted all the reinforcements to our army, after the battle of Chancellorsville, and previous to the campaign into Pennsylvania. Longstreet's two absent divisions were now brought back and moved up toward Culpepper Courthouse, and General Lee entered on a campaign of even greater boldness than that of the previous year.

"While Hooker's army yet occupied the Stafford Heights, our army was put in motion for Pennsylvania, on the 4th of June, Hill's corps being left for a while to watch Hooker. This movement was undertaken because the interposition of the Rappahannock, between the two armies, presented an insurmountable obstacle to offensive operations, on our part, against the enemy in the position he then occupied, and General Lee was determined not to stand on the defensive, and give the enemy time to mature his plans and accumulate a larger army for another attack on him.

"The enemy was utterly bewildered by this new movement, and, while he was endeavoring to find out what it meant, the advance of our army, Ewell's corps, composed of three of Jackson's old divisions, entered the Valley and captured, at Winchester and Martinsburg, about four thousand prisoners, twenty-nine pieces of artillery, about four thousand stand of small arms, a large wagon train, and many stores. It then crossed the Potomac, and two divisions went to Carlisle, while another went to the banks of the Susquehanna, through York. The two other corps soon followed, and this movement brought the whole of Hooker's army across the Potomac in pursuit. The two armies concentrated, and encountered each other at Gettysburg, east of the South Mountain, in a battle extending through three days, from the 1st to the 3d of July, inclusive. On the first day, a portion of our army, composed of two divisions of Hill's corps, and two divisions of Ewell's corps, gained a very decided victory over two of the enemy's corps, which latter were driven back, in great confusion, through Gettysburg, to the heights, immediately south and east of the town, known as Cemetery Hill. On the second and third days, we assaulted the enemy's position at different points, but failed to dislodge his army, now under Meade, from its very strong position on Cemetery and the adjacent hills. Both sides suffered very heavy losses, that of the enemy exceeding ours.

"Our ammunition had drawn short, and we were beyond the reach of any supplies of that kind. General Lee therefore desisted from his efforts to carry the position, and, after straightening his line, he confronted Meade for a whole day, without the latter's daring to move from his position, and then retired toward the Potomac, for the purpose of being within reach of supplies. We halted near Hagerstown, Maryland, and when Meade, who had followed us very cautiously, arrived, battle was offered him, but he went to fortifying in our front. We confronted him for several days, but, as he did not venture to attack us, and heavy rains had set in, we retired across the Potomac to avoid having an impassable river in our rear.

"The campaign into Pennsylvania and the battle of Gettysburg have been much criticized, and but little understood. The magnanimity of General Lee caused him to withhold from the public the true causes of the failure to gain a decisive victory at Gettysburg. Many writers have racked their brains to account for that failure. Some have attributed it to the fact that the advantage gained on the first day was not pressed immediately; and among them is a Northern historian of the war (Swinton), who says: 'Ewell was even advancing a line against Culp's Hill when Lee reached the field and stayed the movement.' There is no foundation for this statement. When General Lee, after the engagement, reached the part of the field where Ewell's command had fought, it was near dark, and no forward movement was in progress or contemplated. Two fresh corps of the enemy, Slocum's and Sickles's, had arrived at five o'clock, at least two hours before General Lee came to us after the engagement. There was a time, as we know now, immediately after the enemy was driven back, when, if we had advanced vigorously, the heights of Gettysburg would probably have been taken, but that was not then apparent. I was in favor of the advance, but I think it doubtful whether it would have resulted in any greater advantage than to throw back the two routed corps on the main body of their army, and cause the great battle to be fought on other ground. Meade had already selected another position, on Pipe Clay Creek, where he would have concentrated his army, and we would have been compelled to give him battle or retire. Moreover, it is not impossible that the arrival of the two fresh corps may have turned the fate of the day against the troops we then had on the field, had we pressed our advantage. General Lee had ordered the concentration of his army at Cashtown, and the battle on this day, brought on by the advance of the enemy's cavalry, was unexpected to him. When he ascertained the advantage that had been gained, he determined to press it as soon as the remainder of his army arrived. In a conference with General Ewell, General Rhodes and myself, when he did reach us, after the enemy had been routed, he expressed his determination to assault the enemy's position at daylight on the next morning, and wished to know whether we could make the attack from our flank—the left—at the designated time. We informed him of the fact that the ground immediately in our front, leading to the enemy's position, furnished much greater obstacles to a successful assault than existed at any other point, and we concurred in suggesting to him that, as our corps (Ewell's) constituted the only troops then immediately confronting the enemy, he would manifestly concentrate and fortify against us, during the night, as proved to be the case, according to subsequent information. He then determined to make the attack from our right on the enemy's left, and left us for the purpose of ordering up Longstreet's corps in time to begin the attack at dawn next morning. That corps was not in readiness to make the attack until four o'clock in the afternoon of the next day. By that time, Meade's whole army had arrived on the field and taken its position. Had the attack been made at daylight, as contemplated, it must have resulted in a brilliant and decisive victory, as all of Meade's army had not then arrived, and a very small portion of it was in position. A considerable portion of his army did not get up until after sunrise, one corps not arriving until two o'clock in the afternoon, and a prompt advance to the attack must have resulted in his defeat in detail. The position which Longstreet attacked at four was not occupied by the enemy until late in the afternoon, and Round Top Hill, which commanded the enemy's position, could have been taken in the morning without a struggle. The attack was made by two divisions, and, though the usual gallantry was displayed by the troops engaged in it, no very material advantage was gained. When General Lee saw his plans thwarted by the delay on our right, he ordered an attack to be made also from our left, to be begun by Johnson's division on Culp's Hill, and followed up by the rest of Ewell's corps, and also by Hill's. This attack was begun with great vigor by Johnson, and two of my brigades, immediately on his right, which were the only portion of the division then available, as the other two brigades had been sent off to the left to watch the York road, moved forward promptly, climbed the heights on the left of Gettysburg, over stone and plank fences, reached the summit of Cemetery Hill, and got possession of the enemy's works, and his batteries there posted. One of my other brigades had been sent for, and got back in time to be ready to act as a support to those in front: but, though Johnson was making good progress in his attack, there was no movement on my right, and the enemy, not being pressed in that direction, concentrated on my two brigades in such overwhelming force as to render it necessary for them to retire. Thus, after having victory in their grasp, they were compelled to relinquish it, because General Lee's orders had again failed to be carried out; but one of those brigades brought off four captured battle flags from the top of Cemetery Hill. This affair occurred just a little before dark.

"On the next day, when the assault was made by Pickett's division in such gallant style, there was again a miscarriage, in not properly supporting it according to the plan and orders of the commanding general. You must recollect that a commanding general cannot do the actual marching and fighting of his army. These must, necessarily, be entrusted to his subordinates, and any hesitation, delay, or miscarriage in the execution of his orders, may defeat the best-devised schemes. Contending against such odds as we did, it was necessary, always, that there should be the utmost dispatch, energy, and undoubting confidence, in carrying out the plans of the commanding general. A subordinate who undertakes to doubt the wisdom of his superior's plans, and enters upon their execution with reluctance and distrust, will not be likely to insure success. It was General Jackson's unhesitating confidence and faith in the chances of success that caused it so often to perch on his banners, and made him such an invaluable executor of General Lee's plans. If Mr. Swinton has told the truth, in repeating in his book what is alleged to have been said to him by General Longstreet, there was at least one of General Lee's corps commanders at Gettysburg who did not enter upon the execution of his plans with that confidence and faith necessary to success, and hence, perhaps, it was that it was not achieved. Some have thought that General Lee did wrong in fighting at Gettysburg, and it has been said that he ought to have moved around Meade's left, so as to get between him and Washington. It is a very easy matter to criticize and prophesy after events happen; but it would have been manifestly a most dangerous movement for him to have undertaken to pass Meade by the flank with all his trains. In passing through the narrow space between Gettysburg and the South Mountain, we would have been exposed to an attack under very disadvantageous circumstances. I then thought, and still think, that it was right to fight the battle of Gettysburg, and I am firmly convinced that, if General Lee's plans had been carried out in the spirit in which they were conceived, a decisive victory would have been obtained, which perhaps would have secured our independence. Our army was never in better heart, and, when it did retire, it was with no sense of defeat. My division brought up the rear of the army, and it did not leave the sight of the enemy's position until the afternoon of the 5th. One of Meade's corps followed us most cautiously, at a respectful distance, and when, at Fairfield, near the foot of the mountain, I formed line of battle to await it, no advance was made. There were none of the indications of defeat in the rear of the army on the march, and, when we took position near Hagerstown to await Meade's attack, it was with entire confidence in our ability to meet it with success.

"Meade's army at Gettysburg numbered at least one hundred thousand men in position. The whole force in the Department of Northern Virginia, at the close of May, four days before our movement north began, was sixty-eight thousand, three hundred and fifty-two. No reinforcements were received after that time, and, of course, the whole force was not carried out of Virginia. General Lee's army at Gettysburg numbered considerably less than sixty thousand men of all arms.

"This campaign did not accomplish all that we desired, but, nevertheless, it was not unattended with great and advantageous results. It certainly had the effect of deferring, for one year at least, the advance on the Confederate capital, and had it not been for the fall of Vicksburg at the same time, and the consequent severance of all the states beyond the Mississippi from the Confederacy, for all practical purposes, the public would not have taken as gloomy a view of the results of the campaign as it did.

"So far from our army being defeated or broken in spirit, when the invading army of the enemy again advanced into Virginia, General Lee intercepted it, and, taking position on the south bank of the Rapidan, effectually prevented any further advance until May 1864, when, as I will show you, the power of the Confederacy had been so crippled in other quarters as to allow an unusual accumulation of men and resources against the Army of Northern Virginia.

"You must understand that the line of the Rappahannock and the Rapidan was the only practicable line of defense in Northern Virginia, because the possession and control of the Potomac and Chesapeake Bay, which the enemy's monitors and iron-clads gave him, without let or hinderance, would enable him to flank and turn any line of defense which might be assumed north of those rivers. Beyond that line General Lee, in 1862, had driven the invading army, and there he had retained it up to the time of which I am speaking. This was all that a defensive policy could accomplish, and it was only when he assumed the offensive, as in the campaigns of Maryland and Pennsylvania, that the enemy could be hurled back on his own border, in order to defend his territory and capital. The results of the campaign into Pennsylvania left General Lee in possession of his legitimate line of defense, with the enemy's plans all thwarted for that year. In fact, so satisfied was the latter of his inability to accomplish anything, by an attempt to advance on Richmond, that two of Meade's corps were detached for the purpose of reinforcing Rosecrans at Chattanooga, and General Lee held his own line by such a certain tenure that he was able to detach Longstreet's corps, and send two divisions to Bragg, and one, first to the south side of James River, and then to North Carolina. After Longstreet had gone, occurred the movement which caused Meade to retire to Centerville, and about the last of November he crossed the Rapidan and moved to Mine Run, but retired just in time to avoid an attack which General Lee had prepared to make on his flank.

"At the close of the year 1863 the enemy was no farther advanced in his oft-repeated effort to capture the Confederate capital, than when Manassas was evacuated, early in the spring of 1862; but, in the Southwest, the fall of Vicksburg, the disaster of Missionary Ridge, and the failure of the campaign in Eastern Tennessee, had not only severed the trans-Mississippi region from the remainder of the Confederacy, but had left all Kentucky and Tennessee firmly in the power of the enemy, and rendered all the lower basin of the Mississippi practically useless to us. The main army of the West had been compelled to retire to Dalton, in the northwestern corner of Georgia, and, for all useful purposes, the Confederacy was confined to Georgia, North and South Carolina, and the portion of Virginia held by us. It is true that we held posts and had troops in Alabama, Florida, and Mississippi, but they could contribute nothing to the general defense, and the resources of those states were substantially lost to us, at least so far as operations in Virginia were concerned. This state of things left the enemy at liberty to concentrate his resources against the two principal armies of the Confederacy. Grant was made commander-in-chief of all the armies of the enemy in the spring of 1864, and took his position with the Army of the Potomac in the field, while Sherman was assigned to the command of the army at Chattanooga, which was to operate against ours at Dalton.

"By the 1st of May Grant had accumulated an army of more than one hundred and forty-one thousand men on the north bank of the Rapidan; and General Lee's army on the south bank, including two of Longstreet's divisions, which had returned from Tennessee, was under fifty thousand men of all arms.

"Grant's theory was to accumulate the largest numbers practicable against us, so as, by constant 'hammering,' to destroy our army 'by mere attrition if in no other way.' Besides the army under Grant, in Culpepper, there were near fifty thousand men in Washington and Baltimore, and the military control of the railroads and the telegraph, as well as an immense number of steam transports, rendered it an easy matter to reinforce him indefinitely.

"On the 4th of May he crossed the Rapidan on our right to the Wilderness, to get between us and Richmond. General Lee advanced promptly to attack him and thwart his purpose; and then ensued that most wonderful campaign from the Rapidan to the James, in which the ever-glorious Army of Northern Virginia grappled its gigantic antagonist in a death struggle, which continued until the latter was thrown off, crippled and bleeding, to the cover of the James and Appomattox Rivers, where it was enabled to recruit and renew its strength for another effort.

"Two days of fierce battle were had in the Wilderness, and our little army never struck more rapid and vigorous blows. Grant was compelled to move off from our front, and attempt to accomplish his purpose by another flank movement, but General Lee promptly intercepted him at Spottsylvania Courthouse; where again occurred a series of desperate engagements, in which, though a portion of our line was temporarily broken, and we sustained a loss which we could ill afford, yet Grant's army was so crippled that it was unable to resume the offensive until it had been reinforced from Washington and Baltimore to the full extent of forty thousand men. But General Lee received no reinforcements; and yet Grant, after waiting six days for his, when they did arrive, was again compelled to move off from us, and attempt another flank movement, under cover of the network of difficult watercourses around and east of Spottsylvania Courthouse. Never had the wonderful powers of our great chief, and the unflinching courage of his small army, been more conspicuously displayed than during the thirteen days at this place. One of his three corps commanders had been disabled by wounds at the Wilderness, and another was too sick to command his corps, while he himself was suffering from a

most annoying and weakening disease. In fact, nothing but his own determined will enabled him to keep the field at all; and it was there rendered
more manifest than ever that he was the head and front, the very life and
soul, of his army. Grant's new movement was again intercepted at Hanover
Junction, and from that point he was compelled to retire behind the North
Anna and Pamunkey, to escape his tenacious adversary by another ma-
neuver. He was again intercepted at Pole Green Church; and at Bethesda
Church, and on the historic field of Cold Harbor, occurred another series
of most bloody battles, in which such carnage was inflicted on Grant's
army that, when orders were given for a new assault, his troops in sullen
silence declined to move; and he was compelled to ask for a truce to bury
his dead. Though largely reinforced from Butler's army, Grant was now
compelled to take refuge on the south side of James River, at a point to
which he could have gone, by water, from his camps in Culpepper, without
the loss of a man. His original plan of the campaign was thus completely
thwarted, and he was compelled to abandon the attempt to take Richmond
by the land route, after a loss in battle of more men than were in General
Lee's whole army, including the reinforcements received at Hanover Junction and Cold Harbor, which latter consisted of two divisions, a brigade,
and less than three thousand men under Breckenridge, from the Valley.
When we consider the disparity of the forces engaged in this campaign,
the advantages of the enemy for reinforcing his army, and the time consumed in actual battle, it must rank as the most remarkable campaign of
ancient or modern times. We may read of great victories, settling the fate
of nations, gained by small armies of compact, well-trained, and thoroughly disciplined troops, over immense and unwieldy hordes of untrained
barbarians, or of demoralized soldiers, sunk in effeminacy and luxury; but
where shall we find the history of such a prolonged struggle, in which
such enormous advantages of numbers, equipments, resources and supplies, were on the side of the defeated party? The proximity of a number
of watercourses, navigable for steam vessels, and patrolled by Federal
gunboats, had enabled Grant to keep open his communications with the
sources of his supplies, and to receive constant accessions of troops, so
that it was impossible to destroy his army; but, if the contest, as in most
campaigns of former times, had been confined to two armies, originally
engaged in it, there can be no question but that Grant's would have been,
in effect, destroyed. As it was, his whole movement, after the first encounter in the Wilderness, was but a retreat by the flank, the Potomac, the

Rappahannock, the York and Pamunkey, and the James, in succession, furnishing him a new base to retire on, for the receipt of supplies and reinforcements, and the resumption of operations. The boldness and fertility of the strategy employed by our glorious chieftain, during this campaign, were indeed marvelous; and such was the disparity of numbers that it appears like romance, and men are disposed to turn an incredulous ear when the truth is told. In fact, General Lee himself was aware of the apparent improbability which a true statement of the facts would present, and in a letter to me, during the winter of 1865–66, he said:

" 'It will be difficult to get the world to understand the odds against which we fought.'

"Notwithstanding the disparity which existed, he was anxious, as I know, to avail himself of every opportunity to strike an offensive blow; and, just as Grant was preparing to move across James River with his defeated and dispirited army, General Lee was maturing his plans for taking the offensive; and, in stating his desire for me to take the initiative with the corps I then commanded, he said:

" 'We must destroy this army of Grant's before he gets to James River. If he gets there, it will become a siege, and then it will be a mere question of time.'

"He knew well that, with the army Grant then had, he could not take Richmond, but he also knew that, if that army could be placed on the south of the James and east of the Appomattox, where it would be out of the reach of ours for offensive operations, it could be reinforced indefinitely, until, by the process of attrition, the exhaustion of our resources, and the employment of mechanism and the improved engines of war against them, the brave defenders of our cause would gradually melt away. In fact, he knew that it would then become a contest between mechanical power and physical strength, on the one hand, and the gradually diminishing nerve and sinew of Confederate soldiers on the other, until the unlimited resources of our enemies must finally prevail over all the genius and chivalric daring which had so long baffled their mighty efforts in the field. It was from such considerations as these that he had made his great and successful effort to raise the siege in 1862; his subsequent campaign into Maryland; and his campaign into Pennsylvania in 1863.

"Before the contemplated blow against Grant was struck, the startling intelligence of Hunter's operations in the Valley was received, and it became necessary to detach, first Breckenridge's command, and then my corps, to meet the new danger threatening all of our communications.

"This enabled Grant to reach his new position unmolested, the movement toward which began on the night I received my orders to move by three o'clock next morning for the Valley. Finding it necessary to detach my command on a work of pressing urgency, General Lee determined to combine with the movement a daring expedition across the Potomac, to threaten the enemy's country and capital; about the conduct and results of which I will merely say that there has been much misunderstanding and ignorant misrepresentation. After reaching the south bank of the James, Grant made a dash for the purpose of capturing Petersburg, which was thwarted by the good soldier who had already baffled and defeated Butler. The enemy, now having found it impossible to capture the Confederate capital in a campaign by land, resorted to a combined operation of his army and navy, by the way of the James. The condition of things in the South and Southwest enabled him to still further strengthen Grant's army after its junction with Butler's; and the fall of Atlanta, in September, severed the greater part of Georgia practically from the Confederacy. There were no means of recruiting General Lee's army, to any considerable extent, after its union with Beauregard's small force, which, with the division and brigade of the Army of Northern Virginia returned at Hanover Junction, and the division received at Cold Harbor, did not reach twenty thousand men, while my corps had been detached. For nine long months was the unequal contest protracted by the genius of one man, aided by the valor of his little force, occupying a line of more than thirty miles, with scarcely more than a respectable skirmish line. During this time, there were many daring achievements and heroic deeds performed by the constantly diminishing survivors of those who had rendered the Army of Northern Virginia so illustrious; but, finally, constant attrition and lingering starvation did their work. General Lee had been unable to attack Grant in his stronghold, south of the James and east of the Appomattox, where alone such a movement was practicable, because a concentration for that purpose, on the east of the later river, would have left the way to Richmond open to the enemy. When, by the unsuccessful expedition into Tennessee, the march of Sherman through the center of Georgia to the Atlantic, his subsequent expedition north through South Carolina into North Carolina, and the consequent fall of Charleston and Wilmington, the Confederacy had been practically reduced to Richmond City, the remnant of the Army of Northern Virginia, and the very narrow slips of

country bordering on the three railroads and the canal running out of that
city into the Valley, southwestern Virginia, and North Carolina, the struggle in Virginia, maintained so long by the consummate ability of our
leader, began to draw to a close. To add to his embarrassments, he had
been compelled to detach a large portion of his cavalry to the aid of the
troops falling back before Sherman in his march northward, and a portion
of his infantry to the defense of Wilmington; and at the close of March
1865, Sherman had approached as far north as Goldsborough, North Carolina, on his movement to unite with Grant.

"It was not till then that Grant, to whose aid an immense force of
superbly equipped cavalry had swept down from the Valley, was able to
turn General Lee's flank and break his attenuated line. The retreat from
the lines of Richmond and Petersburg began in the early days of April,
and the remnant of the Army of Northern Virginia fell back for more than
one hundred miles, before its overpowering antagonist, repeatedly presenting front to the latter, and giving battle so as to check its progress.
Finally, from mere exhaustion, less than eight thousand men, with arms
in their hands, of the noblest army that had ever fought 'in the tide of
times,' were surrendered at Appomattox to an army of one hundred and
fifty thousand men; the sword of Robert E. Lee, without a blemish on it,
was sheathed forever; and the flag, to which he had added such luster,
was furled, to be henceforth embalmed in the affectionate remembrance
of those who had remained faithful during all our trials, and will do so to
the end.

"Who is it that stands out the grandest figure in that last sad scene of
the drama? Is it the victor? Victor over what? Can it be possible that any
adherent to the cause of our enemies can recur to that scene at Appomattox
Courthouse without blushing? On that occasion, the vast superiority of
the Confederate commander over his antagonist, in all the qualities of a
great captain, and of the Confederate soldier over the Northern, was made
most manifest to the dullest comprehension; and none were made more
sensible of it than our adversaries. General Lee had not been conquered
in battle, but surrendered because he had no longer an army with which
to give battle. What he surrendered was the skeleton, the mere ghost of
the Army of Northern Virgina, which had been gradually worn down by
the combined agencies of numbers, steampower, railroads, mechanism,
and all the resources of physical science. It had, in fact, been engaged in
a struggle, not only against the mere brute power of man, but against all

the elements of fire, air, earth, and water; and even that all-pervading and subtle fluid, whose visible demonstrations the ancients designated 'the thunderbolt of the gods,' had been led submissive in the path of the opposing army, so as to concentrate with rapidity and make available all the other agencies.

"It was by the use of these new adjuncts to the science of war, that McClellan and Pope had escaped destruction in 1862; the Federal capital been saved, after the terrible chastisement inflicted on their armies; Pennsylvania also saved in 1863, and Meade enabled to fight a drawn battle at Gettysburg; Grant's army preserved from annihilation in 1864, and enabled to reach the welcome shelter of the James and Appomattox; and now, they had finally produced that exhaustion of our army and resources, and that accumulation of numbers on the other side, which wrought the final disaster.

"When we come to estimate General Lee's achievements and abilities as a military commander, all these things must be taken into consideration.

"I have now given you a condensed sketch of General Lee's military career, and I am aware that what I have said falls short of the real merits of the subject. My estimates of the enemy's strength are taken from their own reports and statements. In the last interview I had with General Lee, since my return to the country, I mentioned to him my estimates of his strength at various times, and he said that they fully covered his force at all times, and in some instances were in excess. They are those I have now given you.

"From the facts I have presented, I think you will have no difficulty in discerning that the fall of Richmond, and the surrender of the Army of Northern Virginia, were the consequences of events in the West and Southwest, and not directly of the operations in Virginia. I say this, without intending to cast any reproach, directly or by implication, on the commanders or the rank and file of our armies operating in those quarters. For them I have a profound respect and admiration, and I am ever ready to receive and acknowledge them as worthy coadjutors and comrades of the Army of Northern Virginia. They had, also, the disadvantage of overwhelming numbers, and the other agencies I have mentioned, to contend against, and a truthful history of their deeds will confer upon them imperishable renown. I do not feel that it is necessary or just to attempt to build up the reputation of the Army of Northern Virginia or its commander, at the expense of our comrades who battled so gloriously and vigorously on other fields for the same just and holy cause. What I have said is not mentioned with any such purpose, but simply to note what I conceive to be an apparent and indisputable historic fact, that ought not to be overlooked in a review of General Lee's military record.

"At the close of the war, the deportment and conduct of our noble and honored leader were worthy of his previous history; and in that dignified and useful retirement to which he devoted the remainder of his days, in your midst, the true grandeur of his soul shone out as conspicuously as had his transcendent military genius in his campaigns; but I leave the duty of illustrating that to others.

"There have been efforts to draw parallels between our illustrious chief and some of the renowned commanders of former times, but these efforts have always proved unsatisfactory to me.

"Where shall we turn to find the peer of our great and pure soldier and hero? Certainly, we shall not find one among the mythic heroes of Homer, the wrath of the chief of whom was—

> '. . . . to Greece the direful spring
> Of woes unnumbered. . . .'

"Nor shall we find one among the Grecian commanders of a later period, though in the devotion of the hero of Thermopylæ, and the daring of the victor of Marathon, may be found similes for the like qualities in our hero. But there is too much of fable and the license of the heroic verse, in the narrations of their deeds, to make them reliable.

"Shall we take Alexander, who, at the head of his serried phalanxes, encountered the effeminate masses of Asia and scattered them like sheep before a ravening wolf? While sighing for new worlds to conquer, he could not control himself, but fell a victim to his own excesses.

"In the march of Hannibal, the great Carthaginian patriot and hero, over the Alps, and his campaigns in Italy, we might find a similarity to General Lee's bold strategy, but the system of warfare in those days, the implements of war, and the mode of maintaining armies in the field, which had neither baggage nor supply trains, but foraged on the country in which they operated, make such a vast difference, that the parallel ceases at the very beginning. Besides, Carthage and Rome were then nearly equal in power, and Hannibal was enabled to receive reinforcements from Carthage by sea, as the Carthaginians were a great maritime people; and the hostile neighbors to Rome readily furnished him with allies and auxiliaries.

"We will not find in republican Rome a parallel. Certainly not in Julius Cæsar, the greatest of Roman generals, who, at the head of the legions of 'the mistress of the world,' overran the countries of barbarians, and then turned his sword against the liberties of his country.

"We shall search in vain for one among the generals of the Roman Empire, either before or after its partition; nor shall we find one among the leaders of the barbaric hordes which overran the territories of the degenerate Romans; nor in the Dark Ages; nor among the Crusaders, who, under the standard of the Cross, committed such crimes against religion and humanity; nor among the chieftains of the Middle Ages, to advance whose ambitious projects the nations of Europe were, by turns, torn and ravaged.

"Perhaps, in the champion of Protestantism, from the north of Europe, Gustavus Adolphus, there might be found no unworthy parallel for our great leader, as well in regard to purity and unselfishness of character, as heroic courage and devotion, and the comparison has not inaptly been drawn; but the career of the heroic king of Sweden was cut short by death in battle, at so early a period, and before he had stood the test of adversity, that the materials for completing the parallel are wanting.

"Some have undertaken to draw the parallel between our pure chieftain and Marlborough, who owed his rise, in the first place, to the dishonor of his family, and the patronage of a debauched court favorite. I utterly repudiate that comparison. Besides, Marlborough commanded the armies of the greatest maritime power in the world, in alliance with all the rest of Europe, against France alone. Shall we compare General Lee to the great Napoleon, or his successful antagonist, Wellington? Napoleon was a captain of most extraordinary genius, but success was always necessary to him. As long as he had what Forest, with such terse vigor, if inelegance, would call 'the bulge,' he did wondrously, but he could never stand reverses; and the disastrous retreat from Moscow, and the shameful flight from Waterloo, must always be blots on his military escutcheon. He would have been unable to conduct the campaigns of General Lee against the constantly accumulating and ever-renewing armies of the enemy, and none of his own campaigns were at all similar to them. He played a bold game for empire and self-aggrandizement, regardless of the lives, liberties, or happiness of others, and the first adverse turn of the wheel of fortune ruined him. 'The Hundred Days' constituted but the last desperate effort of a ruined gambler.

"Wellington was a prudent, good soldier, at the head of the armies of a most powerful nation, 'the mistress of the seas,' in alliance with all Europe against Napoleon in his waning days. He was emphatically a favorite child of Fortune, and won his chief glory in a game against the desperate gambler whose last stake was up, when he had all the odds on his side. 'The Iron Duke,' though almost worshiped and overwhelmed with honors and riches by the British nation, does not furnish a suitable parallel for the great Confederate commander.

"In regard to all I have mentioned, and all other renowned military chieftains of other days, in the Old World, it must be recollected that they did not have to contend against the new elements in the art of war which were brought to bear against our armies and their commanders.

"Coming now to this side of the water, we may draw a parallel between General Lee and our great Washington in many respects; for, in their great self-command, in their patriotism, and in their purity and unselfishness of character, there was a great similarity; but the military operations of General Lee were on so much grander a scale than those of Washington, and the physical changes in the character of the country, wrought by the adaptation of steam power, and the invention of railroads and the telegraph, were so great, that there cease to be any further points of comparison between them as soldiers. It was the physical difficulty of penetrating the country, backed by the material aid, in men, money, and ships-of-war, of a powerful European nation, which enabled the states to win their independence under Washington; while the facilities for rapid communication and concentration, in connection with the aid received by our enemies, in men and money, from all Europe, which was a recruiting ground for them, caused our disasters and lost us our liberties, in a contest in which we stood alone.

"There is no occasion to draw a parallel between General Lee and our dead heroes, Sidney Johnston and Jackson. The career of the former, whose dawn gave such bright promise, was, unfortunately, cut off so soon, that the country at large did not have an opportunity of learning all of which those who knew him believed him to be capable.

"Whoever shall undertake to draw a parallel between General Lee and his great lieutenant, for the purpose of depreciating the one or the other, cannot have formed the remotest conception of the true character of either of those illustrious men, and congenial Christian heroes. Let us be thankful that our cause had two such champions, and that, in their characters, we can furnish the world at large with the best assurance of the rightfulness of the principles for which they and we fought. When asked for our vindication, we can triumphantly point to the graves of Lee and Jackson and look the world squarely in the face. Let them, the descendant of the Cavalier from tidewater, and the scion of the Scotch-Irish stock from the mountains of northwestern Virginia, lie here, in this middle ground, and let their memories be cherished and mingled together in that harmony which characterized them during their glorious companionship in arms.

"Nor would it be at all profitable to institute a comparison between General Lee and any of our living commanders. Let us be rejoiced that those still survive who were worthy defenders of our cause, and not unfit comrades of Lee, Sidney Johnston, and Stonewall Jackson.

"Shall I compare General Lee to his successful antagonist? As well compare the great pyramid, which rears its majestic proportions in the valley of the Nile, to a pigmy perched on Mount Atlas.

"No, my friends, it is a vain work for us to seek anywhere for a parallel to the great character which has won our admiration and love. Our beloved chief stands, like some lofty, column which rears its head among the highest, in grandeur, simple, pure and sublime, needing no borrowed lustre; and he is all our own."

The gallant and accomplished General John B. Gordon of Georgia, who developed such military genius as to place him in the very forefront of the soldiers of mark during the war, thus speaks of General Lee as a soldier:

"But, as one of the great captains of the world, he will first pass review and inspection before the criticism of history. We will not compare him with Washington. The mind revolts instinctively at the comparison and competition of two such men, so equally and gloriously great. But with modest, yet calm and unflinching confidence, we place him by the side of the Marlboroughs and Wellingtons, who fill such high niches in the Pantheon of immortality.

"Let us dwell for a moment, my friends, on this thought. Marlborough never met defeat, it is true. Victory marked every step of his triumphant march, but when, where, and whom, did Marlborough fight? The ambitious and vain but able Louis XIV had already exhausted the resources of his kingdom before Marlborough stepped upon the stage. The great Marshals Turenne and Condé were no more, and Luxemburg, we believe, had vanished from the scene. Marlborough, preeminently great, as he certainly was, nevertheless led the combined forces of England and of Holland, in the freshness of their strength, and the fullness of their financial ability, against prostrate France, with a treasury depleted, a people worn out, discouraged, and dejected.

"But let us turn to another comparison. The great Von Moltke, who now 'rides upon the whirlwind and commands the storm' of Prussian invasion, has recently declared that General Lee, in all respects, was fully the equal of Wellington, and you may the better appreciate this admission, when you remember that Wellington was the benefactor of Prussia, and probably Von Moltke's special idol. But let us examine the arguments ourselves. France was already prostrate when Wellington met Napoleon. That great emperor had seemed to make war upon the very elements themselves, to have contended with Nature, and to have almost defied Providence. The Nemesis of the North, more savage than Goth or Vandal, mounting the swift gales of a Russian winter, had carried death, desolation, and ruin, to the very gates of Paris. Wellington fought, at Waterloo, a bleeding and broken nation—a nation electrified, it is true, to almost superhuman energy, by the genius of Napoleon; but a nation prostrate and bleeding, nevertheless. Compare this, my friends, the condition of France, with the condition of the United States, in the freshness of her strength, in the luxuriance of her resources, in the lustihood of her gigantic youth, and tell me where belongs the chaplet of military superiority, with Lee or with Marlborough or Wellington? Even that greatest of captains, in his Italian campaigns, flashing his fame, in lightning splendor, over the world, even Bonaparte met and crushed in battle but three or four (I think) Austrian armies; while our Lee, with one army, badly equipped, and in time incredibly short, met and hurled back, in broken and shattered fragments, five admirably prepared and most magnificently appointed invasions. Yes, more, he discrowned, in rapid succession, one after another of the United States' most accomplished and admirable commanders.

"Lee was never really beaten. Lee could not be beaten! Overpowered, foiled in his efforts, he might be, but never defeated until the props which supported him gave way. Never until the platform sank beneath him, did any enemy ever dare pursue. On that most melancholy of pages, the downfall of the Confederacy, no Leipsic, no Waterloo, no Sedan, can ever be recorded."

Colonel Charles S. Venable, of General Lee's staff, made in Richmond, on the 30th of October, 1873, an address before the "Association of the Army of Northern Virginia," in which he gave a sketch of the campaign from the Wilderness to Petersburg. His summing up was as follows:

"On the 4th of May, four radiating invading columns set out, simultaneously for the conquest of Virginia. The old state, which had for three years known little else save the tramp of armed legions, was now to be closed in by a circle of fire, from the mountains to the seaboard.

"Through the southwestern mountain passes; through the gates of the lower Valley; from the battle-scarred vales of the Rappahannock; from the Atlantic seaboard to the waters of the James, came the serried hosts on field and flood, numbering more than two hundred and seventy-five thousand men (including in this number also reinforcements sent during the campaign). No troops were ever more thoroughly equipped, or supplied with a more abundant commissariat. For the heaviest column transports were ready to bring supplies and reinforcements to any one of three convenient deep-water bases—Aquia Creek, Port Royal, and the White House.

"The column next in importance had its deep-water base within nine miles of a vital point in our defenses. In the cavalry arm (so important in a campaign in a country like ours) they boasted overwhelming strength. The Confederate forces in Virginia, or which could be drawn to its defense from other points, numbered not more than seventy-five thousand men. Yet our great commander with steadfast heart, committing our cause to the Lord of battles, calmly made his disposition to meet the shock of the invading hosts. In sixty days the great invasion had dwindled to a siege of Petersburg (miles from deep water) by the main column, which, 'shaken in its structure, its valor quenched in blood, and thousands of its ablest officers killed or wounded, was the Army of the Potomac no more.'

"Mingled with it in the lines of Petersburg lay the men of the second column, which for the last forty days of the campaign had been held in inglorious inaction at Bermuda Hundreds by Beauregard, except when a portion of it was sent to share the defeat of June 3d on the Chickahominy, while the third and fourth columns, foiled at Lynchburg, were wandering in disorderly retreat through the mountains of West Virginia, entirely out of the area of military operations.

"Lee had made his works at Petersburg impregnable to assault, and had a movable column of his army within two days' march of the Federal capital. He had made a campaign unexampled in the history of defensive warfare."

Colonel Venable thus concluded his address on his occasion:

"My comrades, I feel that I have given but a feeble picture of this grand period in the history of this time of trial of our beloved South—a history which is a great gift of God, and which we must hand down as a holy heritage to our children, not to teach them to cherish a spirit of bitterness or a love for war, but to show them that their fathers bore themselves worthily in the strife when to do battle became a sacred duty. Heroic history is the living soul of a nation's renown. When the traveler in Switzerland beholds the monument to the thirteen hundred brave mountaineers who met the overwhelming hosts of their proud invaders, and as he reads in their epitaph, 'who fell unconquered, but wearied with victory, giving their souls to God and their bodies to the enemy'; or when he visits the places sacred to the myth of William Tell, transplanted by pious, patriotic friends from the legends of another people to inspire the youth of that mountain land with a hatred of tyrants and a love of heroic deeds; or when he contemplates that wonderful monument by Thorwaldsen on the shores of Lake Lucerne in commemoration of the fidelity in death of the Swiss Guard of Louis XVI—a colossal lion, cut out of the living rock, pierced by a fatal javelin, and yet in death protecting the lily of France with his paw—he asks himself, how many men of the nations of the world have been inspired with a love of freedom by the monuments and heroic stories of little Switzerland?

"Comrades, we need not weave any fable borrowed from Scandinavian lore into the woof of our history to inspire our youth with admiration of glorious deeds in freedom's battles done. In the true history of this Army of Northern Virginia, which laid down its arms not conquered, but wearied with victory, you have a record of deeds of valor, of unselfish consecration to duty, and faithfulness in death, which will teach our sons and our sons' sons how to die for liberty. Let us see to it that it shall be transmitted to them."

*   *   *

In an address before the "Society of Confederate Soldiers and Sailors," in Baltimore, October 12, 1871, that accomplished soldier, General Wade Hampton of South Carolina, thus sums up the result of the campaign of 1862:

"Thus it will be seen that Lee, in the short space of two months, with a force at no time exceeding seventy-five thousand (75,000) men, defeated in repeated engagements two Federal armies, each of which was not less than one hundred and twenty thousand (120,000) strong, relieved the Southern capital from danger, and even threatened that of the North. But the campaign, great as it had been, was not to end here. Throwing his army into Maryland, Lee swept down from that state on Harper's Ferry, capturing it, with its garrison of eleven thousand (11,000) men, and seventy-two (72) guns; and then again concentrating his troops on the north of the Potomac, he fought the brilliant and bloody battle of Sharpsburg. In this great fight—for great it was, though the Southern arms failed to gain so decisive a victory as had so generally attended them—Lee, with only thirty-seven thousand (37,000) men, repulsed every attack of the enemy, who brought into the field an army three times as strong as his own. Is this not glory enough for one campaign, for one army—for one man? Yet the story of these great deeds is scarcely begun—the glory not yet at its zenith. Before even this campaign ended, 'Fredericksburg' was to be inscribed on those Southern banners which were already so covered by names of victories as scarcely to leave room for another."

After quoting the simple but beautiful orders in which General Lee announced to his troops the results of this campaign, General Hampton continues:

"These words, brief and simple as they are, record deeds rarely equaled. What was accomplished by Lee in the brief period embraced in this order will be more readily comprehended by giving the actual results of the campaign. These were, besides a series of brilliant victories to the Confederate arms, losses to the enemy of seventy-five thousand (75,000) men, one hundred and fifty-four (154) pieces of artillery, and seventy thousand (70,000) small arms. If to this list, so glorious to the Army of Northern Virginia, be added the Federal loss in the battle of Fredericksburg, we shall have the enormous number of eighty-seven thousand, five hundred (87,500) men killed, wounded, and captured by this army in one short campaign."

General Hampton then shows the superiority of Lee's generalship, in an able sketch of his subsequent campaigns, and makes the following comparison between him and his finally successful antagonist:

"What did Lee effect with the Army of Northern Virginia?

"In the three years he commanded that army, he inflicted a loss on the enemy of not less, and perhaps more, than three hundred thousand (300,000) men, besides taking guns and small arms almost beyond computation. In his last campaign, with a force at no time exceeding forty-five thousand (45,000), and often far less than that number, he destroyed one hundred and twenty thousand (120,000) of the enemy, and he held for nine months a weak line against an army quadruple his own. These are, in brief, the actual, palpable, enduring results of his generalship.

"What did Grant effect during those same eleven months of carnage embraced in the last campaign, to prove his generalship? He began his movement with upward of one hundred and forty thousand (140,000) men, and he was able, on account of his great resources, to keep his army up to this number, at least, to the close. In the first month of the campaign his loss was so heavy that, had his dead and wounded been placed touching each other, they would literally have formed one long, continuous, gory line from the Wilderness to Cold Harbor! They at least had fought it out 'on that line.' In the whole campaign he lost not less than one hundred and twenty thousand, (120,000) men, and he finally, by mere weight of numbers—for his generalship could never have accomplished this—overwhelmed his antagonist. But in order to bring this question down to narrower limits, let us suppose that the relative numbers and positions of the opposing armies had been reversed, and that Grant, with thirty-five thousand (35,000) men, had occupied a line forty miles long, while Lee confronted him with one hundred and forty thousand (140,000) Southern troops: can any imagination, however wild, stretch so far as to conceive that he could have held that line for nine months? The proposition is too absurd for serious consideration. He would not have held it for one month, not for one day, no, not for one hour!"

Want of space compels the omission of the testimony of others of the ablest soldiers of the Confederate army. Suffice it to say, that they all concur in the opinion which Stonewall Jackson once expressed: *"General Lee is a phenomenon. He is the only man whom I would be willing to follow blindfold."*

Indeed, it has been rarely the fortune of a military chieftain to inspire his subordinates with such implicit confidence in his ability; and Lee's soldiers thought that he could accomplish *anything* which his judgment would allow him to undertake.

Equally decided were the opinions of civilians who were in position to fully appreciate his merits. The able soldier-statesmen who presided over the fortunes of the Confederacy, the Cabinet, the Congress, the press, and the people, were well-nigh unanimous in pronouncing on his unrivaled merits.

John Mitchell, the Irish patriot, thus wrote of him in the *New York Citizen*:

"The highest head, the noblest and grandest character of our continent, the most conscientious, humane, and faithful soldier, the most chivalrous gentleman in this world, the best, the most superb sample of the American warrior, has fallen like a mighty tree in the forest; and men wonder, after the first shock of the news, to find that there is such a gap, such a blank in the world.

"What is there wanting to the fame of this illustrious American?"

One other extract from the countless expressions of his friends is sub-joined. An able writer in the *Southern Review* makes the following comparison between the achievements of Lee and Wellington: "As compared with those of General Lee, they seem, including even Waterloo, absolutely insignificant. General Lee, with a force not so large as the Anglo-Portuguese regular army, which Wellington had under him when he encountered Massena in 1809—not half so large as his whole force, if the Portuguese militia be taken into the account—in the space of twenty-eight days, in three battles, killed and wounded more men than Wellington ever killed and wounded during his whole career from Assaye to Waterloo, both inclusive. In one of these battles he killed and wounded more men by nine thousand (9,000) than the French army lost, including prisoners, in the whole campaign of Waterloo, and the pursuit to the gates of Paris. In the same battle he killed and wounded more men than Wellington, Blucher, and Napoleon, all three together, lost in killed and wounded in the battle of Waterloo, by five thousand (5,000) men. In the second of these battles he killed and wounded the same number that both the opposing armies lost in the battle of Waterloo; and in the third he killed and wounded more men, by seven thousand (7,000), than the French alone lost in the battle of Waterloo. In the three battles together, Lee killed and wounded more men, by at least thirty thousand (30,000), than the allies and the French lost in the whole campaign, including prisoners. The force with which Lee operated never amounted at one time to fifty thousand (50,000) men; the force with which Wellington and Blucher acted was, even according to English estimates, one hundred and ninety thousand (190,000) strong. The force to which Lee was opposed was from first to last two hundred and forty thousand (240,000) strong; the force to which Wellington and Blucher were opposed was but one hundred and twenty-two thousand (122,000) strong. When Massena invaded Portugal, in 1810, Wellington had thirty thousand (30,000) British troops and twenty-five thousand (25,000) Portuguese regulars, who, in the battle of Busaco, according to Wellington's own account, 'proved themselves worthy to fight side by side with the British veterans'; besides forty thousand (40,000) admirable Portuguese militia. He had Lisbon for his base, with a British war fleet riding at anchor, and innumerable vessels of other descriptions plying between the port and England, and bringing the most abundant supplies of arms, provisions, and munitions of war. He had surrounded the port with the most tremendous system of fortifications known in modern times, and his task was to defend the strongest country in Europe. In Lee's case the enemy had possession of the sea, and could and did land a powerful army to attack the very basis of his operations, while he was fighting another of still greater strength in front. It is probably not altogether just to Wellington to institute this comparison. If his deeds look but commonplace beside the achievements of this campaign, so do all others. The history of the world cannot exhibit such a campaign as that of Lee in 1864."

If it be objected that the opinions above cited are those of too-partial friends, the ready reply is to quote from those who adhered to the North in the great struggle.

In an address at Louisville, Kentucky, General Preston thus gives the opinion of General Winfield Scott of his favorite officer:

"I remember when General Lee was appointed lieutenant-colonel, at the same time when Sidney Johnston was appointed colonel, and General Scott thought that Lee should have been colonel. I was talking with General Scott on the subject long before the late struggle between the North and South took place, and he then said that Lee was the greatest living soldier in America. He didn't object to the other commission, but he thought Lee should be first promoted. Finally, he said to me, with emphasis, what you will pardon me for relating: '*I tell you that if I were on my deathbed tomorrow, and the president of the United States should tell me that a great battle was to be fought for the liberty or slavery of the country, and asked my judgment as to the ability of a commander, I would say with my dying breath, Let it be Robert E. Lee.*' "

In his address at a memorial meeting in Baltimore, Hon. Reverdy Johnson bore the following testimony:

"It was his good fortune to know him many years since, before the Mexican War, immediately preceding the great struggle, and after it. The conduct of General Lee at every period was every thing that could command the respect, admiration, and love of man. He (Mr. Johnson) had been intimate with the late General Scott, commander of the Army of Mexico, and served with him as a *quasi*-professional adviser in Washington, and he had heard General Scott more than once say that his success was largely due to the skill, valor, and undaunted energy of Robert E. Lee. It was a theme upon which he (General Scott) liked to converse, and he stated his purpose to recommend him as his successor in the chief command of the army.

"He (Mr. Johnson) was with General Scott in April 1861, when he received the resignation of General Lee, and witnessed the pain it caused him. It was a sad blow to the success of that war, in which his own sword had as yet been unsheathed. Much as General Scott regretted it, he never failed to say that he was convinced that Lee had taken that step from an imperative sense of duty. General Scott was consoled in a great measure by the reflection that he would have as his opponent a soldier worthy of every man's esteem, and one who would conduct the war upon the strictest rules of civilized warfare. There would be no outrages committed upon private persons or private property which he could prevent . . .

"Robert E. Lee is worthy of all praise. As a man, he was peerless among men. As a soldier, he had no superior and no equal. As a humane and Christian soldier, he towers high in the political horizon. He remembered with what delight, while he was the representative of the country at the court of Great Britain, he heard the praises of General Lee's character and fame from eminent soldiers and statesmen of that country. The occasion does not require any comparisons that were made between the generals of the North and Lee by the public opinion of England. There was not one of them who was the superior of Robert E. Lee. It was not only the skill with which he planned his campaigns, it was the humane manner in which he carried them out. He heard the praises which were bestowed upon Lee's order of June 26, 1863, issued in Pennsylvania, to his army, in which he told his men not to forget that the honor of the army required them to observe the same humanity in the country of the enemy as in their own."

As confirmatory of the statements of General Scott's opinion of Lee, I give in full the following letter:

> "HEADQUARTERS OF THE ARMY,
> *May* 8, 1857.
>
> "*Hon.* J. B. FLOYD, *Secretary of War.*
>
> "SIR: I beg to ask that one of the vacant second-lieutenantcies may be given to W. H. F. Lee, son of Brevet-Colonel R. E. Lee, at present on duty against the Comanches.
>
> "I make this application mainly on the extraordinary merits of the father—*the very best soldier that I ever saw in the field*—but the son is himself a very remarkable youth, now about twenty, of a fine stature and constitution, a good linguist, a good mathematician, and about to graduate at Harvard University. He is also honorable, and amiable like his father, and dying to enter the army. I do not ask this commission as a favor, though if I had influence I should be happy to exert it in this case. My application is in the name of national justice, in part payment (and but a small part) of the debt due to the invaluable services of Colonel Lee.
>
> "I have the honor to be, with high respect.
>
> "Your obedient servant,
> "WINFIELD SCOTT."

Rev. Dr. Brantley stated, in a memorial discourse at Atlanta, that in a conversation with him General George Meade, of the United States Army, had stated as his very emphatic opinion that Lee was "by far the ablest Confederate general which the war produced."

*   *   *

In an editorial upon his death the *New York World* said: "Every man is to be judged, so far as human judgment may be passed upon him at all, by the tenor of the motives to which the main current of his days has responded. Judged by this standard, the career of Robert E. Lee must command the deliberate admiration even of those who most earnestly condemn the course upon which he decided in the most solemn and imperative crisis of his life. Of his genius as a military commander we do not speak. To that the unanimous voice of all the true and gallant men who fought our long battle out with him and his untiring army has borne abundant witness. The events which evoked it are still too near to us, too many melancholy memories still cluster about the names of those prodigious battlefields of Virginia, to make it natural or possible for a Northern pen to dwell with complacency upon the strategic resources, the inexhaustible patience, the calm determination, of our most illustrious antagonist. But if the testimony of all honorable men who contended against the great Southern general agrees with the verdict of all competent foreign critics in awarding to him a place among the most eminent soldiers of history, the concord is not less absolute of all who knew the man in the private and personal aspects of his life, as to his gentleness, his love of justice, his truth, and his elevation of soul."

The *New York Sun,* edited by Charles A. Dana—Mr. Lincoln's Assistant Secretary of War—thus concludes its notice:

"His death will awaken most profound and honest manifestations of grief throughout the entire South, and very many people in the North will forget political differences beside the open grave of the dead chieftain, and drop a tear of sorrow on his bier. And whatever may be the verdict as to his career in public life, the universal expression will be that in General Lee an able soldier, a sincere Christian, and an honest man, has been taken from earth."

The *New York Herald* thus announced his death:

"On a quiet autumn morning, in the land which he loved so well, and, as he held, served so faithfully, the spirit of Robert Edward Lee left the clay which it had so much ennobled, and traveled out of this world into the great and mysterious land. The expressions of regret which sprang from the few who surrounded the bedside of the dying soldier and Christian, on yesterday, will be swelled today into one mighty voice of sorrow, resounding throughout our country, and extending over all parts of the world where his great genius and his many virtues are known. For not to the Southern people alone shall be limited the tribute of a tear over the dead Virginian. Here in the North, forgetting that the time was when the sword of Robert Edward Lee was drawn against us—forgetting and forgiving all the years of bloodshed and agony—we have long since ceased to look upon him as the Confederate leader, but have claimed him as one of ourselves; have cherished and felt proud of his military genius as belonging to us; have recounted and recorded his triumphs as our own; have extolled his virtue as reflecting upon us—for Robert Edward Lee was an American, and the great nation which gave him birth would be today unworthy of such a son if she regarded him lightly.

"Never had mother a nobler son. In him the military genius of America was developed to a greater extent than ever before. In him all that was pure and lofty in mind and purpose found lodgment. Dignified without presumption, affable without familiarity, he united all those charms of manners which made him the idol of his friends and of his soldiers, and won for him the respect and admiration of the world. Even as, in the days of his triumph, glory did not intoxicate, so, when the dark clouds swept over him, adversity did not depress. From the hour that he surrendered his sword at Appomattox to the fatal autumn morning, he passed among men, noble in his quiet, simple dignity, displaying neither bitterness nor regret over the irrevocable past. He conquered us in misfortune by the grand manner in which he sustained himself, even as he dazzled us by his genius when the tramp of his soldiers resounded through the valleys of Virginia.

"And for such a man we are all tears and sorrow today. Standing beside his grave, men of the South and men of the North can mourn with all the bitterness of four years of warfare erased by this common bereavement. May this unity of grief—this unselfish manifestation over the loss of the Bayard of America— in the season of dead leaves and withered branches which this death ushers in, bloom and blossom like the distant coming spring into the flowers of a heartier accord!

". . . In person General Lee was a notably handsome man. He was tall of stature, and admirably proportioned; his features were regular and most amiable in appearance, and in his manners he was courteous and dignified. In social life he was much admired. As a slaveholder, he was beloved by

his slaves for his kindness and consideration toward them. General Lee
was also noted for his piety. He was an Episcopalian, and was a regular
attendant at church. Having a perfect command over his temper, he was
never seen angry, and his most intimate friends never heard him utter an
oath. Indeed, it is doubtful if there are many men of the present generation
who unite so many virtues and so few vices in each of themselves as did
General Lee. He came nearer the ideal of a soldier and Christian general
than any man we can think of, for he was a greater soldier than Havelock,
and equally as devout a Christian. In his death our country has lost a son
of whom she might well be proud, and for whose services she might have
stood in need had he lived a few years longer, for we are certain that, had
occasion required it, General Lee would have given to the United States
the benefit of all his great talents."

The *Philadelphia Age* thus concluded an extended criticism of his military career:

"His best-fought fields were on the Peninsula and at Chancellorsville
and Fredericksburg, and the long, desperate, brilliant, unequal struggle,
the successes of which will fill the soldier with admiration and wonder,
though to the popular eye they are merged in the fall of Richmond and
the capitulation of his army. As a great master of defensive warfare, Lee
will probably not be ranked inferior to any general known in history.
Whether those for whom he fought will rank him ultimately above Johnston and Jackson, or how he will stand on the page of history, in comparison with his great opponents, we have neither ability nor inclination
to discuss. It is not our aim today to criticize, nor to broach political
questions, but to pay our tribute of respect and honor to a great man, who
fought fairly and nobly on the side he took, sincerely believing it to be,
according to his light, the side to which patriotism and honor summoned
him. There are too many men in the world who willfully go wrong from
base and venal and selfish motives. Let us be charitable to the brave and
good, who, if they err, err because human judgment is fallible, the circumstances of their position difficult, and the path of duty, which they
wish to follow, is not, to their eyes, clearly discernible."

The *Cincinnati Inquirer* paid him the following tribute:
"The world knows of his virtues and his private worth, and the
men who have commanded armies can bear witness to his valor and skill

as a man of arms. He was the great general of the 'Rebellion.' It was his strategy and superior military knowledge which kept the banner of the South afloat so long, and the campaign of the Wilderness, the defense of Richmond, and the bold advances into Maryland and Pennsylvania, which only failed because of insufficient numbers, established him long before the close of the war as one whom the powerful press of England might well proclaim 'the great captain of the age.' There is no man so bigoted today as not to believe that if Grant had commanded the ill-provided, half-fed army which stood like a wall of fire around Richmond, and the command of that grand army which went down into the Wilderness could have been given to Lee, the flag of the Union would have floated over the Confederate capital long before it did."

Horace Greeley can be suspected of no undue partiality to Lee, and his book, *The American Conflict,* is very far from fair to the Confederates, but in his account of the closing scene at Appomattox he is constrained to say: "The parting of Lee with his devoted followers was a sad one. Of the proud army which, dating its victories from Bull Run, had driven McClellan from before Richmond, and withstood his best effort at Antietam, and shattered Burnside's host at Fredericksburg, and worsted Hooker at Chancellorsville, and fought Meade so stoutly, though unsuccessfully, before Gettysburg, and baffled Grant's bounteous resources and desperate efforts in the Wilderness, at Spottsylvania, on the North Anna, at Cold Harbor, and before Petersburg and Richmond, a mere wreck remained. It is said that twenty-seven thousand were included in Lee's capitulation; but of these not more than ten thousand had been able to carry their arms thus far on their hopeless and almost foodless flight. Barely nineteen miles from Lynchburg when surrendered, the physical possibility of forcing their way thither even at the cost of half their number no longer remained. And if they were all safely there, what then? The resources of the Confederacy were utterly exhausted. Of the one hundred and fifty thousand men whose names were borne on its muster rolls a few weeks ago, at least one-third were already disabled or prisoners, and the residue could neither be clad nor fed—not to dream of their being fully armed or paid; while the resources of the loyal states were scarcely touched, their ranks nearly or quite as full as ever, and their supplies of ordnance, small arms, munitions, etc., more ample than in any previous April. Of the million or so borne on our muster rolls, probably not more than half were in active service, with half so many more able to take the field at short notice. The rebellion had failed and gone down; but the rebel army of Virginia and its commander had *not* failed. Fighting sternly against the inevitable; against the irrepressible tendencies—the generous aspirations of the age, they had been proved unable to succeed when success would have been a calamity to their children, to their country, and to the human race. And when the transient agony of defeat had been endured and passed, they all experienced a sense of relief as they crowded around their departing chief, who, with streaming eyes, grasped and pressed their outstretched hands, at length finding words to say: 'Men, we have fought through the war together. I have done the best that I could for you.' There were few dry eyes among those who witnessed the scene."

Swinton, in his *Army of the Potomac,* a book of considerable ability, which, while making grave errors, has some show of fairness to the South, pays frequent and high tribute to Lee's ability as a soldier; on page 16 he writes as follows: "Nor can there fail to arise the image of that other army, that was the adversary of the Army of the Potomac, and which who can ever forget that once looked upon it?—that array of tattered uniforms and bright muskets—that body of incomparable infantry, the Army of Northern Virginia, which for four years carried the revolt on its bayonets, opposing a constant front to the mighty concentration of power brought against it; which, receiving terrible blows, did not fail to give the like; and which, vital in all its parts, died only with its annihilation."

If it be said that even the opinions of Northern writers are biased by the fact that Lee was an *American,* and that they really exalt their own soldiers in proportion to the high estimate they place on their great antagonist, we have only to quote from foreign writers, who may be supposed to be entirely impartial.

The Halifax (Nova Scotia) *Morning Chronicle* of October 14, 1870, contained a most beautiful tribute to General Lee, from which the following extract is taken:

" 'Ah, Sir Lancelot,' he said, 'thou wert head of all Christian knights; and now, I dare say,' said Sir Ector, 'thou, Sir Lancelot, there thou liest, that thou wert never matched of earthly knights' hand; and thou wert the courtliest knight that ever bare shield . . . and thou wert the kindest man that ever strake with sword; and thou wert the goodliest person that ever came among press of knights; and thou wert the meekest man and the gentliest that ever ate in hall among ladies; and thou wert the sternest knight to thy mortal foe that ever put spear in rest.'—*The Mort d' Arthur* of Sir Thomas Malory.

"With reverence and regret we repeat today Sir Ector's words of sorrow for the great Sir Lancelot, and apply them to the man who died yesterday—the noblest knight of our generation. The hero of the Arthurian legends, as he lay dead in Joyous-Gard with the record of a life made splendid by great deeds, might have revived other than kindly or ennobling recollections in the mourner's mind; for the wronged king, and the breaking up of the goodly fellowship of the Round Table could not be forgotten, but lay like shadows upon the dead knight. But in the life of Robert Edward Lee there was no reproach of man or woman; his deeds were dimmed by no wrong done or duty unfulfilled; there was no stain upon his honor, and no unrighteous blood upon his hands. He was, indeed, a good knight, noble of heart and strong of purpose, and both a soldier and a gentleman. The age that knew him, if not the age of chivalry, will yet be remarkable for having produced in him a man as chivalric as any that lives in history. He, too, was one, and the greatest one, of a goodly fellowship that was broken up and scattered about the world. Some of these Southern knights have gone before him, and with him departs the last remnant of the cause for which they fought and the strength that so long upheld it.

"Only nine years ago he was a colonel of cavalry in the United States army, and yesterday he died the greatest soldier in the world. Four years' service in the field at the head of an army gained for him this reputation, and though he was worsted at the last, it was a reputation that he did not lose with his losses. It is strong praise to give to him, but nonetheless deserved, for even his former enemies must concede to him the first place in the civil war, and we know of no living European general who possesses to the same extent those attributes of a soldier which so distinguished the Confederate leader. It is true that Europe has yet Napier, and McMahon, and Von Moltke, and that America has also Sherman and Sheridan and Longstreet, but all these men and all their fellow soldiers lack the grandeur which was inherent in Lee.

"In every particular he possessed the requisites of a true soldier. He was brave; his whole military record and his life-long scorn of danger alike bear testimony to his bravery. He was wise; his great successes against great odds, and his almost constant anticipation of the enemy's movements, were proofs of his wisdom. He was skillful; his forced marches and unexpected victories assert his skill. He was patient and unyielding; his weary struggle against the mighty armies of the North, and his stern defense of Richmond, will forever preserve the memory of his patience and resolution. He was gentle and just; the soldiers who fought under him and who came alive out of the great fight, remembering and cherishing the memory of the man, can one and all testify to his gentleness and his justice. Above all, he was faithful; when he gave up his sword there was no man in his own ranks or in those of the enemy that doubted his faith, or believed that he had not done all that mortal could do for the cause for which he had made such a noble struggle. . . .

"His military genius derives its most important proof from the fact that, from the time of his appointment to the position of Confederate commander-in-chief until the close of the war, the appointment was never changed. There were many talented and brave men in the South—men like Longstreet and Polk, and the two Johnstons, and that one who took with him to a soldier's grave the love of the whole world, and the name of Stonewall Jackson. But there was only one Lee, and to him the South knew must her safety and her hopes be committed. He failed to realize these hopes, but he gained, if not for his cause, at least for his country and himself, a glory imperishable and unclouded by his defeat. On the other hand, the army of the North was compelled to endure a long succession of leaders, one as incapable as the other, until men of real worth were discovered at last. It seems incredible, on looking back to that wartime, that Lee should have held his own so long and so bravely, when he was opposed to ever-changing tactics, and a force immensely superior in numbers. Only a king of men could have possessed such courage and endurance, and his whole life is a proof that among the brotherhood of men Lee was indeed a king.

"When the last chance was gone, and all hope was at an end, the old hero bowed to a higher will than his own, and accepted the fate of the South with calm grandeur. But he was done with all his wars. He could never take the field again; he knew that it was not for him to see the act of secession upheld by the South and recognized by the North, and after the failure of his own countrymen he was too old and war-worn to draw his sword in a foreign quarrel. He passed from the fever of the camp into the quiet of the cloister, and as the president of Washington College, in

Virginia, spent the remaining portion of his sixty-three years in working for the good of his native state.

"We cannot express all the truth that could be told about Lee, nor can we do justice to his worth and fame, but perhaps the few words of Sir Ector are the best after all. He was a good knight, a true gentleman; knowing this, let us leave him with fame and posterity; with the rest, the light, the Resurrection and the Life."

On the announcement of the illness of General Lee, the London *Standard* paid him a glowing tribute, from which the following extract is taken:

"Whatever differences of opinion may exist as to the merits of the generals against whom he had to contend, and especially of the antagonist by whom he was at last overcome, no one pretending to understand in the least either the general principles of military science, or the particular conditions of the American war, doubts that General Lee gave higher proofs of military genius and soldiership than any of his opponents. He was outnumbered from first to last; and all his victories were gained against greatly superior forces, and with troops deficient in every necessary of war except courage and discipline. Never perhaps was so much achieved against odds so terrible. The Southern soldiers—'that incomparable Southern infantry' to which a late Northern writer renders due tribute of respect—were no doubt as splendid troops as a general could desire, but the different fortune of the war in the East and in the West proves that the Virginian army owed something of its excellence to its chief. Always outnumbered, always opposed to a foe abundantly supplied with food, transports, ammunition, clothing, all that was wanting to his own men, he was always able to make courage and skill supply the deficiency of strength and of supplies; and from the day when he assumed the command after the battle of Seven Pines, where General Joseph Johnston was disabled, to the morning of the final surrender at Appomattox Courthouse, he was almost invariably victorious in the field. At Gettysburg only he was defeated in a pitched battle; on the offensive at the Chickahominy, at Centreville, and at Chancellorsville; on the defensive at Antietam, Fredericksburg, the Wilderness, and Spottsylvania, he was still successful. But no success could avail him anything from the moment that General Grant brought to bear upon the Virginia army the inexhaustible population of the North, and, employing Sherman to cut them off from the rest of the

Confederacy, set himself to work to wear them out by the simple process of exchanging two lives for one. From that moment the fate of Richmond and of the South was sealed. When General Lee commenced the campaign of the Wilderness he had, we believe, about fifty thousand men—his adversary had thrice that number at hand, and a still larger force in reserve. When the Army of Virginia marched out of Richmond it still numbered some twenty-six thousand men; after a retreat of six days, in the face of an overwhelming enemy, with a crushing artillery—a retreat impeded by constant fighting, and harassed by countless hordes of cavalry—eight thousand were given up by the capitulation of Appomattox Courthouse. Brilliant as were General Lee's earlier triumphs, we believe that he gave higher proofs of genius in his last campaign, and that hardly any of his victories were so honorable to himself and his army as that six days' retreat."

The *Montreal* (Canada) *Telegraph* published during the war the following, which not a few intelligent foreigners will heartily indorse:

"Posterity will rank General Lee above Wellington or Napoleon, before Saxe or Turenne, above Marlborough or Frederick, before Alexander or Cæsar. Careful of the lives of his men, fertile in resource, a profound tactician, gifted with the swift intuition which enables a commander to discern the purpose of his enemy, and the power of rapid combination which enables him to oppose to it a prompt resistance; modest, frugal, self-denying, void of arrogance or self-assertion, trusting nothing to chance; among men noble as the noblest, in the lofty dignity of the Christian gentleman; among patriots less self-seeking, and as pure as Washington; and among soldiers combining the religious simplicity of Havelock with the genius of Napoleon, the heroism of Bayard and Sidney, and the untiring, never-faltering duty of Wellington: in fact, Robert E. Lee, of Virginia, is the greatest general of this or any other age. He has made his own name, and the Confederacy he served, immortal."

Colonel Charles Cornwallis Chesney, the reputed author of the *Battle of Dorking* and perhaps the most distinguished of the English military critics, has recently published a volume of *Military Biography,* from which we take the following extracts:

"... Lee's first battle, in fact, was as striking a success, and as well earned, as any of the more famous victories in after-days which have been so widely studied and so often extolled. No word henceforward from his government of any want of confidence in his powers, or fear of his over-caution. From that hour he became the most trusted, as well as the most noted, general of the Confederacy. As to his soldiery, his hardy bearing, free self-exposure, and constant presence near their ranks, completed the influence gained by that power of combining their force to advantage which they instinctively felt without fully understanding. From man to man flew the story of the hour. The subtle influence of sympathy, which wins many hearts for one, was never more rapidly exercised. Like Napoleon, his troops soon learned to believe him equal to every emergency that war could bring. Like Hannibal, he could speak lightly and calmly at the gravest moments, being then himself least grave. Like Raglan, he preserved a sweetness of temper that no person or circumstance could ruffle. Like Caesar, he mixed with the crowd of soldiery freely, and never feared that his position would be forgotten. Like Blucher, his one recognized fault was that which the soldier readily forgives—a readiness to expose his life beyond the proper limits permitted by modern war to the commander-in-chief. What wonder, then, if he thenceforward commanded an army in which each man would have died for him; an army from which his parting wrung tears more bitter than any the fall of their cause could extort; an army which followed him, after three years of glorious vicissitudes, into private life without one thought of further resistance against the fate to which their adored chief yielded without a murmur?"

He thus speaks of the dark days of the winter of 1864–'65:

"Not in the first flush of triumph when his army cheered his victory over McClellan; not when hurling back Federal masses three times the weight of his own on the banks of the Rappahannock; nor even when advancing, the commander of victorious legions, to carry the war away from his loved Virginia into the North, had Lee seemed so great, or won the love of his soldiers so closely, as through the dark winter that followed. Overworked his men were sadly, with forty miles of entrenchments for that weakened army to guard. Their prospects were increasingly gloomy as month passed by after month, bringing them no reinforcements, while their enemy became visibly stronger. Their rations grew scantier and poorer, while the jocund merriment of the investing lines told of abundance often raised to luxury by voluntary tribute from the wealth of the North. The indiscipline, too long allowed, told on them; and, with the pangs of hunger added, led to desertion, formerly almost unknown in the Army of Virginia.

But the confidence of the men in their beloved chief never faltered. Their sufferings were never laid on 'Uncle Robert.' The simple piety which all knew the rule of his life, acted upon thousands of those under him with a power which those can hardly understand who know not how community of hope, suffering, and danger, fairly shared, amid the vicissitudes of war, quickens the sympathies of the roughest and lowest as well as of those above them. He who was known to every soldier under him to have forbidden his staff to disturb the impromptu prayer-meeting which stopped their way when hurrying to the fierce battle in the Wilderness; he whose exposure was seen by all to grow only greater as the hour grew darker; he who was as constant in the lines during the monotonous watch against the foe that never attacked as he had been when Grant hurled fresh legions on him day after day in the blood-stained thickets of Spottsylvania; he who, in short, had long lived up to the motto he had commended to his son on entering life, as the only sure guide, 'Duty is the sublimest word in our language'; now illustrated in his own person that other motto which he bequeathed to the army when it dissolved, 'Human virtue should be equal to human calamity.' The vision of becoming the new Washington of a new republic—had he ever entertained it—had faded away with all its natural ambition. The very hope of saving from humiliation the state for whose safety and honor he had sacrificed his high prospects in the army of the Union, must now be despaired of. Yet the firmness of his bearing, and his unfaltering attention to the hourly business of his office, never declined for a moment, and impressed alike the falling government of the Confederacy, the dejected citizens of its capital, and the humblest soldiers of its army."

He thus closes his honest soldier's tribute to the great Confederate chieftain:

"So passed away the greatest victim of the Civil War. Even in the farthest North, where he had once been execrated as the worst enemy of the Union, the tidings caused a thrill of regret. But though America has learned to pardon, she has yet to attain the full reconciliation for which the dead hero would have sacrificed a hundred lives. Time can only bring this to a land which in her agony bled at every pore. Time, the healer of all wounds, will bring it yet. The day will come when the evil passions of the great civil strife will sleep in oblivion, and North and South do justice to each other's motives, and forget each other's wrongs. Then history will speak with clear voice of the deeds done on either side, and the citizens of the whole Union do justice to the memories of the dead, and place above all others the name of the great chief of whom we have written. In strategy mighty, in battle terrible, in adversity as in prosperity a hero indeed, with the simple devotion to duty and the rare purity of the ideal Christian knight, he joined all the kingly qualities of a leader of men.

"It is a wondrous future indeed that lies before America; but in her annals of years to come, as in those of the past, there will be found few names that can rival in unsullied luster that of the heroic defender of his native Virginia, Robert Edward Lee."

Another English soldier—Colonel Lawler—who visited General Lee at his headquarters during the war, and conceived the warm admiration for him of everyone who came into personal contact with him, thus wrote in *Blackwood's Magazine*:

"One of England's greatest soldiers, Sir Charles James Napier, exclaims, 'How much more depends upon the chief than upon the numbers of an army! Alexander invaded Persia with only thirty thousand foot and five thousand horse; Hannibal entered Italy with twenty thousand foot and six thousand horse, having lost thirty thousand men in crossing the Alps. What did he attempt with this small army? The conquest of Italy from the Romans, who with their allies could bring into the field eight hundred thousand men in arms; and he maintained the war there for fifteen years.' Without maintaining that General Lee, who was neither an Alexander nor a Hannibal, had such odds against him as these two great captains of ancient history, we doubt whether any general of modern history ever sustained for four years—a longer time nowadays than Hannibal's fifteen years in the remote past—a war in which, while disposing of scanty resources himself, he had against him so enormous an aggregate of men, horses, ships, and supplies. It is an under- rather than overestimate of the respective strength of the two sections to state that during the first two years the odds, all told, were ten to one, during the last two twenty to one, against the Confederates. The prolongation of the struggle is in no slight degree attributed to Mr. Jefferson Davis, whose high character and unselfishness are, even now, undervalued by Confederates, and totally denied by his conquerors. The courage of the rank and file of the rebel army is refreshing to contemplate in these days, which have seen a European war between two nations equal in numbers and resources triumphantly closed in seven months, and stained by the three unprecedented capitulations of Sedan, Metz, and Paris. But, after all, the one name which, in connection with the great American Civil War, *posteris narratum atque traditum superstes erit,* is the name of Robert Edward Lee."

He concludes his criticism by saying:

"The fame and character of General Lee will hereafter be regarded in Europe and in America under a dual aspect. In Europe we shall consider him merely as a soldier; and it is more than probable that within the present century we shall have accustomed ourselves to regard him as third upon the list of English-speaking generals, and as having been surpassed in soldierly capacity by Marlborough and Wellington alone. In America, when the passions of the great Civil War shall have died out, Lee will be regarded more as a man than as a soldier. His infinite purity, self-denial, tenderness, and generosity, will make his memory more and more precious to his countrymen when they have purged their minds of the prejudices and animosities which civil war invariably breeds. They will acknowledge before long that Lee took no step in life except in accordance with what he regarded as, and believed to be, his duty."

The London *Times,* in an able review of Colonel Chesney's book, after an extended notice of Grant, concludes as follows:

"This determined soldier is not, however—and Colonel Chesney agrees with our judgment—to be compared with his greatest opponent, in the highest attainments of the military art; and as Hannibal, notwithstanding Zama, towers over the very inferior Scipio, the figure of Lee eclipses Grant, though Lee succumbed to the Northern chief. Colonel Chesney's essay on the brilliant career of the renowned leader of the Virginian army is too short to do the theme justice, but it is very attractive and full of interest. We have no space to notice the pleasing description he has given us of the private life of Lee, nor yet to comment on the public virtues of the high-minded citizen who drew his sword reluctantly in what he thought the rightful cause, and bore himself like a true patriot when reproach and disaster gathered around him. A few words are all that we can devote to the military powers of this great captain; and they are, indeed, superfluous, for their best monument is the battlefields of the American War. It may be said, however, that Lee has a place in the foremost rank of modern strategists; he possessed in the very highest degree ability for the great operations of war; few generals have ever, in Colonel Hamley's phrase, 'interpreted the theatre' with equal insight and known as well how to turn it to account; and no one certainly since the time of Napoleon has conquered against such immense odds, and has so long and fiercely disputed the prize of victory with failing resources. His combinations, indeed, bear a striking resemblance in many particulars to those of the emperor; like him, he gained astonishing success by the well-planned use of interior lines and bold movements against divided foes; like him, he avoided the timid system of passive defense as a general rule, and seemed the assailant, though on the defensive; like him, he possessed a fund of resources in his own genius which effected wonders; like him, too, he was swift and terrible in availing himself of the mistakes of an enemy. Thus it has happened that his campaigns have much in common with those of Napoleon, and fascinate the reader for the same reasons. They exhibit the triumph of profound intelligence, of calculation, and of well-employed force over numbers, slowness, and disunited counsels, like those of 1796 and 1814; and his victory on the Chickahominy in 1862, and the outmaneuvering of Grant in 1864, may fitly compare with Arcola or Rivoli and with the immortal struggle on the Marne and Seine. Lee, too, has never been surpassed in the art of winning the passionate love of his troops, and, as with all generals of a high order, his lieutenants looked up to him with perfect confidence, and saw in his commands a presage of victory."

The following inscription and poem accompanied the presentation of a perfect copy of the "Translation of the Iliad of Homer, into Spenserian Stanza," by Philip Stanhope Worsley, Fellow of Corpus Christi College, Oxford—a scholar and poet whose untimely death, noticed with deepest regret throughout the literary world in England, has cut short a career of the brightest promise:

"To General R. E. Lee—the most stainless of living commanders, and, except in fortune, the greatest—this volume is presented with the writer's earnest sympathy, and respectful admiration:

" ' . . . οἶος γὰρ ἐρύετο Ἰλιου Ἕκτωρ.' "

Iliad, vi., 403.

"The grand old bard that never dies,
Receive him in our English tongue!
I send thee, but with weeping eyes,
The story that he sung.

"Thy Troy is fallen, thy dear land
*   Is marred beneath the spoiler's heel.*
I cannot trust my trembling hand
*   To write the things I feel.*

"Ah, realm of tombs!—but let her bear
*   This blazon to the last of times:*
No nation rose so white and fair,
*   Or fell so pure of crimes.*

"The widow's moan, the orphan's wail,
*   Come round thee; yet in truth be strong!*
Eternal right, though all else fail,
*   Can never be made wrong.*

"An angel's heart, an angel's mouth,
*   Not Homer's, could alone for me*
Hymn well the great Confederate South,
*   Virginia first, and* LEE.

                           "P. S. W."

Professor George Long, of England—the great scholar and high-toned gentleman—has, in a note to the second edition of his translation of the "Thoughts of the Emperor M. Aurelius Antoninus," the following graceful tribute: ". . . I have never dedicated a book to any man, and if I dedicated this I should choose the man whose name seemed to me most worthy to be joined to that of the Roman soldier and philosopher. I might dedicate the book to the successful general who is now President of the United States, with the hope that his integrity and justice will restore peace and happiness, so far as he can, to those unhappy States who have suffered so much from war, and the unrelenting hostility of wicked men. But as the Roman poet said, 'Victrix causa deis placuit, sed victa Catoni'; and if I dedicated this little book to any man, I would dedicate it to him who led the Confederate armies against the powerful invader, and retired from an unequal contest defeated, but not dishonored; to the noble Virginian soldier, whose talents and virtues place him by the side of the best and wisest man who sat on the throne of the imperial Cæsars."

If such is the opinion of disinterested foreign critics (who have been compelled to receive their information in large measure through Northern sources, and who have not been able, therefore, to do full justice to his transcendent abilities), we cannot doubt that the future historian, when he scans carefully all of the facts, will rank our noble chief *the peer, if not the superior, of any soldier of either ancient or modern times* —that the world will one day indorse the estimate of the London *Standard*, "A country which has given birth to men like him, and those who followed him, may look the chivalry of Europe in the face without shame; for *the fatherlands of Sidney and of Bayard never produced a nobler soldier, gentleman, and Christian, than* General ROBERT E. LEE."

Chapter II

THE COLLEGE PRESIDENT

A mong my most cherished "personal reminiscences" of this great man are those last years of his life at Lexington, when he toiled for the young men of the country as the quiet but able and laborious president of Washington College.

But, instead of my own recollections of how grandly he accomplished his work, I deem myself fortunate in being permitted to present papers prepared by two members of the able and accomplished faculty which General Lee called around him. The following sketch was (at the request of the faculty) written by the Rev. Dr. J. L. Kirkpatrick for the projected "Memorial Volume," and the ms has been kindly placed at my disposal. It is given (without essential abridgment) as a deeply interesting, accurate, and authorized account of his career as a *college president:*

"In the sketch which follows, nothing further will be attempted than a brief and simple exhibition of that portion of General Lee's life which was passed at Washington College, and of this only as it relates to his official work as president of that institution.

"SOME INCIDENTS IN THE HISTORY OF THE COLLEGE.

"Washington College is the outgrowth of an academy founded in the year 1749. This was the first classical school opened in the Valley of Virginia. Under a succession of principals, and with several changes of site, the academy at length acquired such a reputation as to attract the attention of General Washington, from whom it received a munificent endowment, and its subsequent name. The endowment was the gift of one hundred shares of what was known as the 'Old James River Company,' tendered him by the Legislature of Virginia, and accepted by him on the condition that he should be allowed to appropriate it 'to some public purpose in the upper part of the State, such as the education of the children of the poor, particularly of such as have fallen in the defense of their country.' This fact in the history of the institution is believed to have had no small influence on the mind of General Lee, in disposing him to accept its presidency, and in prompting him to the measures which he inaugurated for its further endowment and usefulness. His profound veneration for the character and his desire to perpetuate the deeds and virtues of Washington were a controlling impulse of his own moral nature.

"At the time of General Lee's accession to the presidency, the college had, through the calamities of the civil war, reached the lowest point of depression it had ever known. In addition to the calamities common to the whole country, against which it manfully struggled until further effort was shown to be unavailing, it suffered during the war the spoliation of its buildings, library, and apparatus, at the hands of a hostile soldiery left free to sack and plunder at their pleasure; and, at the close of the war, through the impoverishment of the State and the country, its invested funds were rendered unproductive, with the gravest uncertainty as to their ultimate value. Four professors remained at their post, and about forty students were gathered, chiefly from the region contiguous to the college.

"In such a state of affairs and with such prospects, it seemed a bold if not a presumptuous step to invite General Lee to assume the headship of the institution. So it impressed the minds of the people at large. There was a general expectation that he would decline the position—as not sufficiently lucrative, if his purpose was to repair the ruins to his private fortunes resulting from the war; as not lifting him conspicuously enough in the public gaze, if he was ambitious of office or further distinction; or as involving too great labor and anxiety, if he coveted repose after the terrible contest from which he had just emerged.

"As far as it is now known, the person first to suggest an effort to obtain the services of General Lee for the vacant presidency was the Hon. Bolivar Christian, of Staunton, a member of the board of trustees. He mentioned the subject to some confidential friends near him, one of whom wrote to General Lee, then in Cumberland County, where with his family he had made a home for the time. Owing to the deficiencies in the mail facilities, the answer which was expected to this letter did not reach Staunton until after Colonel Christian had left home to attend a meeting of the board of trustees, convened for the purpose of electing a president. The answer had been written and mailed, and such was its tenor that, had it been received in due time, it is almost certain the thought of securing General Lee for the college would have been abandoned as hopeless. The board assembled, and Colonel Christian proposed General Lee for the presidency. The proposition, received at first with surprise, was weighed long and anxiously by the body; not, of course, that there was any hesitation as to the desirableness of obtaining his services, or that there was any other man whom any member would have preferred for the place; but in view of the probabilities of a failure, should the effort be made, and of the effect of such failure on the interests of the college. Besides, the accession of General Lee to the presidency would carry with it extensive modifications of the scheme of instruction as previously in operation, and these would demand an enlargement of the resources of the institution which, in the existing condition of the country, it might have seemed mere rashness to attempt to provide. But the board had faith in the Providence which, as they interpreted its signs, pointed to General Lee for the position, had faith in the man himself, and in the disposition of our people toward an institution with which he should be so prominently associated. Among other proceedings of the body, bearing the date August 4, 1865, appears this simple record: 'The order of the day was resumed, and General Robert E. Lee, being put in nomination by Mr. Christian, was unanimously chosen president.' The Hon. John W. Brockenbrough, the rector of the board, was appointed by the body to convey in person to General Lee the notification of his election, and lay before him such information respecting the history of the college, its existing condition and future plans, as he might desire to possess. The mission was one grateful to the feelings of the distinguished gentleman to whom it was entrusted, and was discharged with promptness, ability, and success.

"Those who are acquainted with the modesty which was a ruling characteristic of General Lee in all the positions he was called to occupy, and with his thorough conscientiousness, will not be surprised to learn that he was, at first, strongly disinclined to accept the appointment, which, as already intimated, he had wished to arrest, and probably supposed he had arrested, in its inception. Nor will *they* be surprised to learn that the grounds of his reluctance were wholly different from those which strangers to his true character, judging him by the standard applicable to men generally, would have assigned as the cause of his hesitancy. These grounds are explicitly set forth in his letter of acceptance, which, as being of much interest to others as well as to the authorities of the college, is here given at length:

" 'POWHATAN COUNTY,
August 24, 1865.

" 'GENTLEMEN: I have delayed for some days replying to your letter of the 5th inst., informing me of my election, by the board of trustees, to the presidency of Washington College, from a desire to give the subject due consideration. Fully impressed with the responsibilities of the office, I have feared that I should be unable to discharge its duties to the satisfaction of the trustees, or to the benefit of the country. The proper education of youth requires not only great ability, but, I fear, more strength than I now possess, for I do not feel able to undergo the labor of conducting classes in regular courses of instruction; I could not therefore undertake more than the general administration and supervision of the institution. There is another subject which has caused me serious reflection, and is, I think, worthy of the consideration of the board. Being excluded from the terms of amnesty in the proclamation of the president of the United States, of the 29th of May last, and an object of censure to a portion of the country, I have thought it probable that my occupation of the position of president might draw upon the college a feeling of hostility; and I should therefore cause injury to an institution which it would be my highest desire to advance. I think it the duty of every citizen, in the present condition of the country, to do all in his power to aid in the restoration of peace and harmony, and in no way to oppose the policy of the state of general government, directed to that object. It is particularly incumbent on those charged with the instruction of the young to set them an example of submission to authority, and I could not consent to be the cause of animadversion upon the college.

" 'Should you, however, take a different view, and think that my services in the position tendered to me by the board will be advan-

tageous to the college and country, I will yield to your judgment,
and accept it; otherwise I must most respectfully decline the office.

" 'Begging you to express to the trustees of the college my heartfelt gratitude for the honor conferred upon me, and requesting you
to accept my cordial thanks for the kind manner in which you have
communicated their decision, I am, gentlemen, with great respect,

" 'Your most obedient servant,

" 'R. E. LEE.

" 'Messrs. JOHN W. BROCKENBROUGH, Rector; S.McD. ⎫
    REID; ALFRED LEYBURN; HORATIO THOMPSON, D.D., ⎬ *Committee.'*
    BOLIVAR CHRISTIAN; T. J. KIRKPATRICK,   ⎭

"As still further exhibiting the state of mind and views with which
General Lee accepted the position tendered to him, an extract will be here
made from an address on the occasion of his death, by Bishop Wilmer,
of Louisiana, at the 'University of the South,' Sewannee, Tennessee, where
the bishop received the sad intelligence. The address is a most beautiful
and touching tribute to the memory of one whom the author loved as a
personal friend, as well as admired for his exalted virtues. Space can be
obtained for only one passage directly pertinent to the subject in hand,
the use now made of which, it is hoped, the author will readily pardon;
as also a remark it seems proper to connect with the quotation, namely,
that those who had enjoyed fuller opportunities than he had probably possessed, for becoming acquainted with the history of Washington College,
prior to the recent change in its circumstances, will be disposed to claim
for it a somewhat higher position among the institutions of learning in the
country than his language would indicate that he had done.

" 'I was seated,' says Bishop Wilmer, 'at the close of the day, in my
Virginia home, when I beheld, through the thickening shades of evening,
a horseman entering the yard, whom I soon recognized as General Lee.
The next morning he placed in my hands the correspondence with the
authorities of Washington College at Lexington. He had been invited to
become president of that institution. I confess to a momentary feeling of
chagrin at the proposed change (shall I say *revulsion?*) in his history. The
institution was one of local interest, and comparatively unknown to our
people. I named others more conspicuous which would welcome him with
ardor as their presiding head. I soon discovered that his mind towered
above these earthly distinctions; that, in his judgment, the *cause* gave

dignity to the institution, and not the wealth of its endowment, or the renown of its scholars; that this door and not another was opened to him by Providence; and he only wished to be assured of his competency to fulfill the trust, and thus to make his few remaining years a comfort and blessing to his suffering country. I had spoken to his human feelings; he had now revealed himself to me as one "whose life was hid with Christ in God." My speech was no longer restrained. I congratulated him that his heart was inclined to this great cause, and that he was spared to give to the world this august testimony to the importance of Christian education. How he listened to my feeble words; how he beckoned me to his side, as the fullness of heart found utterance; how his whole countenance glowed with animation as I spoke of the Holy Ghost as the great Teacher, whose presence was required to make education a blessing, which otherwise might be the curse of mankind; how feelingly he responded, how *eloquently,* as I never heard him speak before—can never be effaced from memory; and nothing more sacred mingles with my reminiscences of the dead.'

"The board of trustees having notified to General Lee their entire and cordial agreement with him in the sentiments he had expressed in his letter of conditional acceptance, with respect to the duties of those charged with the instruction of the young in the existing condition of the country, and their opinion that his personal relations to the government of the United States did not constitute any obstacle to the prosperity of the college, General Lee at once prepared to enter on the duties of the office to which he was chosen. Accordingly, on the 2d of October (1865), in the presence of the trustees, professors, and students then on the ground, after solemn and appropriate prayer by the Rev. W. S. White, D. D., the oldest Christian minister of the town, he took the oath of office as required by the laws of the college, and was thus legally inaugurated as president. The whole scene was characterized by a dignity which was rendered the more impressive by the absence of the formality and pomp usual on similar occasions.

"THE WORK TO BE DONE BY THE NEW PRESIDENT.

"It would occupy too much space to exhibit in detail the various improvements which were instituted by the president, many of which were conducted by himself in person, and all under his supervision. The buildings, which had been partially repaired from the ravages of war and the waste of years of neglect, were to be restored to their former comfort and sightliness; accommodations for an increased number of students and instructors were to be provided; the apparatus in the departments of Chemistry and Natural Philosophy, which had been totally destroyed by the soldiers of the Federal Army, was to be repaired, with such additions as the progress of these branches of science rendered necessary; the library, which had been pillaged, and the contents of which, when not destroyed or carried out of the state, had been scattered over the town and its vicinity, and were then in the possession of those who, for the most part, felt no interest in restoring them to the college, was to be reformed as far as possible out of the old materials and enlarged by fresh additions; the scheme of instruction was to be revised and essentially modified, so as to adapt it more fully to the necessities of the times and of the country, and especially to admit of a ready incorporation with it of the several new departments which were proposed to be added, some forthwith, and others as soon as practicable; and all this with an empty treasury, and in a time of financial distress, of social disorders, and political turbulence, such as had never before existed in the country. The clear, penetrating judgment, and the habits of calm, dispassionate forecast for which he was distinguished throughout his life of varied experiences, forbade the supposition that the president was not fully aware of the magnitude of his undertaking, and of the difficulties to be overcome in its accomplishment. Quietly he set to work, availing himself of whatever assistance the trustees or professors could afford in maturing or in executing his plans. It was a pleasure to any of his associates in these enterprises to offer suggestions to him, so ready was he to listen to them and discuss them in all their bearings; but those approaching him with such suggestions usually discovered, before the conversation ended, that measures which they supposed were fresh and original with themselves, had been thoroughly canvassed by him; and they always learned, then or afterward, that no measure, however plausible, or from whatever source it came, would be adopted by him until he had carefully examined it in all its parts.

"THE CHANGES AND IMPROVEMENTS INTRODUCED
BY GENERAL LEE.

"In presenting the chief modifications of the instruction and government of the college, which were made during the administration of General Lee, it is proper to premise that it is not possible to determine in every case whether the new feature originated with him or was merely approved and adopted by him from the suggestions of others. It is, however, safe to say that where he was not the immediate author of any measure, it would not have been carried into effect without his concurrence and the weight of his influence. The credit and responsibility for the changes in view as truly belonged to him, as in the affairs of a government they belong to the supreme ruler, or, in the conduct of a military campaign, to the commander-in-chief.

"Prior to General Lee's presidency, there were five chairs of instruction—that of Mental and Moral Science and Political Economy, filled by the president, and those of the Latin Language and Literature, of the Greek Language and Literature, of Mathematics, and of the Physical Sciences—chemistry and natural philosophy—filled each by a professor. As General Lee had made it a condition of his taking the office that he should not be required to teach, but be allowed to devote all his time and labors to the superintendency of the institution, it became necessary to appoint a professor for the branches which had been in charge of the president. This was done soon after his accession; and, at the same time, three new chairs of instruction were instituted and professors elected to them, viz.: the chair of Natural Philosophy, embracing, in addition to physics, acoustics, optics, etc., the various subjects of rational and applied mechanics; the chair of Applied Mathematics, embracing the subjects required in civil and military engineering, and also astronomy; the chair of Modern Languages, to which was attached English philology. These four chairs were filled during the first year of General Lee's incumbency. Before the close of the second year the chair of History and English Literature was also filled. About the same time the department of Law and Equity was added by attaching to the college the Lexington Law School, which had for many years been in successful operation under the charge of Judge John W. Brockenbrough, LL. D. A few months before his death, General Lee was permitted to realize the completion of his plans respecting this department, by the appointment and acceptance of a second law professor.

"Two other chairs were included in the president's scheme: the one, of the English Language, as a study to receive equal attention and honor with the most favored branches of instruction; the other, of Applied Chemistry, in which should be taught metallurgy, and the relations of chemistry to agriculture, mining, and manufactures, together with vegetable and animal physiology.

"Wide as is the range of educational facilities already mentioned, it does not embrace all that the president contemplated. He took the initiatory steps toward the establishment of a School of Commerce of so thorough and elevated a character that a student, while pursuing the branches which would impart discipline and culture to the mind, might receive special instruction and systematic training in whatever pertains to business, in the most enlarged sense of the term. It was also his purpose to connect with the college a School of Medicine, a plan for which, with full details, was drawn up under his eye, to be kept in readiness until the funds of the institution should permit its being carried into effect.

"It was proper that these various schemes, as well as those which the want of the requisite funds and his death have left but partially accomplished, as those which were set in full operation during his presidency, should have been placed distinctly before the reader. Without a knowledge of them, the energy General Lee displayed, the labor he performed, and his comprehensive views of what is required of an institution offering to the public the full advantages of a literary and scientific education, cannot be duly appreciated.

"There is danger, however, that the foregoing recital may lead the casual reader into error as to General Lee's conception of what constitutes an education, referring here only to its intellectual aspects—such as it was his desire and purpose to promote in the institution over which he presided. As nearly all the new chairs of instruction and plans for further enlargement relate to a scientific or a professional education, it might be inferred that he did not place an equal value on classical studies. No misapprehension would be greater than this, as all who had the privilege of being associated with him in regulating the studies of the college well understood. Himself acquainted with the ancient languages, Latin and Greek, much beyond what is usual with those of his former profession, or what might have been expected of one so constantly employed as he had been in the kind of public service required by that profession, he set the highest estimate on them as themselves the surest means of a refined mental culture, and as affording the soundest mental discipline for successful attainments in the studies that should be subsequently undertaken. Hence, in cases in which the selection of the studies was left to him, unembarrassed by the wishes of parents or the circumstances of the pupil, he invariably advised and urged a thorough course in the ancient languages. He was aware that in this he had the concurrence of the professors in the scientific branches no less than of those in the classical. The fact that, when he came to the college, he found the classical department competently provided for, explains why his attention was directed chiefly to the expansion of those departments in which deficiencies existed.

"Yet it is due to candor and to his memory to add, if, indeed, it is necessary after what has already been stated, that General Lee was a strong advocate of 'practical education,' in the true sense of the phrase—a practical education founded on systematic mental discipline and a thorough knowledge of the principles and facts of science. This, which is of priceless value at all times, he held to be peculiarly important to his own loved South in the present crisis of her affairs. In a letter to his esteemed friend and former companion in arms, General John B. Gordon of Georgia (December 30, 1867), he writes in general terms: 'The thorough education of all classes of the people is the most efficacious means, in my opinion, of promoting the prosperity of the South; and the material interests of its citizens, as well as their moral and intellectual culture, depend upon its accomplishment. The textbooks of our schools, therefore, should not only be clear, systematic, and scientific, but they should be acceptable to parents and pupils in order to enlist the minds of all in the subjects.' And more specifically in a letter to a friend in Baltimore engaged in practical science (January 1867): 'I agree with you fully as to the importance of a more practical course of instruction in our schools and colleges, which, while it may call forth the genius and energies of our people, will tend to develop the resources and promote the interests of the country.'

"CHANGES IN THE SYSTEM OF INSTRUCTION.

"With the accession of General Lee to the presidency, important changes were made in the system of instruction. One of these was the substitution of what is known as the elective system for a uniform and compulsory curriculum. Without discussing the advantages of the one or the other of the two methods, it is sufficient to remark here that the change which was introduced was the necessary result of the enlarged basis of instruction implied in the addition of the new branches and professors just enumerated. The aim was to secure, alike in the instruction by the professor and in the acquisitions of the student, the highest attainable development. Hence, each branch of study was organized into a distinct and, in a sense, an independent department or school. Students who were prevented, by whatever cause, from pursuing a full course, could enjoy the best advantages for a partial course in special directions, and receive certificates of proficiency, degrees, or titles corresponding to the character and extent of the attainments they should actually make.

"General Lee, however, was not inattentive to the evils that might arise from allowing to students the free, uncontrolled selection of the branches they should pursue. The choice accorded to them was restricted to the schools or departments they were to enter. Within each school a rigid classification was made. No student was admitted into a class for which he was not prepared, and, when admitted, each was required to pursue the prescribed order of subjects. When found deficient he was liable to be transferred to a lower class, and when prepared he could, at any time, be promoted to a higher class, in each case, of the same school; but no promotion was allowed, either at the close of the session or during its progress, except on the ground of proficiency actually made. By these means the professor in charge of a school was enabled to secure an approximation to that which all teachers so earnestly desire—uniformity in proficiency and progress among the members of each class, so that he may adapt his instructions to the ascertained wants of all.

"GENERAL LEE'S MODE OF DISCIPLINE.

"The next topic to be noticed is the mode of discipline adopted and administered by General Lee. For this, it may be said, he was responsible, in a higher and more exclusive sense, than perhaps for any other feature of the college, for it was shaped and controlled with little assistance from any source.

"The immediate ends of college discipline are attention to study, and good order as necessary to such diligence. Its higher and more comprehensive end is attention to study and good order obtained by means which will cultivate virtuous principles and correct habits, not merely for the brief period of a college course, but also for subsequent life. As nothing has occasioned as much trouble in the management of colleges as the discipline, so nothing has yielded so unsatisfactory results. Between the two systems which have been tried—the one of a control, scarcely nominal in pretense, and certainly not more than nominal in reality; the other characterized by a multiplicity of petty, artificial 'rules and regulations,' enforced by vigorous, unremitting *espionage*—it would be difficult to make a choice, whether one judges by the dictates of reason and common sense, or by the light of experience. If the former allows too much license to the unreflecting follies and wayward passions of youth, the latter errs on the other extreme by attempting to impose restraints which, as on the one hand they can never be effectually maintained, assail the young with a temptation to seek to elude them, in order to show their independence of spirit, their skill and daring; and which, just so far, on the other hand, as they are even partially maintained, chafe the student's pride, excite his disgust, and create in the mind a stronger proclivity to the errors and vices they are intended to prevent. It will be found, on a careful review of the history of colleges in our country, that the larger number of the disturbances by which their quiet has been interrupted, and sometimes their exercises suspended, have originated in such arbitrary, mechanical, and yet impotent regulations.

"Those who were acquainted with General Lee only through the incidents of his public career may have expected that he would frame the discipline of the college over which he presided in accordance with the system pursued at the institution (West Point) in which he was educated, and of which he was for some years the superintendent, and in accordance with the order and practice to which, as a military man, he had been so long accustomed. His explanation of the reasons for not adopting a discipline so familiar to him, and that in his hands would have been so easily administered, was, that he did not propose to train men for the army, but for the pursuits of civil life, and that, in his view, the discipline fitted to make soldiers was not best suited to qualify young men for the duties of the citizen. Throughout his official and his private intercourse with the students, his aim was to cultivate in them a nice sense of propriety and a strong sense of duty. Hence he treated each one, not as a machine to move only as external force should impel it forward, nor as a delinquent already convicted as such, and therefore to be suspected and watched at every step; but, until the contrary should be manifested, as a young gentleman of good breeding, veracity, self-respect, and possessing correct principles, honorable impulses, and a conscience, with whom it was sufficient that right and wrong, duty and obligation, should be distinctly made known. Of course, he was aware that, in assuming this of every one, he was liable to be mistaken in some instances. The effect, however, on the minds of all, except the incurably vicious, was most salutary. It caused them to feel that they had a character to maintain, and inspired them with an ambition to vindicate and strengthen the confidence which was reposed in them. Thus, from the beginning, it contributed greatly to the end which the president kept steadily in view in every disciplinary measure he framed or employed—to foster habits of self-control, of intelligent self-government, as the result, not of compulsion or penalties, but of reflection and choice. On the principle of inducing those under his charge to govern themselves by giving scope and opportunity to think for themselves, it was his custom to refrain from interposing with any demonstration of his wishes or authority as long as it could be done with safety. Never was there a president of a college or other ruler who made less display of his official power, or *seemed* to exercise less control. Yet no one, it may be confidently asserted, ever exerted an influence which was more widely and powerfully felt in every department it was designed to embrace.

"Before specifying the particular methods employed by General Lee to establish and preserve an effectual discipline in the college, in accordance with the general principle just stated, it is proper to refer to two circumstances which combined to render the task especially difficult, and should be estimated in determining the degree of credit due him for the success he attained. One of these arose from the character of a portion of the students who came under his charge. They were, indeed, with few if any exceptions, from families of respectability, many of them from families of refined culture and high social position. But for several years—with them the critical years in their moral history—they had been exposed to the disastrous effects of the Civil War, which, in the excitement it created and the exhaustion of the resources of the country, disbanded schools, weakened parental authority, relaxed family government, and disorganized society to an extent that can scarcely be overstated. With the spirit and habits such a state of things might be expected to induce in the minds of youths under twenty years of age, and without time or opportunity for the mitigation of the evil, they were sent to college to be reduced to subordination, to regular application to routine studies, and to a patient endurance of the drudgery (as to them it must appear) of such a life. Nor is it a matter of mere suspicion that some of them were placed under the charge of General Lee in the forlorn hope that his great name and great wisdom might avail for that which all other means had failed to accomplish.

"These remarks, so far as they imply a deterioration of character, are not to be construed as applying to all the students, nor even to a majority of them. It is a gratifying fact in respect to Washington College, as it is believed also to other similar institutions of the South since the war, that the most of the students have evinced an earnestness of purpose and a manly propriety of demeanor never surpassed, if ever equaled, in our country before. This is emphatically true of those of them who were personally engaged in active military service.

"The other circumstance referred to as uniting with that just mentioned to render the task before General Lee more difficult, originated in the emancipation of the slaves in the South. Young men naturally partook deeply of the feelings which were almost universal in the class of society to which they belonged, that this measure was unjust, oppressive, and injurious. They were not likely to be as prudent in giving utterance to their sense of the wrong as others of more experience and self-control. On the other hand, the late slaves, suddenly elevated to a position which they had scarcely ventured to dream would be possible to them, were, as may be supposed, greatly elated by the change; and they too were not always as prudent in giving expression to their feelings as a calmer judgment would have shown them was best. The two inflammable classes being unavoidably brought into proximity to each other, it was hardly possible to prevent occasional collisions. The danger engaged the most assiduous attentions of General Lee, especially during the first three years of his administration. That so few instances of actual violence occurred, is to be ascribed to his untiring energy and consummate skill.

"It is due alike to the students and to the freedmen to say that it is believed some, if not all, of the disturbances between them would have been avoided, if the latter had been left to pursue their usually quiet and inoffensive demeanor, without extraneous efforts to poison their minds and embitter their feelings toward the whites of the South. Such efforts, however, were made, publicly and privately, by those, or their hired emissaries, who had constituted themselves the special guardians of the freed population of the country. General Lee was too conspicuous an object to escape the designs of men who were seeking notoriety for themselves— a notoriety which might be turned to their pecuniary or political advantage. As he was shielded from direct attack by the serene dignity of his character and his scrupulous attention to all his obligations as a member of society and citizen of the country, the only way to reach him was through the institution over which he presided and to the reputation of which he was known to be keenly sensitive. Rumored disorders among the students would react on him; a conflict between them and the laws, or the official representatives of the government, would involve him. To no other cause does it seem possible to ascribe the numerous false and injurious reports that found circulation through the press, of improper conduct on the part of the students of 'General Lee's College'; the frequent 'official' representations addressed to him of rumored disorderly or unlawful acts which they were going to commit, not one of which was ever ascertained or believed to have been founded in truth; or the complaints made to the authorities, civil or military, as happened at the time to be their character, on which, once and again, formal commissions were sent to the place to investigate charges against the students. However frivolous such complaints were in themselves, and however groundless he believed them to be, whenever they came from a source possessing even the semblance of official authority, General Lee received them with scrupulous courtesy, and immediately took steps to have them thoroughly investigated. The results of the inquiry were in every instance creditable alike to the president and the students, as was, on more than one occasion, formally certified by officers of the government. Still, it can readily be seen that the effect of such repeated complaints and investigations on the minds of young men would be, to provoke them to the very course of conduct it ought to have been the wish of all to prevent. There were instances—not more than two or three in all—in which students were guilty of improper conduct toward the negroes. In each case, without any prompting from others, the president, having ascertained the facts, required the offenders to leave the college.

"General Lee bore these annoyances with his accustomed equanimity. That they were aimed at himself, he was fully aware; but, when any of those with whom he allowed himself to converse on the subject expressed the indignation they could but feel at such attempts to harass him and at the indignity to which he was subjected in having to deal, on even the formal terms of official intercourse, with a class of men who were wholly incapable of understanding the motives by which he was governed, he would, at one time, pass the subject by with some pleasantry, and at another would seek to allay the irritation in *their* breast by reminding them that, in the existing condition of the country, such things were perhaps unavoidable, and that it was the duty of all to submit patiently to evils for which time was the only cure.

"While discarding, as has been mentioned, all devices for maintaining the discipline of the college which he supposed would tend to the deg-radation of either officers or students, and while encouraging, in every possible way, habits of subordination, correctness of demeanor, and dili-gent attention to study, as the result of their own conviction of duty and regard for their own reputation, the president, nevertheless, exercised a constant vigilance over the students through means which he believed were not only compatible with the latter end, but also most effectual in its accomplishment. His method of practical operation was simple, and, as the results show, effective.

"As the first step, he sought to become acquainted with each student. He had an office in the college buildings in which he remained, unless called out by public business, from 8 o'clock A.M. to 2 P.M., of each of six days in the week. To this room free access was offered to the students. Here, on their arrival at the place, they were expected to report to the president in person, and he availed himself, as far as was possible, of these earliest interviews, to obtain such knowledge of the several appli-cants for admission as would enable him to adapt whatever disciplinary appliances might be afterward found advisable to the peculiar circum-stances of each one. In the large number of students entering the institution every year, this may be deemed an impracticable task; with ordinary men, it would have been such. No one, however, who was ever associated with General Lee in the management of any enterprise, could fail to observe and admire the remarkable tenacity and accuracy of his memory. He ap-peared never to forget anything, however comparatively insignificant, which it was with him a matter of concern to remember. Hence, until the last year of his presidency, when, on account of his failing health, he was frequently absent from his office, he knew every student in the college, and would greet each one by name whenever they met. One fact, among many others illustrating the point in view, may not be out of place. At one of the meetings of the faculty, held, as was the custom, at short in-tervals, for reviewing the roll of the college in order to ascertain whether all the students were attending the required number of lectures, a name was read out which was not familiar to his ear. He requested that it should be repeated, and then repeated it himself with a slow and heavy emphasis on each syllable, adding with evident surprise, not without a tincture of self-reproach: 'I have no recollection of a student of that name. It is very strange that I have forgotten him. I thought I knew everyone in the college. How long has he been here?' Nor would he be satisfied until it was ascertained by an investigation that the student had recently entered, and was admitted in the president's absence; so that, in fact, the latter had never seen him.

"This personal acquaintance with them was itself felt by the students as a moral power greatly augmenting the influence of the president over them; when there was added to it the effect of the kind words of inquiry, advice, and encouragement, he was wont to address to them, and of the affectionate, sympathetic, and often playful manner in which those words were uttered, when they were admitted into college, when they visited him in his office or his residence, or when he met them on the lawn or in the streets, it is not difficult to understand how their sentiments of reverence and admiration for his character would be heightened into love for him as a man. It was true—and they felt it to be true—that each of them was the object of a solicitude fervent and tender, like that of a father or mother.

"Knowing that idleness is the most fruitful source of temptation to the young, the president was peremptory in requiring that every student should undertake a sufficient number of branches to occupy all his time, and that he should attend regularly on all the exercises of his several classes. Absence from the latter, without a satisfactory reason, was held to be a delinquency that called for prompt and decisive notice. In order that he might be prepared to give due attention to every instance of the kind, each professor and assistant professor made a weekly report, in tabular form, of all the absences occurring in his classes. The president examined these reports with the minutest care, and made memoranda of all cases which called for special inquiry. The delinquents were then summoned to his office, one by one, for a private interview.

"What took place at these conferences was seldom known, except as the student himself might reveal it; for, unless it became necessary from the conduct of the delinquent afterward, the president never alluded to the subject. The young, however, with the ingenuousness which is one of their most pleasing qualities, are naturally inclined to be communicative; and in this way enough transpired to leave no room to doubt that the president's reproofs, admonitions, and counsels, were characterized by a pointedness which could not be evaded, and, at the same time, with a tenderness and affection none but the most hardened could resist. That aspect of indifference and bravado, whether real or affected, so often witnessed in the countenance and bearing of students returning among their companions from a compulsory interview with the authorities of a college,

was never seen on the face of one leaving General Lee's office; but, instead, were often exhibited the unmistakable signs of recent weeping, and
always those of a spirit that had been subdued by its own emotions. Not
an instance is known in which a student complained of injustice or harsh-
ness, or in which the effect on his mind was not a profounder respect and
affection for the president. It was seldom that anything additional to the
penalty, if it may be so called, of being cited to one of these interviews,
was required in order to secure the ends of discipline. Indeed, with the
great majority of the students it was quite sufficient to know that any
delinquencies on their part would subject them to a notice from the president to see him in his office.

"Still there were cases of neglect of duty which the influence of General
Lee, exerted in the manner here explained, did not avail to correct. After
a sufficient number of trials to satisfy him that nothing could be hoped
for from personal admonitions of this character, the parent or guardian
was informed of the fact, and requested to co-operate with the authorities
of the college in a further effort on behalf of the delinquent student. This
final measure failing, as sometimes, though rarely, it did, the parent was
requested to withdraw his son from the institution, on the grounds that he
was spending time and money without remunerative benefit, and that his
example of idleness and irregular attendance on the exercises was injurious to his fellow students. Communications of such tenor are unavoidably
painful to parents receiving them; they were scarcely less so to the president when making them. Hence he sought, in every way, to render them
as kind and tender as possible. He was unwilling, if it could be avoided,
to send any youth from the college with a stigma on his reputation which
would injure him in future life, and in order to prevent this he gave the
parent the opportunity of withdrawing his son when it became necessary
that the latter should be separated from the institution, rather than subject
him to the disgrace of a formal or public dismissal. Unless, indeed, the
student himself or his friends at home made it known, the reason for his
leaving the college would seldom transpire beyond the circle of the parties
immediately concerned.

"The following letter, which explains its own design and contents, illustrates the manner in which the president dealt with a class of cases that
sometimes came under his notice:

" 'LEXINGTON, VA.,
December 12, 1867.

" 'MY DEAR SIR: I am glad to inform you that your son———has made more progress in his studies during the month of November than he did in October, and, as far as I can judge from the reports of his professors, he is fully capable of acquiring a sound education, provided he will faithfully apply himself. I am sorry, however, to state that he has been absent several times from his lectures in the month of November. Thirteen times he tells me he was prevented from attending by sickness, but five times, he says, he intentionally absented himself. He absented himself in the same way several times in October; and I then explained to him the necessity of punctual and regular attendance in his classes, which he promised to observe.

" 'I have again impressed upon him this necessity, and again he promises amendment; but I have thought it proper to write to you on the subject, that you might use your authority with him: for I have been obliged to give him to understand that, if this conduct is repeated, I shall be obliged to return him to you.

" 'Hoping that I may be spared the necessity, I remain,

" 'With great respect, your obedient servant,

" 'R. E. LEE.

" 'To——— ———, Esq.'

"In addition to the weekly reports of absences, the professors laid before the president, at the close of every month, a tabular exhibit of the standing and grade of each student in his respective classes, as determined by the daily marks given in the lecture room. These also he examined with close attention, so as to inform himself of the progress of the students, and then passed the reports over to the clerk, to be transferred to a permanent register arranged in such a manner as to present, at one view, the standing of every student in each of his studies for the month. A copy of the record in the register was then forwarded to the parent or guardian of the student.

"At the close of the two general examinations which were held during the annual sessions—the one in the middle and the other at the end—similar reports were presented, examined, recorded, and forwarded to parents, exhibiting a conspectus of the results and delinquencies for each half-session; the latter, those also of the entire year.

"It would be difficult to suggest any method by which more particular or complete information could be furnished to parents than those frequent and systematized reports supplied. If, however, there was occasion for any additional facts to be stated, the president inserted it with his own hand, or signed it when entered under his direction by the clerk. Especially at the close of the session, when on a review of the year's work it was seen that some of the students were entitled to special commendation for their deportment and proficiency, and that others, although they had not failed in their studies to an extent that rendered their withdrawal from the college necessary during the session, had not made such progress as to afford ground for the hope that their longer continuance in it would result in advantages to them commensurate with the expenditures of time and money it would involve, letters in his own hand, or with his signature, were addressed to the parents, setting forth the views of the president and the professors in relation to the individuals composing the one class or the other.

"The labor involved in the system of discipline was very great; but General Lee thought it necessary to the faithful discharge of the trust he had assumed. He did not shrink from it, nor complain of it. He seemed never to have overlooked anything. When the members of the faculty assembled in his office to lay before him the reports for the week just closed, he was invariably found prepared to receive them, having disposed of all the business which those of the week before had imposed on him, and being now in full and cheerful readiness for any work, though much of it was sheer drudgery, which the new reports might require. Was such an amount of irksome labor necessary? He believed—and often so expressed himself—that it was. He felt that too much vigilance and care could not be bestowed on those who, in the most critical period of their lives, had been committed to his charge, in holding them up to the regular discharge of their duties. He felt too, that the utmost candor and particularity were due from him to the parents who had entrusted him with the oversight of their sons. Having discarded, as already stated, all secret appliances for maintaining an espionage over the students, he felt that it was the more incumbent on him to exercise, with all possible promptness and regularity, the open, manly method of discipline which he had substituted for it.

"As allusion has been made to the frequent complaints made to General Lee of acts of disorder which it was rumored the students had committed, or were about to commit, it may be well to insert here a specimen of the replies and addresses to which such complaints gave rise. The following letter to an officer of the government requires no introduction:

" 'WASHINGTON COLLEGE, LEXINGTON, VA.,
November 20, 1868.
" 'COLONEL: I have received your letter of the 19th inst., which gave me the first intimation I had received of the proposed meeting of the colored people of Lexington.

" 'The faculty and students of the college to whom the subject has been mentioned, were equally ignorant of the contemplated assembly; and I do not think the students have any intention of disturbing the meeting.

" 'Every thing, however, in our power will be done by the faculty as well as myself to prevent any of the students attending; and I heartily concur with you in the hope that the peace and quiet of the community may at all times be preserved.

" 'I have the honor to be, with much respect,
" 'Your obedient servant,
" 'Colonel———.   R. E. LEE.'

"That he might leave no part of his duty unperformed, the president issued the following address to the students, and had it posted on the bulletin board, so as to be seen by all of them:

" 'WASHINGTON COLLEGE,
November 20, 1868.
" 'It has been reported to the faculty of Washington College that some of the students have threatened to disturb a public meeting of the colored people of Lexington, to be held at the fairgrounds this evening, the 20th inst.

" 'It is not believed that the students of this college, who have heretofore conducted themselves in such an exemplary manner, would do any thing to disturb the public peace, or bring discredit on themselves or the institution to which they belong; but it is feared that some, prompted by curiosity, or a desire to witness the proceedings, may be present. The president, therefore, requests all students to abstain from attending this and all similar meetings; and thinks it only necessary to call their attention to the advantages of attending strictly, as heretofore, to their important duties at the college, and of, in no way, interfering with the business of others. From past experience they may feel certain that, should any disturbance occur, efforts will be made to fix the blame on Washington College. It therefore behooves every student to keep away from all such assemblies.

" 'Respectfully,

" 'R. E. LEE, President of Washington College.'

"Two other of his addresses are here inserted, as illustrating further the president's method of operating on the minds of the students either for the purpose of reproving them for improper acts they had committed, or for preventing such as he apprehended they might commit. The first relates to one of the occurrences so well known to all who reside in 'college towns,' which, originating in a mere desire for harmless sport, through the excitement that is generated in their progress, frequently culminate in real annoyances to the community. One such having taken place in Lexington, and the students being suspected of participating in it, General Lee issued the following address, which, after being read out in the chapel at the morning service, was posted on the bulletin board:

" 'WASHINGTON COLLEGE,

November 26, 1866.

" 'The faculty desire to call the attention of the students to the disturbances which occurred in the streets of Lexington on the nights of Friday and Saturday last. They believe that none can contemplate them with pleasure, or can find any reasonable grounds for their justification. These acts are said to have been committed by students of the college, with the apparent object of disturbing the peace and quiet of a town whose inhabitants have opened their doors for their reception and accommodation, and who are always ready to administer to their comfort and pleasure.

" 'It requires but little consideration to see the error of such conduct, which could only have proceeded from thoughtlessness and a want of reflection. The faculty therefore appeal to the honor and self-respect of the students to prevent any similar occurrence, trusting that their sense of what is due to themselves, their parents, and the institution to which they belong, will be more effectual in teaching them what is right and manly, than anything they can say.

" 'There is one consideration connected with these disorderly proceedings, which the faculty wish to bring to your particular notice: the example of your conduct, and the advantage taken of it by others to commit outrages for which you have to bear the blame. They therefore exhort you to adopt the only course capable of shielding you from such charges—the effectual prevention of all such occurrences in future.

" 'R. E. LEE, *President of Washington College.*'

"The second of the addresses referred to was published to the students the day preceding Christmas. The pertinency of it will be recognized by all who are familiar with the customs which prevail in the South. Prior to General Lee's connection with the college, a recess had always been given at Christmas, of not less than eight or ten days. Coming in the midst of the session, this was at best a serious interruption to the exercises. But the evil was much aggravated by the fact that those students who visited their homes, seldom returned promptly at the close of the recess; and those who spent the recess at the college, being released from the obligation to attend lectures, and having at their command time they knew not how to dispose of, became the readier victims to the temptations that so abound at that season of the year. During General Lee's presidency, the recess was limited to one or two days. The following brief address will show what means he employed to guard the students against the dangers to which he knew they would be exposed:

" 'WASHINGTON COLLEGE, VA.,
December 24, 1869.

" 'Academic exercises will be suspended from the 25th to the 27th inclusive, to enable the students to join in the rites and services appropriate to the occasion; and, while enjoying these privileges with grateful hearts, all are urged to do or countenance nothing which may disturb the peace, harmony, and happiness, that should pervade a Christian community.

" 'R. E. LEE, *President.*'

"It seems proper here to remark, with reference to the foregoing addresses, or, as the students familiarly styled them, 'general orders,' and to others of similar character issued from time to time as there was occasion for them, that in no instance did they fail to accomplish the end which the president desired. Indeed, it would have been almost impossible for any student to have withstood the moral sentiment they created among the students at large.

"GENERAL LEE'S EFFORTS ON BEHALF OF RELIGION.

"In other parts of this volume, the religious character of General Lee is brought prominently into view. It will here be referred to only as it respects his efforts on behalf of the religious welfare of the students.

"The passage cited, in the early part of this sketch, from the address of Bishop Wilmer, and several incidents mentioned in the other portions of the volume, show that he assumed the position of presiding officer in the institution with the profoundest convictions of its responsibilities in view of the influence it would enable him to exert in molding the characters and forming the habits of the young men under his charge, in those higher aspects of both which pertain to religion. The same convictions characterized his administration to its close.

"Seeing, during the first year, that the chapel of the college would not afford accommodations for the number of students who might be expected to attend the institution, he urged the immediate erection of another and separate building, to be devoted to religious purposes. There were many objects calling for a far greater outlay of money than the resources of the college permitted; but he regarded this as of paramount importance, and accordingly others were held in abeyance to its prior claims. He chose the site for the new chapel, in front of the row of the other buildings and facing them, in order that it might occupy the more conspicuous position. The plan of the house was drawn by himself or under his eye, in a style of architecture plain indeed, but still more attractive than that of the other buildings, that even this incidental honor might be given to it. Owing to the deficiency of funds necessary for its completion, the progress of the work was retarded much beyond his expectations, but this seemed only to increase his interest in the enterprise. He gave it his personal superintendence, from the first to the last, visiting it every day, and frequently several times in the day. When, at length, the house was finished, it was opened, under his special direction, for religious worship by appropriate services conducted by the pastors of the several churches in the town. This was the first of a series of public exercises, extending through five days, which were connected with the annual commencement of the college, and it was observed by all present that none of the exercises which followed those of the 'chapel dedication' seemed to awaken in his mind a more lively sensibility or to afford him a more heartfelt gratification. Thereafter, as indeed had been previously the case, no religious service, whether that of daily worship on the part of the professors and students, or occasional worship of a more general character, was ever held in the chapel, at which he was not present, unless when absent from home or prevented by sickness. He thus gave to the students every day an example of the value he attached to religion.

"In the basement of this edifice on which he bestowed so much attention, and in which he so often mingled with the professors and students in acts of divine worship, his mortal remains now repose. There it is proposed to erect a mausoleum, and deposit such other tributes to his name as shall perpetuate the memory of his great services to the college, and of the veneration and love of his countrymen for his character and deeds. By the authority of the board of trustees the entire building has been consecrated as a 'memorial chapel.'

"At an early period of General Lee's connection with the college, the students who were communicants in the church, formed an association among themselves for the cultivation of personal piety, and as the means of exerting a favorable influence on others. Coming from different parts of the country and from different religious communions, it was seen to be desirable that they should be drawn together and united in the fellowship of those great doctrines, hopes, and aims, which were common to them all. Thus they would the sooner become acquainted with one another; the timid among them would be encouraged the more distinctively to avow their Christian profession; opportunities would be the more readily afforded for devotional exercises, at times and under circumstances best suited to their needs; and such of them as might be qualified by age or experience for engaging in efforts for the religious welfare of others, through Sunday-schools and devotional meetings held in the destitute neighborhoods in the vicinity of the college, could prosecute their labors with the greater system and efficiency.

"It is not known whether General Lee was the first to propose the organization of this society in Washington College; but, if he did not suggest it, he gave it a warm and active encouragement from its inception. From every source accessible to him, he sought, in advance, minute information as to the best form of organization, and the most effective methods of carrying out its designs. He made to its funds an annual contribution in money, and always a liberal one. On at least one occasion he placed in its library a collection of suitable books, which he had purchased with that view. In his annual reports to the board of trustees, he always made emphatic mention of the association, and gave a particular account of its operations and progress, as data indicating the religious condition of the college, and as constituting in part the grounds of his confidence respecting its future prosperity.

"There being no regular chaplain of the college, the pastors of the several churches in the town kindly consented, at General Lee's request, to hold religious services every morning in the chapel, under such a division of the time as they found most convenient to themselves. The four largest denominations in the country had each a church, with its pastor, in the place, so that this arrangement precluded all objection on the score of sectarian partiality or advantage. It also offered to each of the students, with perhaps not two exceptions out of a hundred of them, the satisfaction of attending, for one fourth of the time, on devotional exercises conducted by a minister of the church of his parents or of his own preference. A special advantage resulting from it, and one that the president sought in every possible way to render effective, was, that it created a tie between the ministers and the students similar to that subsisting between a pastor and his spiritual charge. This was, indeed, the idea he endeavored to impress on both of the parties. Hence he invited the ministers to visit the students freely in their rooms, and advised the students to become members of the Bible classes and to attend the different services conducted by the ministers. The following letter, which is only one of several of the same import that might be inserted, will best exhibit his views on this subject:

" 'WASHINGTON COLLEGE, LEXINGTON, VA.,
September 11, 1869.

" 'REVEREND AND DEAR SIRS: Desirous of making the religious exercises of the college advantageous to the students, and wishing to use all means to inculcate among them the principles of true religion, the faculty tender to you their cordial thanks for your past services, and request you to perform in rotation the customary daily exercises at the college chapel. The hour fixed for these services is forty-five minutes past seven o'clock every morning, except Sunday, during the session, save the three winter months, December, January, and February, when the hour for prayer will be forty-five minutes past eight. The hours for lectures are fixed at eight and nine o'clock respectively during these periods. On Sundays the hour for prayer during the whole session is fixed at nine o'clock.

" 'The faculty also request that you will extend to the students a general invitation to attend the churches of their choice regularly on Sundays and other days; and invite them to join the Bible classes established in each; that you will, as may be convenient and necessary, visit them in sickness and in health; and that you will in every proper manner urge upon them the great importance of the Christian religion.

" 'The faculty further asks that you will arrange among yourselves, as may be most convenient, the periods of the session during which each will perform chapel services, and that during those periods the officiating minister will consider himself chaplain of the college, for the purpose of conducting religious worship, prayers, etc.

" 'The present session will open on the 16th inst., and close on the 25th of June, 1870.

" 'I am, with great respect, your obedient servant,
" 'R. E. LEE.

" 'To the ministers of the Baptist, Episcopal, Methodist, and Presbyterian Churches in Lexington, Va.'

"In order that the minister might be enabled the more effectively to carry out the pious designs set forth in the foregoing letter, General Lee was accustomed to inquire of each student, when entering the college, to what religious denomination his parents belonged, or what church they usually attended. He would then, as far as practicable, introduce the student to the pastor of the same denomination in the town, and thus from the beginning seek to impress the student with the conviction that he might enjoy in the college pastoral privileges similar to those he had enjoyed in the home of his parents. On some occasions, he was known to make a memorandum of the denominations from which the new students came, and to furnish the ministers respectively with a list of such as he desired they should take under their special charge.

"No public worship, except the morning prayers referred to in the foregoing letter, was held in the chapel on the Sabbath. Had the income of the college permitted the employment of a permanent chaplain, it would have been impracticable to have such service except at an hour which would have brought it into conflict with the public services of one or more of the churches in the town; and this would have obliged a portion of the students to absent themselves either from the worship in the chapel, or from that of the church which their parents or themselves preferred they should attend. Lodging, as the most of them did in private, families, in all parts of the town, it was quite as convenient for them to attend the latter as the former. It was believed, also, that they would derive more profit and would be under more wholesome restraints from worshiping with the members of the community in which they resided, and of the families in which they were domiciled, in the church and under the minister of their own preference, than in the chapel where the assembly would consist almost exclusively of their fellow students, and where it would be almost impossible to divest themselves of the impression that it was still but a college duty on which they were attending. If required by the authorities of the institution to be present at the chapel on the occasion of such worship, they would feel aggrieved that they were not permitted to unite with the congregation of their own persuasion. If not so required, they would, for many and obvious reasons, attend the church instead of the chapel, and leave the latter meagerly supplied with worshipers. Besides, a distinct service in the chapel would have gone far to defeat the object the president had so much at heart—the establishment and growth of a pastoral sympathy and obligation between the ministers of the town and the students of the college.

"As would naturally be inferred from what has been stated respecting the method which General Lee pursued in administering the discipline of the college, it was his constant aim to secure from the students a regular attendance on religious services through a conviction of duty, and an experience of the benefits and enjoyment derived from them, rather than by the interposition of authority and penalties. And truly it may be said that he found much in the results of his policy to confirm his opinion of its propriety, as these results were developed from year to year under his eye. It is doubtful whether any measures, compulsory in reality or in appearance, that could have been adopted, would have secured so large and uniform an attendance on public worship. Certainly, they would not have secured an attendance so favorable to the highest spiritual benefit. The demeanor of the students during worship was characterized by so much decorum, and evinced so deep an interest in the services, as to have been the subject of frequent remarks alike by citizens and strangers—it presented so striking a contrast to what they had been accustomed to witness among the same class, when under the operation of a different management. The reader will find a full confirmation of these remarks in the following extract from General Lee's last annual report to the board of trustees, dated the 21st of June, 1870:

" 'Prayers have been offered every morning in the college chapel by clergymen of the different denominations in Lexington, who volunteered at the beginning of the session to perform this service in rotation. The students were in this way introduced to their acquaintance, and were invited to attend the churches of their preference, and to join Bible classes organized in each for their instruction. They are thus early surrounded by favorable influences which in many cases end in the happiest results. The Young Men's Christian Association of the college continues to prosper, and is productive of much good. There are eighty-eight members of the association this year. There is an assembly for prayer every night, and a general prayer meeting once a week. A Sabbath school house has been built near House Mountain by the association, and a Sunday school organized near Thorn Hill. Fifty students are engaged in teaching in Sunday schools and Bible classes. There are twenty-one candidates for the ministry in the college this year, and one hundred and nine church members, nineteen of whom have joined the churches in Lexington during this session. A general and active religious feeling exists among the students, and missionary meetings are held once a month.'

"The following brief letter, so characteristic of the writer in the beauty and comprehensiveness of its diction, will form a fitting close to the subject now in hand:

" 'LEXINGTON,
September 19, 1867.

" 'MY DEAR SIR: I beg you will accept my sincere thanks for the beautiful Bible which you have presented to me—a book which supplies the place of all others, and one that cannot be replaced by any

other. I will place it in the chapel of Washington College, as you
desire, where I trust its simple truths will be daily learned and thoroughly appreciated by all the students.

" 'Very respectfully,

R. E. LEE.

" 'Colonel F. R. FARRAR.'

"Much might be said and many facts cited in illustration of General
Lee's invariable courtesy and kindness to those who were associated with
him in the daily conduct of the college, of his delicate consideration for
their feelings and convenience, and of his special regard to whatever might
tend to uphold and strengthen their influence over the students. Of all this,
and of the many acts of his unselfish devotion to the institution which
they witnessed and in whose benefits they themselves largely shared, they
will carry with them to their graves the most tender and grateful recollections. But these things are of a nature to be laid up and cherished in the
sanctuary of their own bosoms. It is scarcely proper to expose them to
the eye of the public.

"There is, however, one fact in his official relations to the college that
presents an aspect of his character it would not seem right to conceal.
During the last winter of his presidency, his health began to decline in a
way that excited alarm among his friends. They privately urged him to
lay aside his work and try the effect of travel and a sojourn in a warmer
latitude. With his wonted gentleness of manner, and yet with a tone indicating a firmness of purpose not to be mistaken, he declined to adopt
their advice. The professors, suspecting that his reluctance arose from an
unwillingness by his absence to impose additional labor and responsibility
on them, united in a formal request to the same purport, accompanying
the request with a scheme for so distributing the duties of his office among
themselves that, for the month or two of his absence, no onerous burden
would devolve on any of them, and no serious detriment result to the
college. He saw that his compliance would gratify them, and he yielded
without further objection. During his absence, the board of trustees convened, and determined that the time had come for distinctly announcing
to him a purpose they had previously formed—that of providing a home
for his family, with an annuity for their support. They regarded this as a
simple act of justice—a debt they owed him of far higher sanction than

any mere legal obligation could confer. His response to the announcement appears in the following letter written after his return from the South:

" 'WASHINGTON COLLEGE, VA.,
May 28, 1870.
" '*Hon.* JOHN W. BROCKENBROUGH, *Rector, Washington College, Va.*

" 'MY DEAR SIR: I received with feelings of deepest gratitude the resolutions of the board of trustees of Washington College, at their meeting on the 19th ult. The warm sympathy expressed at my sickness, and the cordial approval of my absence, rendered more grateful to me the generous provision for the support of my family. Though fully sensible of the kindness of the board, and justly appreciating the manner in which they sought to administer to my relief, I am unwilling that my family should become a tax to the college, but desire that all its funds should be devoted to the purposes of education. I know that my wishes on this subject are equally shared by my wife, and I therefore request that the provisions of the fourth and fifth resolutions, adopted at the session of the 19th of April, may not be carried into effect. I feel full assurance that, in case a competency should not be left to my wife, her children would never suffer her to want.

" 'With my warmest gratitude for the consideration of the board of trustees and my special thanks for the kind manner in which you have communicated to me their action,

" 'I am, with the highest respect, your obedient servant,
" 'R. E. LEE.'

"With reference to the subject of the foregoing letter, it is only necessary to state that the board of trustees, in terms of the utmost respect and delicacy, declined to recede from the position they had taken, and thus the matter stood at the time of General Lee's death. But Mrs. Lee, catching the spirit of her illustrious husband, always declined the annuity until her lamented death settled the question.

"Another letter from General Lee must be given. It places in a strong light the same aspect of his character which is exhibited in the one just inserted. But it does far more. It reveals more clearly and deeply the inner man in several of its most striking traits, than any thing that has yet been published from his pen. It sets forth his views of the great needs of the institution to which he devoted the anxieties and labors of the last five years of his life and proposed to devote all of whatever years, few or many, Providence should allot to him. It breathes the spirit of pure and enlightened patriotism—the true love of country—for which the wise and good of the land admired him while living and now revere his memory. It answers the question which has so often been asked by his loving countrymen: 'Was General Lee contented and happy in the position and employments of his latter days?' It is doubted whether in the whole range of epistolary literature any thing can be found that tells more in the same compass, and tells it more beautifully. The distinguished gentleman to whom the letter is addressed, and who is honored by the expressions of confidence and affection it contains, has since passed to his reward, and there is, therefore, no impropriety in copying the letter in full from the private letter book of the writer.

" 'WASHINGTON COLLEGE, LEXINGTON, VA.,
                            March 3, 1868.

" 'MY DEAR GENERAL: I have just seen a letter from General Lilly, stating that you had given five hundred dollars to the endowment of Washington College, with the condition that it be applied to increasing my salary. This generous donation on your part was not necessary to convince me of the lively interest you retain for the institutions of your native state, or of your friendly consideration for myself. I fully appreciate the kind motives which prompted you thus to appropriate it. But, when I tell you that I already receive a larger amount from the college than my services are worth, you will see the propriety of my not consenting that it should be increased.

" 'The great want of the college is more extensive buildings, suitable libraries, cabinets, philosophical and chemical apparatus, etc. A liberal endowment will enable it to enlarge the means of its usefulness, to afford the facilities of education to worthy young men who might not otherwise obtain one, and, as we must look to the rising generation for the restoration of the country, it can do more good in this way than in any other.

" 'I hope, now that your care and toils are over, that your health, under the pleasing influences of your present life, has been greatly improved. For my own part, I much enjoy the charms of civil life, and find too late that I have wasted the best years of my existence.

" 'I beg that you will remember me most kindly to Mrs. Ewell, Mrs. Turner, and Major Brown; and believe me, truly,

" 'Your friend,

R. E. LEE.

" 'General R. S. EWELL.' "

The other paper to which allusion is made above was prepared by the facile pen of Prof. Edward S. Joynes, and was published, soon after General Lee's death, in the *University Monthly*. Although touching on some of the points presented by Dr. Kirkpatrick, it will be read with deep interest, especially by those in any way connected with the great cause of education:

". . . General Lee accepted the presidency of Washington College, in the first place, from a profound and deliberate *sense of duty*. The same high principle of action that had characterized his conduct in the gravest crises of public affairs, marked his decision here; and here, as ever, *duty* alone determined his choice. There was absolutely nothing in this position that could have tempted him. Not only was it uncongenial with all the habits of his past life, and remote from all the associations in which he had formally taken pleasure; but it was, at that time, most uninviting in itself. The college to which he was called was broken in fortune and in hope. The war had practically closed its doors. Its buildings had been pillaged and defaced, and its library scattered. It had now neither money nor credit, and it was even doubtful whether it would be shortly reopened at all for the reception of students. The faculty were few in number, disorganized, and dispirited. Of the slender endowment that had survived the war, hardly any thing was available, and ready money could not be secured even for the most immediate and pressing wants of the college. Under these circumstances the offer of the presidency to General Lee seemed wellnigh presumptuous; and surely it was an offer from which he had nothing to expect either of fortune or of fame. The men, however, who had made this election, the trustees of Washington College—ever honored be their memory for their noble conception!—had not calculated in vain in their estimate of General Lee's character. They felt that his position, however humble it might seem, would afford to him what from their knowledge of the man they felt would be the most acceptable to him—a *sphere of duty,* in which he could spend his days in the service of his beloved people; and, though the country looked on astonished and incredulous, the result showed that they had not been mistaken.

"General Lee received the announcement, which was conveyed to him in person by the rector, Hon. John W. Brockenbrough, with surprise and with deep feeling. He was at first disposed to decline the offer; but the distinguished Virginian who represented the trustees urged it upon him, and dwelt earnestly upon the high motives which had prompted their choice. These were motives to which General Lee could not be indifferent; and at last, reserving his answer, he promised to reflect upon the subject. Here, as ever, he was deliberate as well as conscientious. Finally, after several days' consideration, he accepted the position. Suffice it to say here that it was a deliberate sense of duty to his fellow countrymen, and a desire to pay back, as far as he could, through their sons, the sufferings and sorrows of his own generation in the South, that determined his decision. He had already fully resolved not to leave Virginia under any circumstances; and this position, humble as it seemed to be, gave him the wished-for opportunity of laboring for her people, and for the South. Therefore he accepted it.

"The profound sense of duty which marked General Lee's acceptance of this office, characterized also his whole administration of it. He entertained the profoundest convictions on the importance of educational influences, both to individuals and to the country, and the deepest sense of personal responsibility in his own office. He felt that an institution like Washington College owed duty, not only to its own students, but to the whole country; and that its moral obligations were not only supreme within its own sphere, but were attached to the wider interests of public virtue and of true religion, among all the people. Everybody around him felt unconsciously that he was actuated by these principles, and all were impressed by his high conceptions of duty, and the singleness of his devotion to it. Nothing else, indeed, could have sustained him so serenely through so many and so constant details of labor and of trial. Nothing else, in such a man, could have held his thoughts so high or kept his heart so strong, in the midst of daily tasks, always so severe, often so trivial and discouraging. But he never flagged; and, though he fully comprehended the difficulties of his office, and was often wearied with its incessant labors, no word of despondency fell from his lips. He felt that he was doing his duty. 'I have,' he said, as reported by the Hon. Mr. Hilliard, 'a self-imposed task, which I cannot forsake'; and in this spirit he met all the details of his daily labors cheerfully to the last. Again and again, during his life at Lexington, were tempting offers urged upon him—offers of large income, with comparative ease and more active and congenial employment; but, though he fully appreciated these considerations, and was not indifferent to the attractions presented by such offers, he turned from them all, with the same reply. He had chosen his post of duty, and he clung to it. Year by year the conception of his duty seemed to grow stronger with him; and year by year, the college, as its instrument and representative, grew dearer to him. And as, gradually, the fruits of his labors began to be manifest, and the moral and intellectual results of his influence approved themselves even to his own modest self-estimate, his heart grew only warmer, and his zeal more earnest in his work.

"His sense of personal duty was also expanded into a warmer solicitude for all who were associated with him. To the faculty he was as an elder brother, beloved and revered, and full of all tender sympathy. To the students he was as a father, in carefulness, in encouragement, in reproof. Their welfare, and their conduct and character as gentlemen, were his chief concern; and this solicitude was not limited to their collegiate years, but followed them abroad into life. He thought it to be the office of a college not merely to educate the intellect, but to make Christian men. The moral and religious character of the students was more precious in his eyes even than their intellectual progress, and was made the special object of his constant personal solicitude. In his annual reports to the trustees, which are models of clear and dignified composition, he always dwelt with peculiar emphasis upon these interests; and nothing in the college gratified him more than its marked moral and religious improvement during his administration. To the Rev. Dr. White he said, as affectively narrated by that venerable minister soon after his death: 'I shall be disappointed, sir—I shall fail in the leading object that brought me here, unless these young men all become consistent Christians.' Other expressions, bearing eloquent witness to the same truth, might be quoted; but none could be more eloquent than the steady tenor of his own life, quietly yet constantly devoted to the highest ends of duty and of religion.

"Such were the principles which actuated General Lee, as president of Washington College; and their effects showed themselves in all the details of his administration. In the discipline of the college his moral influence was supreme. A disciplinarian, in the ordinary sense of the term, as it is often most unworthily applied, he was not. He was no seeker-out of small offenses, no stickler for formal regulations. In the construction of college rules, and in his dealing with actions generally, he was most liberal; but in his estimate of motives, and in the requirement of principle and honor, he was exacting to the last degree. Youthful indiscretion found in him the most lenient of judges; but falsehood or meanness had no toleration with him. He looked rather to the principles of good conduct than to mere outward acts. He was most scrupulous in exacting a proper obedience to lawful authority; but he was always the last to condemn, and the most just to hear the truth, even in behalf of the worst offender. Hence in the use of college punishment he was cautious, forbearing, and lenient; but he was not the less firm in his demands, and prompt, when need was, in his measures. His reproof was stern, yet kind, and often even melting in its tenderness; and his appeals, always addressed to the noblest motives, were irresistible. The hardiest offenders were alike awed by his presence, and moved, often even to tears, by his word; and there was no student who did not dread a reproof from General Lee more than every other punishment. In all his official action, and indeed in all his intercourse with the students, he looked to the elevation of the tone of principle and opinion among themselves, as the vital source of good conduct, rather than to the simple repression of vice. His discipline was moral rather than punitive. Hence there were few cases of dismission, or other severe punishment, during his administration; and hence, also, the need for such punishments became ever less and less. The influence of this policy, aided especially by the mighty influence of his personal character, was all-powerful. The elevation of tone, and the improvement in conduct, were steady and rapid. Immediately after the war, the young men of the South were wild and unrestrained, and acts of disorder were frequent; in the latter years of his administration hardly a single case of serious discipline occurred. We doubt, indeed, whether at any other college in the world so many young men could have been found as free from misconduct, or marked by as high a tone of feeling and opinion, as were the students of Washington College during these latter years of General Lee's life. The students felt this, and were proud of it; and they were proud of themselves and of their college, as representatives of the character and influence of Lee.

"Yet not the less was he rigidly exacting of duty, and scrupulously attentive to details. By a system of reports, weekly and monthly—almost military in their exactness—which he required of each professor, he made himself acquainted with the standing and progress of every student in every one of his classes. These reports he studied carefully, and was quick to detect shortcomings. He took care, also, to make himself acquainted with each student personally, to know his studies, his boardinghouse, his associations, disposition, and habits; and, though he never obtruded this knowledge, the students knew that he possessed it, and that his interest followed them everywhere. Nor was it a moral influence alone that he exerted in the college. He was equally careful of its intellectual interests. He watched the progress of every class, attended all the examinations, and strove constantly to stimulate both professors and students to the highest attainments. The whole college, in a word, felt his influence as an ever-present motive, and his character was quietly yet irresistibly impressed upon it, not only in the general working in all its departments, but in all the details of each.

"Of this influence, General Lee, modest as he was, was perfectly aware, and, like a prudent ruler, he husbanded it with a wise economy. He preferred to confine his direct interposition to purely personal acts; and rarely, and then only on critical occasions, did he step forward to present himself before the whole body of students in the full dignity of his presidential office. On these occasions, which in the latter years hardly ever occurred, he would quietly post an address to the students, in which, appealing only to the highest principles of conduct, he sought to dissuade them from threatened evil. These addresses, which the boys designated as his 'general orders,' were always of immediate efficacy. No single case ever occurred in which they failed of instant and complete effect; and no student would have been tolerated by his fellow students who would have dared to disregard such an appeal from General Lee. . . .

"General Lee was also most laborious in the duties of his office as a college president. He gave himself wholly to his work. His occupations were constant, almost incessant. He went to his office daily at eight o'clock, and rarely returned home until one or two. During this time, he was almost incessantly engaged in college matters, giving his personal attention to the minutest details, and always ready to receive visitors on college business. It has sometimes been sneeringly alleged that General Lee was only a *figurehead* at Washington College, kept there merely for the attraction of his splendid name. Never was slander more false; for it was a slander upon him, more even than a slur upon the college. Never was a college president more laborious than he. He gave all his powers

entirely to his work. Though ably assisted by subordinate officers, whom
he well knew how to employ, he yet had an eye for the supervision of
every detail. The buildings, the repairs, the college walks and grounds,
the wood yard, the mess hall, all received his attention, and a large portion
of his time was given to the purely business affairs of the college. His
office was always open to students or professors, all of whose interests
received his ready consideration. His correspondence meanwhile was very
heavy, yet no letter that called for an answer was ever neglected. It has
been recently stated by an editor that, to a circular letter of general educational interest, addressed by him to a large number of college presidents,
General Lee was the only one that replied; yet he was the greatest and
perhaps the busiest of them all. In addition to the formal circulars, which
he always revised and signed himself, his correspondence with the parents
and guardians of students was intimate and explicit, on every occasion
that required such correspondence. Many of these letters are models of
beautiful composition and noble sentiment. . . .

"But General Lee was not only earnest and laborious, he was also *able,*
as a college president. He was perfectly master of the situation, and thoroughly wise and skillful in all its duties of organization and of policy, as
well as of detail. To this let the results of his administration bear testimony.
He found the college practically bankrupt, disorganized, deserted; he left
it rich, strong, and crowded with students. It was not merely numbers that
he brought to it, for these his great fame alone would have attracted; he
gave it organization, unity, energy, and practical success. In entering upon
his presidency, he seemed at once fully to comprehend the wants of the
college; and its history during the next five years was but the development
of his plans and the reflection of his wise energy. And these plans were
not fragmentary, nor was this energy merely an industrious zeal. He had
from the beginning a distinct *policy,* which he had fully conceived, and
to which he steadily adhered; so that all his particular measures of progress
were but consistent steps in its development. His object was nothing less
than to establish and perfect an institution which should meet the highest
needs of education in every department. At once, and without waiting for
the means to be provided in advance, he proceeded to develop this object.
Under his advice new chairs were created, and professors called to fill
them; so that, before the end of the first year, the faculty was doubled in
numbers. Still additional chairs were created, and finally a complete system of schools was established and brought into full operation. To these

schools, or distinct departments, each one of which was complete in itself and under the individual control of its own professor, he gave a compact and unique organization into a system of complete courses, with corresponding diplomas and degrees, which, securing the perfect distinctness and responsibility of each school, gave a perfect unity to them all. These courses were so adapted and mutually arranged, under their common organization and his general control, as to escape alike the errors of the purely elective system on the one hand and of the close curriculum on the other, and to secure, by a happy compromise, the best advantages of both. So admirably was this plan conceived and administered by General Lee that, heterogeneous as were the students, especially in the earlier years, each one found at once his proper place, and all were kept in the line of complete and systematic study. Under this organization, and especially under the inspiration of his central influence, the utmost harmony and the utmost energy pervaded all the departments of the college. The highest powers of both professors and students were called forth, under the fullest responsibility. The standards of scholarship were rapidly advanced; and soon the graduates of Washington College were the acknowledged equals of those from the best institutions elsewhere, and were eagerly sought after for the highest positions as teachers in the best schools. These results, which, even in the few years of his administration, had become universally acknowledged throughout the South, were due, directly and immediately, more than to all other causes, to the personal ability and influence of General Lee as president of the college.

"General Lee's plans for the development of Washington College were not simply progressive; they were distinct and definite. He aimed to make this college represent at once the wants and the genius of the country. He fully realized the needs of the present age, and he desired to adapt the education of the people to their condition and their destiny. He was the ardent advocate of complete classical and literary culture. Under his influence, the classical and literary schools of the college were fully sustained. Yet he recognized the fact that material well-being is, for a people, a condition of all high civilization, and therefore, though utterly out of sympathy with the modern advocates of materialistic education, he sought to provide all the means for the development of science, and for its practical applications. He thought, indeed, that the best antidote to the materialistic tendencies of a purely scientific training was to be found in the liberalizing influences of literary culture, and that scientific and profes-

sional schools could best be taught when surrounded by the associations
of a literary institution. He sought, therefore, to establish this mutual connection, and to consolidate all the departments of literary, scientific, and
professional education under a common organization. Hence, at an early
day, he called into existence the Schools of Applied Mathematics and
Engineering, and of Law, as part of the collegiate organization; and, later,
he submitted to the trustees a plan for the complete development of the
scientific and professional departments of the college, which will ever
remain as an example of his enlarged wisdom, and which has anticipated,
by many years, we fear, the practical attainments of any school in this
country. In addition to all the other reasons for mourning the death of
Lee, it is to be deeply regretted, not only for Washington College, but for
the sake of the education of the country, that he did not live to complete
his great designs. Had he done so, he would probably have left behind
him an institution of learning which would have been a not less illustrious
monument of his character than his most brilliant military achievements.
As it is, Washington College, henceforth forever associated with his name,
will also be inseparably associated with the memory of his noble influence
and of his wise and far-sighted plans. Had this been the profession of his
life, General Lee would have been not less famous, relatively, among
college presidents than he is now among soldiers. *Now,* after having won,
in other fields, a worldwide fame, he has, in this last labor of his life,
displayed an ability and developed a power for the highest achievements,
such as form no small part of the fame even of his distinguished career.

"Such, briefly and imperfectly sketched, was General Lee as a college
president. And surely this part of his life deserves to be remembered and
commemorated by those who hold his memory dear. In it he exhibited all
those great qualities of character which had made his name already so
illustrious; while, in addition, he sustained trials and sorrows without
which the highest perfections of that character could never have been so
signally displayed. This life at Washington College, so devoted, so earnest,
so laborious, so full of far-reaching plans and of wise and successful effort,
was begun under the weight of a disappointment which might have broken
any ordinary strength, and was maintained, in the midst of public and
private misfortune, with a serene patience, and a mingled firmness and
sweetness of temper, that give additional brilliancy even to the glory of
his former fame. It was his high privilege to meet alike the temptations
and perils of the highest stations before the eyes of the world, and the

cares and labors of the most responsible duties of private life, under the most trying circumstances, and to exhibit in all alike the qualities of a great and consistent character, founded in the noblest endowments, and sustained by the loftiest principles of virtue and religion. It is a privilege henceforth for the teachers of our country that their profession, in its humble yet arduous labors, its great and its petty cares, has been illustrated by the devotion of such a man. It is an honor for all our colleges that one of them is henceforth identified with the memory of his name and of his work. It is a boon for us all; an honor to the country, which in its whole length and breadth will soon be proud to claim his fame; an honor to human nature itself, that this great character, so often and so severely tried, has thus approved itself consistent, serene, and grand, alike in peace and in war, in the humblest as well as in the highest offices. Among the monuments which shall perpetuate his fame, not the least honorable will be that which shall commemorate his life at Washington College; and among the materials out of which the historian shall construct his future biography, not the least interesting, we are sure, will be the simple record of these last years of silent but sublime labor—of peaceful yet noble and far-reaching aspiration—in behalf of his beloved and suffering people of the South."

I will add to these sketches of those who helped him in his work, that, as I was permitted to see, during five years, the daily effects of his power in the college—the skill with which he managed its affairs, and the enthusiasm with which he inspired all who came in contact with him, until he had one of the hardest-working faculties, and one of the most orderly, studious bodies of young men in the country—I was impressed with the conviction that he was not only the best soldier, but also *the best college president,* whom this country has ever produced.

The following incidents may be given as illustrating an important fact stated above by Dr. Kirkpatrick. Happening into his office one day, I heard a visitor inquire how a certain student was getting on, when President Lee promptly replied: "He is a very quiet, orderly young man, but seems very careful *not to injure the health of his father's son.* He got last month only forty on his Greek, thirty-five on his mathematics, forty-seven on his Latin, and fifty on his English, which is a very low stand, as one hundred is our maximum. Now, I do not want our young men to really injure their health; but I wish them to come as near it as possible."

Very much surprised at his being able, without reference to memoranda, to thus give the class standing of one out of four hundred students, I related the incident to one of the professors, and asked if this was not an isolated case. He replied that the general could not, of course, always recollect the exact "class mark" of every student, but that he never failed to know the general standing of a student, and would frequently say, when a name was called at the faculty meeting, "He does his mathematics pretty well, but is neglecting his Latin and Greek;" or, "He is making good progress in the languages, but is deficient in his mathematics and the sciences." Upon one occasion, when a certain name was called, General Lee remarked, "I am sorry to see that he has fallen back so far in his mathematics." "You are mistaken, general," said the professor; "he is one of the very best men in my class." "He only got fifty-four last month," was the reply, and upon looking at the consolidated report it was found that there had been a mistake in copying, and that General Lee was correct according to the record.

As a fitting conclusion to this chapter, the following extract from an eloquent sermon, preached in the Citadel Square Baptist Church, Charleston, S.C., by Rev. Dr. E. T. Winkler, may be subjoined:

"When I seek to penetrate into the mind of our great leader, to understand how he, who failed to save the country by the sword, still hoped to save its laws, its institutions, its customs, its sciences, its letters, its magistracies, its altars—all that has been overwhelmed by a fierce and tumultuous democracy—I admire the simple and noble expedient to which he resorted. General Lee established new claims to the reverence of his countrymen when he exchanged the camp for the college, and the sword for the pen.

"Men have praised his modest retirement to scholastic retreats when the war was over, his silence amid political clamors, his labors in failing health, his devotion to the interests of peace, and virtue, and religion. How few realize that, in the quiet hall of the lecturer and professor, he renewed the war, transferring it to the sphere of mind! A year before his death, Washington liberally endowed the college that bears his name in Lexington, a town situated on the high western bank of North River, a little over a hundred miles from Richmond. The Virginia Military Institute is there, where Stonewall Jackson taught, and there is that lamented warrior's grave. There his commander now reposes.

" 'They were swifter than eagles, they were stronger than lions. Lovely and pleasant in their lives, in their deaths they are not divided.' Lexington is the parable of the great Virginia soldiers. In that quiet scholastic retreat, in that city set upon a hill and crowned with martial trophies, they, being dead, yet speak. Richmond desires his body. It is natural that the metropolis he defended so bravely, and so long, should yearn for that mighty presence. But the removal of his remains from Lexington would obscure the final lesson of his career. At Lexington the Southern leader entrenched himself upon the battlefield of intelligence, and gathered around him the ardent youth of a new generation, and the spirits of the illustrious dead, for the redemption of his conquered country. Lexington is the capital upon the column, otherwise incomplete, of an harmonious and beautiful patriotism.

"The earthworks he erected are fast disappearing. The fields he glorified by his valor have wept away the stains of heroic blood, and are now robed as with a golden vesture in the yellow autumnal grain. The cause for which he contended is lost. Yet the great character is immortal, and the great lesson remains. O ye, in whose service that perfect mechanism was worn out, for whom he endured sleepless nights, watchful days; for whom he planned and marched; for whom he encountered exposures, and perils, and privation, and combats, until defense after defense of Nature was carried, and the citadel of life was assailed, and the spotless sword was surrendered to the grim conqueror, revere that last legacy, so simple, as coming from the war-worn soldier: Take care of your institutions of learning. Esteem education, mental, moral, and religious, as the only bulwark of the republic. Regard service and sacrifice, not as the means of success, but as the true glory of life. And think of manliness as attaining its noblest elevation when it bows before the cross of Jesus Christ.

"As David composed 'The Song of the Bow,' to celebrate the glory of that warrior king who had checked the invaders of Palestine, and at last fell upon the memorable mountains of Gilboa, so will the people of this land, for countless generations, celebrate the memory of the consummate soldier who resisted the overwhelming flood of our enemies, and guarded for years the vast bulwarks of our country, until, battle-spent, he died—a nobler chief than Saul—a hero adorned with religion, and vindicating his country less by his prowess than by his pure virtues. Favored land, which has produced so rare a spirit, which encircles by its boundaries the fields of his shining valor, which has so long beheld a monument to the glory of religion in the person of her most honored son! Favored land, where the echoes of his prayers still linger, after the trumpets of his charging squadrons have died away! Favored land, where the laurels, and the standards, and the spoils of war lie low before the Mercy-Seat! Favored land, where the spirit of her greatest son is expressed in the inspired ascription of old: 'Not unto us, O Lord, not unto us, but unto Thy name give glory!' "

Chapter III

DUTY, THE KEYNOTE OF HIS LIFE

If asked to name in a single word the controlling principle of General Lee's life, we should unhesitatingly answer, DUTY. Whether as a youth meeting his obligations to his aged mother, and passing through the military academy without a single demerit; or serving in the United States Army; or directing the forces of his native South; or quietly working in the college at Lexington for the good of the young men of the country—*duty* was the star which guided him throughout his eventful career. The letter which has been so widely published, purporting to have been written by General Lee at Arlington to his son Custis at West Point, is unquestionably spurious. But the expression, "Duty is the sublimest word in the English language," did occur in a letter to his son, and it is very certain that he regulated his own life by this noble sentiment.

General Magruder related a characteristic incident, which was thus given by the *Norfolk Virginian:*

"After the fall of Mexico, when the American army was enjoying the ease and relaxation which it had bought by toil and blood, a brilliant assembly of officers sat over their wine, discussing the operations of the siege, and indulging hopes of a speedy return to the United States.

"One among them rose to propose the health of the captain of engineers, who had found a way for the army within the city; and then it was remarked that Captain Lee was absent. Magruder was dispatched to bring him to the hall, and, departing on his mission, at last found the object of his search in a remote room of the palace, busy on a map.

"Magruder accosted his friend, and reproached him for his absence.

"The earnest worker looked up from his labors with a calm, mild gaze, which we all remember, and, pointing to his instruments, shook his head.

" 'But,' said Magruder, in his impetuous way, 'this is mere drudgery! Make somebody else do it, and come with me.'

" 'No,' was the reply—'no, I am but doing my duty.' "

We give, in his own words, an incident related by ex-President Jefferson Davis, in his address at the Lee Memorial Meeting held in Richmond, November 3, 1870:

"An attempt has been made to throw a cloud upon his character because he left the army of the United States to join in the struggle for the liberty of his state. Without entering into politics, I deem it my duty to say one word in reference to this charge. Virginian born, descended from a family illustrious in the colonial history of Virginia, more illustrious still in her struggle for Independence, and most illustrious in her recent effort to maintain the great principles declared in 1776, given by Virginia to the service of the United States, he represented her in the Military Academy at West Point. He was not educated by the Federal government, but by Virginia; for she paid her full share for the support of that institution, and was entitled to demand in return the services of her sons. Entering the army of the United States, he represented Virginia there also, and nobly performed his duty for the Union of which Virginia was a member, whether we look to his peaceful services as an engineer, or to his more notable deeds upon foreign fields of battle. He came from Mexico crowned with honors, covered by brevets, and recognized, young as he was, as one of the ablest of his country's soldiers. And to prove that he was estimated then as such, not only by his associates, but by foreigners also, I may mention that when he was a captain of engineers, stationed in Baltimore, the Cuban Junta in New York selected him to be their leader in the revolutionary effort in that island. They were anxious to secure his services, and offered him every temptation that ambition could desire, and pecuniary emoluments far beyond any which he could hope otherwise to acquire. He thought the matter over, and, I remember, came to Washington to consult me as to what he should do. After a brief discussion of the complex character of the military problem which was presented, he turned from the consideration of that view of the question, by stating that the point on which he wished particularly to consult me was as to the propriety of entertaining the proposition which had been made to him. He had been educated in the service of the United States, and felt it wrong to accept place in the army of a foreign power, while he held his commission. Such was his extreme delicacy, such the nice sense of honor of the gallant gentleman we deplore. But when Virginia—the state to which he owed his first and last allegiance—withdrew from the Union, and thus terminated his relations to it, the same nice sense of honor and duty, which had guided him on a former occasion, had a different application, and led him to share her fortune for good or for evil."

It cost General Lee a severe struggle to leave the old army. He had never been a politician, but was ardently attached to the Union, and earnestly opposed to secession as a remedy for the grievances of the South.

Besides his published utterances, a few extracts from his private letters to his wife will abundantly show this. From "Camp Cooper, on the Clear Fork of the Brazos," under date of "August 4, 1856," he writes as follows: "... I hope your father enjoyed his usual celebration of the 4th of July. My 4th was spent (after a march of thirty miles) on a branch of the Brazos, under my blanket, which was elevated on four sticks driven in the ground as a sunshade. The sun was fiery hot, the atmosphere like the blast from a hot-air furnace, the water salt; still my feelings for my country were as ardent, my faith in her future as true, and my hopes for her advancement as unabated, as if called forth under more propitious circumstances."

Under date of "December, 1856," he writes from Fort Brown, Texas:

"... We get plenty of papers, but all of old dates. Things seem to be going on as usual in the states. Mr. Buchanan, it appears, is to be our next president. I hope he will be able to extinguish fanaticism North and South, cultivate love for the country and Union, and restore harmony between the different sections. . . ."

He wrote as follows on the eve of the great catastrophe which was to drench the land in blood:

"FORT MASON, TEXAS,
January 23, 1861.

"I received Everett's *Life of Washington* which you sent me, and enjoyed its perusal. How his spirit would be grieved could he see the wreck of his mighty labors! I will not, however, permit myself to believe, until all ground of hope is gone, that the fruit of his noble deeds will be destroyed, and that his precious advice and virtuous example will so soon be forgotten by his countrymen. As far as I can judge by the papers, we are between a state of anarchy and civil war. May God avert both of these evils from us! I fear that mankind will not for years be sufficiently Christianized to bear the absence of restraint and force. I see that four states have declared themselves out of the Union; four more will apparently follow their example. Then, if the border States are brought into the gulf of revolution, one half of the country will be arrayed against the other. I must try and be patient and await the end, for I can do nothing to hasten or retard it. . . ."

Under the same date, he wrote thus to his son:

"The South, in my opinion, has been aggrieved by the acts of the North, as you say. I feel the aggression, and am willing to take every proper step for redress. It is the principle I contend for, not individual or private benefit. As an American citizen, I take great pride in my country, her prosperity and institutions, and would defend any state, if her rights were invaded. But I can anticipate no greater calamity for the country than a dissolution of the Union. It would be an accumulation of all the evils we complain of, and I am willing to sacrifice every thing but honor for its preservation. I hope, therefore, that all constitutional means will be exhausted before there is a resort to force. Secession is nothing but revolution. The framers of our Constitution never exhausted so much labor, wisdom, and forbearance in its formation, and surrounded it with so many guards and securities, if it was intended to be broken by every member of the Confederacy at will. It was intended for 'perpetual union,' so expressed in the preamble, and for the establishment of a government, not a compact, which can only be dissolved by revolution, or the consent of all the people in convention assembled. It is idle to talk of secession. Anarchy would have been established, and not a government, by Washington, Hamilton, Jefferson, Madison, and the other patriots of the Revolution. . . . Still a Union that can only be maintained by swords and bayonets, and in which strife and civil war are to take the place of brotherly love and kindness, has no charm for me. I shall mourn for my country and for the welfare and progress of mankind. If the Union is dissolved, and the government disrupted, I shall return to my native state and share the miseries of my people, and save in defense will draw my sword on none."

Three weeks after this letter was written, he received orders "to report to the commander-in-chief at Washington," and hastened to obey the summons—reaching there on the 1st of March, just three days before the inauguration of President Lincoln. Here he had the strongest pressure brought to bear upon him to induce him to side with the North in the impending struggle. General Scott, who had been his warm personal friend, and to whom he was most sincerely attached, used all of his powers of persuasion to induce him to "stand by the old flag." We have the authority of Hon. Montgomery Blair for saying that the supreme command of the United States Army was offered him by Mr. Lincoln. He knew that in the Southern army several other officers (by a law already passed by the Confederate Congress) would rank him. He appreciated, as few others did, the magnitude of the war which was about to burst forth, the fearful odds against which the South would contend, and the uncertainty of the issue. His beautiful home at Arlington, around which clustered so many hallowed associations, must fall within the Federal lines, and he must lose his splendid estate if he sided with the South. But "none of these things moved him"—his only desire was *to know that he might walk the path of duty.*

To Mr. Lincoln's messenger (the elder Blair) he said: "Mr. Blair, I look upon secession as anarchy. If I owned the four millions of slaves in the South, I would sacrifice them all to the Union—but how can I draw my sword upon Virginia, my native state!" To all of General Scott's entreaties he made similar replies; and when on the 17th day of April, 1861, the Virginia Convention (which had stood firm in its adherence to the Union, and exhausted every means of pacification), in reply to Mr. Lincoln's call for troops to coerce the seceded states, passed its ordinance of secession and called upon the sons of Virginia to rally to her standard, the course of R. E. Lee was decided.

He turned his back upon wealth, rank, and all that a mighty nation could offer him, severed the strong ties which bound him to the "old service" and his brother officers, and offered his stainless sword to his mother state.

The following letter to General Scott explains the feelings with which he left the United States Army:

"ARLINGTON, VA.,
April 20, 1861.

"GENERAL: Since my interview with you on the 18th instant, I have felt that I ought not longer to retain my commission in the army. I therefore tender my resignation, which I request you will recommend for acceptance. It would have been presented at once, but for the struggle it has cost me to separate myself from a service to which I have devoted all the best years of my life, and all the ability I possessed.

"During the whole of that time—more than a quarter of a century—I have experienced nothing but kindness from my superiors, and the most cordial friendship from my comrades. To no one, General, have I been as much indebted as to yourself for uniform kindness and consideration, and it has always been my ardent desire to meet your approbation. I shall carry to the grave the most grateful recollections of your kind consideration, and your name and fame will always be dear to me.

"Save in defense of my native state, I never desire again to draw my sword. Be pleased to accept my most earnest wishes for the continuance of your happiness and prosperity, and believe me most truly yours,

R. E. LEE."

To a sister in Baltimore he wrote as follows, under the same date as the above:

"MY DEAR SISTER: I am grieved at my inability to see you. . . . I have been waiting for a more 'convenient season,' which has brought to many before me deep and lasting regret. We are now in a state of war which will yield to nothing. The whole South is in a state of revolution, into which Virginia, after a long struggle, has been drawn; and though I recognize no necessity for this state of things, and would have forborne and pleaded to the end for redress of grievances, real or supposed, yet in my own person I had to meet the question whether I should take part against my native state. With all my devotion to the Union, and the feeling of loyalty and duty of an American citizen, I have not been able to make up my mind to raise my hand against my relatives, my children, my home. I have, therefore, resigned my commission in the army, and save in defense of my native state—with the sincere hope that my poor services may never be needed—I hope I may never be called upon to draw my sword.

"I know you will blame me; but you must think as kindly of me as you can, and believe that I have endeavored to do what I thought right. To show you the feeling and struggle it has cost me, I send a copy of my letter of resignation. I have no time for more. . . .

"May God guard and protect you and yours, and shower upon you everlasting blessings, is the prayer of

"Your devoted brother,
"R. E. LEE."

Immediately upon his arrival in Richmond, the governor nominated him to the chief command of the Virginia forces, and the convention unanimously confirmed the nomination. On the 23d of April he was enthusiastically received by the convention, and their president (the venerable John Janney) made him an eloquent address of welcome, concluding as follows:

"Sir, we have by this unanimous vote expressed our convictions that you are at this day, among the living citizens of Virginia, 'first in war.' We pray to God most fervently that you may so conduct the operations committed to your charge that it may soon be said of you that you are 'first in peace'; and when that time comes, you will have earned the still prouder distinction of being 'first in the hearts of your countrymen.'

"Yesterday your mother, Virginia, placed her sword in your hand, upon the implied condition, that we know you will keep to the letter and in spirit, that you will draw it only in defense, and that you will fall with it in your hand rather than that the object for which it was placed there shall fail."

General Lee replied with characteristic modesty and said: "Mr. President and gentlemen of the Convention—Profoundly impressed with the solemnity of the occasion, for which I must say I was not prepared, I accept the position assigned me by your partiality. I would have much preferred had your choice fallen upon an abler man. Trusting in Almighty God, an approving conscience, and the aid of my fellow citizens, I devote myself to the service of my native state, in whose behalf alone will I ever again draw my sword."

Men may differ as to the rightfulness of the course on which General Lee decided; but no one who knew him could ever doubt that he acted from the highest conviction that he was but doing his duty.

The following letter will be a valuable contribution to history, not only as giving General Lee's own version of the important events mentioned, but also as refuting certain misrepresentations of him which have been widely circulated:

"LEXINGTON, VA.,
February 25, 1868.
"Hon. REVERED JOHNSON, *U.S. Senate, Washington, D.C.*

"MY DEAR SIR: My attention has been called to the official report of the debate in the Senate of the United States of the 19th instant, in which you did me the kindness to doubt the correctness of the statement made by the Hon. Simon Cameron in regard to myself. I desire that you may feel certain of my conduct on the occasion referred to, so far as my individual statement can make you.

"I never intimated to any one that I desired the command of the United States Army, nor did I ever have a conversation but with one gentleman, Mr. Francis Preston Blair, on the subject, which was at his invitation, and, as I understood, at the instance of President Lincoln.

"After listening to his remarks, I declined the offer he made me, to take command of the army that was to be brought into the field, stating, as candidly and as courteously as I could, that, though opposed to secession and deprecating war, I could take no part in an invasion of the Southern states.

"I went directly from the interview with Mr. Blair to the office of General Scott; told him of the proposition that had been made to me, and my decision.

"Upon reflection after returning to my home, I concluded that I ought no longer to retain any commission I held in the United States Army, and, on the second morning thereafter, I forwarded my resignation to General Scott.

"At the time, I hoped that peace would have been preserved; that some way would have been found to save the country from the calamities of war; and I then had no other intention than to pass the remainder of my life as a private citizen.

"Two days afterward, upon the invitation of the governor of Virginia, I repaired to Richmond, found that the convention then in session had passed the ordinance withdrawing the state from the Union, and accepted the commission of commander of its forces which was tendered me.

"These are the simple facts of the case, and they show that Mr. Cameron has been misinformed.

"I am, with great respect, your obedient servant,
"R. E. LEE."

But it is proper to add that, when his course was once decided upon, he never faltered, and never for a moment regretted his decision, or doubted that he was treading the path of duty.

In June 1868, when speaking to his trusted lieutenant—the gallant and accomplished General Wade Hampton—of the war and its results, and of the part he bore in it, he said, with emphasis: *"I did only what my duty demanded; I could have taken no other course without dishonor. And if all were to be done over again, I should act in precisely the same manner."*

In reference to General Lee's views and feelings at the breaking out of the war, Bishop Joseph P. B. Wilmer, of Louisiana, in a memorial address, testifies as follows:

"In what temper of mind he entered this contest, I can speak with some confidence, from personal interviews with him soon after the commencement of hostilities. 'Is it your expectation,' I asked, 'that the issue of this war will be to perpetuate the institution of slavery?'

" 'The future is in the hands of Providence,' he replied, 'but, if the slaves of the South were mine, I would surrender them all without a struggle, to avert this war.'

"I asked him, next, upon what his calculations were based in so unequal a contest, and how he expected to win success; was he looking to divided counsels in the North, or to foreign interposition? His answer showed how little he was affected by the hopes and fears which agitated ordinary minds. 'My reliance is in the help of God.'

" 'Are you sanguine of the result?' I ventured to inquire. 'At present I am not concerned with results. God's will ought to be our aim, and I am quite contented that his designs should be accomplished and not mine.' "

And so, all through that great contest (in the hour of victory and the hour of defeat alike), he seemed animated only by a desire *to do his duty,* whatever others might think.

This is illustrated by an incident of the surrender, related by Colonel C. S. Venable, a gallant and accomplished member of his personal staff, in his address at the Lee Memorial Meeting in Richmond, November 3, 1870:

"At three o'clock on the morning of that fatal day, General Lee rode forward, still hoping that we might break through the countless hordes of the enemy which hemmed us in. Halting a short distance in rear of our vanguard, he sent me on to General Gordon to ask him if he could break through the enemy. I found General Gordon and General Fitz Lee on their front line in the dim light of the morning, arranging an attack. Gordon's reply to the message (I give the expressive phrase of the gallant Georgian) was this: 'Tell General Lee I have fought my corps to a frazzle, and I fear I can do nothing unless I am heavily supported by Longstreet's corps.' When I bore this message back to General Lee, he said: 'Then there is nothing left me but to go and see General Grant,[1] and I would rather die a thousand deaths.' Convulsed with passionate grief, many were the wild words which we spoke, as we stood around him. Said one, 'O General, what will history say of the surrender of the army in the field?' He replied: 'Yes, I know they will say hard things of us; they will not understand how we were overwhelmed by numbers; but that is not the question, Colonel; the question is, is it right to surrender this army? If it is right, then *I* will take *all* the responsibility.'

"Fellow soldiers, though he alone was calm, in that hour of humiliation the soul of our great captain underwent the throes of death for his grand old army surrendered, and for his people so soon to lie at the mercy of the foe; and the sorrows of this first death at Appomattox Courthouse, with the afflictions which fell upon the devoted South, weighed upon his mighty heart to its breaking, when the welcome messenger came from God to translate him to his home in heaven."

One day in 1866 the writer was conversing with General Lee in ref-

---

[1] Field's and Mohone's divisions of Longstreet's corps, stanch in the midst of all our disasters, were holding Meade back in our rear, and could not be spared for the attack.

erence to certain results of the war, when he said, very emphatically: "Yes! all that is very sad, and might be a cause of self-reproach, *but that we are conscious that we have humbly tried to do our duty.* We may, therefore, with calm satisfaction, trust in God, and leave results to him."

General Gordon testifies that in the deep agony of spirit with which Lee witnessed the grief of his soldiers at the surrender, he exclaimed, "I could wish that I were numbered among the slain of the last battle," but that he at once recalled the wish, and said, "No! we must live for our afflicted country."

And one of his officers relates that during those hours of terrible suspense, when he was considering the question of surrender, he exclaimed from the depths of a full heart: "How easily I could get rid of this and be at rest! I have only to ride along the lines, and all will be over. But," he quickly added, "*it is our duty to live*—for what will become of the women and children of the South if we are not here to support and protect them?"

So, too, after the surrender, he determined that it was *his duty* to remain in his native state, share her fortunes, and abide all the perils of personal danger which then seemed to surround him.

He said to an intimate friend who visited him in Richmond soon after the surrender: "What course I shall pursue I have not decided upon, and each man must be the judge of his own action. We must all, however, resolve on one thing—not to abandon our country. Now, more than at any other time, Virginia and every state in the South needs us. We must try and, with as little delay as possible, go to work to build up their prosperity. The young men especially must stay at home, bearing themselves in such a manner as to gain the esteem of every one at the same time that they maintain their own self-respect."

It was my sad privilege, not long after General Lee's death, to look over some papers found in his army satchel, together with his parole, and other things which had not been disturbed since his return from Appomattox Courthouse. On loose sheets he had written—evidently to amuse a leisure hour in camp—a great many maxims, proverbs, quotations from the Psalms, selections from standard authors, and reflections of his own. On one sheet was found, in his well-known handwriting, the following:

"The warmest instincts of every man's soul declare the glory of the soldier's death. It is more appropriate to the Christian than to the Greek to sing:

> *'Glorious his fate, and envied is his lot,*
> *Who for his country fights and for it dies.'*

"There is a true glory and a true honor: the glory of duty done—the honor of the integrity of principle."

On another sheet he had written: "Private and public life are subject to the same rules; and truth and manliness are two qualities that will carry you through this world much better than *policy,* or *tact,* or *expediency,* or any other word that was ever devised to conceal or mystify a deviation from a straight line."

In finally deciding upon his course after the surrender—in refusing the many tempting offers that were made him, turning aside from wealth and honors still within his grasp, and going of his own free choice to the quiet town of Lexington to devote his remaining years to the interest of Washington College—he but acted on the guiding principle of his life.

To his lifelong friend, General W. N. Pendleton, he wrote, in reference to accepting the presidency of Washington College:

"If I thought I could be of any benefit to our noble youth, I should not hesitate to give my services."

Hon. H. W. Hilliard, ex-member of the Federal Congress, made a speech in Augusta, Ga., at the meeting there held to do honor to the memory of General Lee, in which he said:

"An offer, originating in Georgia, and I believe in this very city, was made to him to place an immense sum of money at his disposal if he would consent to reside in the city of New York and represent Southern commerce. Millions would have flowed to him. But he declined. He said: 'No; I am grateful, but I have a self-imposed task, which I must accomplish. I have led the young men of the South in battle; I have seen many of them fall under my standard. I shall devote my life now to training young men to do their duty in life.' "

Chapter IV

HIS MODEST HUMILITY, SIMPLICITY, AND GENTLENESS

If ever there lived a man who might of right be *proud,* it was General Lee! Descended from a long line of illustrious ancestors—allied by marriage to the family of George Washington—of manly beauty, rarely equaled—with honors constantly clustering around his brow, until his fame was coextensive with two continents—it would surely have been excusable had he exhibited, if not a haughty spirit, at least a *consciousness* of his superiority and his fame.

But modest humility, simplicity, and gentleness, were most conspicuous in his daily life.

Scrupulously neat in his dress, he was always simply attired, and carefully avoided the gold-lace and feathers in which others delighted. During the war, he usually wore a suit of gray, without ornament, and with no insignia of rank save three stars on his collar, which every Confederate colonel was entitled to wear. But he always kept a handsomer (though equally simple) uniform, which he wore upon occasions of ceremony. General W. N. Pendleton—chief of artillery of the Army of Northern Virginia—relates that on the morning of the surrender he found him before daybreak dressed in his neatest style, and that to his inquiries he pleasantly replied: "If I am to be General Grant's prisoner today, I intend to make my best appearance."

There was a smaller number of attendants about General Lee's headquarters, and less display of "the pomp and circumstance of war," than about the quarters of many officers of inferior rank. He was frequently seen riding alone among the troops, or attended by a single courier; more than half the time with hat lifted in response to loving salutations or enthusiastic cheers from his ragged soldiers.

An intelligent gentleman at whose house Major General John Pope once had his headquarters—on that famous campaign in 1862, during which Stonewall Jackson rudely broke in upon his dream of victory and compelled him, despite his general orders, to look to his "line of retreat"—

gave the writer a vivid conrast between the regal splendor in which this officer moved, and the modest simplicity observed at the headquarters of the great Confederate leader.

One of his brigadiers asked him one day, "Why is it, General, that you do not wear the full insignia of your rank, but content yourself with the stars of a colonel?" " 'Oh,' replied the modest chieftain, 'I do not care for display. And the truth is, that the rank of colonel is about as high as I ought ever to have gotten; or, perhaps, I might manage a good cavalry brigade if I had the right kind of subordinates.' "

No name (certainly no name of like rank) appears so conspicuously in General Scott's reports of his Mexican campaign as that of the young engineer officer, R. E. Lee. At Cerro Gordo, General Scott wrote: "I am compelled to make special mention of Captain R. E. Lee, engineer. This officer greatly distinguished himself at the siege of Vera Cruz; was again indefatigable during these operations in reconnaissances, as daring as laborious, and of the utmost value. Nor was he less conspicious in planting batteries, and in conducting columns to their stations under the heavy fire of the enemy." General Scott says of him at Chapultepec, that he was "as distinguished for felicitous execution as for science and daring." Again: "Captain Lee, so constantly distinguished, also bore important orders from me, until he fainted from a wound and the loss of two nights' sleep at the batteries." This distinguished service made him a name among his comrades, and famous throughout the country.

In 1869 I heard General Lee, in conversing with a visiting minister, who had the day before fainted in the pulpit, allude to the incident which General Scott speaks of in such high praise. But he spoke of "going up to the gates of the city," and having a "tedious season," and "a slight wound" which brought on a "fainting-spell," in such quiet, modest phrase that no one unacquainted with the facts would have supposed for a moment that he was then winning the brightest laurels and laying deep the foundations of his imperishable fame.

Indeed, he rarely alluded at all to his own exploits, and never spoke of them except in the most modest, becoming manner.

I cannot better illustrate these points further than by giving an extract from the eloquent address of Colonel Charles Marshall—the accomplished military secretary of General Lee—delivered at the Soldiers' Memorial Meeting in Baltimore:

"We recall him as he appeared in the hour of victory, grand, imposing, awe-inspiring, yet self-forgetful and humble. We recall the great scenes of his triumph, when we hailed him victor on many a bloody field, and when above the pæans of victory we listened with reverence to his voice as he ascribed 'all glory to the Lord of hosts, from whom all glories are.' We remember that grand magnanimity that never stooped to pluck the meaner things that grow nearest the earth upon the tree of victory, but which, with eyes turned to the stars, and hands raised toward heaven, gathered golden fruits of mercy, pity, and holy charity, that ripen on its topmost bough beneath the approving smile of the great God of battles.

"We remember the sublime self-abnegation of Chancellorsville, when, in the midst of his victorious legions, who, with the light of battle still on their faces, hailed him conqueror, he thought only of his great lieutenant lying wounded on the field, and transferred to him all the honor of that illustrious day.

"I will be pardoned, I am sure, for referring to an incident which affords to my mind a most striking illustration of one of the grandest features of his character.

"On the morning of May 3, 1863, as many of you will remember, the final assault was made upon the Federal lines at Chancellorsville.

"General Lee accompanied the troops in person, and as they emerged from the fierce combat they had waged in 'the depths of that tangled wilderness,' driving the superior forces of the enemy before them across the open ground, he rode into their midst. The scene is one that can never be effaced from the minds of those who witnessed it. The troops were pressing forward with all the ardor and enthusiasm of combat. The white smoke of musketry fringed the front of the line of battle, while the artillery on the hills in the rear of the infantry shook the earth with its thunder, and filled the air with the wild shrieks of the shells that plunged into the masses of the retreating foe. To add greater horror and sublimity to the scene, the Chancellorsville house and the woods surrounding it were wrapped in flames. In the midst of this awful scene General Lee, mounted upon that horse which we all remember so well, rode to the front of his advancing battalions. His presence was the signal for one of those uncontrollable outbursts of enthusiasm which none can appreciate who have not witnessed them.

"The fierce soldiers, with their faces blackened with the smoke of battle, the wounded, crawling with feeble limbs from the fury of the devouring flames, all seemed possessed with a common impulse. One long, unbroken cheer, in which the feeble cry of those who lay helpless on the earth blended with the strong voices of those who still fought, rose high above the roar of battle, and hailed the presence of the victorious chief. He sat in the full realization of all that soldiers dream of—triumph; and as I looked upon him in the complete fruition of the success which his genius, courage, and confidence in his army had won, I thought that it must have been from some such scene that men in ancient days ascended to the dignity of the gods.

"His first care was for the wounded of both armies, and he was among the foremost at the burning mansion where some of them lay. But at that moment, when the transports of his victorious troops were drowning the roar of battle with acclamations, a note was brought to him from General Jackson. It was brought to General Lee as he sat on his horse, near the Chancellorsville house, and, unable to open it with his gauntleted hands, he passed it to me with directions to read it to him. The note made no mention of the wound that General Jackson had received, but congratulated General Lee upon the great victory.

"I shall never forget the look of pain and anguish that passed over his face as he listened. With a voice broken with emotion he bade me say to General Jackson that the victory was his, and that the congratulations were due to him. I know not how others may regard this incident, but, for myself, as I gave expression to the thoughts of his exalted mind, I forgot the genius that won the day in my reverence for the generosity that refused its glory.

"There is one other incident to which I beg permission to refer, that I may perfect the picture. On the 3d day of July, 1863, the last assault of the Confederate troops upon the heights of Gettysburg failed, and again General Lee was among his baffled and shattered battalions as they sullenly retired from their brave attempt. The history of that battle is yet to be written, and the responsibility for the result is yet to be fixed.

"But there, with the painful consciousness that his plans had been frustrated by others, and that defeat and humiliation had overtaken his army, in the presence of his troops he openly assumed the entire responsibility of the campaign, and of the last battle. One word from him would have relieved him of this responsibility, but that word he refused to utter until it could be spoken without fear of doing the least injustice. Thus, my fellow soldiers, I have presented to you our great commander in the supreme moments of triumph and of defeat. I cannot more strongly illustrate his character. Has it been surpassed in history? Is there another instance of such self-abnegation among men? The man rose high above victory in the one instance, and, harder still, the man rose superior to disaster in the other. It was such incidents as these that gave General Lee the absolute and undoubting confidence and affection of his soldiers."

To Jackson's note informing him that he was wounded General Lee replied: "I cannot express my regret at the occurrence. Could I have directed events I should have chosen, for the good of the country, to have been disabled in your stead. I congratulate you on the victory which is due to your skill and energy." It was on the reception of these touching words that the wounded chieftain exclaimed: "Better that ten Jacksons should fall than one Lee."

Several days afterward, when his great lieutenant was reported to be doing well, Lee playfully sent him word: "You are better off than I am; for while you have only lost your *left,* I have lost my *right* arm."

Hearing soon after that Jackson was growing worse, he expressed the deepest concern and said: "Tell him that I am praying for him as I believe I have never prayed for myself."

The 10th of May, 1863, was a beautiful Sabbath day, and Rev. B. T. Lacy, at the special request of the dying chieftain, left his bedside to hold his usual services at the headquarters of the Second Corps. General Lee was present at the service, and at its conclusion he took Mr. Lacy aside to inquire particularly after Jackson's condition. Upon being told that he would not probably live through the day, he exclaimed: "Oh, sir, he must not die. Surely God will not visit us with such a calamity. If I have ever prayed in my life, I have pleaded with the Lord that Jackson might be spared to us." And then his heart swelled with emotion too deep for utterance, and he turned away to weep like a child.

The warm friendship which existed between Lee and Jackson is in beautiful contrast with the petty jealousies and bickering which have not unfrequently marked the relations and interfered with the success of military chieftains.

The rising fame of Jackson excited no envy in the bosom of Lee; but the praises of the lieutenant were most heartily endorsed by the commander-in-chief, who gave him his full confidence and warm personal friendship. He announced to the troops the death of Jackson in the following order:

"General Order No. 61.

"HEADQUARTERS ARMY OF NORTHERN VIRGINIA, *May* 11, 1863.

"With deep grief the commanding general announces to the army the death of Lieutenant General T. J. Jackson, who expired on the 10th inst., at a quarter past 3 P.M. The daring, skill, and energy of this great and good soldier are now, by the decree of an all-wise Providence, lost to us. But, while we mourn his death, we feel that his spirit still lives, and will inspire the whole army with his indomitable courage, and unshaken confidence in God as our hope and strength. Let his name be a watchword to his corps, who have followed him to victory on so many fields. Let his officers and soldiers emulate his invincible determination to do everything in the defense of our beloved country.

R. E. LEE, *General.*"

In a private letter to his wife General Lee wrote:

"CAMP NEAR FREDERICKSBURG,

May 11, 1863.

". . . In addition to the death of officers and friends consequent upon the late battle, you will see that we have to mourn the loss of the great and good Jackson. Any victory would be dear at such a price. His remains go to Richmond today. I know not how to replace him; but God's will be done! I trust He will raise up some one in his place. The papers will give you all the particulars. I have no time to narrate them."

The following extract from an article in the *Southern Magazine* on "Stonewall Jackson between his Deathbed and his Grave," by Major H. Kyd Douglas, of Jackson's staff, well illustrates this point:

"On Monday morning, at the request of the officer in command of the Stonewall Brigade, I went to ask General Lee if in his judgment it was proper to permit the old brigade, or a part of it, to accompany the remains of General Jackson to Richmond as an escort. I found the commander-in-chief walking in front of his tent, looking sad and thoughtful. He listened attentively to my request, and then, in a voice as gentle and sad as his looks, replied: 'I am sure no one can feel the loss of General Jackson more deeply than I do; for no one has the same reason. I have lost a dear friend and an invaluable officer. I can fully appreciate the feelings of the men of his old brigade; they have reason to mourn for him, for he was proud of them. They have been with him and true to him since the beginning of the war. I should be glad to grant any request they might make, the object of which was to show their regard for their lost general; and I am sorry that the situation of affairs will not justify me in permitting them to go with his corpse, not only to Richmond, but to Lexington, that they might see it deposited in its last resting-place. But it may not be. Those people over the river are again showing signs of movement, and it is so necessary for me to be on hand that I cannot leave my headquarters long enough to ride to the depot and pay my dear friend the poor tribute of seeing his body placed upon the cars.' Then, after stating what orders he had sent to Richmond for the reception of the remains, he said: 'His friends of the Stonewall Brigade may be assured their general will receive all the honor practicable. But as General Jackson himself never neglected a duty while living, he would not rest the quieter in his grave because even his old brigade had left the presence of the enemy to see him buried. Tell them how I sympathize with them, and appreciate the feelings which prompted their request. Tell them for me, that deeply as we all lament the death of their general, yet if his body is only to be buried and his spirit remains behind to inspire his corps and this whole army, we may have reason to hope that in the end his death may be as great a gain to us as it certainly is to himself.' "

I am indebted to my friend Rev. J. P. Smith, of Fredericksburg, Va. (who served on Jackson's staff during the whole of his brilliant career), for the following copy of an autograph letter from Lee to Jackson, written on the night of the battle of Fredericksburg:

"HEADQUARTERS,
December 13, 1862.

"GENERAL: Will you direct your ordnance officer, Major Bier, to send to Guinney's Depot *immediately* all the empty ordnance wagons he can, to be replenished with ammunition, for which they must remain there till loaded? To obtain as many wagons as possible, let him empty all he can in replenishing the ammunition of men and batteries.

"Very respectfully,
R. E. LEE.

"P. S.—I need not remind you to have the ammunition of your men and batteries replenished tonight—everything ready by daylight tomorrow. I am truly grateful to the Giver of all victory for having blessed us thus far in our terrible struggle. I pray He may continue to do so.

R.E.L.

"General Jackson commanding."

His full confidence in Jackson's skill was illustrated in the playful reply he made to one of his aides who came to his tent, on April 29, 1863, to inform him that the enemy had crossed the river in heavy force: "Well, I *heard* firing, and I was beginning to think it was time some of you lazy young fellows were coming to tell me what it was all about. *Say to General Jackson that he knows just as well what to do with the enemy as I do.*"

To one of his trusted officers he said, after Jackson's death: "I had such implicit confidence in Jackson's skill and energy, that I never troubled myself to give him detailed instructions. The most general suggestions were all that *he* needed."

In speaking of Jackson one day not long before his own fatal illness, and of the irreparable loss the South sustained in his death, General Lee said, with emphasis: "If I had had Stonewall Jackson at Gettysburg, we should have won a great victory. And I feel confident that a complete success there would have resulted in the establishment of our independence."

And this affectionate confidence of his chief was fully reciprocated by Jackson. In the summer of 1862 (soon after General Lee had taken command of the army) some officer ventured to intimate in his presence that the new commander was "slow," and that the army needed such an active leader as the one who had just double-quicked his "foot cavalry" through the splendid "Valley campaign." Instead of being pleased at the compliment intended to be paid him, Jackson replied, in indignant tones: "General Lee is *not* 'slow.' No one knows the weight upon his heart—his great responsibilities. He is commander-in-chief, and he knows that if his army is lost, it cannot be replaced. No! there may be some persons whose good opinion of me may make them attach some weight to my views, and if you ever hear that said of General Lee, I beg that you will contradict it in my name. I have known General Lee for five-and-twenty years. He is cautious. He ought to be. But he is *not* 'slow.' Lee is a phenomenon. He is the only man whom I would follow blindfold."

The opinion thus expressed in the early days of their service together during the late war (they were comrades in Mexico) seems to have strengthened up to the death of Jackson, and it has been said by a gallant soldier and facile writer (Colonel John Esten Cooke), who knew them both well, that the lieutenant always thought what the chief directed or suggested *the very best thing to do,* and that about the only occasion upon which he openly expressed dissent from Lee's opinions was when he said, on receiving his note of congratulation on the victory of Chancellorsville, '*General Lee should give the glory to God.*'"

In several private letters to Mrs. Jackson, General Lee expressed his warmest admiration and regard for her "great and good husband."

The following is given in full, and will be read with deep interest by many old soldiers who so well remember the coat:

"LEXINGTON, VA.,
January 18, 1868.
"*Mrs.* M. A. JACKSON, *Care of James P. Irwin, Charlotte, N.C.*

"MY DEAR MRS. JACKSON: In compliance with your wishes, as expressed in your note of the 6th inst., I forward by express, to the care of Mr. James P. Irwin, Charlotte, N. C., the overcoat sent to me by Mr. J. R. Bryan, of Virginia.

"It has appeared to me most proper that this relic of your husband, though painfully recalling his death, should be possessed by you, and I take great pleasure in transmitting it to you.

"I enclose you an extract from Mr. Bryan's letter, describing how the coat came into his possession, etc.

"It is a familiar object to my sight, and must recall sad reminiscences to the mind of every soldier of the Army of Northern Virginia.

"With my most earnest wishes for the welfare and happiness of yourself and daughter, I am, with great respect,

"Your most obedient servant,
"R. E. LEE."

The following gives pleasing evidence of his deep interest in all details concerning the history of his great lieutenant:

"LEXINGTON, VA.,
March 5, 1866.

"Mr. D. CREEL, Chillicothe, Ohio.

"MY DEAR SIR: I have received your letter of the 24th ult., and thank you for the interesting account of the early history of General T. J. Jackson. It is as pleasant as profitable to contemplate his character, to recall his patriotism, his piety, and his unselfish nature. The early instructions of his mother, whom he seems never to have forgotten, may have had great influence in shaping his course through life, and that mother may have been greatly indebted to you for qualifying her for the discharge of her important duty. I hope that the remainder of your days may be passed in peace and rest; and that the merciful God who has given you such length of days, and protected you amid so many dangers, may comfort and support you to the end.

"With great respect, your obedient servant,
"R. E. LEE."

It is due alike to General Lee and to the truth of history that the following letter should be given in full; and I do so on my own responsibility, hoping that the distinguished gentleman to whom it is addressed will pardon the liberty I take:

"LEXINGTON, VA.,
October 28, 1867.

"Dr. A. T. BLEDSOE, Office of Southern Review, Baltimore, Md.

"MY DEAR SIR: I regret that I am unable to comply with your request to write a review of Hozier's Seven Weeks' War, but my time is so much occupied that I could not sufficiently study the campaign, or inform myself of the incidents of the war.

"At the time of the occurrence, I thought I saw the mistake committed by the Austrians; but I did not know all the facts, and you are aware that, though it is easy to write on such a subject, it is difficult to elucidate the truth.

"In reply to your inquiry, I must acknowledge that I have not read the article on Chancellorsville in the last number of the *Southern Review,* nor have I read any of the books published on either side since the termination of hostilities. I have as yet felt no desire to revive my recollections of those events, and have been satisfied with the knowledge I possessed of what transpired. I have, however, learned, from others that the various authors of the *Life of Jackson* award to him the credit of the success gained by the Army of Northern Virginia where he was present, and describe the movements of his corps or command as independent of the general plan of operations, and undertaken at his own suggestion, and upon his own responsibility. I have the greatest reluctance to do anything that might be considered as detracting from his well-deserved fame, for I believe that no one was more convinced of his worth, or appreciated him more highly, than myself; yet your knowledge of military affairs, if you have none of the events themselves, will teach you that this could not have been so. Every movement of an army must be well considered, and properly ordered; and everyone who knows General Jackson must know that he was too good a soldier to violate this fundamental military principle. In the operations round Chancellorsville I overtook General Jackson, who had been placed in command of the advance as the skirmishers of the approaching armies met, advanced with the troops to the Federal line of defenses, and was on the field until their whole army recrossed the Rappahannock. There is no question as to who was responsible for the operations of the Confederates, or to whom any failure would have been charged. What I have said is for your own information. With my best wishes for the success of the *Southern Review,* and for your own welfare, in both of which I take a lively interest, I am, with great respect, your friend and servant,

"R. E. LEE."

Those who have attempted to institute comparisons between Lee and Jackson, or to exalt one at the expense of the other, have utterly misapprehended the character of both. They were, indeed, *par nobile fratrum.* They worked together for the cause they loved—their bodies sleep near each other in the beautiful "Valley of Virginia"—and it is a pleasing fancy that, when Lee "struck his tent" and "crossed over the river to rest under the shade of the trees," Jackson was the first to greet and welcome him to those fadeless joys.

And these pleasant relations between these two great men were by no means exceptional. Lee bore himself in the same manner toward all of his officers, and none of them could charge that he ever sought for himself honor or credit which justly belonged to others. But, on the contrary, he sometimes suffered himself to be censured when, by a word, he could have transferred the blame to others.

We have seen, above, what a member of his staff says of his conduct, as he moved among his shattered battalions after their unsuccessful assault on the heights of Gettysburg. And, lest it be thought that he looked through the eyes of too-partial friendship, we give the following from an account of the same scene written by Colonel Freemantle, of the English army, who was also an eyewitness:

"I joined General Lee, who had, in the meanwhile, come to the front on becoming aware of the disaster. General Lee was perfectly sublime. He was engaged in rallying and encouraging the broken troops, and was riding about a little in front of the wood, quite alone—the whole of his staff being engaged in a similar manner farther to the rear. His face, which is always placid and cheerful, did not show signs of the slightest disappointment, care, or annoyance; and he was addressing to every soldier he met a few words of encouragement, such as 'All this will come right in the end; we'll talk it over afterward; but, in the meantime, all good men must rally. We want all good and true men just now,' etc. He spoke to all the wounded men that passed him, and the slightly wounded he exhorted to 'bind up their hurts and take a musket' in this emergency. Very few failed to answer his appeal, and I saw badly wounded men take off their hats and cheer him. General—— now came up to him, and, in very depressed tones of annoyance and vexation, explained the state of his brigade. But General Lee immediately shook hands with him, and said, in a cheerful manner: 'Never mind, General. All this has been my fault. It is I that have lost this fight, and you must help me out of it the best way you can.' In this manner did General

Lee, wholly ignoring self and position, encourage and reanimate his somewhat dispirited troops, and magnanimously take upon his own shoulders the whole weight of the repulse. It was impossible to look at him, or to listen to him, without feeling the strongest admiration."

The effect of his conduct on the troops was electrical: the broken commands were rallied, and his army soon presented such a determined front, that General Meade did not deem it prudent to attack.

When General Lee reached Hagerstown in his retrograde movement, the Potomac was past fording. Meade's army was close upon his rear; the Northern press were clamorous for the capture of "Lee's beaten, dispirited ragamuffins," and another battle seemed imminent. The following stirring order was issued:

"General Order No. 16.

"HEADQUARTERS ARMY OF NORTHERN VIRGINIA, *July* 11, 1863.

"After the long and trying marches, endured with the fortitude that has ever characterized the soldiers of the Army of Northern Virginia, you have penetrated to the country of our enemies, and recalled to the defense of their own soil those who were engaged in the invasion of ours. You have fought a fierce and sanguinary battle, which, if not attended with the success that has hitherto crowned your efforts, was marked by the same heroic spirit that has commanded the respect of your enemies, the gratitude of your country, and the admiration of mankind.

"Once more you are called upon to meet the enemy from whom you have torn so many fields—names that will never die. Once more the eyes of your countrymen are turned upon you, and again do wives and sisters, fathers and mothers, and helpless children, lean for defense on your strong arms and brave hearts. Let every soldier remember that on his courage and fidelity depends all that makes life worth having, the freedom of his country, the honor of his people, and the security of his home. Let each heart grow strong in the remembrance of our glorious past, and in the thought of the inestimable blessings for which we contend; and, invoking the assistance of that heavenly Power which has so signally blessed our former efforts, let us go forth in confidence to secure the peace and safety of our country. Soldiers! your old enemy is before you. Win from him honor worthy of your right cause, worthy of your comrades dead on so many illustrious fields.

"R. E. LEE, *General commanding.*"

This address was received with the greatest enthusiasm. That army was never more eager to fight, or more confident of victory, than it was that day, and General Meade showed his able generalship in not making the attack.

In the winter of 1864 the following incident went the rounds of the Southern press:

"One very cold morning a young soldier on the cars to Petersburg was making fruitless efforts to put on his overcoat, with his arm in a sling. His teeth, as well as his sound arm, were brought into use to effect the object; but in the midst of his efforts an officer rose from his seat, advanced to him, and very carefully and tenderly assisted him, drawing the coat gently over his wounded arm, and buttoning it comfortably; then, with a few kind and pleasant words, returned to his seat.

"Now the officer in question was not clad in gorgeous uniform, with a brilliant wreath upon the collar, and a multitude of gilt lines upon the sleeves, resembling the famous labyrinth of Crete, but he was clad in 'a simple suit of gray,' distinguished from the garb of a civilian only by the three stars which every Confederate colonel is, by the regulations, entitled to wear. And yet he was no other than our chief general, Robert E. Lee, who is not braver than he is good and modest."

It is related that during the seven days' battle he was quietly sitting under a tree, the approaching shades of evening concealing even his stars, and none of his aides or couriers being present, when an impetuous surgeon galloped up and abruptly said: "Old man, I have chosen that tree for my field-hospital, and I want you to get out of the way."

"I will cheerfully give place when the wounded come, Doctor, but in the meantime there is a plenty of room for both of us," was the meek rejoinder. The irate surgeon was about to make some harsh reply, when to his utter consternation a staff officer rode up and addressed his "old man" as General Lee. To his profuse apologies and explanations, the general quietly replied: "It is no matter, Doctor; there is plenty of room for both of us until your wounded are brought."

The following was found in his own handwriting on one of the loose sheets in the satchel to which I have before referred:

"The forbearing use of power does not only form a touchstone, but the manner in which an individual enjoys certain advantages over others is a test of a *true gentleman*.

"The power which the strong have over the weak, the magistrate over

the citizen, the employer over the employed, the educated over the unlet-
tered, the experienced over the confiding, even the clever over the silly—
the forbearing or inoffensive use of all this power or authority, or a total
abstinence from it when the case admits it, will show the gentleman in a
plain light. The gentleman does not needlessly and unnecessarily remind
an offender of a wrong he may have committed against him. He cannot
only forgive, he can forget; and he strives for that nobleness of self and
mildness of character which impart sufficient strength to let the past be
but the past. *A true man of honor feels humbled himself when he cannot
help humbling others.*"

The following incident is from the *Norfolk Virginian* of October, 1870:

"Some years ago we stood, in company with General Lee, watching a
fire in the mountains, which blazed out with a baleful glare on the darkness
of a winter's night. The scene was as picturesque as any Salvator ever
painted, and the conversation naturally turned on its beauty. At last appealed to for an opinion, the general replied: 'It is beautiful, but I have
been thinking of the poor animals which must perish in the flames.' There
was no affection in this. His tone was simple and earnest—his manner a
complete negation of all art. With this wealth of tenderness, added to his
grand and knightly attributes of character, it is no wonder that his people
loved him with all their hearts, and cherish his memory with a passionate
devotion."

An officer who witnessed the incident relates that on one occasion in
1864, when General Lee was visiting Captain G———'s battery, on the
lines below Richmond, the soldiers gathered near him so as to attract the
enemy's fire.

Turning to them he said, in a very quiet tone and manner: "Men, you
had better go into the backyard; they are firing up here, and you are
exposing yourselves to unnecessary danger."

The men obeyed the order, but saw their loved general walk across the
yard (as if entirely unconscious of any personal danger), and stoop down
to pick up tenderly some small object, and place it gently upon a tree over
his head.

It was afterward ascertained that the object which had thus attracted
his attention under the enemy's fire, was *an unfledged sparrow* that had
fallen from its nest.

That loving Father, without whose knowledge not even a sparrow falleth to the ground, gave to the stern warrior a heart so tender that he could pause amid the death-dealing missiles of the battlefield to care for a helpless little bird.

His letters to his family were full of expressions of interest in birds and animals, or flowers. In a letter from Fort Brown, Texas, December 1856, he says:

"... I am able to give you but little news, as nothing of interest transpires here, and I rarely see anyone outside the garrison. My daily walks are alone, up and down the banks of the river, and my pleasure is derived from my own thoughts, and from the sight of the flowers and animals I there meet with. The birds of the Rio Grande form a constant source of interest, and are as numerous as they are beautiful in plumage. I wish I could get for you the roots of some of the luxuriant vines that cover everything, or the seeds of the innumerable flowers."

He paused amid his pressing duties at Gettysburg, to reprove an officer who was beating an unruly horse. For the noble animal which bore him through so many of his campaigns he cherished the tenderest regard. In a letter written from the Springs to his clerk in Lexington, he says: "How is Traveler? Tell him I miss him dreadfully, and have repented of our separation but once, and that is the whole time since we parted."

To those who knew his affection for this favorite horse it was very touchingly appropriate to see him, with saddle and accoutrements draped, led in the funeral procession by two old soldiers, and we could almost fancy that Traveler appreciated his loss, and entered keenly into the common sorrow.

His modest humility was very evident in his correspondence, and many letters illustrating it might be given. The several following must suffice:

"LEXINGTON, VA.,
September 26, 1866.
"Mr. EDWARD A. POLLARD, *Care of L. S. Palmer & Co.,* }
104 *West Baltimore St., Baltimore, Md.* }

"DEAR SIR: I return to you my thanks for the compliment paid me by your proposition to write a history of my life. It is a hazardous undertaking to publish the life of anyone while living, and there are but few who would desire to read a *true* history of themselves. Independently of the few national events with which mine has been connected, it presents little to interest the general reader. Nor do I know where to refer you for the necessary materials; all my private as well as public records have been destroyed or lost, and, except what is to be found in published documents, I know of nothing available for the purpose. Should you, therefore, determine to undertake the work, you must rely upon yourself, as my time is so fully occupied that I am unable to promise you any assistance.

"Very respectfully,

"R. E. Lee."

"Lexington, Va.,
March 21, 1866.

"Mrs. Emma Willard, *Troy, N.Y.*

"I received, by the last mail, the package containing your letter of the 15th inst. I have mailed to Generals Johnston, Beauregard, and Bragg, the letters for them. The address of the first is Richmond, Va., and of the second, New Orleans, La. Not knowing the address of the third, I have forwarded his letter to a friend in New Orleans, who will give it the proper destination. I know of no one here who can give you as correct a history of the life of General T. J. Jackson as that written by the Rev. Dr. Dabney, which, I understand, is now in process of publication by Blelock & Co., of New York City. I am obliged to you for your proposition as regards myself, but it is not in my power to give you the account you require; my time is too fully occupied to permit me to undertake it, even if I were able to make it of value.

"With great respect, your obedient servant,

"R. E. Lee."

In response to another letter from a Virginian lady, asking permission to visit him at his home in order to gather materials for writing his biography, he wrote the following:

"Lexington, Va.,
December 7, 1869.

"Miss———: I have received your letter of the 3d inst., and am sensible of the implied compliment in your proposal to write a history of my life.

"I should be happy to see you in Lexington, but not on the errand you propose, for I know of nothing good I could tell you of myself, and I fear I should not like to say any evil. The few incidents of interest in which I have been engaged are as well known to others as to myself, and I know of nothing I could say in addition.

"With great respect, your obedient servant,

"R. E. LEE."

Chapter V

HIS SPIRIT OF SELF-DENIAL FOR THE GOOD OF OTHERS

Closely allied to General Lee's modest humility was his spirit of self-denial. He never presumed upon his position to infringe the rights of others, and never called on his soldiers to make sacrifices or endure privations which he was not willing to share.

Hon. A. H. Stephens says, in his *War between the States,* that when he first came to Richmond as a commissioner of the Confederate states, to induce Virginia to join the Confederacy and turn over to it her army, he was met by a serious difficulty in the rank of General Lee.

By vote of the Virginia Convention, he had been made commander-in-chief of the forces of that state, and his friends were unwilling for him to have less rank, while on the other hand there were other officers already commissioned who would rank him in the Confederate army. Mr. Stephens sought an interview with General Lee and explained to him the difficulty. He at once said that no personal interest of his should for a single moment stand in the way of the interests of the state; that he was willing to take *any* position—even in the ranks as a private soldier—in which he could best serve the common cause; and that his rank should not for a moment bar the desired union. By General Lee's personal influence all difficulty was removed, and the fortunes of Virginia were blended with those of the other Southern states. A distinguished gentleman, who at the time held an important state office, has given the writer the following incident, of which he was personally cognizant: Before Virginia united with the Confederacy, President Davis had offered General Lee a position in the Confederate army, which he declined on the ground that he held a position under state authority. Mr. Davis did not formally renew the offer after the union was consummated, because he took it for granted that General Lee would come into his proper rank in the Confederate army. But General Lee did not so understand it; he was not the man to seek place for himself either directly or indirectly; and he was quietly getting positions for his staff, and arranging to enlist as a private soldier in a cavalry company, when, through mutual friends, the mistake was discovered and rectified.

Soon after his West Virginia campaign, when—strange as it seems now—the newspapers and many of the people were severely censuring him for not fighting Rosecrans, he said to an intimate friend: "I could have fought, and I am satisfied that I could have gained a victory. But the nature of the country was such that it would have proved a barren victory, and I had rather sacrifice my military reputation and quietly rest under this unjust censure than to unnecessarily sacrifice the life of a single one of my men."

Ex-President Davis said, in his speech at the great Memorial Meeting in Richmond, that on General Lee's return from that campaign he gave him a statement of the facts, which showed beyond all cavil that the failure was due to others and not to himself. And yet he urged Mr. Davis not to repeat his statement, as he would rather rest under censure himself than injure in the public esteem any who were bravely striking for the common cause.

General Lee rarely slept in a house—never outside of his lines—during the war, and when on the march some convenient fence-corner would be his most frequent place of bivouac. The writer has not unfrequently seen some colonel, or major-quartermaster, entertained in princely style at some hospitable mansion, while nearby the commander-in-chief would bivouac in the open air.

He never allowed his mess to draw from the commissary more than they were entitled to, and not unfrequently he would sit down to a dinner meager in quality and scant in quantity.

He was exceedingly abstemious in his own habits. He never used tobacco, and rarely took even a single glass of wine. Whiskey or brandy he did not drink, and he did all in his power to discourage their use by others.

In the spring of 1861, while on an inspection tour to Norfolk, a friend there insisted that he should take two bottles of very fine old "London Dock" brandy, remarking that he would be certain to need it, and would find it very difficult to obtain so good an article. General Lee declined the offer, saying that he was sure he would not need it. "As proof that I will not," he said, "I may tell you that, just as I was starting to the Mexican War, a lady in Virginia prevailed on me to take a bottle of fine old whiskey, which she thought I could not get on without. I carried that bottle all through the war without having had the slightest occasion to use it, and on my return home I sent it back to my good friend, that she might be convinced that I could get on without liquor."

But the gentleman still insisted, and the general politely yielded and took the two bottles.

At the close of the war he met a brother of this gentleman (from whom I get the incident) in Lexington, and said to him: "Tell your brother that I kept the brandy he gave me all through the war, and should have it yet, but that I was obliged to use it last summer in a severe illness of one of my daughters."

I was walking with him one day in Lexington, during the sway of the military, when, seeing a young man stagger out of one of the bar rooms, he seemed very much annoyed by the spectacle, and said: "I wish that these military gentlemen, while they are doing so many things which they have no right to do, would close up all of these grog shops which are luring our young men to destruction."

That he felt a lively interest in promoting sobriety among the young men of the college, the following letter will show:

"WASHINGTON COLLEGE, VA.,
December 9, 1869.
"*Messrs.* S. G. M. MILLER, J. L. LOGAN, T. A. ASHBY, *Committee.*

"GENTLEMEN: The announcement, in your letter of the 8th inst., of an organization of the 'Friends of Temperance' in the college, has given me great gratification; I sincerely hope that it may be the cause of lasting good, not only to the members themselves, but to all those with whom they associate to the extent of their influence and example. My experience through life has convinced me that, while moderation and temperance in all things are commendable and beneficial, abstinence from spirituous liquors is the best safeguard to morals and health. The evidence on this subject that has come within my own observation is conclusive to my mind, and, without going into the recital, I cannot too earnestly exhort you to practice habitual temperance, so that you may form the habit in youth, and not feel the inclination, or temptation, to depart from it in manhood. By so doing your health will be maintained, your morals elevated, and your success in life promoted. I shall at all times, and in whatever way I can, take great pleasure in advancing the object of your society, and you may rely on my cooperation in the important work in which you have engaged.

"Very respectfully, your obedient servant,

"R. E. Lee."

During the war he was accustomed to do everything in his power, both by precept and example, to prevent drunkenness among his officers and men, and more than once he refused to promote an officer who drank too freely, saying, "I cannot consent to place in the control of others one who cannot control himself."

It may be worthwhile for me to digress so far as to say that Stonewall Jackson, "Jeb" Stuart, and a large number of the most distinguished of the Confederate officers, imitated the example of their chief, and were strict temperance men. Upon one occasion Jackson was suffering so much from fatigue, and severe exposure, that his surgeon prevailed on him to take a little brandy. He made a very wry face as he swallowed it, and the doctor asked: "Why, general, is not the brandy good? It is some that we have recently captured, and I think it very fine." "Oh, yes!" was the reply, "it is very good brandy. I like liquor—its taste and its effects—and *that is just the reason why I never drink it.*" Upon another occasion, after a long ride in a drenching rain, a brother officer insisted upon Jackson's taking a drink with him, but he firmly replied: "No, sir, I cannot do it. I tell you *I am more afraid of King Alcohol than of all the bullets of the enemy.*"

The young men of the country who think that it is *manly* to drink, and cowardly to refuse, would do well to study and imitate the example of these two great men.

A great deal has been written of the famous dinner of sweet potatoes to which Marion, the American partisan, invited the British officer. General Lee considered himself fortunate when he had a good supply of sweet potatoes or a jug of buttermilk.

General Ewell told the writer, not long before his death, that "being at

General Lee's headquarters before the evacuation of Petersburg, and being unable to remain to dinner, the general insisted upon his taking his lunch, which he found to be two cold sweet potatoes, of which he said he was very fond."

Upon another occasion General Lee proposed to "treat" some of his officers, remarking, "I have just received a demijohn which I know *is of the best.*" The demijohn, tightly corked, was produced, drinking vessels were brought out, and all gathered around in eager expectancy, when the general filled the glasses and cups to the brim—not with old "Cognac" or "Bourbon"—but with *fresh buttermilk,* which a kind lady, knowing his taste, had sent him. He seemed to enjoy greatly the evident disappointment of some of the company when they ascertained the true character of their "treat."

Luxuries which friends sent for his mess table went regularly to the sick and wounded in the hospitals, and he was accustomed to say, "I am content to share the rations of my men."

As showing the impression which Lee's mode of living made upon a disinterested foreigner, we give an extract from an account of a visit to his headquarters in the autumn of 1862, written by an English officer:

"In visiting the headquarters of the Confederate generals, but particularly those of General Lee, anyone accustomed to see European armies in the field cannot fail to be struck with the great absence of all the 'pomp and circumstance of war' in and around their encampments. Lee's headquarters consisted of about seven or eight pole tents, pitched with their backs to a stake fence, upon a piece of ground so rocky that it was unpleasant to ride over it, its only recommendation being a little stream of good water which flowed close by the general's tent. In front of the tents were some three four-wheeled wagons, drawn up without any regularity, and a number of horses roamed loose about the field. The servants, who were of course slaves, and the mounted soldiers, called 'couriers,' who always accompany each general of division in the field, were unprovided with tents, and slept in or under the wagons. Wagons, tents, and some of the horses, were marked U.S., showing that part of that huge debt in the North has gone to furnishing even the Confederate generals with camp equipments. No guard or sentries were to be seen in the vicinity: no crowd of aides-de-camp loitering about, making themselves agreeable to visitors, and endeavoring to save their general from receiving those who have no particular business. A large farmhouse stands close by, which, in any other army, would have been the general's residence, *pro tem.;* but, as no liberties are allowed to be taken with personal property in Lee's army, he is particular in setting a good example himself. His staff are crowded together, two or three in a tent; none are allowed to carry more baggage than a small box each, and his own kit is but very little larger. Every one who approaches him does so with marked respect, although there is none of that bowing and flourishing of forage caps which occurs in the presence of European generals; and, while all honor him and place implicit faith in his courage and ability, those with whom he is most intimate feel for him the affection of sons to a father."

He always manifested the liveliest interest in the welfare of his men, and was deeply touched by their hardships and privations. Being invited upon one occasion to dine at a house where an elegant dinner was served, it is related that he declined all of the rich viands offered him, dined on bread and beef, and quietly said in explanation to the lady of the house, "I cannot consent to be feasting while my poor soldiers are nearly starving."

In the same spirit he wrote to some young officers who were getting up a grand military ball: "I do not think this a fit time for feasting or unseemly merry-making. I am always gratified to see your names figure among the gallant defenders of the country. I confess that I have no desire just now to see them conspicuous among the promoters of a 'Grand Military Ball,' or anything of that character."

In November 1863, the City Council of Richmond passed a resolution to purchase for him an elegant mansion, as a small token of the high esteem in which he was held by the city which he had so long defended. "Arlington" was in the hands of the United States Government, the "White House" on York River (the house of Washington's early wedded life) had been ruthlessly burned by Federal soldiers, his splendid estate had nearly all passed from his control, and his salary, in Confederate scrip, was utterly inadequate to support in proper style his invalid wife and accomplished daughters. These facts were known to the city authorities, and they but reflected the popular wish in the action which they took.

But, when General Lee heard of it, he wrote as follows to the president of the council:

"I assure you, sir, that no want of appreciation of the honor conferred upon me by this resolution, or insensibility to the kind feelings which prompted it, induces me to ask, as I most respectfully do, that no further proceedings be taken with reference to the subject. The house is not necessary to the use of my family, and my own duties will prevent my residence in Richmond.

"I should, therefore, be compelled to decline the generous offer, and I trust that whatever means the city council may have to spare for this purpose may be devoted to the relief of the families of our soldiers in the field, who are more in want of assistance, and more deserving of it, than myself."

At the close of the war, offers of pecuniary assistance poured in upon him from all quarters, but he steadfastly refused to received them. An English nobleman, thinking that he would rejoice in some place of retreat, wrote to offer him a splendid country seat and a handsome annuity. He replied: "I am deeply grateful, but I cannot consent to desert my native state in the hour of her adversity. I must abide her fortunes and share her fate."

Soon after he went to Lexington, he was visited by an agent of a certain insurance company, who offered him their presidency, at a salary of *ten thousand* dollars per annum; he was then receiving only *three thousand* from the college.

He told the agent that he could not give up the position he then held, and could not properly attend to the duties of both.

"But, general," said the agent, "we do not want you to discharge any duties. We simply wish the use of your name; *that* will abundantly compensate us."

"Excuse me, sir," was the prompt and decided rejoinder; "I cannot consent to receive pay for services I do not render."

His letter book is full of responses to letters offering him direct assistance, or positions where he could realize large pecuniary returns. A few of these will serve as specimens of the whole:

"WHITE SULPHUR SPRINGS, W. VA.,
August 26, 1869.

"*Mr.* R. W———.

"MY DEAR SIR: I received, this mail, your letter of the 19th inst.; and though truly sensible of your kindness, and highly appreciating the feelings which prompted your offer, I am compelled most reluctantly to decline it. I will retain your letter as a mark of your esteem, and the most pleasing evidence of your regard; and though my losses by the war have been heavy, as you state, they are light in comparison to other things all have to bear, and are not worth consideration. Thanking you most sincerely for your generous purpose,

"I am most truly yours,
"R. E. LEE."

"LEXINGTON, VA.,
May 21, 1866.

"*Mr.* H. R.———, *Salem, Franklin County, Tenn.*

"MY DEAR SIR: I have received your letter of the 12th inst., and thank you most cordially for your kind proposition. I shall be unable to take any part in the conduct of the business in which you propose to engage, or to render any adequate service in return for the benefits I might receive. With a due sense, therefore, of your generous offer, and a grateful appreciation of the motives which induced it, I am constrained to decline it.

"Wishing you every success in the prosecution of your purpose, and all happiness in its accomplishment,

"I am, very respectfully, your obedient servant,
"R. E. LEE."

The following reply to an earnest call made upon him by old friends speaks for itself:

"LEXINGTON, VA.,
March 18, 1870.

"*General* CORSE, FRANCIS L. SMITH, R. H. MILLER, C. S. LEE, }
    EDGAR SNOWDEN, *etc., Alexandria, Va.*   }

"GENTLEMEN: I am deeply sensible of the kind feelings which prompted your communication of the 12th inst.; any proposition emanating from the citizens of Alexandria would command my earnest consideration, but one fraught with so much interest to the city, and filled with such considerate kindness to myself, demands my serious attention and frank reply. There is no community to which my affections more strongly cling than that of Alexandria, composed of my earliest and oldest friends, my kind school fellows, and faithful neighbors. Its interests and prosperity are of such paramount importance to me that it is my desire to do any thing to promote them. It is on this account that I must decline the proposition you have made me. I do not feel able to undertake the business you would assign me, and it would not be honest in me to accept it. My health has been so feeble this winter that I am only waiting to see the effect of the opening spring before relinquishing my present position. I am admonished by my feelings that my years of labor are nearly over, and my inclinations point to private life. You require the energy of a younger man to push forward your communications with the interior of the country, to economize the construction and working of your roads, and to afford cheap transportation for the products of agriculture to your port, and the articles of commerce in return to the interior. Without knowing more than any other deeply interested in the welfare of your city, the president of your roads seems to me to have been earnest and indefatigable in their advancement, and I would recommend him for the office rather than myself.

"With my earnest wishes for the prosperity of Alexandria, and the individual happiness of you all,

"I am, with great regard, your obedient servant,

"R. E. Lee."

Nearly every mail brought him some such proposition, and just a short time before his death a large and wealthy corporation in the city of New York offered him a salary of *fifty thousand dollars* per annum if he would consent to become their president.

But he steadfastly refused all such offers, and quietly pursued his chosen path of duty.

He did accept, not long before his death, the presidency of the Valley Railroad Company; but in this he yielded his personal wishes to the views of the warmest friends of the college, who urged that his acceptance of the position was necessary to the construction of the road, and that this was essential to the development of the resources of the Valley, and the highest prosperity of Lexington and of the college itself.

When the board of trustees of Washington College called General Lee to its presidency, they were anxious to fulfill the wishes and expectations of the Southern public by paying such salary as his wide reputation and invaluable services were entitled to receive. This feeling increased as they saw the college expand under his magic touch, until, from an institution with five professors and some sixty students, it numbered more than twenty instructors and over four hundred students. But they always found an insurmountable difficulty in the steadfast refusal of General Lee to receive a salary beyond what he conceived the funds of the institution and fairness to the other members of the faculty would justify. It was in vain that the faculty united with the trustees in urging that the prosperity of the college was due to his influence; that his name had secured the endowment whereby the additional professors were appointed, and had attracted young men from every state; that they were offering him no gratuity, but simply a compensation for his invaluable services. His firm reply was, "My salary is as large as the college ought to pay."

The trustees were anxious to have built for him a handsome residence, and friends in different sections contributed funds for the purpose, but he insisted that other buildings were needed far more than a new house for himself. The trustees finally made the appropriation without his knowledge, and he then superintended the building himself, reduced its cost considerably below the amount appropriated, and was very careful always to speak of it not as his own (as the trustees meant it to be), but as "the president's house."

In the spring of 1870 the Board of Trustees delicately deeded to Mrs. Lee this house, and settled on her an annuity of three thousand dollars. When the general heard of it, he wrote, in Mrs. Lee's behalf, a polite but firm letter, declining the offer.

The trustees still delicately adhered to their purpose, had the deed quietly recorded, and after General Lee's death sent Mrs. Lee a check for the annuity. But this noble Virginia matron had caught the spirit of her husband, and returned the check with a beautiful letter declining to allow any of the funds of the college to be diverted to her private use, or to receive for her family any part of the property of the institution.

Certain wealthy friends and admirers of General Lee one summer, at the White Sulphur Springs, put on foot a scheme to raise fifty thousand dollars which they designed to be used by the college for his benefit during his life, and to revert to his family at his death. He declined to allow this fund to be raised, except on the condition that, instead of going to the benefit of his family, it should be a *permanent endowment* of the president's chair of the college.

An agent of the college had been, without authority, making very free use of General Lee's name in his efforts to secure contributions; and, when the general heard of it, he promptly wrote the following protest:

"WASHINGTON COLLEGE, LEXINGTON, VA.,
March 1, 1866.

"*Hon.* JOHN W. BROCKENBROUGH, *Rector,* ⎫
Washington College, Lexington, Va. ⎭

"MY DEAR SIR: My attention has been called to the enclosed slip, which seems to have been taken from a Memphis paper. I do not know what instructions the Rev. Mr.——— received from the board of trustees; but he certainly had no authority from me to use my name in soliciting contributions to the college with a view of increasing my salary. If such is the 'main object' of his mission, as stated, he cannot hope to succeed; and I should regret if any friend of mine gave a dollar for the purpose.

"It is difficult to know to what extent Mr.——— is responsible for the statement; but it is calculated to injure the college, and I request that the committee of the board of trustees will take measures to prevent my being presented to the country in so reprehensible a manner.

"Very respectfully, your obedient servant,
"R. E. LEE."

The following endorsement upon a letter from Rev. S. D. Stuart to the rector of the college will further illustrate the feelings of this noble man:

"LEXINGTON, VA.,
January 23, 1866.

"The letter of the Rev. S. D. Stuart, of the 15th inst., is respectfully returned to Judge John W. Brockenbrough.

"I am deeply sensible of my obligations to the Hon. B. Wood for his good opinion, his interest in the South, and for the repetition of his conditional offer of aid to Washington College. Upon giving the subject additional reflection, I cannot reach the conclusion that any acceptance of his proposition would be beneficial. The college would gain the sum of money he generously proposes to give, but it would lose a great amount in other respects. I am not in a position to make it proper for me to take a public part in the affairs of the country.

"I have done, and continue to do, in my private capacity, all in my power to encourage our people to set manfully to work to restore the country, to rebuild their homes and churches, to educate their children, and to remain with their states, their friends and countrymen. But, as a prisoner on parole, I cannot with propriety do more; nor do I believe it would be advantageous for me to do so.

"R. E. LEE."

The refusal of General Lee to receive presents or gratuities was but one of the many points in which he resembled George Washington, "the Father of his Country." How far he differed from many of our leading public men of the present day, in this respect, we will not here discuss.

Up to his fatal illness, General Lee was busily engaged in collecting material, and seemed very anxious to write a history of his campaigns; but his object was to vindicate *others rather than himself.* He said to one of his generals, in a letter asking for his official reports: "I shall write this history, not to vindicate myself, or to promote my own reputation. I want that the world shall know what my poor boys, with their small numbers and scant resources, succeeded in accomplishing."

He sent out to many of his old officers the following circular:

"NEAR CARTERSVILLE, CUMBERLAND COUNTY, VA.,
July 31, 1865.

"GENERAL: I am desirous that the bravery and devotion of the Army of Northern Virginia be correctly transmitted to posterity. This is the only tribute that can now be paid to the worth of its noble officers and soldiers. And I am anxious to collect the necessary information for the history of its campaigns, including the operations in the Valley and western Virginia, from its organization to its final surrender. I have copies of my reports of the battles, commencing with those around Richmond in 1862, to the end of the Pennsylvania campaign; but no report of the campaign in 1864, and of the operations of the winter of 1864–'65, to the 1st of April, 1865, has been written; and the corps and division reports of that period which had been sent to headquarters before the abandonment of the lines before Petersburg, with all the records, returns, maps, plans, etc., were destroyed the day before the army reached Appomattox Courthouse. My letter books, public and confidential, were also destroyed, and the regular reports and returns transmitted to the adjutant-general at Richmond have been burned or lost. Should you have copies of the reports of the operations of your command within the period specified (from May 1, 1864, to April 1, 1865), or should you be able to renew them, I will be greatly obliged to you to send them to me. Should you be able to procure other reports of other commands, returns of the effective strength of the army of any of the battles from the first Manassas to the 1st of April, 1865, or copies of my official orders, letters, etc., you will confer an additional favor by sending them to me.

"Very respectfully and truly,

"R. E. LEE."

To his trusted lieutenant, General J. A. Early, who was at this time in voluntary exile, he wrote the following letter:

"LEXINGTON, VA.,

November 22, 1865.

"*General* J. A. EARLY.

"MY DEAR GENERAL: I received last night your letter of the 30th ult., which gave me the first authentic information of you since the cessation of hostilities, and relieved the anxiety I had felt on your account. I am very glad to hear of your health and safety, but regret your absence from the country, though I fully understand your feelings on the subject. I think the South requires the presence of her sons more now than at any period of her history, and I determined at the outset of her difficulties to share the fate of my people.

"I wish you every happiness and prosperity wherever you may go, and in compliance with your request enclose a statement of your services, which I hope may answer your purpose. You will always be present to my recollections.

"I desire, if not prevented, to write a history of the campaign in Virginia. All my records, books, orders, etc., were destroyed in the conflagration and retreat from Richmond. Only such of my reports as were printed are preserved.

"Your reports of your operations in 1864 and '65 were among those destroyed.

"Cannot you repeat them, and send me copies of such letters, orders, etc., of mine (including that last letter to which you refer), and particularly give me your recollection of our effective strength at the principal battles?

"My only object is to transmit the truth, if possible, to posterity, and do justice to our brave soldiers.

"Most truly your friend,
"R. E. LEE."

He delayed the fulfillment of this cherished purpose because he was refused copies of his captured official papers which are under charge of the War Department in Washington, and was unwilling to write his history without these.

But he would sometimes make it an objection to writing at all, that he would be obliged to relate facts which would cause the conduct of others to be subjected to criticism and censure. No man was ever more careful of the feelings or reputation of others, or more ready to submit quietly to wrong himself rather than have censure cast upon his comrades or subordinates.

General Lee had nothing of *nepotism* about him, but meted out the evenest justice to all, except that he did not promote his relatives as rapidly as he did others.

His son Robert served as a private in the ranks of the Rockbridge Artillery, sharing with his comrades of that crack corps all of their dangers, hardships, drudgery, and privations, when a hint from his father would have secured him promotion to some place of honor. The general told, with evident relish, that during the battle of Sharpsburg he became very uneasy about Robert—knowing that his battery had suffered severely, and not hearing anything from him. At last he made it convenient to ride up to the battery, which had just been relieved from a very perilous position where it had suffered fearful loss, and had his fears increased by not recognizing his son among the men. To the hearty greeting of the brave fellows he replied, "Well! you have done nobly today, but I shall be compelled to send you in again."

"Will you, general?" said a powder-begrimed youth whom he did not recognize, until he spoke, as his son Robert. "Well, boys! come on; the general says we must go in again, and you know he is in the habit of having his own way about such matters."

Thus the anxiety of the commander-in-chief was relieved, and his son went gaily to work at his gun and contributed his full share toward "keeping those people back."

I have the following from the lips of the distinguished officer who related it:

When General——— was compelled by failing health to ask to be relieved from a certain important command, he went to Richmond to confer with President Davis as to his successor, and to endeavor to impress upon him the very great importance of the district, and of the commander being a man of fine abilities. Mr. Davis fully sympathized with his views, and, after reflection, said: "I know of no better man for that position than General Custis Lee. To show you my estimate of his ability, I will say that, when some time ago I thought of sending General Robert Lee to command the Western Army, I had determined that his son Custis should succeed him in command of the Army of Northern Virginia. Now, I wish you to go up and see General Lee, tell him what I say, and ask him to order General Custis Lee to the command of that department. Tell him I will make his son major general, lieutenant general, or, if need be, full general, so that he may rank any officer likely to be sent to that department."

General——— promptly sought Lee's headquarters, delivered Mr. Davis's message, and urged a compliance.

But to all of his arguments and entreaties the old chieftain had but one reply: "I am very much obliged to Mr. Davis for his high opinion of Custis Lee. I hope that, if he had the opportunity, he would prove himself in some measure worthy of that confidence. But he is an untried man in the field, and I cannot appoint him to that command. Very much against his wishes and my own, Mr. Davis has kept him on his personal staff, and he has had no opportunity to prove his ability to handle an army in the field. Whatever may be the opinion of others, I cannot pass by my tried officers and take for that important position a comparatively new man—especially when that man is my own son. Mr. Davis can make the assignment if he thinks proper—I shall certainly not do so."

The records of the Confederate War Department would be searched in vain for any word of General Lee seeking place either for himself or his sons.

Rev. Dr. T. V. Moore, so long pastor of the First Presbyterian Church in Richmond, and who recently died in Nashville, Tenn., related the following in his memorial sermon:

"After the cartel for the exchange of prisoners during the war was suspended, one of his own sons was taken prisoner. A Federal officer of the same rank in Libby Prison sent for me, and wished me to write to General Lee, begging him to obtain the consent of the Confederate authorities to his release, provided he could, as he felt sure would be the case, induce the United States authorities to send General Lee's son through the lines to effect this special exchange.

"In a few days a reply was received in which, with the lofty spirit of a Roman Brutus, he respectfully but firmly declined *to ask any favor for his own son that could not be asked for the humblest soldier in the army.* The officer, while disappointed, was yet so struck with the unselfish nobleness of the reply, that he begged the letter from me as a memento of General Lee, adding, with deep emphasis, 'Sir, I regard him as the greatest man now living.' "

It will add greatly to the force of the above incident to recall the fact that the son (General W. H. F. Lee) was at home, severely wounded, at the time he was captured; that his accomplished wife was lying at the point of death, and actually died before his release (the Federal authorities refusing to allow General Custis Lee to take the place of his brother, as he nobly offered to do) and that he was closely confined in a casemate at Fortress Monroe, and threatened with death by hanging, in retaliation for alleged cruelty on the part of the Confederate authorities toward certain Federal prisoners.

Only those who know how devoted to his children General Lee was can appreciate the noble self-denial which he exercised when, under these circumstances, the tenderest feelings of the loving father were sacrificed to his sense of duty to his country.

Not long after his West Virginia campaign, he was recommending a certain officer for promotion, when a friend urged him to do so, alleging that this officer was accustomed to speak very disparagingly and disrespectfully of General Lee. The quick reply was, "The question is not what he thinks or is pleased to say about me, but what I think of him. I have a high opinion of this officer as a soldier, and shall most unquestionably recommend his promotion, and do all in my power to secure it."

Surely the pages of the world's history afford no nobler example of self-denial for the good of others than that of the modest, unobtrusive life of the Christian soldier and patriot—R. E. LEE.

Chapter VI

HIS WANT OF BITTERNESS TOWARD THE NORTH, BUT DEVOTION TO THE INTERESTS OF THE SOUTH

General Lee was conspicuous for a want of bitterness toward the United States authorities and the people of the North. He certainly had much which others would have taken as an occasion of bitterness, if not absolute hatred. While he was suffering privation and hardship, and meeting danger in opposing what he honestly believed to be the armed hosts of oppression and wrong, his home was seized (and held) by the government, and his property destroyed. When at the close of the war he faithfully and scrupulously sought to carry out his parole, avoided the popular applause that his people were everywhere ready to give him, and sought a quiet retreat where he could labor for the good of the young men of the South, his motives were impugned, his actions were misrepresented, and certain of the Northern journals teemed with bitter slanders against him, while a United States grand jury (in violation of the terms of his parole, as General Grant himself maintained) found against him an indictment for "treason and rebellion." And yet amid all these provocations he uttered no word of bitterness, and always raised his voice for moderation and charity.

Upon several occasions, the writer has heard him rebuke others for bitter expressions, and the severest terms he was accustomed to employ were such as he used to his son Robert, to whom he said one day, as he was bravely working one of the guns of the Rockbridge Artillery which was engaged in a fierce fight with the enemy: "That's right, my son; drive those people back."

When told of Jackson's wound, and of his plan to cut Hooker off from the United States ford, and drive back his army on Chancellorsville, the eye of the great captain sparkled, and his face flushed as he remembered that in the loss of his lieutenant he had been "deprived of his right arm"; but his quiet reply was, "General Jackson's plans shall be carried out—those people shall be driven today."

He used to sometimes speak of the enemy as "General Meade's people," "General Grant's people," or "our friends across the river."

When in 1863 the head of the Army of Northern Virginia was turned northward, and it was understood that an invasion of Pennsylvania was contemplated, there resounded through the South a cry for retaliation there for the desolation inflicted by the Federal armies upon our own fair land. The newspapers recounted the outrages that we had endured, painted in vivid colors the devastation of large sections of the South, reprinted the orders of Pope, Butler, and others of like spirit, and called upon the officers and men of the Army of Northern Virginia to remember these things when they reached the rich fields of Pennsylvania, arguing that the best way of bringing the war to a successful termination was to let the people of the North feel it as we had done. Prominent men urged these views on General Lee, and it would not have been surprising if he had so far yielded to the popular clamor as to have at least winked at depredations on the part of his soldiers. But he did not for a single moment forget that he led the army of a people who professed to be governed by the principles of Christian civilization, and that no outrages on the part of others could justify him in departing from these high principles. Accordingly, as soon as the head of his column crossed the Potomac, he issued a beautiful address, in which he called upon his men to abstain from pillage and depredations of every kind, and enjoined upon his officers to bring to speedy punishment all offenders against this order. If this had been intended for *effect* merely, while the soldiers were to be allowed to plunder at will, nothing further would have been necessary. But we find him publishing the following, which forms one of the brightest pages in the history of that unhappy strife, will go down to coming ages in vivid contrast with the orders of Pope, Butler, Sheridan, and other Federal generals, and will for all time reflect the highest honor alike upon our Christian chieftain and the army he led:

"General Order No. 73.

"HEADQUARTERS ARMY OF NORTHERN VIRGINIA
CHAMBERSBURG, PA., *June* 27, 1868.

"The commanding general has observed with marked satisfaction the conduct of the troops on the march, and confidently anticipates results commensurate with the high spirit they have manifested. No troops could have displayed greater fortitude, or better have performed the arduous marches of the past ten days. Their conduct in other respects has, with few exceptions, been in keeping with their character as soldiers, and entitles them to approbation and praise.

"There have been, however, instances of forgetfulness on the part of some that they have in keeping the yet unsullied reputation of the army, and that the duties exacted of us by civilization and Christianity are not less obligatory in the country of the enemy than in our own. The commanding general considers that no greater disgrace could befall the army, and through it our whole people, than the perpetration of the barbarous outrages upon the innocent and defenseless, and the wanton destruction of private property, that have marked the course of the enemy in our own country. Such proceedings not only disgrace the perpetrators and all connected with them, but are subversive of the discipline and efficiency of the army, and destructive of the ends of our present movements. It must be remembered that we make war only upon armed men, and that we cannot take vengeance for the wrongs our people have suffered without lowering ourselves in the eyes of all whose abhorrence has been excited by the atrocities of our enemy and offending against Him to whom vengeance belongeth, and without whose favor and support our efforts must all prove in vain.

"The commanding general, therefore, earnestly exhorts the troops to abstain, with most scrupulous care, from unnecessary or wanton injury to private property; and he enjoins upon all officers to arrest and bring to summary punishment all who shall in any way offend against the orders on this subject.

"R. E. LEE, General."

That these orders were in some instances violated is not denied, but both General Lee and his officers exerted themselves to have them carried out, and with almost perfect success, as even the Northern press abundantly testified at the time.

No blackened ruins, desolated fields, or wanton destruction of private property, marked the line of his march. His official dispatches are blotted by no wicked boast of the number of barns burned, and the amount of provisions destroyed, until he had made the country "such a waste that even a crow flying over would be compelled to carry his rations!" But the order above quoted not only expressed the feelings of the commander-in-chief, but was an index to the conduct of his officers and the troops under their command.

When General John B. Gordon, at the head of his splendid brigade of Georgians, entered York, there was great consternation among the people, and he sought to quiet their fears by making the following address to a crowd of women gathered on the street: "Our Southern homes have been pillaged, sacked, and burned; our mothers, wives, and little ones, driven forth amid the brutal insults of your soldiers. Is it any wonder that we fight with desperation? A natural revenge would prompt us to retaliate in kind, but we scorn to war on women and children. We are fighting for the God-given rights of liberty and independence, as handed down to us in the Constitution by our fathers. So fear not: if a torch is applied to a single dwelling, or an insult offered to a female of your town by a soldier of this command, point me out the man, and you shall have his life."

Other officers were equally earnest in carrying out General Lee's orders and allaying the fears of the citizens, who were expecting to see the same depredations committed by the rebels, that had marked the course of the Union troops all through the South.

The people were utterly astonished at their lenient treatment, and were loud in their praise of "Lee and his hungry rebels." One intelligent and wealthy citizen wrote: "If it were not for the name of the thing, I would much rather have the rebels than the Union troops to camp on my premises. The former committed much fewer depredations than the latter."

It is said that one day General Lee dismounted and began with his own hands to put up a fence that had been left down; and that several times he went in person and had soldiers arrested for slight depredations.

No man, living or dead, ever heard General Lee utter an unkind word to a prisoner, or saw him maltreat in the slightest degree any who fell into his power. And, when he was charged by the radical press with being responsible for alleged "cruel treatment" of prisoners, he quietly said: "I court the most searching investigation into this matter."

The following extract from his testimony before the congressional "reconstruction" committee may be appropriately introduced in this connection:

"*Question.* By Mr. Howard: 'I wish to inquire whether you had any knowledge of the cruelties practiced toward the Union prisoners at Libby Prison and on Belle Isle?' *Answer.* 'I never knew that any cruelty was practiced, and I have no reason to believe that it was practiced. I can believe, and have reason to believe, that privations may have been experienced by the prisoners, because I know that provision and shelter could not be provided for them.'

"*Q*. 'Were you not aware that the prisoners were dying from cold and starvation?' *A*. 'I was not.'

"*Q*. 'Did these scenes come to your knowledge at all?' *A*. 'Never. No report was ever made to me about them. There was no call for any to be made to me. I did hear—it was mere hearsay—that statements had been made to the War Department, and that everything had been done to relieve them that could be done, even finally so far as to offer to send them to some other points—Charleston was one point named—if they would be received by the United States authorities and taken to their homes; but whether this is true or not I do not know.'

"*Q*. 'And of course you know nothing of the scenes of cruelty about which complaints have been made at those places (Andersonville and Salisbury)?' *A*. 'Nothing in the world, as I said before. I suppose they suffered from want of ability on the part of the Confederate States to supply their wants. At the very beginning of the war I knew that there was suffering of prisoners on both sides, but as far as I could I did everything in my power to relieve them, and to establish the cartel which was agreed upon.'

"*Q*. 'It has been frequently asserted that the Confederate soldiers feel more kindly toward the government of the United States than any other people of the South. What are your observations on that point?' *A*. 'From the Confederate soldiers I have heard no expression of any other opinion. They looked upon the war as a necessary evil, and went through it. I have seen them relieve the wants of Federal soldiers on the field. The orders always were, that the whole field should be treated alike. Parties were sent out to take the Federal wounded as well as the Confederate, and the surgeons were told to treat the one as they did the other. These orders given by me were respected on every field.'

"*Q*. 'Do you think that the good feeling on their part toward the rest of the people has continued since the close of the war?' *A*. 'I know nothing to the contrary. I made several efforts to exchange the prisoners after the cartel was suspended. I do not know to this day which side took the initiative. I know there were constant complaints on both sides. I merely know it from public rumors. I offered to General Grant, around Richmond, that we should ourselves exchange all the prisoners in our hands. There was a communication from the Christian Commission, I think, which reached me at Petersburg, and made application to me for a passport to visit all the prisoners South. My letter to them, I suppose, they have. I told them I had not that authority, that it could only be obtained from the War Department at Richmond, but that neither they nor I could relieve the sufferings of the prisoners; that the only thing to be done for them was, to exchange them; and, to show that I would do whatever was in my power, I offered them to send to City Point all the prisoners in Virginia and North Carolina over which my command extended, provided they returned an equal number of mine, man for man. I reported this to the War Department, and received for answer that they would place at my command all the prisoners at the South if the proposition was accepted. I heard nothing more on the subject.' "

The charge made against General Lee in some of the Northern papers of complicity, if not chief responsibility, in the alleged cruel treatment of prisoners was very annoying to one of his high sense of right; but he did not permit himself to enter into any public defense. He did, however, express himself quite freely to his friends, and the following letter is now for the first time given to the public:

"LEXINGTON, VA.,

April 17, 1867.

"Dr. CHARLES CARTER, *No.* 1632 *Walnut Street, Philadelphia, Pa.*

"MY DEAR DR. CARTER: I have received your letter of the 9th inst., inclosing one to you from Mr. J. Francis Fisher, in relation to certain information which he had received from Bishop Wilmer. My respect for Mr. Fisher's wishes would induce me to reply fully to all his questions, but I have not time to do so satisfactorily; and, for reasons which I am sure you both will appreciate, I have a great repugnance to being brought before the public in any manner. Sufficient information has been officially published, I think, to show that whatever sufferings the Federal prisoners at the South underwent, were incident to their position as prisoners, and produced by the destitute condition of the country, arising from the operations of war. The laws of the Confederate Congress and the orders of the War Department directed that the rations furnished prisoners of war should be the same in quantity and quality as those furnished enlisted men in the army of the Confederacy, and that the hospitals for prisoners should be placed on the same footing as other Confederate States hospitals in all respects. It was the desire of the Confederate authorities to effect a continuous and speedy exchange of prisoners of war; for it was their true policy to do so, as their retention was not only a calamity to them, but a heavy expenditure of their scanty means of subsistence, and a privation of the services of a veteran army. Mr. Fisher or Bishop Wilmer has confounded my offers for the exchange of prisoners with those made by Mr. Ould, the commissioner of the Confederate States. It was he that offered, when all hopes of effecting the exchange had ceased, to deliver all the Federal sick and wounded, to the amount of fifteen thousand, without an equivalent, provided transportation was furnished. Previously to this, I think, I offered to General Grant to send into his lines all the prisoners within my department, which then embraced Virginia and North Carolina, provided he would return me man for man; and, when I informed the Confederate authorities of my proposition, I was told that, if it was accepted, they would place all the prisoners at the South at my disposal. I offered subsequently, I think to the committee of the United States Sanitary Commission, who visited Petersburg for the purpose of ameliorating the condition of their prisoners, to do the same. But my proposition was not accepted. I understand that Mr. Pollard, in his *Lost Cause,* has devoted a chapter of his work to the subject of the exchange of prisoners; I have not read it, but, in a letter received from Mr. Ould, he stated that he had furnished Mr. Pollard with the facts for his chapter, and could vouch for their accuracy. Dr. Joseph Jones has recently published a pamphlet termed "Researches upon Spurious Vaccination," etc., issued from the University Medical Press, at Nashville, Tenn., in which he treats of certain diseases of the Federal prisoners at Andersonville and their causes, which I think would be interesting to you as a medical man, and would furnish Mr. Fisher with some of the information he desires. I therefore refer you to both of these works. And now I wish you to understand that what I have written is for your personal information and not for publication, and to send as an expression of thanks to Mr. Fisher for his kind efforts to relieve the sufferings of the Southern people.

"I am very much obliged to you for the prayers you offered for us in the days of trouble. Those days are still prolonged, and we earnestly look for aid to our merciful God. Should I have any use for the file of papers you kindly offer me, I will let you know.

"All my family unite with me in kind regards to your wife and children. And I am, very truly, your cousin,

"R. E. LEE."

As this charge of cruelty to Federal prisoners has been again and again reiterated, and as the direct charge against General Lee is again produced in a book just issued from the press, the following facts, which can be proved before any fair tribunal, should go on the record:

1. The Confederate authorities gave to prisoners in their hands *the same rations which they issued to their own soldiers, and gave them the very best accommodations which their scant means afforded.*

2. *They were always anxious to exchange prisoners, man for man, and, when this was rejected by the Federal authorities, they offered to send home the prisoners in their hands without any equivalent.*

3. *By refusing all propositions to exchange prisoners, and declining even to receive their own men without equivalent, the Federal authorities made themselves responsible for all the suffering, of both Federal and Confederate prisoners, that ensued.*

4. And yet, notwithstanding these facts, it is susceptible of proof, from the official records of the Federal Department, that *the suffering of Confederate prisoners in Federal prisons was much greater than that of Federal prisoners in Confederate prisons.* Without going more fully into the question, the following figures from the report of Mr. Stanton, secretary of war, in response to a resolution of the House of Representatives calling for the number of prisoners on both sides and their mortality, are triumphantly submitted:

	In Prison.	Died.
U.S. soldiers	260,940	22,526
Confederates	200,000	26,500

That is, the Confederate States held as prisoners sixty-one thousand men more than the Federals held of the Confederates; and yet the deaths of Federal prisoners fell below those of Confederates by *four thousand.*

Two Federal prisoners died out of every twenty-three; while two out of every fifteen Confederates died in Federal prisons. The mortality was fifty percent greater in Federal prisons than in ours! And, even if all that is charged against us were true, General Lee was in no way responsible, as he had no control whatever over the prisoners after they were turned over to the authorities at Richmond.

Soon after the grand jury found its indictment against General Lee, at a time when President Andrew Johnson was showing a purpose to carry out his threat to "make treason odious by hanging the chief of the rebel leaders," and when ultra men at the North were clamoring for vengeance for what they claimed as "the complicity of the South" in the assassination of Mr. Lincoln, a party of friends were spending an evening at his house in Richmond, and the conversation naturally turned on these matters. Rev. Dr.——— led the conversation in expressing, in terms of decided bitterness, the indignation of the South at the indictment of General Lee. The general pleasantly remarked, "Well! it matters little what they may do to me; I am old, and have but a short time to live anyhow," and very soon turned the conversation into other channels. Presently Dr.——— got up to go, and General Lee followed him out to the door and said to him very earnestly: "Doctor, there is a good old book which I read, and you preach from, which says, 'Love your enemies, bless them that curse you, do good to them that hate you, and pray for them which despitefully use you and persecute you.' Do you think your remarks this evening were quite in the spirit of that teaching?"

Dr.——— made some apology for the bitterness which he felt and expressed, and General Lee added, with that peculiar sweetness of tone and manner that we remember so well: "I have fought against the people of the North because I believed they were seeking to wrest from the South dearest rights. But I have never cherished toward them bitter or vindictive feelings, and have never seen the day when I did not pray for them."

If the world's history affords a sublimer spectacle than that of this stern warrior teaching a minister of the gospel of peace the duty of love to enemies, the present writer has failed to note it.

It is related that one day during the war, as they were reconnoitering the countless hosts opposed to them, one of his subordinates exclaimed in bitter tones, "I wish those people were all dead!" General Lee, with that inimitable grace of manner peculiar to him, promptly rejoined: "How can you say so, General? Now, I wish that they were all at home attending to their own business, and leaving us to do the same."

One day in the autumn of 1869, I saw General Lee standing at his gate, talking to a humbly clad man, who turned off, evidently delighted with his interview, just as I came up. After exchanging salutations, the general pleasantly said, pointing to the retreating form, "That is one of our old soldiers who is in necessitous circumstances." I took it for granted that it was some veteran Confederate, and asked to what command he belonged, when the General quietly and pleasantly added, *"He fought on the other side, but we must not remember that against him now."*

The man afterward came to my house and said to me, in speaking of his interview with General Lee: "Sir, he is the noblest man that ever lived. He not only had a kind word for an old soldier who fought against him, but he gave me some money to help me on my way."

What a beautiful illustration of the teaching of the apostle: "If thine enemy hunger, feed him; if he thirst, give him drink!"

Upon the occasion of the delivery of an address at Washington College by a certain distinguished orator, General Lee came to the writer and said: "I saw you taking notes during the address. It was in the main very fine; but, if you propose publishing any report of it, I would suggest that you leave out all the bitter expressions against the North and the United States government. They will do us no good under our present circumstances, and I think all such expressions undignified and unbecoming."

Soon after the passage of some of the most objectionable of the so-called "Reconstruction Acts," two of the professors of the college were conversing with him, when one of them expressed himself in very bitter terms concerning the dominant party and their treatment of the people of the South. General Lee quietly turned to his table, and, picking up a manuscript (which afterward proved to be his memoir of his father), read the following lines:

> *"Learn from you Orient shell to love thy foe,*
> *And store with pearls the hand that brings thee woe:*
> *Free like you rock, from base, vindictive pride,*
> *Emblaze with gems the wrist that rends thy side;*
> *Mark where you tree rewards the stony shower*
> *With fruit nectareous, or the balmy flower,*
> *All Nature cries aloud: shall man do less*
> *Than heal the smiter, and the railer bless?"*

He then said that these lines were written "in Arabia and by a Mussulman, the poet of Shiraz—the immortal Hafiz," and quietly asked,

"Ought not we who profess to be governed by the principles of Christianity to rise at least to the standard of this Mohammedan poet, and learn to forgive our enemies?"

The conduct of Lee's soldiers, after the close of the war, has excited the attention and elicited the admiration of the world. There was much in the state of things, just after the surrender, to excite the serious apprehension of thinking men that these disbanded soldiers would render the condition of the South far worse by entering upon a career of lawlessness. After long exposure to the demoralizing influences of the camp, and a long cessation from any industrial pursuit, these young men returned to find their fondly cherished hopes blighted, their fortunes ruined, their fields laid waste, and, in not a few instances, blackened ruins marking the spot of their once-happy homes. It would not have been surprising if they had yielded to despair, and had sought redress by taking the law into their own hands. I claim to have thoroughly known the veterans of Lee's army, and to have had some peculiar opportunities of seeing them after the close of the war. In traveling very extensively through the South, I made it a point always to inquire after them, and the invariable response was, "They have gone to work, and are quiet, orderly members of society." Many of them, who had been raised in luxury and ease, took off their coats and went into the corn, tobacco, or cotton fields of the South, or entered upon other pursuits, with a zeal and earnestness truly marvelous to those who did not know the stuff of which these heroic men were made.

They "accepted the situation," and, amid provocations and insults not a few, have proved themselves "loyal" to their every pledge—law-abiding citizens of whom any community might be proud.

If asked the explanation of this, the simplest answer would be, *"The soldiers have continued to follow their commander-in-chief."* General Lee was most scrupulous in observing the terms of his parole. He refused to attend political gatherings, avoided discussing the war, or its issues (except with intimate friends, and in the freedom of private intercourse), and gave the young men of the South a striking example of quiet submission to the United States authorities.

He was accustomed to say: "I am now unfortunately so situated that I can do no good; and, as I am anxious to do as little harm as possible, I deem it wisest for me to remain silent." And yet, as has been intimated, the good order and law-abiding spirit of the soldiers and people of the South were due, in no small measure, to the quiet example and influence of this noble man.

His spirit and conduct at this critical period, when all eyes were turned to him, may be best illustrated by quoting freely from his private correspondence.

And it may be well to give first the following letters, in which he endeavors to ameliorate the condition of some of his old soldiers:

"RICHMOND, VA.,
April 25, 1865.

"Lieutenant General U. S. GRANT, *commanding* }
the Armies of the United States.   }

"GENERAL: I have awaited your arrival in Richmond to propose that the men and officers of the Army of Northern Virginia, captured or surrendered on the 2d and 6th of April, or since that time, may be granted the same terms as given to those surrendered by me on the 9th. I see no benefit that will result by retaining them in prison, but, on the contrary, think good may be accomplished by returning them to their homes. Indeed, if all now held as prisoners of war were liberated in the same manner, I think it would be advantageous. Should there, however, be objections to this course, I would ask that exceptions be made in favor of the invalid officers and men, and that they be allowed to return to their homes on parole. I call your attention particularly to General Ewell, the members of the reserves, local defense troops, naval battalion, etc. The local troops were not performing military duty, and the naval battalion fell in the line of march of the army for subsistence and protection. Understanding that you may not reach Richmond for some days, I take the liberty to forward this application for your consideration.

Very respectfully your obedient servant,
"R. E. LEE, *General.*"

"RICHMOND, VA.,
April 25, 1865.

"Lieutenant General U. S. GRANT, *commanding* }
the Armies of the United States.   }

"GENERAL: I transmit for your perusal a communication just received, and ask your interposition in behalf of the authors. Similar statements have been made to me by officers of rank, which I have not thought it necessary to trouble you with, believing that the obstacles mentioned would be removed as soon as possible. This is still my conviction, and I should consider it unnecessary to call your attention to the subject, had I not been informed of orders issued by the military commanders at Norfolk and Baltimore, requiring oaths of paroled soldiers before permitting them to proceed on their journey. Officers and men on parole are bound in honor to conform to the obligations they have assumed. This obligation cannot be strengthened by any additional form or oath, nor is it customary to exact them.

"Very respectfully your obedient servant,
"R. E. LEE, *General*."

A good deal has been said about General Lee's application for "amnesty." I am enabled to publish, for the first time, both his letter to General Grant and his application to the president. He made this application not because he ever, for a single moment, admitted that he needed "pardon" for his course during the war, but simply that he might show to the world that he had no spirit of hostility to the government, and give to his own people an example of quiet submission to "the powers that be."

"RICHMOND, VA.,
June 13, 1865.

"*Lieutenant General* U. S. GRANT, *commanding* }
     the Armies of the United States.   }

"GENERAL: Upon reading the president's proclamation of the 29th ult. I came to Richmond to ascertain what was proper or required of me to do, when I learned that, with others, I was to be indicted for treason by the grand jury at Norfolk. I had supposed that the officers and men of the Army of Northern Virginia were, by the terms of their surrender, protected by the United States government from molestation so long as they conformed to its conditions. I am ready to meet any charges that may be preferred against me, and do not wish to avoid trial; but, if I am correct as to the protection granted by my parole, and am not to be prosecuted, I desire to comply with the provisions of the president's proclamation, and therefore enclose the required application, which I request in that event may be acted on. I am, with great respect,

> "Your obedient servant,
> "R. E. Lee."

> "Richmond, Va.,
> *June* 13, 1865.

"His Excellency Andrew Johnson, *President of the United States.*

"Sir: Being excluded from the provisions of amnesty and pardon contained in the proclamation of the 29th ult., I hereby apply for the benefits and full restoration of all rights and privileges extended to those included in its terms. I graduated at the Military Academy at West Point in June, 1829; resigned from the United States Army, April, 1861; was a general in the Confederate Army, and included in the surrender of the Army of Northern Virginia, April 9, 1865.

"I have the honor to be, very respectfully,

> "Your obedient servant,
> "R. E. Lee."

In the uncertainty as to the future of the South, just after the close of the war, many of our best men were seriously thinking of seeking homes in foreign lands. General Lee's influence, more than anything else, prevented this. The following is one of many letters which he wrote on that subject:

> "Near Cartersville, Va.,
> *July* 31, 1865.

"Colonel Richard L. Maury, *University of Virginia.*

"My dear Colonel: I received, by the last packet from Richmond, your letter of the 22d, enclosing an extract from a letter of your father to you, dated June 27th, and a project of a decree of the Emperor of Mexico, to encourage emigration of the planters of the South to that country. I was very glad to learn of the well-being of your father, and of his safe arrival in Mexico; and have felt assured that, wherever he might be, he deeply sympathized with the suffering of the people of the South, and was ready to do all in his power to relieve them. I do not know how far their emigration to another land will conduce to their prosperity. Although prospects may not now be cheering, I have entertained the opinion that, unless prevented by circumstances or necessity, it would be better for them and the country to remain at their homes and share the fate of their respective states. I hope the efforts of your father will, however, facilitate the wishes and promote the welfare of all who may find it necessary or convenient to expatriate themselves, but should sincerely regret that either he or his should be embraced in that number. I beg you will present to him my most cordial thanks for his sympathy and interest in our welfare, and my best wishes for his happiness. For your own kind expressions toward me and my family, please accept my grateful thanks. My daughters unite with me in kindest regards to Mrs. Maury, and I am most truly and

> "Respectfully yours,
> "R. E. LEE."

The following letter, to the distinguished gentleman who so ably filled the governor's chair of Virginia during the greater part of the war, will be read with interest, and gives a full view of his feelings and purposes at the time:

> "NEAR CARTERSVILLE, VA.,
> *August* 28, 1865.

"*Hon.* JOHN LETCHER, *Lexington, Va.*

MY DEAR SIR: I was much pleased to hear of your return to your home, and to learn by your letter of the 2d of the kindness and consideration with which you were treated during your arrest, and of the sympathy extended to you by your former congressional associates and friends in Washington. The conciliatory manner in which President Johnson spoke of the South must have been particularly agreeable to one who has the interest of its people so much at heart as yourself. I wish that spirit could become more general. It would go far to promote confidence, and to calm feelings which have too long existed. The questions which for years were in dispute between the state and general government, and which unhappily were not decided by the dictates of reason, but referred to the decision of war, having been decided against us, it is the part of wisdom to acquiesce in the result, and of candor to recognize the fact.

"The interests of the state are therefore the same as those of the United States. Its prosperity will rise or fall with the welfare of the country. The duty of its citizens, then, appears to me too plain to admit of doubt. All should unite in honest efforts to obliterate the effects of war, and to restore the blessings of peace. They should remain, if possible, in the country; promote harmony and good feeling; qualify themselves to vote; and elect to the state and general legislatures wise and patriotic men, who will devote their abilities to the interests of the country, and the healing of all dissensions. I have invariably recommended this course since the cessation of hostilities, and have endeavored to practice it myself. I am much obliged to you for the interest you have expressed in my acceptance of the presidency of Washington College. If I believed I could be of advantage to the youth of the country, I should not hesitate. I have stated to the committee of trustees the objections which exist in my opinion to my filling the position, and will yield to their judgment. Please present me to Mrs. Letcher and your children, and believe me most truly yours,

                                                    "R. E. LEE."

The following characteristic letter illustrates several points of his character:

                                        "NEAR CARTERSVILLE, VA.,
                                           September 4, 1865.

"*Mr.* A. M. KEILEY, *Petersburg, Va.*

"MY DEAR SIR: I only received yesterday your letter of the 11th ult. I am exceedingly obliged to you for your kind proposition, and beg you to accept my sincere thanks for the manner in which it was conveyed. I am compelled to decline your offer, and, as I feel convinced that my services would be of no advantage to your enterprise, I do so with the less regret. I trust, however, you will carry out your design. A journal such as you propose will be of incalculable benefit to the country. It should be the object of all to avoid controversy, to allay passion, give full scope to reason and every kindly feeling. By doing this, and encouraging our citizens to engage in the duties of life with all their heart and mind, with a determination not to be turned aside by thoughts of the past and fears of the future, our country will not only be restored in material prosperity, but will be advanced in science, in virtue, and in religion.

"Wishing you every success, I am most truly yours,

"R. E. LEE."

The following letter explains itself:

"NEAR CARTERSVILLE, VA.,
September 4, 1865.
"*To the* COUNT JOANNES, *No. 37 East 27th Street, City of New York.*

"SIR: I received a few days since your communication of the 14th ult., transmitting a copy of your published letter to the president of the United States.

"Your arguments and conclusions are duly appreciated, and I am exceedingly obliged to you for the offer of your legal services to defend me against the charge of treason. Should they become necessary, they will be gratefully accepted.

"In your letter to me you do the people of the South but simple justice in believing that they heartily concur with you in opinion in regard to the assassination of the late President Lincoln. It is a crime previously unknown to this country, and one that must be deprecated by every American.

"I am, very respectfully,
"R. E. LEE."

The following, to a distinguished naval officer, will show the character of the influence which General Lee exerted:

"NEAR CARTERSVILLE, VA.,
September 7, 1865.

"*Captain* JOSIAH TATNALL, *Savannah, Ga.*

"SIR: I have received your letter of the 23d ult., and in reply will state the course I have pursued under circumstances similar to your own, and will leave you to judge of its propriety. Like yourself, I have, since the cessation of hostilities, advised all with whom I have conversed on the subject, who come within the terms of the president's proclamations, to take the oath of allegiance, and accept in good faith the amnesty offered. But I have gone further, and have recommended to those who were excluded from their benefits, to make application under the *proviso* of the proclamation of the 29th of May, to be embraced in its provisions. Both classes, in order to be restored to their former rights and privileges, were required to perform a certain act, and I do not see that an acknowledgment of fault is expressed in one more than the other. The war being at an end, the Southern states having laid down their arms, and the questions at issue between them and the Northern states having been decided, I believe it to be the duty of everyone to unite in the restoration of the country, and the reestablishment of peace and harmony. These considerations governed me in the counsels I gave to others, and induced me on the 13th of June to make application to be included in the terms of the amnesty proclamation. I have not received an answer, and cannot inform you what has been the decision of the president. But, whatever that may be, I do not see how the course I have recommended and practiced can prove detrimental to the former president of the Confederate States. It appears to me that the allayment of passion, the dissipation of prejudice, and the restoration of reason, will alone enable the people of the country to acquire a true knowledge and form a correct judgment of the events of the past four years. It will, I think, be admitted that Mr. Davis has done nothing more than all the citizens of the Southern states, and should not be held accountable for acts performed by them in the exercise of what had been considered by them unquestionable right. I have too exalted an opinion of the American people to believe that they will consent to injustice; and it is only necessary, in my opinion, that truth should be known, for the rights of every one to be secured. I know of no surer way of eliciting the truth than by burying contention with the war. I enclose a copy of my letter to President Johnson, and feel assured that, however imperfectly I may have given you my views on the subject of your letter, your own high sense of honor and right will lead you to a satisfactory conclusion as to the proper course to be pursued in your own case.

"With great respect and esteem, I am your most obedient servant,

"R. E. LEE."

The following letter to the great scientist whom the whole world honored, and whose death was so widely deplored—who was General Lee's intimate friend, and in whose society in Lexington he seemed so much to delight—will be read with peculiar interest:

"NEAR CARTERSVILLE, VA.,
September 8, 1865.

"*Captain* M. F. MAURY.

"MY DEAR CAPTAIN: I have just received your letter of the 8th ult. We have certainly not found our form of government all that was anticipated by its original founders; but that may be partly our fault in expecting too much, and partly in the absence of virtue in the people. As long as virtue was dominant in the republic, so long was the happiness of the people secure. I cannot, however, despair of it yet. I look forward to better days, and trust that time and experience, the great teachers of men, under the guidance of an ever-merciful God, may save us from destruction, and restore to us the bright hopes and prospects of the past. The thought of abandoning the country and all that must be left in it is abhorrent to my feelings, and I prefer to struggle for its restoration and share its fate, rather than to give up all as lost. I have a great admiration for Mexico; the salubrity of its climate, the fertility of its soil, and the magnificence of its scenery, possess for me great charms; but I still look with delight upon the mountains of my native state. To remove our people with their domestics to a portion of Mexico which would be favorable to them, would be a work of much difficulty. Did they possess the means, and could the system of apprenticeship you suggest be established, the United States government, I think, would interpose obstacles;

and under the circumstances there would be difficulty in persuading the freedmen to emigrate. Those citizens who can leave the country, and others who may be compelled to do so, will reap the fruits of your considerate labor; but I shall be very sorry if your presence be lost to Virginia. She has now need for all of her sons, and can ill afford to spare you. I am very much obliged to you for all you have done for us, and hope your labors in the future may be as efficacious as in the past, and that your separation from us may not be permanent. Wishing you every prosperity and happiness,

> "I am most truly yours,
> "R. E. LEE."

The following, to the gallant and distinguished soldier with whom General Lee always preserved the kindliest relations, will be appropriately introduced in this connection:

> "LEXINGTON, VA.,
> *October* 3, 1865.

"*General* G. T. BEAUREGARD, *New Orleans, La.*

"MY DEAR GENERAL: I have received your letter of the 1st ult., and am very sorry to learn that the papers of yourself and Johnston are lost, or at least beyond your reach; but I hope they may be recovered. Mine never can be, though some may be replaced. Please supply all you can; it may be safer to send them by private hands, if practicable, to Mr. Caskie, at Richmond, or to me at this place. I hope both you and Johnston will write the history of your campaigns. Every one should do all in his power to collect and disseminate the truth, in the hope that it may find a place in history, and descend to posterity. I am glad to see no indication in your letter of an intention to leave the country. I think the South requires the aid of her sons now more than at any period of her history. As you ask my purpose, I will state that I have no thought of abandoning her unless compelled to do so.

"After the surrender of the Southern armies in April, the revolution in the opinions and feelings of the people seemed so complete, and the return of the Southern states into the Union of all the states so inevitable, that it became in my opinion the duty of every citizen, the contest being virtually ended, to cease opposition, and place himself in a position to serve the country. I therefore, upon the promulgation of the proclamation of President Johnson, of 29th of May, which indicated his policy in the restoration of peace, determined to comply with its requirements, and applied on the 13th of June to be embraced within its provisions. I have not heard the result of my application. Since then, I have been elected to the presidency of Washington College, and have entered upon the duties of the office, in the hope of being of some service to the noble youth of our country. I need not tell you that true patriotism sometimes requires of men to act exactly contrary, at one period, to that which it does at another, and the motive which impels them—the desire to do right—is precisely the same. The circumstances which govern their actions, change, and their conduct must conform to the new order of things. History is full of illustrations of this: Washington himself is an example of this. At one time he fought against the French, under Braddock, in the service of the king of Great Britain; at another, he fought with the French at Yorktown, under the orders of the Continental Congress of America, against him. He has not been branded by the world with reproach for this, but his course has been applauded. With sentiments of great esteem,

"I am most truly yours,
"R. E. LEE."

He cherished the liveliest interest in those of his old soldiers who were in voluntary exile. The following, to a gallant gentleman, is a specimen of many such letters which he wrote:

"LEXINGTON, VA.,
December 23, 1865.
"*General* C. M. WILCOX, *City of Mexico.*

"MY DEAR GENERAL: I have just received your letter of the 3d inst., and am very glad to hear of your safety and your health. I enclose a short statement of your military career, which I hope will answer your purpose. My time does not permit my entering into details, you must supply them; neither am I able to advise you on the subject of entering the military service of Mexico, except so far as my judgment and feelings may be inferred from my own action. They do not prompt me to do so, but, on the contrary, impel me to remain with my own people and share their fortunes, unless prevented by inexorable circumstances. I must refer you to the papers for information as to the state of the country. You will see, by the message of President Johnson, his views and policy; to what degree he will be sustained by Congress, I cannot say; as yet, it has shown no favorable disposition that I am aware of. I fear the South has yet to suffer many evils, and it will require time, patience, and fortitude, to heal her afflictions.

"Please present my kindest regards to all our friends near you; I feel a deep interest in their welfare, and hope you and they may enjoy all happiness and prosperity.

"With great respect, your friend and servant,

"R. E. LEE."

The following additional letter to General Beauregard needs no explanation:

"LEXINGTON, VA.,
December 23, 1865.

"*General* G. T. BEAUREGARD, *New Orleans, La.*

"MY DEAR GENERAL: I have just received, by the hands of Captain Hitchens, your letter of the 25th ult., and the copies of your public letters, telegrams, and reports, mentioned in the accompanying list. I am very much obliged to you for them, and hope you may soon be able to send me the remainder of such as I requested in my former letter. I must beg you to present my heartfelt thanks to Miss Blanche Bernard, for her kindness in preparing me the copies on foolscap, and say to her all that I would did opportunity permit.

"I am very glad to learn that you have determined to remain in the country, and have set regularly to work. I think it is the course indicated by true patriotism. My remarks in my former letter were not intended to question the conduct of Southern citizens before the war, but to show that, what patriotism required of them then, it requires of them now; if they do not so read, I beg you will correct them.

"I am, my dear general, most truly yours,

"R. E. LEE."

The following, to a distinguished Northern politician, is a very quiet but emphatic vindication of the course of the South:

"LEXINGTON, VA.,
January 5, 1866.

"*Mr.* CHAUNCEY BURE.

"MY DEAR SIR: I am very much obliged to you for your letter of the 12th ult., and for the number of the *Old Guard* which you kindly sent me. I am glad to know that the intelligent and respectable people at the North are true and conservative in their opinions; for I believe by no other course can the right interest of the country be maintained. All that the South has ever desired was that the Union, as established by our forefathers, should be preserved; and that the government, as originally organized, should be administered in purity and truth. If such is the desire of the North, there can be no contention between the two sections; and all true patriots will unite in advocating that policy which will soonest restore the country to tranquility and order, and serve to perpetuate true republicanism.

"Please accept my thanks for your advocacy of right and liberty, and for the kind sentiments which you express toward myself; and believe me to be, with great respect,

"Your obedient servant,
"R. E. LEE."

The following, to his friend Hon. Reverdy Johnson, expresses very emphatically his views on the "test oath," and other matters:

"LEXINGTON, VA.,
January 27, 1866.

"*Hon.* REVERDY JOHNSON, *Washington City, D.C.*

"MY DEAR SIR: I am very much obliged to you for your kind letter of the 8th inst., and for the opportunity afforded, by the pamphlet which accompanied it, of reading your speech before the Supreme Court, on the subject of the test oath. I should have expressed my thanks to you sooner; but I have but recently returned from a visit to Richmond, where I was detained a week on business connected with Washington College. I have been looking anxiously for a decision of the question by the Supreme Court, and cannot but hope it will be favorable. You have so ably presented the arguments and reasons on the subject, that I trust they may prevail. I have hoped that Congress would have thought proper to have repealed the acts imposing it, and all similar tests. To pursue a policy which will continue the prostration of one-half the country, alienate the affections of its inhabitants from the government, and which must eventually result in injury to the country and the American people, appears to me so manifestly injudicious that I do not see how those responsible can tolerate it. I sincerely thank you for the repetition of your kind offer to aid me in any way in your power. I have been awaiting the action of President Johnson upon my application to be embraced in his proclamation of May 29th, and for my restoration to civil rights, before attempting to close the estate of Mr. G. W. P. Custis, of which I am sole administrator. His servants were all liberated, agreeably to the terms of his will; but I have been unable to place his grandchildren in possession of the property bequeathed them. A portion of his landed property has been sold by the government, in the belief, I presume, that it belonged to me; whereas I owned no part of it, nor had any other charge than as administrator. His will, in his own handwriting, is on file in the court of Alexandria County. Arlington, and the tract on 'Four-Mile Run,' given him by General Washington, he left to his only child, Mrs. Lee, during her life, and, at her death, to his eldest grandson. Both of these tracts have been sold by government. It has also sold Smith's Island (off Cape Charles), which Mr. Custis directed to be sold to aid in paying certain legacies to his granddaughters. If in your opinion there is anything that can be done to enable me to bestow the property as bequeathed by the testator, and to close my administration of his estate, I would be greatly obliged to you to inform me.

"I am, with great esteem, your obedient servant,

"R. E. LEE."

The following, to the wife of President Davis, shows his indisposition to engage in controversy, and his keen sympathy for Mr. Davis in his imprisonment:

"LEXINGTON, VA.,
February 23, 1866.

"*Mrs.* JEFFERSON DAVIS, *Prospect Hill, Ga.*

"MY DEAR MRS. DAVIS: Your letter of the 12th inst. reached Lexington during my absence at Washington. I have never seen Mr. Colfax's speech, and am therefore ignorant of the statements it contained. Had it, however, come under my notice, I doubt whether I should have thought it proper to have replied. I have thought, from the time of the cessation of hostilities, that silence and patience on the part of the South was the true course, and I think so still. Controversy of all kinds will in my opinion only serve to continue excitement and passion, and will prevent the public mind from the acknowledgment and acceptance of the truth. These considerations have kept me from replying to accusations made against myself, and induced me to recommend the same to others.

"As regards the treatment of the Andersonville prisoners, to which you allude, I know nothing, and could say nothing of my own knowledge. I never had anything to do with any prisoners, except to send those taken on the fields where I was engaged, to the provost-marshal-general at Richmond.

"I have felt most keenly the sufferings and imprisonment of your husband; and have earnestly consulted with friends as to any possible mode of affording him relief and consolation. He enjoys the sympathy and respect of all good men; and, if, as you state, his trial is now near, the exhibition of the whole truth in his case will, I trust, prove his defense and justification. With sincere prayers for his health and speedy restoration to liberty, and earnest supplication to God that he may take you and yours under His guidance and protection.

"I am, with great respect, your obedient servant,
"R. E. LEE."

The following, to an old and long-tried friend, will serve to illustrate several points of his character:

"LEXINGTON, VA.,
March 1, 1866.

"*Mr.* E. J. QUIRK, *San Francisco, Cal.*

"MY DEAR SIR: I received with much pleasure your letter of the 20th of January, and am glad to learn that you are well and prosperous. A continuance of the manly exertion and rigid fidelity which you have hitherto practiced will still further advance you in life, and enable you to accomplish much good in the world. Time seems to have fallen lightly on you, and your photograph represents you but little changed from the period when I first met you on the banks of the Mississippi. Yet the fact which you mention, of having a married daughter living in Nevada, shows the length of time which has elapsed. I hope future years will bring you equal happiness, and equal prosperity. In compliance with your request, I send a photograph of myself, taken during the war. I am sure that you will scarcely recognize a single trace of him whom you met at the quarries of St. Louis.

"I am very much obliged to you for your bold defense of me in the New York papers, at a time when many were willing to believe any enormity charged against me.

"This same slander which you at the time denounced as false, was nevertheless circulated at the North, and since the termination of hostilities has been renewed in Europe. Yet there is not a word of truth in it, or any ground for its origin. No servant, soldier, or citizen, that was ever employed by me, can with truth charge me with bad treatment. You must present my kind regards to your daughter. I am glad that you have her near you. I know she will be a great comfort to you.

"With my best wishes for your health, happiness, and prosperity, and many thanks for your kind remembrance of me,

"I am, with much esteem, very truly yours,
"R. E. LEE."

The following indicates his deep interest in the educational interests of the country:

"LEXINGTON, VA.,
March 20, 1866.
"*Rev.* G. W. LEYBURN, *Care of Rev. Dr. Bamsey, Lynchburg, Va.*

"MY DEAR SIR: I have received your letter of the 27th ult., in reference to our conversation upon the subject of the educational interests of the country. So greatly have these interests been disturbed at the South, and so much does its future condition depend upon the rising generation, that I consider the proper education of its youth one of the most important objects now to be attained, and one from which the greatest benefits may be expected. Nothing will compensate us for the depression of the standard of our moral and intellectual culture, and each state should take the most energetic measures to revive its schools and colleges, and, if possible, to increase the facilities of instruction, and to elevate the standard of learning.

"The legislature of Virginia, at its recent session, evinced its sense of the importance of education, by providing for the payment of the interest of its bonds held by the several institutions of learning, and by making the usual annual appropriations to the University of Virginia, and to the Virginia Military Institute, notwithstanding the extreme financial pressure under which the state is suffering. As regards Washington College, you are aware of the efforts which its friends are making to increase its endowment, so as to expand its course of instruction. This is necessary, in my opinion, in order to keep pace with the advancement of science, and to provide for the present wants of the country. If it is accomplished it will be of the greatest advantage, not only to the surrounding community, but to the state and to the South. There are at present representatives at the college from all the Southern states except Arkansas.

"Very respectfully your obedient servant,
"R. E. LEE."

The following, to one of his favorite officers, expresses his feelings very freely on various points of interest:

"LEXINGTON, VA.,
March 15, 1866.
"*General* J. A. EARLY, *Care of J. Anderson, Esq.,* }
Cuidad de Mexico, Mexico. }

"MY DEAR GENERAL: I am very much obliged to you for the copies of my letters forwarded with yours of the 25th January. I hope you will be able to send me reports of the operations of your commands in the campaign from the Wilderness to Richmond, at Lynchburg, in the Valley, Maryland, etc. All statistics as regards numbers, destruction of private property by the Federal troops, etc., I should like to have, as I wish my memory strengthened on those points. It will be difficult to get the world to understand the odds against which we fought; and the destruction, or loss, of all returns of the army embarrasses me very much. I read your letter from Havana, in the New York *News,* with much interest, and was pleased with the temper in which it was written. I have since received the paper containing it, published in the city of Mexico, and also your letter in reference to Mr. Davis. I understand and appreciate the motives which prompted both letters, and think they will be of service in the way you intended. I have been much pained to see the attempts made to cast odium upon Mr. Davis, but do not think they will be successful with the reflecting or informed portion of the country. The accusations against myself I have not thought proper to notice, or even to correct misrepresentations of my words and acts. We shall have to be patient, and suffer for a while at least; and all controversy, I think, will only serve to prolong angry and bitter feelings, and postpone the period when reason and charity may resume their sway. At present the public mind is not prepared to receive the truth. The feelings which influenced you to leave the country were natural, and I presume were uppermost in the breasts of many. It was a matter which each one had to decide for himself, as he could only know the reasons which governed him. I was particularly anxious on your account, as I had the same apprehensions to which you refer. I am truly glad that you are beyond the reach of annoyance, and hope you may be able to employ yourself profitably and usefully. Mexico is a beautiful country, fertile, of vast resources, and, with a stable government and a virtuous population, will rise to greatness. I do not think that your letters can be construed by your former associates as reflecting upon them, and I have never heard the least blame cast, by those who have remained, upon those who thought it best to leave the country. I think I stated in a former letter the reasons which governed me, and will not, therefore, repeat them. I hope in time peace will be restored to the country, and that the South may enjoy some measure of prosperity. I fear, however, much suffering is still in store for her, and that her people must be prepared to exercise fortitude and forbearance. I must beg you to present my kind regards to the gentlemen with you; and, with my best wishes for yourself, and undiminished esteem,

"I am, most truly, yours,

"R. E. LEE."

The following letter is worth preserving:

"LEXINGTON, VA.,

April 6, 1866.

"Mr.————.

"MY DEAR SIR: I have received your letter of the 2d inst., and am obliged to you for your kind offer to reclaim some of the articles that have been taken from Arlington by the soldiers of the United States Army. I fear this would be a task of great trouble, and would not be attended by comparative good; but any articles that fall in your way, such as you describe, and which can be returned to me without inconvenience, I would be glad to get. As regards the advice you ask on the subject of emigrating to Mexico or Brazil, I do not feel competent to give it. Each individual is the best judge of his own feelings, his own conduct, and his own wants, and can best determine such a question for himself. I made up my mind on the subject at the first cessation of hostilities. I considered that the South required the presence of her sons more then than at any former part of her history, to sustain and restore her; that though many might find comfortable homes in a foreign land, what would become of the Southern states, and the citizens who abided in them? I have, therefore, invariably advised all who could remain to adhere to their home and friends; and I have seen no reason to change my opinions, In answer to your question as to what position I hold in the order of Masons, I have to reply that I am not a Mason, and have never belonged to the society. With my best thanks for the kind sentiments you express toward me, and my sincere wishes for your future welfare, I am, very respectfully,

"Your obedient servant,

"R. E. LEE."

The following is a specimen of many similar letters which he wrote:

"LEXINGTON, VA.,
April 13, 1866.

"*Mr.*————.

"MY DEAR SIR: Your letter of the 5th inst., enclosing a slip from the Baltimore *American,* has been received. The same statement, with some variation, has been published at the North for several years. The statement is not true; but I have not thought proper to publish a contradiction, being unwilling to be drawn into a newspaper discussion, believing that those who know me would not credit it, and those who do not would care nothing about it.

"I cannot now depart from the rule I have followed. It is so easy to make accusations against the people at the South upon similar testimony, that those so disposed, should one be refuted, will immediately create another; and thus you would be led into endless controversy. I think it better to leave their correction to the return of reason and good feeling.

"Thanking you for your interest in my behalf, and begging you to consider my letter as intended only for yourself,

"I am, most respectfully, your obedient servant,
"R. E. LEE."

The following was written to one of his oldest and most cherished friends:

"LEXINGTON, VA.,
July 9, 1866.

"*Captain* JAMES MAY, *Rock Island, Ill.*

"MY DEAR SIR: I was truly glad to receive your friendly letter, after so many years of silence and separation; and I rejoice to read in it the expression of the same feeling of kindness and friendship that characterized our intercourse in early life. I assure you these feelings are cordially reciprocated by Mrs. Lee and myself, and we shall never forget the numerous kind acts extended to us by you during our sojourn in the West.

"Your letter deserved and would have received an earlier answer; but when it reached me I was engaged in the annual examination exercises at Washington College, which continued over three weeks, and since their termination I have been continuously occupied in business relating to the institution.

"I must give you my special thanks for doing me the justice to believe that my conduct during the last five eventful years has been governed by my sense of duty. I had no other guide, nor had I any other object than the defense of those principles of American liberty upon which the constitutions of the several states were originally founded; and, unless they are strictly observed, I fear there will be an end to republican government in this country. I concur with you in opinion as to the propriety and duty of all persons uniting in the present posture of affairs for the restoration and reconciliation of the country. I have endeavored to pursue this course myself since the cessation of hostilities, and have recommended it to others. So far as my knowledge extends, there is no opposition at the South to the general government. Everyone approves of the policy of President Johnson, gives him his cordial support, and would, I believe, confer on him the presidency for another term, if it was in his power. I do not know what more you desire, and, even if I possessed the influence you attribute to me, how I could exercise it otherwise than as I have. But I have no influence, and do not feel at liberty to take a more active part in public affairs than I have done.

"The whole attention of the people at the South is confined to their private business. They have no influence in the regulation of public affairs; and, whatever is done, must be accomplished by those who control the councils of the country. You and your friends at the North are the only persons who can exercise a beneficial influence.

"I hope the long years which have passed since we met, have brought you nothing but prosperity and happiness, and that the future may give you tranquility and peace.

"I am, with great regard, your friend and servant,

"R. E. Lee."

The following is all that the most intense "loyalty" could ask:

"LEXINGTON, VA.,
August 16, 1866.

"———, *Esq., New Orleans, La.*

"MY DEAR SIR: Your letter of the 9th inst. has been received. If you intend to reside in this country, and wish to do your part in the restoration of your state and in the government of the country, which I think it the duty of every citizen to do, I know of no objection to your taking the amnesty oath which I have seen. These considerations induced me to make applications to be included in the terms of the proclamation of President Johnson shortly after its promulgation.

"Very respectfully, your obedient servant,
"R. E. LEE."

The following is an emphatic reiteration of his purpose not to suffer himself to be paraded before the public or led into controversy:

"LEXINGTON, VA.,
August 22, 1866.

"*Mr.* HERBERT SAUNDERS, *South Kingston, London, England.*

"MY DEAR MR. SAUNDERS: I received today your letter of the 31st ult. What I stated to you in conversation, during the visit which you did me the honor to pay me in November last, was entirely for your own information and was in no way intended for publication; my only object was to gratify the interest which you apparently evinced on the several topics which were introduced, and to point to facts which you might investigate, if you so desired, in your own way. I have an objection to the publication of my private conversations which are never intended but for those to whom they are addressed. I cannot, therefore, without an entire disregard of the rule which I have followed in other cases, and in violation of my own sense of propriety, assent to what you propose; I hope, therefore, you will excuse me. Whatever you may think proper to publish, I hope will be the result of your own observations and convictions, and not on my authority. In the hasty perusal which I have been obliged to give the manuscript inclosed to me, I perceive many inaccuracies, resulting as much perhaps from my imperfect narration as from misapprehension on your part. Though fully appreciating your kind wish to correct certain erroneous statements as regards myself, I prefer to remain silent rather than do any thing that might excite angry discussion at this time, when strong efforts are being made by conservative men, North and South, to sustain President Johnson in his policy, which I think offers the only means of healing the lamentable divisions of the country, which the result of the late convention at Philadelphia gives great promise of doing.

"Thanking you for the opportunity afforded me of expressing my opinion before executing your purpose,

"I am, yours very truly,

"R. E. LEE."

The following is at the same time a graceful acknowledgment of courtesy and an emphatic avowal of principle:

"LEXINGTON, VA.,

September 27, 1866

"*Mr.* CHARLES W. LAW, 6 *Victoria Street, Westminster* }
  Abbey, S. W., London, England. }

"MY DEAR SIR: Allow me to thank you for your kind letter of the 17th ult., enclosing an article from the London *Standard.* The complimentary remarks of the letter I understand as referring to the cause in which I was engaged, and not to myself. The good opinion of the English people as to the justice of that cause, constitutional government, is highly appreciated by the people of the South; and my thanks are due to you for the sympathy and support you gave it.

"Most truly yours,

"R. E. LEE."

"LEXINGTON, VA.,

October 1, 1866.

"*Mrs.* MARY E.————, *Washington City, D.C.:*

"I have not found time till today to reply to your letter of the 2d ult. I regret that I cannot give you the information you ask in regard to the pictures at Arlington. I have understood that those remaining in the house have been moved from their former positions, and I do not, therefore, recognize them from your description. I cordially unite in your prayer that deeds of kindness and forbearance may be practiced toward each other, by persons of all sections of the country, and that the ravages of war may be speedily obliterated.

"Very respectfully your obedient servant,

"R. E. LEE."

The following endorsement of his narrative of the campaign of 1864 will be appreciated by the many friends of the distinguished soldier to whom it is addressed:

"LEXINGTON, VA.,
October 15, 1866.

"General J. A. EARLY, Toronto, C.W.

"MY DEAR GENERAL: I am much obliged to you for the narrative forwarded with your letter of the 4th ult. I have read it with interest, and have tried to find the means of replying. Not being able do so, I shall wait no longer; but will trust to the mail, hoping it may reach you safely. Your account corresponds generally with my recollection, though I cannot pretend to express an opinion as to the accuracy of your statements, without giving the subject more investigation than I have now time to devote. I have no objection to the publication of the narrative of your operations before leaving the Army of Northern Virginia. I would recommend, however, that, while giving facts which you think necessary for your own vindication, you omit all epithets or remarks calculated to excite bitterness or animosity between different sections of the country.

"With the most sincere wishes for your welfare,

"I am very truly yours,
"R. E. LEE."

The following will be read with deep interest, and will go down to history in vivid contrast with the political ambition of many others:

"LEXINGTON, VA.,
February, 4, 1867.
"*Hon.* ROBERT OULD, *Virginia Senate, Richmond, Va.*

"MY DEAR SIR: I received today your letter of the 31st ult., and the subject to which it relates is so important that, though confined to my room by indisposition, I reply at once. I feel greatly honored at what you say is the prevailing wish of leading men in the state, that I should accept the nomination for the office of governor of Virginia, and I duly appreciate the spirit that has led them to name me for that high position. I candidly confess, however, that my feelings induce me to prefer private life, which I think more suitable to my condition and age, and where I believe I can better advance the interests of my state than in that you propose. You will agree with me, I am sure, in the opinion that this is no time for the indulgence of personal or political considerations in selecting a person to fill that office; nor should it be regarded as a means of rewarding individuals for supposed former services. The welfare of the state and the interests of her citizens should be the only principle of selection. Believing that there are many men in the state more capable than I am of filling the position, and who could do more to promote the interests of the people, I most respectfully decline to be considered a candidate for the office.

"I think it important, in selecting a chief magistrate of the commonwealth, for the citizens to choose one capable of fulfilling its high trust, and at the same time not liable to the misconstruction which their choice of one objectionable to the general government would be sure to create, and thereby increase the evils under which the state at present labors.

"I have no means of knowing, other than are apparent to you, whether my election as governor of Virginia would be personally injurious to me or not, and therefore the consideration of that question in your letter has not been embraced in my reply. But I believe it would be used by the dominant party to excite hostility toward the state, and to injure the people in the eyes of the country; and I therefore cannot consent to become the instrument of bringing distress upon those whose prosperity and happiness are so dear to me. If *my* disfranchisement and privation of civil rights would secure to the citizens of the state the enjoyment of civil liberty and equal rights under the Constitution, I would willingly accept them in their stead.

"What I have written is intended only for your own information. With grateful thanks for your friendly sentiments,

"I am very truly yours,

"R. E. LEE."

The following extract from a speech delivered in Atlanta, Ga., by Hon. B. H. Hill, may be appropriately introduced here:

"When the future historian comes to survey the character of Lee, he will find it rising like a huge mountain above the undulating plain of humanity, and he will have to lift his eyes toward heaven to catch its summit. He possessed every virtue of the great commanders, without their vices. He was a foe without hate; a friend without treachery; a private citizen without wrong; a neighbor without reproach; a Christian without hypocrisy, and a man without guilt. He was a Cæsar without his ambition; a Frederick without his tyranny; a Napoleon without his selfishness; and a Washington without his reward. He was obedient to authority as a servant, and loyal in authority as a true king. He was gentle as a woman in life; modest and pure as a virgin in thought; watchful as a Roman vestal in duty; submissive to law as Socrates; and grand in battle as Achilles.

"There were many peculiarities in the habits and character of Lee which are but little known, and may be studied with profit. He studiously avoided giving opinions upon subjects which it had not been his calling or training to investigate; and sometimes I thought he carried this great virtue too far. Neither the president, nor Congress, nor friends, could get his views upon any public question not strictly military, and no man had as much quiet, unobtrusive contempt for what he called 'military statesmen and political generals.' Meeting him once on the streets of Richmond, I said to him, 'General, I wish you would give us your opinion as to the propriety of changing the seat of government and going farther south.'

" 'That is a political question, Mr. Hill, and you politicians must determine it; I shall endeavor to take care of the army, and you must make the laws and control the government.'

" 'Ah, General,' I said, 'but you will have to change that rule, and form and express political opinions; for, if we establish our independence, the people will make you Mr. Davis's successor.'

" 'Never, sir,' he replied with a firm dignity that belonged only to Lee. 'That I will never permit. Whatever talents I may possess (and they are but limited) are military talents. My education and training are military. I think the military and civil talents are distinct, if not different, and full duty in either sphere is about as much as one man can qualify himself to perform. I shall not do the people the injustice to accept high civil office with whose questions it has not been my business to become familiar.'

" 'Well, but General,' I insisted, 'history does not sustain your view. Cæsar, and Frederick of Prussia, and Bonaparte, were great statesmen, as well as great generals.'

" 'And great tyrants,' he promptly responded. 'I speak of the proper rule in republics, where, I think, we should have neither military statesmen nor political generals.'

" 'But Washington was both, and yet not a tyrant,' I repeated.

"And with a beautiful smile he said, 'Washington was an exception to all rule, and there was none like him.'

"I could find no words to answer further, but instantly I said in thought 'Surely Washington is no longer the only exception, for one like him, if not even greater, is here.' "

"Lexington, Va.,
April 20, 1867.
"*Mr.* Frank Fuller, 57 *Broadway, New York City, N.Y.*

"My dear Sir: I hasten to return my thanks for your invitation to deliver a lecture before the Peabody Institute of New York and Brooklyn, and am much indebted to you for the motives which prompted it. For reasons which I am sure you can appreciate, I have felt great reluctance to appear before the public in any manner, and do not think that I could accomplish any good by departing from this course. My opinions would have no influence in correcting the misunderstanding which has existed between the North and South, and which I fear is still destined to involve the country in greater calamities. Apart from these considerations, my present duties oc-cupy all my time, and I am unable to neglect them without inconvenience to others. I am therefore obliged respectfully to decline your invitation.

"With great respect, your obedient servant,

"R. E. LEE."

The following, to a lady of his acquaintance, will be read with interest:

"LEXINGTON, VA.,

May 21, 1867.

"*Mrs.——, Petersburg, Va.*

"MY DEAR MRS.——: I regret that I have not been able to reply sooner to your kind letter; but my duties are so constant and my correspondence so large, that I am unable to keep pace with their demands. I am very glad to hear from you, and hope that your family are all well. My thoughts often revert to the good people of your city, and I shall never cease to sympathize in everything that concerns them. The present condition of affairs is, as you state, calculated to create much anxiety, but not sufficient, in my opinion, to cause us to despond, or to cease in our effort to direct events to a favorable issue. It is difficult to see now what course will lead certainly to that end, and I cannot pretend to advise, as you suggest, those better qualified to judge than myself. But I know that in pursuing the path dictated by prudence and wisdom, and in endeavoring honestly to accomplish what is right, the darkness which overshadows our political horizon will be dissipated, and the true course to pursue will, as we advance, become visible and clear. I think, however, it must now be apparent to everyone who reflects, that all who are not disfranchised by the present laws should qualify themselves to vote at the approaching elections, and unite in selecting the best available men to represent them in the required convention. Whatever the convention may then adopt as the best under the circumstances for the people and State, irrespective of individuals, should then be accepted and carried out in good faith. Although their decision may not be considered at the time as the most advantageous, it should be recollected that it can be improved as opportunity offers, and in the end I trust all things will work together for our good.

"Above all, I think there should be harmony and good feeling between all citizens, and no division into parties, but all should unite for the common good. For reasons which I think you will understand and appreciate, I have a great reluctance to appear before the public in any manner. I think no good would result from it, and I must, therefore, ask you to consider my letter as private. Please present me most kindly to Mr. W——— and all the members of your household, and say to your kind neighbors, the M———s, B———, and B———s, that I wish much to see them.

"Very respectfully and truly yours,
"R. E. LEE."

The following, to one of the most gallant soldiers and devoted patriots in the South, has been published in the newspapers, but is worth preserving:

"LEXINGTON, VA.,
May 28, 1867.

"MY DEAR GENERAL: I was very glad to hear, from your letter of last month, the prosperous condition of the Southern Hospital Association, and the relief that has already been afforded to disabled and needy men. I trust that, as our political troubles are reconciled, and business becomes reestablished and extended in the South, the sufferings of all may be relieved. I feel assured that, under the present management of the association, all will be done that can be done, and those who are devoting their time and energies to this praiseworthy work will receive from posterity, as well as from the present generation, the thanks which are due.

"As regards the course Virginia may take under the recent laws of Congress, to which you refer, it is difficult to see what may eventually be the best. I think, though, it is plain, in the execution of the laws, that a convention will be called, and a state constitution formed. The question, then, is, Shall the members of the convention be selected from the best available men in the state, or from the worst? Shall the machinery of the state government be arranged and set in motion by the former or by the latter? In this view of the case, I think it is the duty of all citizens not disfranchised to qualify themselves to vote, attend the polls, and elect the best men in their power. Judge Underwood, Messrs. Botts, Hunnicut, etc., would be well pleased, I presume, if the business were left to them and the negroes. But I do not think this course would be either for the interest of the state or country. When the convention assembles, it will be for them to determine what, under the circumstances of the case, it will be best for the people to do, and their decision should be submitted to by all, as the decision of the state. I look upon the Southern people as acting under compulsion, not of their free choice, and that it is their duty to consult the best interests of their states as far as may be in their power to do.

"I hope that all our friends in New Orleans may do well, and that each may succeed in the business which he has undertaken. Every man must now look closely to his own affairs, and depend upon his own good sense and judgment to push them onward. We have but little to do with general politics. We cannot control them, but, by united efforts, harmony, prudence, and wisdom, we may shape and regulate our domestic policy.

"Please present my kindest regards to Generals Beauregard, Longstreet, Hood, Buckner, and all friends.

"Wishing you every happiness, I am truly yours,

"R. E. LEE."

"To General D. H. MAURY."

The following explains itself, and is most significant as showing that, while fully "accepting the situation," he could by no means approve of the course of Southern men who have united with the dominant party:

"LEXINGTON, VA.,

October 29, 1867.

"*General* J. LONGSTREET, 21 *Carondelet Street, New Orleans, La.*

"MY DEAR GENERAL: When I received your letter of the 8th of June, I had just returned from a short trip to Bedford County, and was preparing for a more extended visit to the White Sulphur Springs for the benefit of Mrs. Lee's health. As I could not write such a letter as you desired, and as you stated that you would leave New Orleans for Mexico in a week from the time you wrote, to be absent some months, I determined to delay my reply till my return. Although I have been here more than a month, I have been so occupied by necessary business, and so incommoded by the effects of an attack of sickness, from which I have not yet recovered, that this is the first day that I have been able to write to you.

"I have avoided all discussion of political questions since the cessation of hostilities, and have, in my own conduct, and in my recommendations to others, endeavored to conform to existing circumstances. I consider this the part of wisdom as well as of duty; but, while I think we should act under the law and according to the law imposed upon us, I cannot think the course pursued by the dominant political party the best for the interests of the country, and therefore cannot say so, or give them my approval. This is the reason why I could not comply with the request in your letter. I am of the opinion that all who can, should vote for the most intelligent, honest, and conscientious men eligible to office, irrespective of former party opinions, who will endeavor to make the new constitutions and the laws passed under them as beneficial as possible to the true interests, prosperity, and liberty of all classes and conditions of the people.

"With my best wishes for your health and happiness, and my kindest regards to Mrs. Longstreet and your children, I am with great regard, and very truly and sincerely yours,

"R. E. LEE."

It may be added in this connection, that he was accustomed sometimes to express himself in terms of strongest condemnation of the injustice done the South by some of the ultra measures of Congress. In a word, he never ceased to be a Virginian and a Southron.

The following is in reply to one of many similar letters which he received:

"LEXINGTON, VA.,
January 20, 1868.

"MY DEAR MADAM: I have just received your letter of the 15th inst., and am glad to learn of the interest felt by yourself and friends in the welfare of the South, and hope that your kind efforts to relieve the suffering among its people may be successful.

"I think you need feel no hesitation in calling upon any of the citizens of the cities which you propose to visit, for information or aid to enable you to administer relief to the distressed; and I feel assured that your charitable errand will be commended by the benevolent, and that you will receive a cordial welcome from your former pupils and acquaintances.

"Such great changes have occurred in the condition of Southern families, that I am at a loss to designate those whose hospitality it might be agreeable to you to accept, or convenient to them to extend; but, should you experience any embarrassment on your arrival in Richmond, you can safely go to any of the principal hotels, and I feel certain that Mr. Carrington, of the Exchange, or Mr. Ballard, of the Ballard House, would do everything in his power to promote your comfort and convenience.

"Among the gentlemen to whom you could apply for any information you might want, I can refer you to Messrs. James Lyons and Wm. H. MacFarland, and the Rev. Drs. Hoge and Minnegerode. Should you continue your journey to Wilmington and Charleston, as you intimate, Mr. George Davis, of the former city, and Mr. C. C. Meminger, of the latter, could give you useful information and assistance.

"With my best wishes for your safe journey and successful mission, I am, very respectfully,

"Your obedient servant,
"R. E. LEE."

The following letter shows that he appreciated his legal rights, and purposed at a proper time to maintain them:

"LEXINGTON, VA.,
January 13, 1869.

"*Hon.* J. S. BLACK, *Washington City, D.C.*

"MY DEAR SIR: I received this morning a letter from my friend Captain James May, informing me of the kind interest you expressed in my welfare, and of the generous offer of your professional services for the restoration of the property belonging to the state of Mr. G. W. P. Custis, which was sold by the government during the late war.

"I am deeply sensible of your kindness, and return my grateful thanks to you for your offer of assistance, which at the proper time

I hope it may be convenient for you to give. You have been made aware by the papers in Captain May's possession, that I am not directly interested in this property, except as the executor of Mr. Custis. It will never be of any value to me, but I desire to turn it over to the rightful heir. I have not as yet taken any steps in the matter, under the belief that I could accomplish no good, nor do I wish now to do so, unless in your opinion some benefit would result from it.

"Mr. Francis L. Smith, of Alexandria, my friend and counsel before the war, is acquainted with all the circumstances of Mr. Custis's estate, and will be happy to give you any information you may at any time desire, or to procure you any evidence you may require.

"I hope someday that I may have the pleasure of meeting you again, and of renewing the friendly intercourse that formerly existed, and of thanking you in person for your kindness and consideration.

"With great respect, I am your obedient servant,

"R. E. LEE."

The following, written soon after the action of Congress, preventing the execution of an order to restore the Arlington relics, fully explains itself:

"LEXINGTON, VA.,
March 29, 1869.
"*Hon.* THOMAS LAWRENCE JONES, *Washington City, D.C.*

"MY DEAR SIR: I beg to be allowed to tender you my sincere thanks for your efforts to have restored to Mrs. Lee certain family relics in the patent office in Washington. The facts related in your speech in the House of Representatives on the 3d inst., so far as known to me, are correct; and, had I conceived the view taken of the matter by Congress, I would have endeavored to have dissuaded Mrs. Lee from applying for them. It may be a question with some whether the retention of these articles is more 'an insult,' in the language of the Committee on Public Buildings, 'to the loyal people of the United States,' than their restoration; but of this I am willing that they should be the judge; and, since Congress has decided to keep them, she must submit.

"Her thanks to you, sir, however, are not the less fervent for your kind intercession in her behalf; and, with highest regards, I am, with great respect,

"Your obedient servant,
"R. E. LEE."

The following is one of many similar letters which, although never published, exerted a most potent influence upon public sentiment in Virginia and the South:

"LEXINGTON, VA.,
June 11, 1869.

"*Major*————.

"MY DEAR SIR: Your letter has been received. I have great reluctance to speak on political subjects, because I am entirely withdrawn from their consideration, and therefore mistrust my own judgment. I have, however, said, in conversation with friends, that, if I was entitled to vote, I should vote for the excision of the obnoxious clauses of the proposed constitution, and for the election of the most conservative eligible candidates for Congress and the legislature. I believe this course offers the best prospect for the solution of the difficulties in which the state is involved, accessible to us. I think all who can should register and vote. Very truly yours,

"R. E. LEE."

The following shows his deep interest in all that concerns the material prosperity of the South:

"LEXINGTON, VA.,
September 14, 1869.

"*Colonel* BLANTON DUNCAN, *Chairman Committee*⎫
of Arrangements, Louisville, Ky.   ⎭

"DEAR SIR: I have had the honor to receive your invitation to attend as an honorary member of the Commercial Convention, to assemble at Louisville on the 12th of October next. The important measures proposed to be considered by the convention will attract the earnest attention of the whole country, and, I feel assured, will receive the calm deliberation which so momentous a subject as the advancement of the interests of all the states, the development of the wealth and resources of each, requires from American citizens. If we turn to the first history of the country and compare our material condition with that of our forefathers, when they bravely undertook, in the face of the difficulties which surrounded them, its organization and establishment, it would seem to be an easy task for us to revive what may be depressed, and to encourage what may be languishing in all the walks of life. We shall find it easy, if we cherish the same principles and practice the same virtues which governed them. Every man must, however, do his part in this great work. He must carry into the administration of his affairs industry, fidelity, and economy, and apply the knowledge taught by science to the promotion of agriculture, manufactures, and all industrial pursuits. As individuals prosper, communities will become rich, and the avenues and depots, required by trade and commerce, will be readily constructed. In my particular sphere I have to attend to my proper business, which occupies so much of my attention that I have but little time to devote to other things. I am unable, therefore, to accept your kind invitation, but I am happy in the belief that the enlightened delegates that will be present at the convention will do all that can be done for the good of the country. Thanking you for the kind manner in which your invitation has been extended, I am, with great respect, your obedient servant,

"R. E. LEE."

The following shows how widely his opinions were sought, and how far his influence extended:

"LEXINGTON, VA.,
January 6, 1870.
"DUNLAP SCOTT, *Esq., Georgia Legislature, Macon, Ga.*

"DEAR SIR: Your letter of the 3d has been received. I am very sorry for the new difficulties in which Georgia is involved, but hope that the united wisdom and prudence of her legislature may decide upon a course that will relieve her. What that course shall be I cannot pretend to say. The members of the legislature can alone decide. The responsibility rests solely upon them, and they have at heart the true interests of the state with that of all her people. If you will act in accordance with the dictates of your conscience, to the best of your judgment, and for the whole interests of your state, in her present emergency, unbiased by selfish or party considerations, you will do right. Thanking you for your kind expressions of regard and esteem, I am very truly yours,

"R. E. LEE."

Additional interest is added to the following letter by the death of the distinguished gentleman to whom it is addressed, and by the fact that it is among the last letters of this character which General Lee ever wrote:

"LEXINGTON, VA.,
March 3, 1870.

"*Hon.* JAMES M. MASON, *Alexandria, Va.*

"MY DEAR SIR: I thank you for your letter of the 25th ult., and still more for the kind feelings which prompted it. I rarely read newspaper articles about myself, and feel more humbled by the praise of my friends (knowing how little I merit it) than the censure of my enemies. The one seems to me to be as distant from the truth as the other. I desired to write to you upon your return to Virginia to express my pleasure at the event, and, but that I hoped to have soon seen you, should have done so. I have been so much indisposed this winter that I have not been able to go anywhere, and my regular avocations employed all the time I could devote to them. I hope, should you visit the mountains this summer, that you will come to Lexington to see us. I do not know that I will leave here, but whenever I go to Alexandria I shall take great pleasure in seeing you.

"I desired to attend Mr. Peabody's funeral, simply to show my respect for a man whom Americans might justly honor, and, had I felt able to undertake the journey at that inclement season, I should have gone for that single purpose. When I saw the protracted parade and lingering ceremony which was practiced on the occasion, so opposed to my feelings of sorrow and resignation, I regretted less my inability to attend. Please present my kindest regards to Mrs. Mason, your daughters and family, in which Mrs. Lee and my family cordially unite.

"With my best wishes for your health and happiness, I am most truly yours,

"R. E. LEE."

So careful was General Lee to observe scrupulously the terms of his parole, and to avoid even the appearance of political entanglements of every kind, that he refused to attend all public meetings which had any bearing upon the war or the political status of the country.

At the Virginia Springs, in 1869, a meeting was called to aid the scheme of Rev. Dr. W. F. Broaddus for the education of the orphans of Virginia soldiers. General Lee sympathized most heartily with this enterprise, and with the judicious manner in which it was conducted; he had frequent conferences and correspondence with Dr. Broaddus concerning it, and was accustomed every year to make most liberal contributions to the object. Yet he refused to attend this meeting—assigning as a reason that he desired to avoid all public gatherings that had anything to do with the war. Upon the same principle he refused to attend the "Gettysburg Identification" meeting, and wrote a letter in which he said: "I THINK IT WISEST NOT TO KEEP OPEN THE SORES OF WAR, BUT TO FOLLOW THE EXAMPLE OF THOSE NATIONS WHO ENDEAVORED TO OBLITERATE THE MARKS OF CIVIL STRIFE, AND TO COMMIT TO OBLIVION THE FEELINGS IT ENGENDERED." King William of Prussia has been justly eulogized for forbidding the celebration of the anniversary of Sadowa, "that he might not wound the feelings of any German people." But nobler still is the conduct of this great leader of a "Lost Cause," who would suppress natural resentment against successful wrong, forget the afflictions of the people he loved so well, and, instead of cherishing hatred against the enemies who had triumphed over the liberties of his country, would seek to heal "the sores of war," and "to commit to oblivion the feelings it engendered."

And yet this noble man died "a prisoner of war on parole"—his application for "amnesty" was never granted, or even noticed—and the commonest privileges of citizenship which are accorded to the most ignorant negro were denied to this *king of men.*

Chapter VII

General Lee had a quiet dignity which forbade all undue familiarity, and those who only saw him amid the pressing cares of the war might call him "reserved"; but in the social circle there was about him a charming affability and courtesy which won the hearts of all who had the privilege of meeting him thus.

It is related that, during one of his great marches, a plain old farmer started out from home with the full purpose of seeing General Lee. Riding up to a bivouac fire around which some officers were gathered, he was so courteously received by a plainly dressed "colonel" that he forgot his special mission and accepted an invitation to join the group. Presently he turned to his polite "colonel," and, expressing his great desire to see General Lee, was very much astonished at the quiet reply, "I am General Lee, and I am most happy to have met you."

Even amid his pressing duties at the college he found time to be the most thoroughly polite gentleman in the community. He seemed to think himself called on to visit all strangers who came to Lexington, and frequently surprised and delighted them by his unexpected courtesy. How often have I seen him in the stores and shops of the town, chatting pleasantly with every comer, or walking a mile through mud or snow to call on some humble family, who will hand it down as an event in their history that they had a visit from General Lee!

His house was the abode of real "old Virginia hospitality," and many visitors to Lexington will now recall with sad pleasure the grace and dignity with which they were welcomed to that model home.

Quiet and unobtrusive, a good listener, and always ready to allow others to lead the conversation, General Lee was yet possessed of very fine conversational powers, and showed the greatest tact in adapting himself to the tastes of his guests and making them feel at home. A plain farmer upon whose lands our troops were once camped told the writer that he had less difficulty in gaining access to General Lee, was treated by him with far more courtesy and felt more at home in his tent, than with certain quartermasters with whom he came in contact.

In the spring of 1869 an old gentleman, who was so deaf that it was exceedingly difficult to converse with him, called one evening at General Lee's house. The room was full of company, but the general took his seat beside his deaf visitor, talked to him with apparent ease, chose such topics as he was familiar with, and conducted the conversation with such tact that the old gentleman went away charmed with his visit.

General Lee rarely forgot a face or a name. I have seen him frequently recognize at once some old soldier whom he had barely met during the war, and who would be as surprised as delighted that his loved commander had not forgotten him. He knew by name nearly all of the ladies and children of Lexington and the vicinity, and seemed worried if he ever met one whom he failed to recognize. I remember seeing him once at a public gathering, very much annoyed at not knowing a young lady present, until he learned by diligent inquiry that she was a stranger who had just reached town that evening. The only occasion upon which I ever knew him to fail to recognize an old acquaintance was under the following circumstances: Seeing the general one morning coming down to the chapel with a gentleman who was evidently an Episcopal clergyman, I purposely threw myself in the way in order that I might be introduced, and thus have opportunity to ask him to officiate in my place at the chapel service. Noticing that in the introduction the general called my own name, but did not call that of the visitor, I said: "Excuse me, general, but I did not hear the name." With the inimitable grace peculiar to him, he replied: "It is time for us to go in to the service." As I came down from the pulpit the general (whose seat, by the way, was always near the front) met me and said: "I am ashamed to say, sir, that I do not know the name of that gentleman. And I am so sure that I ought to know him that I should be sorry for him to find out that I do not recognize him. I wish that you would ascertain his name." I immediately approached the gentleman, told him that I did not hear his name when introduced, and thus got him to give it. The general, who had followed within earshot, at once stepped up and began to introduce the gentleman to all around. The next day he said to me: "I was really very much ashamed at not knowing that gentleman yesterday; I ought to have recognized him at once. He spent at least an hour in my quarters in the city of Mexico just after its occupation by the American army, and, although I have never seen him since (and had never seen him before), he made a very agreeable impression upon me, and I ought not to have forgotten him."

I never saw General Lee's courtesy desert him for a moment, even amid the most trying circumstances.

His uniform courtesy and kindness were sometimes abused by thoughtless visitors who obtruded upon him at unseasonable hours, and still more by letters which flooded his mails, and to which he was very careful to reply. While at Washington College he received bushels of letters from all sorts of people on all sorts of subjects, and would worry himself to reply to them, when most men would have passed them by in silence. He one day showed the writer a letter from a distressed damsel in St. Louis, who said that her lover had been a soldier, "either in Mr. Lee's or Mr. Johnston's army"—that she had not heard from him since the close of the war, and that his family reported him dead, but she believed that this was only a trick on their part, to prevent him from marrying her. She wrote to beg that "Mr. Lee" would write her if he knew anything of him, and, if he did not, that he would write for her to "Mr. Johnston," to see if he could give her any information. General Lee made the most diligent inquiries after the man in question, saying that he "would be very glad to relieve the poor woman if he could," and, after all of his inquiries proved futile, he wrote her a kind letter of sympathy.

He received many letters from Federal officers, newspaper men, etc, and the mingled courtesy, tact, and quiet humor with which he would reply, would form a most interesting chapter if it were proper to publish the letters in full.

I cannot, however, refrain from giving the following *verbatim* copy of a reply to a distinguished Federal general, who wrote to propound to him certain questions which are plainly indicated in General Lee's answer:

"LEXINGTON, VA.,
January 18, 1869.

"DEAR SIR: A reply to your letter of the 4th inst. would require more time than I can devote to it, and lead to a discussion of military affairs from which, for reasons that will occur to you, I hope that you will excuse me.

"I will, therefore, only say that the failure of the Confederate army at Gettysburg was owing to a combination of circumstances, but for which success might have been reasonably expected.

"It is presumed that General Burnside had good reasons for his move from Warrenton to Fredericksburg; and, as far as I am able to judge, the earlier arrival of his pontoons at Aquia Creek would not have materially changed the result. Their appearance would only have produced an earlier concentration of the Confederate army at Fredericksburg. As regards General McClellan, I have always entertained a high opinion of his capacity, and have no reason to think that he omitted to do anything that was in his power.

"It is difficult for me to say what success would have attended the execution of your plan of moving the Federal army to Aquia Creek, after its attack on Fredericksburg, and of threatening Richmond from Fortress Monroe with the available troops in that quarter, and then entering the Rappahannock with the main army.

"I do not think that the Confederate army would have retreated to Richmond until the movement developed the necessity.

"After the accomplishment of an event it is so easy, with the aid of our after-knowledge, to correct errors that arise from previous want of information, that it is difficult to determine the weight that should be given to conclusions thus reached.

"Thanking you for your expressions of kindness, and regretting my inability to comply more fully with your wishes,

                              "I am, very truly, your obedient servant,
                                                           "R. E. LEE."

The above letter was *never published;* but it is hoped that the distinguished gentleman to whom it was addressed will pardon its introduction here, as I have carefully suppressed his name. Upon another occasion General Lee received a letter from some spirit-rappers, asking his opinion on a certain great military movement. He wrote in reply a most courteous letter, in which he said that the question was one about which military critics would differ; that his own judgment about such matters was but poor at best, and that inasmuch as they had power to consult (through their mediums) Cæsar, Alexander, Napoleon, Wellington, and all of the other great captains who have ever lived, he could not think of obtruding his opinion into such company. He astonished the writer one day, a few weeks before his death, by showing him a letter from one of the editors of a New York paper, inquiring what battle it was in which General Lee asked of General McClellan a truce to bury his dead—and asking me if

I remembered. Upon replying that it was my very decided conviction that, in all of his contests with General McClellan, the flag of truce had to come *from the other side;* that Sharpsburg was the only battle at which it *could* have occurred, and that there was no formal truce there, though a tacit understanding on a part of the line, by which both parties gathered up their dead and wounded—he quietly replied: "Yes! that is my impression. I remember distinctly that at Sharpsburg we held a large part of the battlefield, that we remained in line of battle the whole of the next day, expecting—*and in fact hoping for*—an attack, and that we only withdrew upon information that the enemy was being largely reinforced. But this gentleman writes to me (I wish he had written to General McClellan, *he* could have told him), and I desired before answering him to confirm my impression by that of others."

Not long after the close of the war General Lee received a letter from General David Hunter, of the Federal army, in which he begged information upon two points:

1. His (Hunter's) campaign in the summer of 1864 was undertaken on information received at the War Department in Washington that General Lee was about to detach forty thousand picked troops to send to General Johnston. Did not his (Hunter's) movements prevent this, and relieve Sherman to that extent?

2. When he found it necessary to retreat from before Lynchburg, did he not adopt the most feasible line of retreat?

General Lee wrote a very courteous reply, in which he said: "The information upon which your campaign was undertaken was erroneous. I had *no troops* to spare General Johnston, and no intention of sending him any—*certainly not forty thousand, as that would have taken about all I had.*

"As to the second point, I would say that I am not advised as to the motives which induced you to adopt the line of retreat which you took, and am not, perhaps, competent to judge of the question; *but I certainly expected you to retreat by way of the Shenandoah Valley,* and was gratified at the time that you preferred the route through the mountains to the Ohio—leaving the valley open for General Early's advance into Maryland."

There was a quiet humor, and upon occasion a keen wit, in General Lee, which was only appreciated by those who came into intimate contact with him. Hon. B. H. Hill, in the speech from which an extract in the previous chapter is taken, gives the following:

"Lee sometimes indulged in satire, to which his greatness gave point and power. He was especially severe on newspaper criticisms of military movements—subjects about which the writers knew nothing.

" 'We made a great mistake, Mr. Hill, in the beginning of our struggle, and I fear, in spite of all we can do, it will prove to be a fatal mistake,' he said to me, after General Bragg ceased to command the Army of Tennessee, an event Lee deplored.

" 'What mistake is that, General?'

" 'Why, sir, in the beginning we appointed all our worst generals to command the armies, and all our best generals to edit the newspapers. As you know, I have planned some campaigns and quite a number of battles. I have given the work all the care and thought I could, and sometimes, when my plans were completed, as far as I could see, they seemed to be perfect. But when I have fought them through, I have discovered defects and occasionally wondered I did not see some of the defects in advance. When it was all over, I found by reading a newspaper that these best editor generals saw all the defects plainly from the start. Unfortunately, they did not communicate their knowledge to me until it was too late.' Then, after a pause, he added, with a beautiful, grave expression I can never forget: 'I have no ambition but to serve the Confederacy, and do all I can to win our independence. I am willing to serve in any capacity to which the authorities may assign me. I have done the best I could in the field, and have not succeeded as I could wish. I am willing to yield my place to these best generals, and I will do my best for the cause editing a newspaper.' "

In the same strain he once remarked to one of his generals: "Even as poor a soldier as I am can generally discover mistakes *after it is all over.* But if I could only induce these wise gentlemen who see them so clearly *beforehand* to communicate with me *in advance,* instead of waiting until the evil has come upon us, to let me know that *they knew all the time,* it would be far better for my reputation, and (what is of more consequence) far better for the cause."

He had a quiet humor in administering his rebukes which made them very keenly felt by those who were so unfortunate as to incur in any way his disapprobation.

The following incidents may serve as specimens of many more that might be given:

After the battle of Malvern Hill had ceased, and McClellan had left the ground of his gallant defense for Harrison's Landing, one of the Confederate commanders, who had not been fortunate in his management of the attack, and was not aware that McClellan had retreated, galloped up to General Lee and exclaimed with considerable vehemence: "If you will permit me, sir, I will charge that hill with my whole force and carry it at the point of the bayonet." "No doubt you could *now* succeed," was the quiet reply, "but I have one serious objection to your making the attack at this time." "May I ask what that objection is?" was the eager question of the ardent soldier, who saw honor and glory before him in the present opportunity. "I am afraid, sir," rejoined the commander-in-chief, with a mischievous twinkle of the eye which all around enjoyed greatly, "that you would hurt my little friend, Captain———. The enemy left about an hour ago, and he is over there with a reconnoitering party."

While at winter quarters at Peterburg, a party of officers were one night busily engaged in discussing, at the same time, a mathematical problem and the contents of a stone jug which was garnished by two tin cups. In the midst of this General Lee came in to make some inquiry. He got the information he wanted, gave a solution of the problem, and went out, the officers expressing to each other the hope that the general had not noticed the jug and cups. The next day one of the officers, in the presence of the others, was relating to General Lee a very strange dream he had the night before. The general listened with apparent interest to the narrative, and quietly rejoined: "That is not at all remarkable. When young gentlemen discuss at midnight mathematical problems, the unknown quantities of which are a stone jug and two tin cups, they may expect to have strange dreams."

One day, at Petersburg, General Lee, who never suffered a day to pass without visiting some part of his lines, rode by the quarters of one of his major generals, and requested him to ride with him. As they were going he asked General——— if a certain work which he had ordered to be pushed was completed. He replied with some hesitation that it was, and General Lee then proposed that they should go and see it. Arriving at the spot it was found that little or no progress had been made since they were there a week before, and General——— was profuse in his apologies, saying that he had not seen the work since they were there together, but that he had ordered it to be completed at once, and that Major——— had informed him that it had been already finished. General Lee said nothing then, except to remark, quietly, "We must give our personal attention to the lines." But, riding on a little farther, he began to compliment General——— on the splendid charger he rode. "Yes, sir," said General———, "he is a splendid animal, and I prize him the more highly because he belongs to my wife, and is her favorite riding horse." "A magnificent horse," rejoined General Lee, "but I should not think him safe for Mrs.——— to ride. He is entirely too spirited for a lady, and I would urge you by all means to take some of the mettle out of him before you suffer Mrs.——— to ride him again. And, by the way, General, I would suggest to you that *these rough paths along these trenches would be very admirable ground over which to tame him.*" The face of the gallant soldier turned crimson; he felt most keenly the rebuke, and never afterward reported the condition of his lines upon information received from Major———, or any one else. His spirited charger felt the effect of this hint from headquarters.

One of the professors in the college was one day making a very earnest speech at a meeting of the faculty on the best means of securing a full attendance of the students at the chapel service. It so happened that this excellent gentleman (as well as some other members of the faculty) was not in the habit of attending chapel himself. When he had finished his speech, President Lee quietly said: "One of the best ways that I know of to induce the students to attend chapel is to be sure that we attend ourselves." And accordingly his seat was never vacant, unless he was kept away by absence from home or sickness.

The general used to enjoy very much a quiet joke at the expense of some overconfident student. The writer heard him, one day, introduce a new student to one of the professors by saying, with a quiet smile: "This young gentleman is going to graduate in one session." "No, General," replied the youth, "you misunderstood me; I did not say that I would graduate in one, but in two sessions." "Ah, he has concluded to postpone it for a session. Well, sir, I wish you the full realization of your hopes; but I must tell you that you will have no time to play baseball."

It may be as well to introduce at this point a number of his private letters, which, written without any expectation that they would ever be published, will be read with deep interest as illustrating not only his social character, but other points as well.

"LEXINGTON, VA.,
October 25, 1865.

"*Messrs.* SCRANTON & BURR, *Hartford, Conn.*

"GENTLEMEN: I have received your letter of the 13th inst., and fear I was not sufficiently explicit in my former communication. I cannot now undertake the work you propose, nor can I enter into an engagement to do what I may never be able to accomplish. I have not read the histories of the late war to which you refer, but think it natural they should be of the character you describe. It will be some time before the truth can be known, and I do not think that period has yet arrived. I am unwilling that you should unnecessarily undertake a wearisome journey; but if, after what I have said, you should still desire an interview with me, it will give me pleasure to see you at this place.

"Very respectfully, your obedient servant,
"R. E. LEE."

"WASHINGTON COLLEGE, LEXINGTON, VA.,
March 22, 1866.

"WARREN NEWCOMB, *Esq., New York City, N.Y.*

"SIR: The pleasing duty of transmitting to you the accompanying copy of the proceedings of the trustees of Washington College, at their meeting on the 10th inst., has been conferred upon me by the board.

"In presenting to you their grateful thanks for your generous aid in behalf of the college, I beg leave to express my sense of your liberality to the cause of education, now so essential to the prosperity of the South. The reestablishment of her colleges upon a broad and enlightened basis, calculated to provide for the proper instruction of her people, and to develop her dormant resources, is one of the greatest benefits that can be conferred upon the country.

"Those contributing to this great result will be ranked by posterity among the most meritorious citizens.

"With sentiments of great esteem, I am your obed't serv't,
"R. E. LEE."

"LEXINGTON, VA.,
March 26, 1866.
"*Mr.* RATHMELL WILSON, 919 *Clinton Street, Philadelphia, Pa.*

"SIR: I have delayed replying to your letter of the 12th inst. until I could inform you of the arrival of the books which you have so generously bestowed upon Washington College. The six (6) boxes described in your letter arrived in safety and good order on Saturday last, and today the books have been properly arranged in a part of the library appropriated to them, where shelves are reserved for the other volumes which you mention. They will be preserved with care, and be designated as 'The Wilson Contribution to the Library of Washington College.'

"They form the most valuable collection in the library, will do much for the advancement of science, give an impulse to the spread and development of that knowledge so highly valued by your esteemed brother, and cause his memory to be revered and cherished by the wise and good.

"I am, with great respect, your obedient servant,
"R. E. LEE."

"LEXINGTON, VA.,
March 27, 1866.
"*Mr.*———, *Louisville, Ky.*

"MY DEAR SIR: In reply to your communication of the 19th inst., stating your kind intentions in behalf of the Literary Societies of Washington College, I have the honor to transmit a letter of thanks from each society. There is scarcely a feature in the organization of the college more improving or beneficial to the students than the exercises and influence of the societies; and the good they accomplish renders them worthy of encouragement by the friends of education.

"I therefore present to you, and to those who are united with you, my cordial thanks for the aid you propose.

"Very respectfully, your obedient servant,
"R. E. LEE."

"Lexington, Va.,
April 5, 1866.

"*Mr.* William H. Hope, *City of New York.*

"My dear Sir: I am greatly obliged to you for your kind letter of the 22d ult., and for the interest you express for the fate of Arlington. I should like to recover it, that I might, as the executor of Mr. G. W. P. Custis, carry out the provisions of his will. I did not know that it had been sold for taxes on the 11th of January, 1864, as stated in the newspaper slip you enclosed. It was seized by the United States troops in the spring of 1861 while in possession of a regularly appointed manager, who was conducting the usual agricultural operations. I should have thought that the use of the grounds, the large amount of wood on the place, the teams, etc., and the sale of the furniture of the house, would have been sufficient to have paid the taxes. I do not know whether the secretary of war would relinquish possession of the estate, or permit its redemption under the Virginia laws. If he did, and should require the $26,860, stated to have been bid for it by the United States, to be refunded, it would be out of my power to redeem it. With my sincere thanks for your friendly letter,

"I am, very truly, your obedient servant,
"R. E. Lee."

"Lexington, Va.,
April, 6, 1866.

"Alfred H. Guernsey, *Care of Harper & Brothers,*
    Franklin Square, New York.

"Sir: I have received your letter of the 22d ult., requesting the numbers of the Confederate army in the battles around Richmond, in 1862. I have not access to the returns of the army at that time, or I would comply with your request.

"Very respectfully, your obedient servant,
"R. E. Lee."

"ROCKBRIDGE BATHS, VA.,
August 4, 1866.

"CHAS. F. DEEMS, D. D., *Editor* Watchman, *New York City.*

"MY DEAR SIR: I am very much obliged to you for your kind letter
of the 27th ult., and beg to return you my thanks for the friendly
sentiments it contained. I have derived much satisfaction from the
numbers of the *Watchman* you have kindly sent me, but it will be
out of my power to contribute anything to its columns. My time is
fully occupied, and I cannot undertake to do more. No one can have
more at heart the welfare of the young men of the country than I
have. It is the hope of doing something for the benefit of those at
the South that has led me to take my present office. My only object
is to endeavor to make them see their true interest, to teach them to
labor diligently for their improvement, and to prepare themselves for
the great work of life. Wishing you every happiness and success, I
am, etc.,

"R. E. LEE."

The two following letters, addressed to the distinguished scholar from
whose tribute to Lee a quotation is made in a previous chapter, will be
read with peculiar interest:

"LEXINGTON, VA.,
February 10, 1866.

"*Mr.* P. S. WORSLEY.

"MY DEAR SIR: I have received the copy of your translation of the
Iliad, which you so kindly presented to me. Its perusal has been my
evening's recreation, and I have never enjoyed the beauty and grandeur of the poem more than as recited by you. The translation is as
truthful as powerful, and faithfully reproduces the imagery and
rhythm of the bold original.

"The undeserved compliment to myself in prose and verse, on the
first leaves of the volume, I receive as your tribute to the merit of
my countrymen who struggled for constitutional government.

"With great respect, your obedient servant,
"R. E. LEE."

"LEXINGTON, VA.,
March 14, 1866.

"*Mr.* P. S. WORSLEY.

"MY DEAR MR. WORSLEY: In a letter just received from my nephew, Mr. Childe, I regret to learn that, at his last accounts from you, you were greatly indisposed. So great is my interest in your welfare, that I cannot refrain, even at the risk of intruding upon your sick room, from expressing my sincere sympathy in your affliction. I trust, however, that ere this you have recovered, and are again in perfect health. Like many of your tastes and pursuits, I fear you may confine yourself too closely to your reading: less mental labor, and more of the fresh air of heaven, might bring to you more comfort, and to your friends more enjoyment, even in the way in which you now delight them. Should a visit to this distracted country promise you any recreation, I hope I need not assure you how happy I should be to see you at Lexington. I can give you a quiet room and careful nursing, and a horse that would delight to carry you over our beautiful mountains. I hope my letter informing you of the pleasure I derived from the perusal of your translation of the *Iliad,* in which I endeavored to express my thanks for the great compliment you paid me in its dedication, has informed you of my high appreciation of the work. Wishing you every happiness in this world, and praying that eternal peace may be your portion in that to come,

"I am, most truly, your friend and servant,
"R. E. LEE."

"LEXINGTON, VA.,
April 16, 1866.

"*Lieutenant* VON CLAUSENITZ, *Germany.*

"SIR: I have had the honor to receive your letter of the 13th of March, offering to translate into German the history of the late war in America, which you understood that I was engaged in writing.

"It has been my desire to write a history of the campaigns in Virginia; but I have not yet been able to commence it, and it is so uncertain that I shall be able to accomplish my purpose, that I think it unnecessary to make any arrangements for its translation into a foreign language. Should circumstances hereafter render such a course proper, I shall not forget your kind proposition.

"Thanking you most cordially for the interest you have taken in the Southern states, and for the kind sentiments you manifest toward myself,

"I am, with great respect, your obedient servant,

"R. E. LEE."

"LEXINGTON VA.,
April 17, 1866.

"Mr.——, New York City, N.Y.

"SIR: I thank you for your offer presented in your note of the 9th inst., but I am now unable to purchase works of art of any kind. The White House of Pamunkey, as it lives in my memory, must suffice for my purpose.

"Very respectfully, your obedient servant,

"R. E. LEE."

"LEXINGTON, VA.,
April 30, 1866.

"Rev. ALEX B. GROSART, 308 *Upper Parliament* ⎫
Street, Liverpool, England. ⎭

"MY DEAR SIR: I have had the pleasure to receive the English Bible which in your note of the 26th ult. you announced had been forwarded to my address. It is one of the best copies of the Holy Scriptures that I have ever seen, and is particularly valuable to me from the circumstances associated with its presentation, and as a token of the generous sympathy of the donors, among whom I perceive the names of some of England's most worthy citizens.

"I hope you will allow me to repeat my request that you will give to them my sincere thanks for a gift so precious.

"I am extremely obliged to you for the set of your writings which accompanied the Bible. After perusal I will place them in the library of Washington College, that all connected with it may partake of their benefit.

"I am, with great respect, most cordially yours,

"R. E. LEE."

"LEXINGTON, VA.,
May 3, 1866.

"*Mrs.*———, *Baltimore, Md.*

"I received this morning the gown presented to me by the ladies of the Northeastern Branch tables, 40 and 42, at the late fair held in Baltimore.

"I beg that you will express to them my grateful thanks for this mark of kindness, which I shall value most highly in remembrance of their munificent bounty bestowed on thousands of destitute women and children by the 'Association for the Relief of Southern Sufferers,' the fruits of which shall live long after those who have received it have mouldered into dust.

"With great respect, your obedient servant,

"R. E. LEE."

"LEXINGTON, VA.,
May 5, 1866.

"C. R. BISHOP, JR., *P.O. Box* 482, *Petersburg, Va.*

"SIR: I have received your letter of the 1st inst., informing me of my election as an honorary member of the Stonewall Literary Society of Petersburg.

"Please present to the society my grateful thanks for associating me in their laudable design of self-improvement, in accomplishing which I can commend to them no more worthy example than his whose name they have adopted.

"Very respectfully,

"R. E. LEE."

"LEXINGTON, VA.,
May 12, 1866.

"The Ladies of the Southern Relief Fair, Baltimore, Md.

"I beg leave to present to the ladies of the Southern Relief Fair my grateful thanks for the handsome saddle and bridle which they have been so kind as to send me from Mr. Farquharson.

"Were I not reminded at every point to which I turn, at the South, of their benevolent labors for its relief, their gift would serve to keep me in mind of their sympathy and generosity.

"With great respect,
"R. E. LEE."

"LEXINGTON, VA.,
May 21, 1866.

"Mr. W. H. NETTLETON, *Care of Southwestern*
Telegraph Office, New Orleans, La.

"SIR: I am very much obliged to you for the kind sentiments expressed in your letter of the 11th inst. toward myself and my native state. Your visit to America must have impressed upon you the fact that, though climate, government, and circumstances have produced changes in the character of the people, yet in all essential qualities they resemble the races from which they are sprung; and that to no race are we more indebted for the virtues which constitute a great people than to the Anglo-Saxon. You will carry back with you to England my best wishes for your future happiness, and

"I am, very respectfully, your obedient servant,
"R. E. LEE."

"LEXINGTON, VA.,
May 23, 1866.

"Mr.———, *Fort Riley, Kansas.*

"MY DEAR SIR: I have received your letter of the 21st ult., and send a prospectus of the course of studies, etc., at Washington College.

"You will see the character of instruction given at the institution, and can judge whether it will suit the views you entertain for the education of your son. If he really desires to learn, I think it will afford him ample opportunity.

"There are other colleges in Virginia where a student anxious for the acquisition of knowledge can be accommodated.

"The University of Virginia at Charlottesville is the largest institution of learning at the South, and has enjoyed the highest reputation. After the attainment of a collegiate education, such as may desire can enter the schools of law or medicine, and acquire the knowledge of a profession.

"At this place there is an excellent law school, of which Judge Brockenbrough is the principal; but there is no school of medicine.

"Hoping that your selection of a school for your son may advance his true interest, I remain, respectfully,

"Your obedient servant,
"R. E. LEE."

"LEXINGTON, VA.,
May 25, 1866.
"*Colonel* ———.

"MY DEAR COLONEL: In compliance with your request of the 21st, I send a general statement of your services while with the Army of Northern Virginia. I hope it may answer your purpose. But I think an old engineer-officer ought to make a good farmer; and I advise you not to abandon such an honorable and independent pursuit, until you are very sure you can do better.

"Very respectfully yours,
"R. E. LEE."

"LEXINGTON, VA.,
June 1, 1866.
"*Messrs.* ——————, *South Sharp Street, Baltimore, Md.*

"GENTLEMEN: I am much obliged to you for your kind offer to send me a hat, and appreciate most highly the motives which prompt it. When so many are destitute, I dislike to have more than I actually require, and yet am unwilling to appear insensible to your sentiments of friendship and sympathy. I have a very good hat, which will answer my purpose the whole year; and would, therefore, prefer you to give to others what I really do not require. If, however, after what I have said, you still wish to present me with what I can well do without, I cannot refuse what you say will be a gratification to you.

"I am, very respectfully, your obedient servant,

"R. E. LEE."

"LEXINGTON, VA.,
June 5, 1866.

"*Colonel*———.

"MY DEAR SIR: I have been intending to write to you for some weeks; but, as I knew that what I desire to say would not be pleasing, I have deferred from day to day, in the hope that the necessity for my letter might be avoided. I think, however, it is better that you should know what I have to relate.

"I fear your son John has not been as attentive to his studies as he might have been. But, however that may be, he certainly has not progressed as I desired him, or as you might wish him. It is true, he has been sick; had an attack of mumps, which caused him to be absent for a time; and indisposition may have rendered him indisposed to study. I have, in a friendly way, called his attention to his apparent neglect of his studies, and to the injury he would thereby do himself, which he received in the same spirit in which it was given, and at the time was, no doubt, in earnest in his intention to change his course. But, as far as I can judge from the reports of his teachers, he is not spending his time profitably; and, unless he should show some marked improvement before the end of the session, I would recommend you to withdraw him from the college. Such, I may add, is the opinion of the faculty. I do not think it would be to his advantage to continue here without reaping an adequate return for the expenditure of his time and money. I hope you will excuse the freedom with which I have written; but I have been prompted by a desire to give you such information as would enable you to direct the course of your son to his own benefit, and your own satisfaction.

"Very respectfully, your obedient servant,

"R. E. LEE."

"LEXINGTON, VA.,
August 11, 1866.

"*Messrs.———————, Richmond, Va.*

"GENTLEMEN: I have received the armchair which you have forwarded to me, at the request of Mr.———, of Baltimore. It possesses
for me now a double value, as recalling its former use and illustrious
associations, with the pleasing remembrance of living friends whose
kindness never ceases and whose thoughtful consideration never
wearies. I beg that you will express to Mr.——— my sense of gratitude for his gift, and that you will accept my thanks for the agreeable manner in which you have presented it.

"I am, very respectfully, yours, etc., etc.,
"R. E. LEE."

"LEXINGTON, VA.,
August 29, 1866.

"———————, *Richmond, Va.*

"GENTLEMEN: I have received your letter of the 28th inst., and thank
you for the compliment tendered me in the proposed name of your
club. While I feel no desire for such distinction, I do not wish to
control your preferences, and therefore leave the matter to your own
decision. It might answer your purposes as well, perhaps, to bestow
upon your club some real appellation, such as 'Virginia,' 'Richmond,' or, if you desire a name more closely connected with my
own, 'Arlington.'

"Very respectfully, etc., etc.,
"R. E. LEE."

"LEXINGTON, VA.,
August 30, 1866.

"*Mr.* WILLIAM B. REED, *Chestnut Hill, near Philadelphia.*

"MY DEAR SIR: I am greatly indebted to you for the package of my
father's letters which you have kindly sent me. They will be doubly
valuable to me, as relics of one whose memory I cherish and venerate, and as mementos of your 'sincere regard.' I shall take renewed
interest in referring to your *Life of General Reed,* and shall endeavor

to procure Mr. Dawson's pamphlet on 'Stony Point.' I have long wished to see some points in the chapter on Sergeant Champe in the *Memoirs* cleared up. Of the main facts I think there can be no reasonable doubt. They are narrated with clearness and distinctness, and it is stated that, soon after the return of Champe, his story became known to the 'Legion,' and that he was introduced to General Greene, who cheerfully complied with the promises of Washington. The *Memoirs* were first published in 1811 or '12. Many officers of the corps must have been then alive—Dr. Irvine certainly was, as also Judge Peter Johnson and Major Gardner. The latter, in his *Anecdotes of the Revolution,* could hardly have restrained the expression of his surprise unless he possessed some knowledge of the truth of the story. The late Judge Brooke, of the Court of Appeals of Virginia, told my brother, C. C. Lee, that he was familiar with Champe's enterprise long before the publication of the *Memoirs,* having learned it from his brother, for whom Champe's brother was overseer. I cannot think, with Colonel Allen McLane, that it is a romance. The fact that he, as commander of Paulus Hook, did not know of the desertion of Champe, is no proof that it did not occur. It is not customary in military operations for post commanders to know everything that happens, nor is it usual for the names or acts of those employed in secret service to be known. Even their immediate commanders are kept in as much ignorance as possible of their movements, and the personal staff of the general-in-chief are as ignorant of them as the private soldier.

"That there was a plan for taking Arnold, is proved by the letter of Washington, in his own handwriting, of the 20th of October, 1780, to Major Lee, in which he gives it his approval, agrees to the promised rewards, adds certain instructions, and directs that under no circumstances should he be put to death. Washington is said to have had other objects in view, in the capture of Arnold, than saving the life of André. The most important was to ascertain the truth of the information received through his confidential agents in New York, that many of his officers were connected with Arnold, and after the execution of André, 13th of October, he commanded Major Lee to communicate it to Champe, with directions to prosecute with vigor the remaining objects of his instructions, and expressed to him his satisfaction, in his letter of the 13th of October (also in his own handwriting), at the reception of the documents from Champe, exculpating the major general who had been named by his agents.

"If, in your reading, you can recall any facts tending to decide the matter, I shall be under additional obligations to you if you will mention them.

"Most truly yours,

"R. E. LEE."

"LEXINGTON, VA.,

September 5, 1866.

"*Hon.* A. J. REQUIER, 81 *Cedar Street, New York.*

"MY DEAR SIR: I am very much obliged to you for your kind letter of the 22d ult. So many articles formerly belonging to me are scattered over the country, that I fear I have not time to devote to their recovery. I know no one in Buffalo whom I could ask to reclaim the Bible in question. If the lady who has it will use it as I hope she will, she will herself seek to restore it to its rightful owner. I will, therefore, leave the decision of the question to her and her conscience. I have read with great pleasure the poem you sent me, and thank you sincerely for your interest in my behalf.

"With great respect, etc.,

"R. E. LEE."

"LEXINGTON, VA.,

September 26, 1866.

"*Mrs.* MILES LELLS, *St. Louis, Mo.*

"I received, this morning, your letter of the 19th inst., and hasten to express my deep sympathy in the object of the Southern Relief Association of St. Louis. A cause so benevolent as the relief of suffering women and children will be sure to elicit the kindest feelings of your great and populous city, and awaken the interest of the whole West in your enterprise. Its success, therefore, cannot be doubtful, and I feel assured the result will equal your highest expectations. You may be certain of the profound gratitude of the people of the South, and of their earnest wishes for your prosperity.

"With great respect, your obedient servant,

"R. E. LEE."

"LEXINGTON, VA.,
November 1, 1866.
"*Mr.* W. PARKER SNOW, *Nyack, N.Y.*

"MY DEAR SIR: I regret that it will be out of my power to furnish you with the information you require for your proposed work. I can readily understand the nature of the difficulties which you will have to encounter, but my time is so fully occupied with my present engagements, that I can scarcely keep pace with my current correspondence. I hope that you will be able to visit the scenes of the events you describe, and to ascertain the true circumstances connected with them. I feel assured that all concerned at the South will take pleasure in giving you any information in their power. As you state that you did not receive my answer to your former letter, I enclose you a copy.

"Very respectfully, your obedient servant,
"R. E. LEE."

"LEXINGTON, VA.,
December 13, 1866.
"*General* THOMAS L. ROSSER, 634 *Lexington Street, Baltimore.*

"MY DEAR GENERAL: I have considered the questions in your letter of the 8th inst., and am unable to advise as to the efficacy of the scheme proposed for the accomplishment of the object in view. That can be better determined by those more conversant with similar plans than I am.

"As regards the erection of such a monument as is contemplated, my conviction is, that, however grateful it would be to the feelings of the South, the attempt, in the present condition of the country, would have the effect of retarding instead of accelerating its accomplishment, and of continuing if not adding to the difficulties under which the Southern people labor. All, I think, that can now be done is to aid our noble and generous women in their efforts to protect the graves and mark the last resting places of those who have fallen, and wait for better times.

"I am very glad to hear of your comfortable establishment in

Baltimore, and that Mrs. Rosser is with you. Please present to her my warm regards. It would give me great pleasure to meet you both anywhere, and especially at times of leisure in the mountains of Virginia, but such times look too distant for me to contemplate, much less for me now to make arrangements for.

"Very truly yours,
"R. E. LEE."

"LEXINGTON, VA.,
December 15, 1865.

"*Mrs.*————.

"I received yesterday your letter of the 6th inst., inviting me to Baltimore, and hasten to return my sincere thanks for the kind and earnest manner in which it was given.

"I am fully aware of the many and repeated acts of sympathy and relief bestowed by the generous citizens of Baltimore upon the people of the South, acts which will always be remembered, but which can never be repaid, and which will forever stand as monuments of their Christian charity and kindness.

"I know, too, that by their munificence they have brought loss and suffering on themselves, for which I trust God will reward them. I need not, I hope, assure you of the pleasure it would give me to express to them the gratitude I feel; but I cannot do it in the way you propose, even if my engagements permitted; and I therefore hope you will excuse me for declining your invitation.

"The exercises of the college are only suspended Christmas day, and my presence here is required.

"With great respect,
"R. E. LEE."

"LEXINGTON, VA.
April 16, 1867.
"*Rev.* JOHN W. BROWN, *Rector of St. Ann's, Middletown, Del.*

"MY DEAR SIR: I have received your letter of the 11th inst., enclosing your draft for eighty dollars for the relief of the suffering people of the South. In its application I will endeavor to select objects worthy of the donation; and I feel assured that the blessing of God will accompany a gift dictated by benevolent motives, and hallowed by pious memories. I sympathize with you deeply in the death of your noble brother, and trust he has received the reward of duty faithfully performed.

"With great respect, your obedient servant,

"R. E. LEE."

The following outburst of feeling on the release of his warm personal friend (ex-President Davis) from prison will be read with deep interest:

"LEXINGTON, VA.,

June 1, 1867.

"*Hon.* JEFFERSON DAVIS.

"MY DEAR MR. DAVIS: You can conceive better than I can express the misery which your friends have suffered from your long imprisonment, and the other afflictions incident thereto. To none has this been more painful than to me, and the impossibility of affording relief has added to my distress. Your release has lifted a load from my heart which I have not words to tell, and my daily prayer to the great Ruler of the world is, that He may shield you from all future harm, guard you from all evil, and give you that peace which the world cannot take away.

"That the rest of your days may be triumphantly happy is the sincere and earnest wish of

"Your most obedient, faithful friend and servant,

"R. E. LEE."

"LEXINGTON, VA.,

June 18, 1867.

"*Mr.* H. S. MCKEE, *Eastman Business College, Poughkeepsie, N.Y.*

"MY DEAR SIR: I beg leave to return my sincere thanks to the 'Lee Association' for the handsome photographic picture of its founders. It will keep in my remembrance the youthful features of those whose friendly sentiments will cause them to live always in my heart.

"With my best wishes for the success of your Association, and for the individual happiness of all its members,

"I am, with great respect, your obedient servant,

"R. E. LEE."

"WASHINGTON COLLEGE, LEXINGTON, VA.,

June 18, 1867.

"*Mr.* E. V. ELLIOT, *President Ghent College,*
Care of James S. Frank, Ghent, Ky. }

"MY DEAR SIR: I have received your letter of the 1st inst., and highly appreciate the invitation of the board of directors of Ghent College, Ky., to visit their institution at its opening on the 1st of September next, and regret that it will not be in my power to do so. I beg, therefore, that you will present to the board my sincere thanks for their invitation, and my earnest wishes for the success of their college.

"At no period in the history of the country was the right education of its youth of so much importance to its welfare as at present, and the establishment of every suitable institution of learning should be a source of congratulation to its citizens.

"Reciprocating all your friendly sentiments, and hoping that our acquaintance may be extended,

"I am, with great respect, your obedient servant,

"R. E. LEE."

"LEXINGTON, VA.,

June 24, 1867.

"*Mrs.* ANN UPSHUR JONES, 156 *Lafayette Avenue, Brooklyn, N.Y.*

"MY DEAR MADAM: I have had the honor to receive your letter of the 17th inst., and send to your address a catalogue of Washington College, and a copy of its charter and laws. On the thirty-seventh page of the former, and the eleventh of the latter, you will find what is prescribed on the subject of religion. I do not know that it ever has been sectarian in its character since it was chartered as a college; but it certainly is not so now. Located in a Presbyterian community, it is natural that most of its trustees and faculty should be of that denomination, though the rector, president, and several of the professors, are members of the Episcopal Church. It is the furthest from my wish to divert any donation from the Theological Seminary at Alexandria, for I am well acquainted with the merits of the institution, have a high respect for its professors, and am an earnest advocate of its object. I only give you the information you desire, and wish you to follow your own preferences in the matter.

"With great respect, your obedient servant,
"R. E. Lee."

The several letters which follow are specimens of a large number of the same character which his rigid conscientiousness compelled him to write:

"Near Cartersville, Va.,
September 4, 1865.

"*Major*————

"MY DEAR MAJOR: I have received your note of the 1st expressing your wish to use my name as reference in the partnership you propose entering into with Captain————, for conducting a general commission business in Richmond. My official intercourse has been so large, and my military connection so extensive with the people of the Southern states, during the last four years, that, were I to begin to endorse all who with equal propriety might apply to me, it would defeat the objects in view. Neither would I know how to discriminate between those who in my opinion possess such great merit, and who have won my admiration and regard. Besides, I know nothing of commercial affairs, and could say nothing as to their business capacity. The endorsation of business men would be far more valuable and appropriate. These considerations have mainly compelled me to decline similar applications that have been made to me. I hope they may be sufficient to excuse me for not violating in your case the rule I have established for my guidance. I will do anything personally I can for your benefit, and you may always be assured of any aid I can with propriety afford. If you will be kind enough to give these reasons to Captain————, from whom I have received a similar application, and of the same date as yours, it will serve as an answer to him. With kindest regards to your mother and sisters.

"I am most truly yours,
"R. E. LEE."

"LEXINGTON, VA.,
March 26, 1866.

"*Mrs.*————.

"MY DEAR MADAM: It would give me much pleasure to do anything in my power for Prof.————, who, from your account, and others that have reached me, I believe showed great kindness to our prisoners at Elmira. For this he deserves, and will no doubt receive, the thanks of the humane, not only at the South, but elsewhere; but of myself I know nothing, and can therefore say nothing. Those who are acquainted with the circumstances, and can state the facts from their own knowledge, are the persons whose testimony would be of weight and value: not those who could only repeat from hearsay. I am sorry to learn that his sympathy with the unfortunate has brought upon him unkind feelings from any quarter, but trust this is only temporary, and that his conduct will yet redound to his credit.

"Mrs. Lee joins me in kind regards to you, and to your family. You must not think I have forgotten you; I have you and yours distinctly in remembrance. As these letters enclosed to me may be of use to you, I return them.

"With great respect, I am very truly yours,
"R. E. LEE."

"LEXINGTON, VA.,
March 21, 1866.

"*Mrs.*————, *Georgetown, D.C.*

"With the kindest feelings toward Prof.————, from your representation of his character, etc., and with sincere wishes for his welfare, I yet have no personal knowledge of his qualifications for the position he seeks, and cannot take the liberty of recommending him. Testimonials, to be of value, should come from persons who can speak positively of his scientific attainments, capacity for imparting knowledge, etc., etc. I cannot state what I do not know. I regret my inability, therefore, to comply with your wishes. With sentiments of high esteem,

"I am, very respectfully, your obedient servant,
"R. E. LEE."

"LEXINGTON, VA.,
May 14, 1867.
"*Mr.————, Oxford, Miss.*

"MY DEAR SIR: I have received your letter of the 28th ult., and regret to have to state that my personal knowledge of your qualifications does not enable me to give the statement you desire, of your fitness to teach fencing. I would recommend you to write to the gentlemen with whom you state you have served, and who doubtless have the necessary information for such evidence as you require.

"Sincerely sympathizing with you on account of your disability, and wishing you every happiness, I am, very respectfully,

"Your obedient servant,
"R. E. LEE."

"LEXINGTON, VA.,
March 20, 1866.
"*Mr.————.*

"MY DEAR SIR: I regret to perceive, by your letter of the 14th inst., that you have been inconvenienced by my silence. My time is so fully occupied, and my correspondence so large, that I am only able to attend to letters of business.

"In your former letter you seemed to desire me to do what I did not consider was in my power. I was very glad to read the high testimonials in your favor, written by gentlemen acquainted with you, who knew what they stated, and what I did not doubt, but of which I had no personal knowledge, and to which I could add nothing. I did not think that the testimony of those gentlemen required the endorsement of any one; and, as I had not the pleasure of your acquaintance, or any knowledge beyond what they stated, I did not see how I could strengthen it. This was the reason of my not replying to your letter.

"Sympathizing with you in the circumstances which render it necessary, in your opinion, for you to leave your home and friends, and wishing you every happiness and success,

"I am, very respectfully, your obedient servant,

"R. E. LEE."

"LEXINGTON, VA.,
May 1, 1867.

"*Mr.* ————.

"MY DEAR SIR: I have been obliged to refuse so many applications from my comrades and friends, to use my name in their business references, for reasons which I think will occur to you, that I hope you will excuse me for not departing from this rule in your case.

"Wishing you all success and happiness, I am, very respectfully, your obedient servant,

"R. E. LEE."

The following will be appreciated by the many friends of the distinguished gentleman to whom it refers:

"LEXINGTON, VA.,
July 5, 1867.

"*Miss* JOSEPHINE SEATON, 131 *St. Paul Street, Baltimore, Md.*

"MY DEAR MISS SEATON: I regret that I am unable to send you any circumstance or event that would give interest to the history that is proposed of your father's life. My acquaintance with him, and your uncle Gales, though of long standing and of the most cordial nature, was altogether social and friendly in its relations; and I have no letters from either on political or national events. I retain the most pleasing recollections of your father's kindness of manner, gentleness of disposition, and character for integrity, and I grieve deeply at his death. You have my sincere sympathy in this afflicting event, and my prayers to Him who cares for the fatherless, that He may guide and protect you.

"With great respect, you obedient servant,

"R. E. LEE."

"LEXINGTON, VA.,
October 4, 1867.

"Colonel C. A. WHITE, *Georgetown, D.C.*

"MY DEAR SIR: Absence has prevented my earlier reply to your letter of the 27th of August. I am unable to refer to official returns, but in a statement made in the fall of 1865, by the officer whose business it was to prepare them, the effective strength of the Army of Northern Virginia, on the 5th of May, 1864, is placed at forty thousand infantry, six thousand cavalry, and four thousand artillery, making fifty thousand in all. This corresponds with my recollection. Longstreet's corps, and a part of Ewell's, were absent on that day, and it was estimated that there were about twenty-five thousand men engaged in the battle.

"Very respectfully your obedient servant,
"R. E. LEE."

"LEXINGTON, VA.,
November 7, 1868.

"Rev. SAMUEL BOYKIN, *Macon, Ga.*

"DEAR SIR: The death of General Howell Cobb was to me, as it must have been to every friend of his country, the cause of great grief. His death at any period would have been a great calamity; but at a time when his wise counsel and sound judgment were so much needed, it is a double source of affliction. My sympathy with his bereaved family is as deep as my admiration for his character is great, and I sincerely deplore the loss sustained by his friends and state. There are none who more highly appreciate his worth than myself; but there are many more capable of writing the sketch of his life which you propose than I am, and to them I must leave it.

"Very respectfully, your obedient servant,
"R. E. LEE."

The following letter in reference to the distinguished Christian soldier who laid his life on the altar of his country, should go on the record, and be handed down to the calm judgment of the future:

"LEXINGTON, VA.,
November 21, 1867.
"Mrs. LEONIDAS POLK, *Care of Rev. George Beckett, Columbia, Tenn.*

"MY DEAR MADAM: I received yesterday your letter of the 15th, and it will give me great pleasure to furnish you such information as I possess of your lamented husband, whose name and character are so dear to the Southern people. I only regret that my intercourse with him was such as to enable me to say but little of my personal knowledge. His career at West Point, if not already familiar to you, can be more fully narrated by his classmates, who were in daily association with him; for, although I was there two years with him, he was in a class two years my senior, and my intercourse with him was not frequent. I can, however, say that he was considered, by the officers and cadets with whom I was acquainted, as a model for all that was soldierly, gentlemanly, and honorable.

"I do not now recollect to have seen him from the time he left West Point until I met him in Richmond at the time he was appointed in the Confederate Army. He then informed me that he had been offered the commission of major general, and that its acceptance was to him a matter of grave consideration. Before accepting it, he intended to have an interview with Bishop Meade, to state to him the impressions of his mind on the whole subject. To his remarks to me, I replied that I could well conceive the difficulties which presented themselves, and that in my opinion he was the only person who could decide the question. I never saw him again after his departure for Tennessee.

"He always possessed my esteem and veneration, and I sympathize with you and the country at his death.

"I am, with great respect, your most obedient servant,
"R. E. LEE."

The following letter, written with no expectation of its ever being published, will be read with deep interest, as throwing light upon various points connected with the campaigns of the Army of Northern Virginia. Everything on the subject coming from General Lee's pen will not only be eagerly read, and implicitly believed, but will increase the general regret that he was not spared to give to the world the history of the Army of Northern Virginia—a book which *the world* would have received as truth:

"LEXINGTON, VA.,
April 15, 1868.

"WM. M. McDONALD, *Cool Spring, near Berryville, Clarke County, Va.*

"MY DEAR SIR: I thank you for your kind letter of the 3d inst., which I have been unable to answer till today. I hope that your school history may be of such character as will insure its broadest circulation, and prove both interesting and instructive to the youth of the whole country.

"As regards the information you desire, if you will refer to my official report of March 6, 1863, which was published in Richmond in 1864, you will find the general reasons which governed my actions; but whether they will be satisfactory to others is problematical. In relation to your first question, I will state that, in crossing the Potomac, I did not propose to invade the North, for I did not believe that the Army of Northern Virginia was strong enough for the purpose, nor was I in any degree influenced by popular expectation. My movement was simply intended to threaten Washington, call the Federal Army north of that river, relieve our territory, and enable us to subsist the army. I considered it useless to attack the fortifications around Alexandria and Washington, behind which the Federal Army had taken refuge, and, indeed, I could not have maintained the army in Fairfax, so barren was it of subsistence, and so devoid were we of transportation. After reaching Frederick City, finding that the enemy still retained his positions at Martinsburg and Harper's Ferry, and that it became necessary to dislodge him in order to open our communication through the Valley for the purpose of obtaining from Richmond the ammunition, clothing, etc., of which we were in great need—after detaching the necessary troops for the purpose, I was left with but two divisions, Longstreet's and D. H. Hill's, to mask the operation. That was entirely too weak a force to march on Baltimore, which you say was expected, even if such a movement had been expedient.

"As to the battle of Gettysburg, I must again refer you to my official accounts. Its loss was occasioned by a combination of circumstances. It was commenced in the absence of correct intelligence. It was continued in the effort to overcome the difficulties by which we were surrounded, and it would have been gained could one determined and united blow have been delivered by our whole line. As it was, victory trembled in the balance for three days, and the battle resulted in the infliction of as great an amount of injury as was received, and in frustrating the Federal campaign for the season.

"I think you will find the answer to your third question in my report of the battle of Fredericksburg. In taking up the position there, it was with the view of resisting General Burnside's advance after crossing the Rappahannock, rather than of preventing its passage.

"The plain of Fredericksburg is completely commanded by the heights of Stafford, which prevented our occupying it in the first instance.

"Nearly the whole loss that our army sustained during the battle arose from the pursuit of the repulsed Federal columns into the plain. To have advanced the whole army into the plain for the purpose of attacking General Burnside, would have been to have insured its destruction by the fire from the continued line of guns on the Stafford Hills. It was considered more wise to meet the Federal army beyond the reach of their batteries than under their muzzles, and even to invite repeated renewal of their attacks. When convinced of their inutility, it was easy for them under cover of a long, dark, and tempestuous night to cross the narrow river by means of their numerous bridges before we could ascertain their purpose.

"I have been obliged to be very brief in my remarks, but I hope that I have been able to present to you some facts which may be useful to you in drawing correct conclusions. I must ask that you will consider what I have said as intended solely for yourself.

"Very respectfully and truly yours,
"R. E. Lee."

The following is of most valuable historic interest, as showing the great disparity of numbers between General Lee's army and that of his adversary:

WARM SPRINGS, VA.,
July 27, 1868.

"*General* WM. S. SMITH.

"MY DEAR SIR: Your letter has been forwarded to me from Lexington. My official records have been destroyed; and in the absence of such other information as is accessible to me, I am obliged to answer your inquiries from memory.

"The number of effective men under my command on May 4, 1864, of all arms, was between forty-five and fifty thousand. The losses in the several battles up to June 17th I do not recollect; but at the time of withdrawing from the lines around Richmond and Petersburg, the number of troops amounted to about thirty-five thousand.

"Notwithstanding the demonstrations made against our front and left at the opening of the campaign of 1864, I believed that General Grant would cross the Rapidan on our right, and resolved to attack him whenever he presented himself.

"As regards the movements of General Sherman, it was easy to see that, unless they were interrupted, I should be compelled to abandon the defense of Richmond, and with a view of arresting his progress I so weakened my force by sending reinforcements to South and North Carolina, that I had not sufficient men to man the lines. Had they not been broken, I should have abandoned them as soon as General Sherman reached the Roanoke.

"I have understood that the Confederate military records are in one of the bureaus at Washington. If so, the official returns of the Army of North Virginia will be found among them, and exact information can be obtained. I regret that my information should be so indefinite; but, such as it is, I send it for your own satisfaction.

"Wishing you health and happiness, I remain very respectfully yours,

"R. E. LEE."

"WASHINGTON COLLEGE, LEXINGTON, VA.,
March 4, 1868.

"MY DEAR SIR: I enclose fifty dollars of the fund contributed by the faculty and students for the religious exercises of the college; not in compensation for your voluntary services, but in grateful testimony of them.

"With great respect, your obedient servant,
"R. E. LEE."

"*Rev.* J. WILLIAM JONES."

"LEXINGTON, VA.,
March 25, 1868.

"MY DEAR SIR: I thank you most cordially for the valuable collection of minerals forwarded with your letter of the 17th ult.

"Notwithstanding their journey from the Pacific, they were so well packed that they arrived in perfect order, and are among the most valuable specimens in our cabinet, as they go far to supply the places of the gold and silver ores carried away during the war.

"As a contribution to Washington College by the son of my friend and comrade General Albert Sidney Johnston—one of the bravest, truest, and noblest men I have ever known—they are particularly prized.

"I beg that you will present my kindest regards to your mother, sister, and brother, and accept my best wishes for your own health and happiness.

"Very truly yours,
"R. E. LEE."

"*Mr.* HANCOCK M. JOHNSTON."

"WASHINGTON COLLEGE, VA.,
June 23, 1868.

"*Dr.* S. MAUPIN, *Chairman of Faculty of University of Virginia.*

"MY DEAR SIR: In compliance with a resolution of the faculty of Washington College, passed at their last regular meeting, I have to present their thanks to the faculty of the University of Virginia for their invitation to attend the closing exercises of the university the present session; and to express their regret that duties, public and private, prevent them from accepting it, though it is hoped that several individual members will be able to be present on that interesting occasion.

"I have the honor to be, with great respect, your obedient servant,

"R. E. LEE."

"LEXINGTON, VA.,
December 18, 1868.

"DEAR SIR: I entirely concur with you in the opinion that the education and advancement of the colored people at the South can be better attended to by those who are acquainted with their characters and wants than by those who are ignorant of both; and I would recommend you to place such funds as you may have for their benefit in the hands of ministers of your own church, who, I am sure, would expend them judiciously, and in whose fidelity you would naturally have faith. You are probably acquainted with many, either personally or by reputation, to whom you might confide the trust. I can name to you two gentlemen of Richmond, Va., the Rev. Drs. Hoge and Brown, on whose judgment, kindness, and integrity, you can safely rely. From their position in the Presbyterian church, and location at Richmond, they may be able to attend to the matter. I could not attend to it—on account of other duties, and my isolated position—nor do I know any colored preacher competent to take charge of the matter. The colored people in this vicinity are doing very well, are progressing favorably, and, as far as I know, are not in want. There is abundance of work for them, and the whites with whom they are associated retain for them the kindest feelings.

"I am, very respectfully, your obedient servant,

"R. E. LEE."

"LEXINGTON, VA.,
January 8, 1869.

"MY DEAR SIR: I am much obliged to you for your letter of the 29th ult., which I am sure has been prompted by the best of motives. I should be glad if General Grant would visit Washington College, when I would endeavor to treat him with the courtesy and respect due the president of the United States. But if I were to invite him to do so, it might not be agreeable to him, and I fear, at this time, my motives might be misunderstood, both by himself and others, and that evil would result instead of good. I will, however, bear your suggestion in mind, and, should a favorable opportunity offer, will be glad to take advantage of it.

"Wishing you happiness and prosperity, I am, very respectfully, your obedient servant,

"R. E. LEE."

"LEXINGTON, VA.,
December 5, 1868.
"*Mr.*——, *Savannah, Ga.*

"MY DEAR SIR: I return you my thanks for the copy of the records of the Union Society of the city of Savannah, an organization almost coeval with the colonization of Georgia, which by its sacred works of charity in which it has been laboring for more than a century has endeared itself to the benevolent throughout the country. In its new career upon the site of the ancient Bethesda, on an enlarged and wider field, I trust that its prosperity may be equal to its former usefulness. In reply to your renewed invitation to deliver before the society the anniversary address, I am unable to give a different an- swer from that I made to your personal application. I regret my inability to comply with your request, and assure you that it would afford me great pleasure to revisit Savannah, a city to which I have been long attached, and in whose citizens I feel the deepest interest. For your cordial invitation to your house, please accept my hearty thanks.

"I am, with great respect, your most obedient servant,
"R. E. LEE."

"LEXINGTON, VA.,
February 12, 1869.
"*Colonel*——.

"MY DEAR SIR: Your generous proposition to give two lectures for the benefit of the Rockbridge Bible Society, has been laid before the executive committee, and I have been requested to thank you most cordially for your kind offer, and to say that, under the constitution and direction of the society, the several churches in the county have been appealed to for the means to accomplish the object in view; and it is hoped that in this manner sufficient funds will be obtained. They therefore consider it inexpedient to resort to other means without express direction from the society.

"In addition to the thanks of the committee, I beg you will accept my personal acknowledgments for your kind expressions toward myself, and will be assured that they are reciprocated. You have my earnest wishes for your success and prosperity in this life, and my fervent prayers for eternal peace and happiness in the world to come.

"Very truly yours,

"R. E. Lee."

"Lexington, Va.,
February 12, 1869.

"My dear Mrs.————: I have received your letter of the 16th inst., and heartily sympathize in your distress concerning your son. I have requested Prof. W———— to communicate to me such information as he has of the street difficulty in which he was involved. His letter, which I enclose, and the resolution passed by the faculty on the subject, contain all the information I have on the subject. On the first arrival of your son at college I was especially impressed with his appearance and manner, and was anxious that he should be favorably located. Until the occurrence which caused him to leave college, I had remarked nothing objectionable in his conduct but what might be attributed to youthful indiscretion and thoughtlessness; and as one of these instances was calculated to teach him to what such conduct would reasonably lead, I was in hopes his own good sense would correct it. I, however, hope that this last occurrence will teach him a lesson that he will never forget, and save him and you from future distress. I hope that he has safely reached you before this, and that his contrition and conduct will relieve you from further anxiety.

"With great respect, your obedient servant,

"R. E. Lee."

"LEXINGTON, VA.,
February 13, 1869.

"MY DEAR MISS JONES: After long and diligent inquiry, I only this moment learned your address, and have been during this time greatly mortified at my inability to acknowledge the receipt and disposition of your valuable and interesting donation to Washington College. The books were arranged in the library on their arrival; the globes in the philosophical department; and the furniture, carpets, sofas, chairs, etc., have been applied to the furnishing of the dais of the audience room of the new chapel, to the comfort and ornament of which they are a great addition. I have yet made no disposition of the plate and table ware, and they are still in the boxes in which they came. I enclose the resolution of thanks passed by the board of trustees of the college at their annual meeting, to which I beg to add my personal acknowledgments and grateful sense of your favor and kindness to this institution, and it would give me great pleasure if you would visit Lexington at the commencement in June next, the third Thursday, that I might then show you the successful operation of the college. Mrs. Lee joins me in sentiments of esteem and regard, praying that the great and merciful God may throw around you his protecting care and love.

"I am, with great respect, your obedient servant,

"R. E. LEE."

"*Miss* ANNE UPSHUR JONES, 88 *Union Square, New York.*"

The following extract contains a bit of quiet humor worth preserving:

"LEXINGTON, VA.,
February 12, 1869.

". . . Mrs. Lee has determined to act upon your suggestion, and apply to President Johnson for such of the relics from Arlington as are in the patent office. From what I have learned, a great many things formerly belonging to General Washington, bequeathed to her by her father, in the shape of books, furniture, camp equipage, etc., were carried away by individuals, and are now scattered over the land. I hope the possessors appreciate them, and may imitate the example of their original owner, whose conduct must at times be brought to their recollection by these silent monitors. In this way they will accomplish good to the country."

"LEXINGTON, VA.,
March 22, 1869.
"*Hon.* GEORGE W. JONES, *P. O. Box* 52, *Dubuque, Iowa.*

"MY DEAR SIR: I am very much gratified at the reception this morning of your letter of the 16th inst., enclosing for my perusal one that you had received from General A. C. Dodge, and which, as you have given me permission, I will retain; not merely for the kind sentiments toward me, which I feel I ill deserve, but in remembrance of the writer.

"Were it worth his while to refer to my political record, he would have found that I was not in favor of secession, and was opposed to war; in fact, that I was for the Constitution and the Union established by our forefathers. No one now is more in favor of that Constitution and that Union; and, as far as I know, it is that for which the South has all along contended; and if restored, as I trust they will be, I am sure there will be no truer supporters of that Union and that Constitution than the Southern people. But I must not wander into politics, a subject I carefully avoid, and will return to your letter. Your communication of the 15th of January last was especially pleasing to me, and I am very glad to have authenticated, under your own name, statements which were made to me at the time of General————'s removal, as well as your high opinion of his character. I have never been associated with a person who, as far as my knowledge extended, labored more earnestly or more honestly for the government and the welfare of the people than he did. When you next come to Virginia, I hope that you will not halt on the borders, but penetrate the interior of the state, and that you will come to Lexington. We shall be very glad to see you, and I hope that you will be repaid for your journey by the pleasure which you will see your visit affords us.

"Though rather late, I must thank you for introducing me to your friend Mrs.————, whom I met last summer at the Warm Springs. We found her and her sister most agreeable companions and charming ladies. I wished to write to you at that time, but they can tell you how closely I was occupied night and day, in nursing a sick daughter. I have thought of your friends very often since their departure, and hope that their health has been permanently benefited by their visit to our mountains, and that they will be encouraged to repeat it.

"Please present my kindest regards to every member of your family, especially to your brave sons who aided in our struggle for states' rights and constitutional government.

"We failed, but in the good providence of God apparent failure often proves a blessing. I trust it may eventuate so in this instance. In reference to certain articles which were taken from Arlington, about which you inquire, Mrs. Lee is indebted to our old friend Captain James May for the order from the late administration for their restoration to her. Congress, however, passed a resolution forbidding their return. They were valuable to her as having belonged to her great-grandmother, and having been bequeathed to her by her father. But, as the country desires them, she must give them up. I hope their presence at the capital will keep in the remembrance of all Americans the principles and virtues of Washington.

"With my earnest prayers for the peace and happiness of yourself and all your family, I am, with true regard,

"Your friend and servant,

"R. E. LEE."

"LEXINGTON, VA.,
March 26, 1869.

"———, *Esq., Fort Laramie, Wyoming Terr.*

"MY DEAR SIR: I am very much obliged to you for the beaver robe which you have been so kind as to send me. It is the handsomest fur robe that I have ever seen, and, while protecting me from the wintry winds of our mountains, will remind me continually of your repeated kindnesses. I sympathized deeply with you and your wife, when your brave son fell at the head of his company, under the gallant Stuart, in the struggle of the Southern states for the right of constitutional government. But he, I trust, is happy, and I pray that you may all be again united in heaven. With my kindest regards and best wishes for your happiness, I am very truly yours,

"R. E. LEE."

The following is in reply to an offer of the artist to present him with his great painting, *The Meeting between Lee and Jackson:*

"WHITE SULPHUR SPRINGS, W. VA.,
August 21, 1869.
"Q. D. JULIO, *St. Louis, Mo.*

"DEAR SIR: I am much obliged to you for the sentiments expressed toward me in your letter of the 10th, and I am grateful for your intention to present to me the picture you describe. It is not that I do not appreciate your feelings, or value your kindness, that I cannot accept your picture, but that I desire you to have all the benefit as well as the credit of your labors. I will retain your letter as the pleasing evidence of your generous purpose, and with my best wishes for the realization of your aspirations and for your complete success in your profession,

"I am, etc.,
"R. E. LEE."

"WASHINGTON COLLEGE, VA.,
September 25, 1869.
"F. POOLE, *Secretary Peabody Institute, Peabody, Mass.*

"DEAR SIR: In compliance with your request, I send a photograph of myself, the last that has been taken, and shall feel honored in its being placed among the 'friends' of Mr. Peabody, for though they can be numbered by millions, yet all can appreciate the man who has illustrated his age by his munificent charities during his life, and by his wise provisions for promoting the happiness of his fellow creatures,

"Very respectfully, your obedient servant,
"R. E. LEE."

"LEXINGTON, VA.,
September 27, 1869.
"*Mr.* GEORGE PEABODY RUSSELL, *Salem, Mass.*

"MY DEAR SIR. Your letter of the 22d reached me by the last mail, and I thank you most sincerely for your interest in Washington Col-

lege, and your desire to insure its endowment. The act of the legislature, passed February 27, 1866, modifying the charter of
Washington College, as you will see by the copies of the charter and
by-laws herewith sent, established its legal title 'Washington College,
Virginia,' which is its corporate name. Should the college never receive the fund generously presented by Mr. Peabody, I shall be as
grateful to him for his kind intentions as if it had; but, if it is realized,
it will enable the college to extend its instructions and enlarge its
usefulness. Last year the college gave about fifty free scholarships,
that is, free tuition to fifty young men, and this year it will have to
exceed that number, or exclude meritorious youths who are unable
to pay for their tuition. These free scholarships embrace the following classes: Young men seeking to enter the Christian ministry of
every denomination; young men intending to make practical printing
and journalism their business in life; meritorious young men who
are unable to pay the college fees. Students standing first in certain
high schools and academies throughout the country receive prize
scholarships as an incentive to study. Honorary scholarships are
awarded to students of the college as a reward for high attainments
in scholarship, and two hundred dollars are annually given to three
graduates of the degree of Master of Arts, who also receive free
tuition to enable them to prosecute certain courses of study. These
free scholarships are granted to promote the cause of education and
of learning, and, to be continued or enlarged, require the appropriation of funds by the college. I send you one of the catalogues of
the college, which, if you have time to examine it, will explain what
we are now doing, and what we propose to do whenever our means
will permit. . . .

"With my best wishes for the health of Mr. Peabody and your
own happiness, I am, with great respect,

"Most truly yours,
"R. E. LEE."

The following graceful acknowledgment of a compliment paid him by
Mr. George Long, Jr. (son of Prof. George Long), of England, is but a
specimen of many similar letters which he wrote:

"Lexington, Va., Washington College,
December 8, 1869.

"Dr. J. L. Cabell, *University of Virginia.*

"My dear Doctor: I am obliged to you for informing me of the desire of George Long, Jr., to possess my photograph, and I take pleasure in forwarding it to one who has so kindly shown his interest in the South, and has extended to her people his warm sympathy. Such liberal conduct is the natural result of an enlarged mind and cultivated intellect, to which he is entitled by inheritance, birth, and education; and it is pleasing to contemplate one in whom all are combined. With my grateful thanks to him and his highly esteemed father, and my sincere regard for yourself and Mrs. Cabell,

"I am very truly yours,
"R. E. Lee."

"Lexington, Va.,
December 14, 1869.

"General J. B. Gordon, *President Southern*
Life Insurance Company, Atlanta, Ga.

"My dear General: I have received your letter of the 3d inst., and am duly sensible of the kind feelings which prompted your proposal. It would be a great pleasure to me to be associated with you, Hampton, B. H. Hill, and the other good men whose names I see on your list of directors, but I feel that I ought not to abandon the position I hold at Washington College at this time or as long as I can be of service to it. Thanking you for your kind consideration, to which I know I am alone indebted for your proposition to become the president of the Southern Life Insurance Company, and with my kindest regards to Mrs. Gordon, and my best wishes for yourself,

"I am very truly yours,
"R. E. Lee."

"Washington College,
January 7, 1870.
"*Messrs.* Lewis Allen, *etc., Committee of Invitation, Peabody, Mass.*

"Gentlemen: In transmitting a copy of the resolutions of the trustees of Washington College in reference to the death and funeral of Mr. George Peabody, I beg leave to express my regret at being prevented by indisposition from uniting with the citizens of his native town in paying the last but grateful respect to his mortal remains, in accordance with your invitation and the request of the trustees of the college. Though debarred from being present at his obsequies, his memory will live in the hearts of the Southern people, and his virtues be revered by unborn generations.

"With great respect, your obedient servant,
"R. E. Lee."

The distinguished gentleman to whom the following was addressed was (together with Prof. Long) one of the able corps of English professors whom Jefferson induced to come as the first faculty of the University of Virginia:

"Washington College, Lexington, Va.,
February 19, 1870.

"*Prof.* J. Hewitt Key, *M.A., F.R.S.,*
21 *Westbourne Square, W. London.*

"Dear Sir: I have received, by the hands of Colonel McCullough, the two volumes you have presented to the library of Washington College, a copy of your *Philological Essays,* and of your *Latin Grammar.* They are highly valued for their intrinsic merit, and for the kind feelings their donation evinces toward a state for whose benefit the labors of your early life were so well bestowed, and by whose people your memory is still warmly cherished. I beg also to return you my sincere thanks for the kindness extended to Colonel McCullough during his visit to London, and for the interest you take in Washington College. You will lay me under additional obligations if you will present my regards to your former colleague, Prof. George Long, and my grateful thanks for his excellent translation of the thoughts of the Emperor M. Aurelius Antoninus, my acknowledgments for which I hope have reached him.

"Wishing you much happiness and continued usefulness, I am, with great respect, your obedient servant,

"R. E. LEE."

"LEXINGTON, VA.,
February 19, 1870.

"Monsieur DEVISMES, *Fabricant des Armes,* }
Boulevard des Italiens, Paris. }

"SIR: Colonel McCullough, since his return from France, has described to me his interesting visit to your laboratory, and your friendly feelings to the people of the Southern states of North America. I am, therefore, induced, in presenting to you my thanks for the skillful workmanship you bestowed upon the beautiful sword sent me by a friend in Paris in 1863, to express to you my gratitude for your kind sentiments toward the people of the South.

"With much respect, your obedient servant,
"R. E. LEE."

"LEXINGTON, VA.,
February 26, 1870.

"General WILLIAM S. HARNEY, *Major General U.S.A.,* }
St. Louis, Mo. }

"MY DEAR GENERAL: I have learned, through a letter from General Lilly to a member of the endowment committee of Washington College, your kind sentiments toward the institution, and of your generous donation for the endowment of the presidential chair. This information recalls so vividly to my mind the kind acts extended to me in former years, that I hope you will allow me, in thanking you in the name of the trustees of the college for your aid in their plans of education, to express to you my individual thanks for the manner in which it has been bestowed.

"Wishing you health and happiness, I am, very respectfully, etc.,
"R. E. LEE."

The following is to the widow of the late Confederate Secretary of War, General Randolph:

"LEXINGTON, VA.,
March 8, 1870.
"*Mrs.* GEO. W. RANDOLPH, 504 *Grace Street, Richmond, Va.*

"MY DEAR MRS. RANDOLPH: I have felt great interest in the success of the scheme of the Hollywood Memorial Association of Richmond, for the removal of the Confederate dead at Gettysburg, since learning of the neglect of their remains on the battlefield. I hope that sufficient funds may be collected to enable the association to accomplish this pious work, and I feel assured that it will receive the grateful thanks of the humane and benevolent. May I request you to apply the enclosed amount to this object?

"I have been greatly pleased to hear of your improved health, and trust, for the benefit of the afflicted, and the comfort of your friends, you may be entirely restored.

"With great respect and esteem, I am your most obedient servant,
"R. E. LEE."

"LEXINGTON, VA.,
March 15, 1870.

"*Hon.* THOMAS MARTIN,
General Assembly of Maryland, Annapolis.

"DEAR SIR: I have read with great pleasure your speech before the House of Delegates of Maryland on the 17th ult., advocating an appropriation for burying the Confederate dead at Point Lookout, in St. Mary's County, Md., which you were so kind as to send me in your letter of the 10th inst. It would be a great relief to the sorrow of the friends of those brave men, should their earthly remains receive the care and respect you propose, and the ladies of your county as well as the people of your generous state would share their heartfelt gratitude.

"The ladies composing the Hollywood Memorial Association in Virginia are endeavoring to remove the neglected bodies of the Confederate dead from the battlefield of Gettysburg to their cemetery at Richmond, but the contributions for this purpose, owing to the poverty of our people, are as yet so small that they are not able to accomplish it. We are, therefore, the more grateful to Maryland for the provision she has made and still contemplates for this object. Those whose final resting place is in her soil, we feel, will be properly cared for.

"Very respectfully, your obedient servant,
"R. E. LEE."

"LEXINGTON, VA.,
March 17, 1870.

"*Mrs.* MARY E. RANDOLPH, 504 *Grace Street, Richmond, Va.*

"MY DEAR MRS. RANDOLPH: My former letter was intended for your own eyes, and I am always reluctant to be brought unnecessarily before the public. Still, if you think its publication will be any aid to the cause which the Hollywood Memorial Association has so kindly undertaken, I cannot refuse the slight assistance in my power. I send you a letter recently received from the Hon. Thomas Martin, of the General Assembly of Maryland, and an article that was sent to me from the Baltimore *Sun,* that you may see what Maryland proposes to do for the decent interment of the Confederate dead on her soil. I think, if the Hollywood Memorial Association would place itself in communication with the committee or trustees charged with the application of the funds appropriated by the state, that it might result to their mutual benefit. To obtain aid from the South, where all have to give out of their poverty, individuals or committees should be delegated in each state, to canvass or otherwise appeal to each county for the small amounts they can spare from their subsistence, with the understanding that what is received from each state will be applied first for the removal of the dead from that state. It is needless to wait for their unsolicited offerings. The Rev. Dr.————, of the Methodist church, an ardent friend of the South, intends visiting different sections in aid of religious objects, and has offered specially to advocate this object. Mrs. Lee sent you his letter, which I hope you have received. This is one way of bringing this enterprise to the notice of the people. I am sorry that you could not confirm the favorable accounts I had received of your health, but I trust you will soon do so.

"You must get well. Mrs. Lee and my daughters send their affectionate love.

"With kindest regards, I am yours most truly,
"R. E. Lee."

Pages more could be easily written illustrating General Lee's polite kindness, his social disposition, and his tender regard for the feelings of others; but the above must suffice, while I pass to another phase of his character equally marked, but not at all inconsistent with this.

Chapter VIII

His Firmness in Carrying Out His Purposes

Yet, while always kind and courteous, and willing to sacrifice personal convenience and feeling for others, General Lee had a proper sense of what was his due, and always, quietly but firmly, demanded this.

A newspaper correspondent once came to Lexington to "interview" him, and when he indicated his purpose the general said: "If you come to see me as one gentleman calls on another, I shall be glad to entertain you, sir; but if you come to report for the newspapers my private conversation, I have nothing further to say." The fellow still persisted, until the old hero arose and with quiet dignity and grace opened the door and bowed him out of the room.

The writer was present upon one occasion when an agent for the sale of a certain catchpenny book about the war called to see him, and the following colloquy ensued:

Agent. "I sent you the other day, General, a copy of this book which I am engaged in selling."

General Lee. "Yes, sir, I received it, and am obliged for your kindness."

Agent. "I called this morning to get you to give me a recommendation of the work. A line from you would be worth a great deal to me."

General Lee. "You must excuse me, sir; I cannot recommend a book which I have not read, and never expect to read."

I have spoken of the modest humility, spirit of self-denial, and gentle meekness, of this great man. But it must not be inferred that he was not, at the same time, firm in maintaining his opinions, and almost severe in carrying out his authority. No one ever bowed more submissively than he to what he recognized as superior authority. Mr. Jefferson Davis, in his eulogy, in Richmond, said that he always found him ready to obey to the letter any orders emanating from his office or that of the Confederate secretary of war, and during his last illness he showed this spirit by taking cheerfully any medicine given him by his attending physicians, although he would sometimes refuse it when offered by others. But when, on the other hand, he was placed in authority, he expected and enforced the most rigid obedience from his subordinates. His staff speak of him as being stern and even severe upon delinquents. And while all this was kept very quiet, it was no uncommon thing for his higher officers to receive from their loved chief the most severe rebukes.

When he first took charge of Washington College he at once, in his quiet way, gave both professors and students to understand that he was *president,* and meant to control the affairs of the institution. He at once introduced sundry reforms, which affected both professors and students; and while he won the love of all by his gentleness, he inspired all with a mortal dread of meeting the disapprobation of "the general." The professors would make any effort, and submit to any sacrifice, rather than incur the slightest censure from their honored president, and the students considered it a great misfortune to be summoned to go to General Lee's office. The result was, that no college in the land had a harder-working faculty, or a better-behaved, more orderly set of students. If he employed workmen, while he was always kind and polite, he gave them to understand distinctly that they must follow to the letter his directions.

In the administration of the affairs of the college, General Lee was very particular about *small* matters, and required that *everything* belonging to it should be properly used, taken care of, and accounted for. His keen eye was sure to detect the slightest departure from this inflexible law. If an old fence was removed, he required that the timbers should be carefully preserved; and when spades, shovels, or axes, were worn out, they had to be collected and disposed of to the best advantage.

Upon one occasion a locust tree had to be cut down to make way for some new walks that were being constructed through the college grounds. The efficient proctor (Captain G———) directed that a maul which was needed to "set" the stone on the walks should be constructed from the butt end of this tree. But the general, who had a great fondness for locust posts, had determined to have some gate posts made from this same tree, and, when he found out what had been done, he said to Captain G————, with some sharpness of tone: "Well, sir, your maul will be an expensive one. You might have ordered one *from New York,* or even imported it *from Liverpool,* at less cost."

During a meeting of the faculty, one of the professors, having occasion to refer to the catalogue of the college, picked up one ready wrapped for mailing, and was about to tear off the wrapper, when the general stopped him, handed him another catalogue, and quietly remarked: "We must take care of these small matters. Many a man has made his fortune by so doing."

A student was once guilty of a gross breach of college law, and brought General Lee a long letter of apology from his father.

One of the professors went into the general's office and found him greatly annoyed and provoked. Showing him the father's letter, he said: "Now it is evident to my mind that this is a disingenuous letter. He does not fairly represent the facts, and will completely ruin his son, as well as seriously interfere with our discipline. Now, sir, I will show you what I have written him in reply." The general's letter was a polite and very keen rebuke to one capable of appreciating it, but the professor happened to know that it would be entirely lost on the man to whom it was addressed. Accordingly he said, pleasantly: "Why, General, he will not appreciate that; he will take it as rather an approval of his course." The old hero looked very much perplexed, but presently replied: "Well, sir, I cannot help it; if a gentleman can't understand the language of a gentleman, he must remain in ignorance, for a gentleman cannot write in any other way."

The system of discipline which he adopted at the college abolished the old custom of turning the faculty into a body of spies, to go at unexpected hours into students' rooms, and to keep a constant watch for opportunities of catching them at some violation of college rules. He used to say, "I have but one rule— deport yourselves as gentlemen"; and he acted upon the presumption that the young men were gentlemen, and would behave as such, unless they should prove the contrary by their conduct. But if he found that a young man would not study, or would not deport himself properly, he would deal with him very promptly and decidedly.

Many incidents are related illustrating not only his firmness in carrying out his purposes, but his retentive memory of, and prompt attention to, *small things.*

The Warrenton (Virginia) *Index* gives the following:

"Early in the fall of 1860 he rode over from Arlington to the iron foundry of Mr. Schneider, corner of Eighteenth Street and Pennsylvania Avenue, and drew from his pocket the draft of a peculiar kind of coulter, which he requested to be cast for him to use in breaking up a lot of heavy meadow sod. The price of the coulter was fixed at two dollars, and the general's old market man called for it a day or two afterward.

"A few months passed, and the peaceful pursuits of agriculture were exchanged for the strife and turmoil of war. General Lee pitched his tent in the South, and the quiet scenes of Arlington knew him no more.

"Late in 1861, amid the stirring events that were enacting around him, and while all the mighty cares and responsibilities of his position were resting upon General Lee, Mr. Schneider received, by the hands of a little boy, two dollar gold pieces, with a brief note of apology for overlooking the little account."

When General Lee came to Richmond to tender his services to his native state, his baggage, which had just reached New York, was seized on and "confiscated." Among other articles was a saddle of peculiar make, which he had become accustomed to riding, and preferred to all others. He at once wrote to the maker in St. Louis that he should be glad to have another like it, if he was willing to risk the chances of getting his pay in those uncertain times. The saddle was promptly sent, and the great soldier was not too much occupied to remember to send through a safe channel the full amount in specie. The general rode this saddle all through the war, and indeed up to the day of his death.

When Mrs. Lee read the above incidents in my manuscript, she expressed herself as particularly gratified that they had been given, saying that *attention to "small" matters* was preeminently characteristic of General Lee; and that she thought that his example in this respect might be most profitably studied by the young people of the present day.

While General Lee, in firmly carrying out his purposes, would sometimes have occasion to rebuke sternly his higher officers, he was always careful not to do it in the presence of others.

Riding with General Gordon one day on an inspection tour, he remarked that certain works were "very badly located"; but, perceiving that some young officers were nearer than he supposed, and had probably overheard the remark, he immediately added: "But these works were located by skillful engineers, who probably know their business better than we do."

One of his generals once tried, in a confidential interview, to get General Lee to express himself in reference to a certain other officer about whom he himself spoke very freely. But the old chief merely replied, with a quiet smile: "Well, sir, if that is your opinion of General————, I can only say that you differ very widely from the general himself."

We have said that General Lee was both firm and persevering in carrying out his purposes. Two incidents of his experience in Mexico, related by the general himself (though of course with a very different object from the one for which we use them), will serve to illustrate this as well as other points in his character.

Not very long before the battle of Buena Vista, General Wool was in doubt as to the movements of the enemy, and found it very difficult to get reliable information. One evening he received the most positive assurances that Santa Anna, with an immense army, had crossed the mountain and was encamped only twenty miles off. Captain R. E. Lee happened to be present, and at once volunteered to ascertain the truth of the report. His offer was gladly accepted, and he was directed to secure a guide, take a company of cavalry which would meet him at the outer picket line, and proceed at once on the scout. Securing, after a good deal of difficulty, a young Mexican who knew the country, Captain Lee quietly showed him his pistols, and told him to expect their contents if he played false. By some means he missed the picket post, and consequently his cavalry escort, and found himself, before he was aware of it, some miles beyond the American lines with no company but his guide. To go back might make it too late to accomplish the scout during the night, and he determined to dash on. When within five miles of the point at which the enemy were reported, he discovered by the moonlight that the road was filled with tracks of mules and wagons, and, though he could see no artillery tracks, he concluded that they had been obliterated by the others, and that these were certainly the traces of a large force that had been sent forward to forage, or to reconnoiter and had now returned to the main army. Most officers (even the most daring) would have returned upon these evidences of the truth of the first information that had been received. But Captain Lee determined to go on until he came to the enemy's picket posts. To his surprise, he did not encounter any pickets, and had concluded that he had somehow missed them as he had his own, and had gotten unawares within the Mexican lines, when this opinion was confirmed by coming in sight of large campfires on a hillside, not far in front of him. His guide, who had been for some time very much alarmed, now begged piteously that he would go back, saying that there was a stream of water just at that point, and he knew that it was Santa Anna's whole army, and that to go on would be certain capture and death. But Captain Lee determined to have a still nearer view, and, allowing the guide to await him at this point, he galloped forward. As he came nearer, he saw what seemed to be a large number of white tents gleaming in the moonlight; and, encountering no pickets, he rode through the little town, and down to the banks of the stream, on the opposite side of which he heard loud talking and the usual noise incident to a large camp. Here he discovered that his "white tents" were an immense *flock of sheep,* and that the supposed army was simply a large train of wagons and a herd of cattle, mules, etc., being driven to market. Conversing with the teamsters and drovers, he ascertained that Santa Anna had not crossed the mountains; and galloped back to relieve his guide, and still more his friends at headquarters, who were having the most serious apprehensions concerning his safety. "But," said General Lee, "the most delighted man to see me was the old Mexican, the father of my guide, with whom I had been last seen by any of our people, and whom General Wool had arrested and proposed to hang if I was not forthcoming." Notwithstanding he had ridden forty miles that night, he only rested three hours before taking a body of cavalry with which he penetrated far beyond the point to which he had before gone, and ascertained definitely the position, force, etc., of the enemy. Soon after this he joined General Scott, and entered upon that brilliant career which illustrated every step of the progress of the American army in its march to the city of Mexico.

At the siege of Vera Cruz, Captain Lee was ordered to throw up such works as were necessary to protect a battery which was to be manned by the sailors of a certain man-of-war, and to use these gallant tars in constructing the work. The time being short, the young engineer pushed on the work very rapidly, and the sons of Neptune began to complain loudly. "They did not enlist to dig dirt, and they did not like to be put under a 'land-lubber' anyhow." At last the captain of the frigate, a thorough specimen of a United States naval officer in the palmy days of the service, came to Captain Lee and remonstrated, and then protested against the "outrage" of putting his men to digging dirt. "The boys don't want any dirt to hide behind," said the brave old tar, with deep earnestness and not a few expletives; "they only want to *get at the enemy;* and after you have finished your banks we will not stay behind them, we will get up on top, where we can have a fair fight." Captain Lee quietly showed his orders, assured the old salt that he meant to carry them out, and pushed on the work, amid curses both loud and deep.

Just about the time the work was completed, the Mexicans opened upon that point a heavy fire, and these gallant sons of the sea were glad enough to take refuge behind their despised "bank of dirt," feeling very much like the ragged Confederate who said one day, as the bullets flew thick against a pit which he had dug the night before, "I don't begrudge now nary cupful of dirt I put on this bank!" Not long afterward the gallant captain, who, by the way, was something of a character, met Captain Lee, and, feeling that some apology was due him, said: "Well! I reckon you were right. I suppose the dirt *did* save some of my boys from being killed or wounded. But I knew that we would have no use for dirt banks on shipboard, that there what we want is clear decks and an open sea. And the fact is, Captain, I don't like this land fighting anyway—*it ain't clean!*"

The general related these incidents with evident relish (he was fond of talking of events that occurred prior to the late war), and gave many details of interest which I am unable to recall.

The following from the San Antonio *Herald* is, I believe, a well-authenticated incident, save that Captain Lee was never a member of General Scott's staff except during the Mexican War:

"The almost uniform success of General Robert E. Lee was due probably to the simplicity of the means he invariably adopted to attain even the most gigantic results. As an evidence of this fact, we would call to mind something that our people have never known, and the people of St. Louis, those most interested, have likely forgotten. Certain it is that by these latter no official recognition of General (then Brevet-Captain) Lee's services was ever made—not even the poor compliment of a notice in the minutes of the Board of Aldermen.

"It will be remembered that many years ago all St. Louis was terrified at the prospect of being isolated by the action of the river current, which up to that time had been striking its banks, as it swayed from side to side, almost in front of the city. But, by washing away the banks on the Illinois side, thereby changing the angles of impingement, the stream commenced to gradually wear away the soil below St. Louis, making its way toward the American bottoms, an alluvial tract, and would have finally reached and emptied into a creek some five miles below the city, diverting the river and leaving St. Louis an inland town.

"The city council and the general government made large appropriations, hired the best engineers, built dikes to find them useless, and were finally obliged to admit that, if there was engineering skill sufficient to avert the calamity, it could not be found. General Scott was consulted to know if he could not recommend some one capable of grappling the problem. The general replied: 'I know of but one officer, a brevet-captain on my staff. He is young, but, if the work can be done, he can do it.'

"Brevet-Captain Robert E. Lee arrived in St. Louis and went to work. Quietly and unostentatiously he prepared his plans, drew his charts, calculated the force and direction of the currents, examined all the discarded plans, and determined on his course. All this took considerable time, because, as he remarked, 'Too much is at stake to trust to any uncertain agencies, or leave anything to fortune.' So noiselessly were his preparations carried on that the citizens began to murmur at the apparent inactivity of the young officer; the *Republican* and other newspapers attacked him, and at last the city withdrew its appropriation.

"Through all this accumulated dissatisfaction Captain Lee pursued the even tenor of his way, merely remarking, when the appropriation was withdrawn by the city: 'They have a right to do as they will with their own; I do not own the city. The government has sent me here as an officer of the army to do a certain work. I shall do it.'

"The careful preparations were at last completed and everything in readiness: a number of flatboats, some partially laden with stones, others fully, according to the depth of water in which they were to sink, moored with strong ropes from each, so that they could be cast loose to the current at one time, by one stroke of an axe, and a plug in each so arranged that at a given signal all the plugs could be withdrawn simultaneously. A man stood ready at each line with a hatchet to cut loose; a watch in his hand, with the hour, minute, and second indicated when to pull the plug. The signal to 'cut loose' was the firing of the captain's pistol, which being given, as with one accord every rope was cut, and the boats, exactly as calculated, swung out toward their proper and destined places. Curving at first by the greater force of the current, so accurately had every ounce of pressure been ascertained and provided for, that when the moment arrived and every plug was withdrawn, the boats went down in a perfect line, at right angles to the current, as intended. Buoys were fixed, and next day Captain Lee paid an early visit to see if all was safe. All was safe, including the city of St. Louis. Day after day, brush, stones, etc., were sunk until the dike thus formed reached the surface of the water. Today cars cross the same structure, to whose existence a proud city owes its great-ness, a silent monument to the genius of one who, though dead, 'still lives.'

"The *Republican,* we believe, managed to say, after the work was com-plete, 'The talented young engineer has succeeded in diverting the current of the river, notwithstanding the fears entertained that such would not be the case.'

"This is but one notable instance of 'Lee's way,' which was ever a successful one, whether grappling with a scientific or military problem, whether planning the saving or reducing of a city. Whether in peace or in war, his means were as simple, direct, speedy, and efficacious, as the results of his efforts were successful, enduring, and glorious."

It has been common in certain quarters to represent that General Lee's heart was not fully enlisted in the Confederate cause; that he entered upon the contest very reluctantly; that he was ready to abandon it long before he did; and that he was prevented by others from doing so.

The truth is that, having once drawn his sword, he "threw away the scabbard," stood firm to the last, and only yielded to "overwhelming num-bers and resources"; that there was not in the whole South a more deter-mined, firmer man than this modest chieftain.

There can be little doubt that General Lee favored the famous "Hamp-ton Roads Conference," and was anxious to obtain for the South honorable terms of peace; and in the same spirit he wrote as follows to General Grant:

"HEADQUARTERS CONFEDERATE STATES ARMIES,
March 2, 1865.
"*Lieutenant General* U. S. GRANT, *commanding United States Armies.*

"GENERAL: Lieutenant General Longstreet has informed me that in a recent conversation between himself and Major General Ord, as to the possibility of arriving at a satisfactory adjustment of the present unhappy difficulties, by means of a military convention, General Ord stated that, if I desired to have an interview with you on the subject, you would not decline, provided I had authority to act. Sincerely desiring to leave nothing untried which may put an end to the ca-lamities of war, I propose to meet you at such convenient time and place as you may designate, with the hope that upon an interchange of views it may be found practicable to submit the subjects of controversy between the belligerents to a convention of the kind mentioned. In such an event I am authorized to do whatever the result of the proposed interview may render necessary or advisable. Should you accede to this proposition, I would suggest that, if agreeable to you, we meet at the place selected by Generals Ord and Longstreet for the interview, at 11 A.M., on Monday next.

"Very respectfully, your obedient servant,

"R. E. LEE."

But, when these overtures had failed, there was no man more determined to fight it out to the end than the commander-in-chief. He said to a Southern senator, "For myself, I intend to die sword in hand rather than to yield," and he went to work to make the best possible disposition of his little army. Hon. R. L. Montague (ex-Lieutenant Governor of Virginia) gives the following incident:

"In 1862 Richmond was besieged. The Federal gunboats were threatening to move up the river, and the army of General McClellan was camped in sight of the capital. General Lee devised the plan of relieving the city. I had visited the general at his room at night on business, and after it had transpired was about to leave, when he desired me to remain. His adjutant then left, and the general detailed to me his entire plan for the relief of the city. I said: 'General, if it fails, what then? Will you abandon Virginia?' He immediately rose from his seat (it was the only time I ever saw him the least excited), and, clinching his fist, and with much animation, exclaimed: 'Never, never! I will fall back to the mountains of Virginia, and if my soldiers will stand by me I will fight these people' (he always spoke of the enemy as 'these people') 'for years to come!' "

Ex-President Davis says that, in the straits to which they were reduced during the latter part of the siege of Petersburg, General Lee said: "With my army in the mountains of Virginia, I could carry on this war for twenty years longer." He had decided to evacuate Richmond and Petersburg, and had made all of his arrangements to do so about the middle of February, 1865. But he was overruled, the movement was stopped, his thin line was finally broken by the overwhelming numbers opposed to him, and he was thus compelled in the face of a victorious enemy of four times his numbers to hastily undertake a movement which he desired to make secretly and at his leisure. And yet he was calm, cheerful, confident, and firm. "I have got my army safe out of its breastworks," he said, "and, in order to follow me, my enemy must abandon his lines and can derive no further benefit from his railroads and James River." It was his purpose to move toward Danville, form a junction with General Johnston, and strike once more for the independence of the Confederacy. But the freshet rendered the streams impassable; this delay enabled General Grant to throw a heavy force between him and Danville; and, worse still, on reaching Amelia Courthouse he found a cruel disappointment awaiting him, in the fact that trains of cars loaded with rations for his men, which he had ordered to that point, had been sent on to Richmond.

As there have been so many erroneous accounts of "the last days of Lee's army" published, and as the writer was so fortunate as to hear General Lee's own description, as he gave it to a party of friends, it will be briefly given here, both as illustrating General Lee's firmness, and as placing right on the record of these great historic events.

I will not sketch the events of the "running fight" from Amelia Springs to Appomattox. Suffice it to say that Grant had been enabled, by having the shorter route, by the delay of General Lee on account of the swollen condition of the streams, and by the necessary halt at Amelia Courthouse, to throw his immense army on the flank and rear of his antagonist, to cut off our line of retreat to Danville, and to be in position to continually harass our jaded, starving troops. The broken-down mules and horses were unable to drag the wagons (even lightly loaded) and artillery along the miry roads. Sheridan's splendidly mounted and equipped cavalry were able to make most advantageous forays upon the trains, and often Lee was obliged to halt for hours and fight eight or ten times his numbers upon most disadvantageous ground, until the jaded teams could pull the trains out of the mud. In all of these contests the Army of Northern Virginia maintained its old prestige; the men fought with heroic courage, and won some most brilliant successes. But the constant marching and fighting without rations or sleep steadily and surely decimated the thin ranks of this noble band. Men who had been true to their colors from the early days of the war, fell out of the ranks and were captured, simply because it was beyond their power of physical endurance to go any farther; many who had been hitherto good soldiers straggled; the devoted and strong found great difficulty in preserving organization and efficiency; and as the retreat rolled on by the light of burning wagons and to the music of hoarse artillery, mingling with the rattle of small arms, the corps commanders saw that the days of that grand old army were numbered.

Accordingly, on Thursday night (the 6th of April), they held a conference, at which they commissioned General W. N. Pendleton (chief of artillery) to inform General Lee that in their judgment the time had come when negotiations should be opened with General Grant.

General Pendleton thus describes the interview: "General Lee was lying on the ground. No other heard the conversation between him and myself. He received my communication with the reply, 'Oh, no! I trust it has not come to that'; and added: 'General, we have yet too many bold men to think of laying down our arms. The enemy do not fight with spirit, while our boys still do. Besides, if I were to say a word to the Federal commander, he would regard it as such a confession of weakness as to make it the occasion of demanding unconditional surrender—a proposal to which I will never listen. I have resolved to die first; and that, if it comes to that, we shall force through or all fall in our places. . . . General, this is no new question with me. I have never believed we could, against the gigantic combination for our subjugation, make good in the long run our independence unless foreign powers should, directly or indirectly, assist us. This I was sure it was their interest to do, and I hoped they would so regard it. But such considerations really made with me no difference. We had, I was satisfied, sacred principles to maintain and rights to defend, for which we were in duty bound to do our best, even if we perished in the endeavor!'

"These were, as nearly as I can recall them, the exact words of General Lee on that most critical occasion. You see in them the soul of the man. What his conscience dictated and his judgment decided, there his heart was."

General Lee did not think proper to comply at once with the suggestion of his corps commanders, but on the night of the next day (the 7th) he received from General Grant the following letter:

"*April 7th.*

"*General* R. E. Lee, *Commander C.S.A.*

"Sir: The result of the last week must convince you of the utter hopelessness of further resistance on the part of the Army of Northern Virginia in this struggle. I feel that it is so, and regard it as my duty to shift from myself the responsibility of any further effusion of blood, by asking of you the surrender of that portion of the Confederate States Army known as the Army of Northern Virginia.

"Very respectfully, your obedient servant,
"U. S. GRANT,

"Lieutenant General, commanding Armies of the United States."

To this General Lee replied as follows:

"April 7th.

"GENERAL: I have received your note of this date. Though not entirely of the opinion you express of the hopelessness of further resistance on the part of the Army of Northern Virginia, I reciprocate your desire to avoid useless effusion of blood, and therefore, before considering your proposition, ask the terms you will offer on condition of its surrender.

"R. E. LEE, *General.*

"*To* Lieutenant General U. S. GRANT, commanding }
    Armies of the United States."

General Grant sent the following reply:

"April 8th.

"*To General* R. E. LEE, *commanding Confederate States Army.*

"GENERAL: Your note of last evening, in reply to mine of same date, asking the condition on which I will accept the surrender of the Army of Northern Virginia, is just received.

"In reply, I would say that, peace being my first desire, there is but one condition that I insist upon, viz.:

"That the men surrendered shall be disqualified for taking up arms against the government of the United States until properly exchanged. I will meet you, or designate officers to meet any officers you may name for the same purpose, at any point agreeable to you, for the purpose of arranging definitely the terms upon which the surrender of the Army of Northern Virginia will be received.

"Very respectfully, your obedient servant,
"U. S. GRANT,

"Lieutenant General, commanding Armies of the United States."

In the meantime General Lee was pressing on toward Lynchburg, and, on the evening of the 8th, his vanguard reached Appomattox Station, where rations for the army had been ordered to be sent from Lynchburg. Four loaded trains were in sight, and the famished army about to be supplied, when the head of Sheridan's column dashed upon the scene, captured the provisions, and drove the vanguard back to Appomattox Courthouse, four miles off. Sheridan's impetuous troopers met a sudden and bloody check in the streets of the village, the colonel commanding the advance being killed. That morning General Lee had divided the remnant of his army into two wings, under Gordon and Longstreet—Gordon having the advance, and Longstreet the rear. Upon the repulse of the cavalry, Gordon's corps advanced through the village and spent another night of sleepless vigilance and anxiety, while Longstreet, four miles in the rear, had to entrench, against the Army of the Potomac under Meade. That night General Lee held a council of war with Longstreet, Gordon, and Fitz Lee, at which it was determined that Gordon should advance early the next morning to "feel" the enemy in his front; that, if there was nothing but cavalry, he should press on, followed by Longstreet; but that, if Grant's infantry had gotten up in too large force to be driven, he should halt and notify General Lee, that a flag of truce might be raised, and the useless sacrifice of life stopped.

Accordingly, on the morning of the memorable 9th of April, Gordon and Fitz Lee attacked Sheridan's splendid cavalry, outnumbering them more than four to one, and flushed with the full confidence of victory and the assurance that, if they needed support, the "Army of the James" was close at hand. Yet, despite these odds and the exhaustion of these famishing men, they went into that fight with the heroic courage which ever characterized that old corps, and proved themselves not unworthy of Stonewall Jackson, Ewell, Early, Gordon, Rodes, Ramseur, Pegram, J. A. Walker, O. A. Evans, and other noble leaders whom they had been wont to follow to victory. Utterly unable to withstand the onset, Sheridan hastened in person to hurry up the Army of the James, while Gordon drove his "invincible troopers" more than a mile, and captured and brought off two pieces of artillery and a large number of prisoners. Had only Sheridan barred the way, the surrender had not occurred at Appomattox Courthouse; but Gordon only drove back the cavalry to find himself confronted by the Army of the James, and the road blocked by ten times his numbers.

At this time occurred the touching incident related by Colonel Venable, which is given in a previous chapter, and this morning General Grant received the following letter, written the day before:

"April 8th.

"GENERAL: I received, at a late hour, your note of today, in answer to mine of yesterday. I did not intend to propose the surrender of the Army of Northern Virginia, but to ask the terms of your proposition. To be frank, I do not think the emergency has arisen to call for the surrender. But, as the restoration of peace should be the sole object of all, I desire to know whether your proposals would tend to that end.

"I cannot, therefore, meet you with a view to the surrender of the Army of Northern Virginia, but so far as your proposition may affect the Confederate States forces under my command, and lead to the restoration of peace, I should be pleased to meet you at 10 A.M. tomorrow, on the old stage road to Richmond, between the picket lines of the two armies.

"Very respectfully, your obedient servant,

"R. E. LEE, *General, Confederate States Armies.*

"*To* Lieut. General GRANT, commanding Armies of the United States."

The following reply was sent and received on the morning of the 9th:

"April 9th.

"*General* R. E. LEE, *commanding C.S.A.*

"GENERAL: Your note of yesterday is received. As I have no authority to treat on the subject of peace, the meeting proposed for 10 A.M. today could lead to no good. I will state, however, General, that I am equally anxious for peace with yourself; and the whole North entertain the same feeling. The terms upon which peace can be had are well understood. By the South laying down their arms, they will hasten that most desirable event, save thousands of human lives, and hundreds of millions of property not yet destroyed.

"Sincerely hoping that all our difficulties may be settled without the loss of another life, I subscribe myself,

"Very respectfully, your obedient servant,

"U. S. GRANT, *Lieutenant General U.S.A.*"

"The situation" when General Lee received this note was simply this: There were only seven thousand, eight hundred and ninety-two jaded, half-famished Confederates with arms in their hands, nearly surrounded by *eighty thousand* Federal troops already in position, with heavy reinforcements hurrying forward. Gordon fell back through the village, and moved to meet an attack of Sheridan on the flank; the Federal infantry was pressing forward, and that heroic remnant of our grand old army seemed about to crown their illustrious deeds with a glorious death, when General Lee determined to "take all of the responsibility" of stopping, if he could, the further effusion of blood. Accordingly, he had a white flag raised, and sent General Grant the following note:

"*April* 9, 1865.

"GENERAL: I received your note this morning, on the picket line, whither I had come to meet you, and ascertain definitely what terms were embraced in your proposition of yesterday with reference to the surrender of this army.

"I now request an interview in accordance with the offer contained in your letter of yesterday for that purpose.

"Very respectfully, your obedient servant,

"R. E. LEE, *General.*

"To LIEUTENANT GENERAL GRANT, commanding United States Armies."

General Grant at once returned the following answer:

"*April 9th.*

"*General* R. E. LEE, *commanding C. S. Armies.*

"Your note of this date is but this moment (11:50 A.M.) received.

"In consequence of my having passed from the Richmond and Lynchburg road to the Farmville and Lynchburg road, I am at this writing about four miles west of Walter's Church, and will push forward to the front for the purpose of meeting you.

"Notice sent to me on this road where you wish the interview to take place, will meet me.

"Very respectfully, your obedient servant,

"U. S. GRANT, *Lieutenant General.*"

That gallant soldier and unconquerable patriot, General J. A. Early, says that, in his last interview with General Lee, he told him, when speaking of the surrender, that he had that morning only *seven thousand, nine hundred* men with arms in their hands, but that, when he went to meet General Grant, he left orders with Gordon and Longstreet to hold themselves in readiness, and that he had determined "to cut his way out at all hazards if such terms were not granted as he thought his army was entitled to demand."

What followed is best given by General Lee himself in the conversation with the company of friends referred to above:

He said that he had for duty that morning not eight thousand men, and that, when he learned from Gordon that there was a heavy infantry force in his front, he decided to see General Grant and ascertain the terms upon which he could end the contest. But, before going to meet him, he left orders with Longstreet and Gordon to hold their commands in readiness, determined as he was to cut his way through, or perish in the attempt, if such terms were not granted as he thought his army entitled to demand. He met General Grant between the picket lines, in the open field, about two hundred yards below Appomattox Courthouse.

"You met under an apple tree, did you not, General?" asked a gentleman present. "No, sir!" was the reply; "we did not meet under an apple tree, and I saw no tree near. It was in an open field not far from the main road." (This explodes the "historic apple tree," about which so much has been said. A gentleman, who was within a few feet of the two generals when they met, pointed out to the writer the exact spot. The apple tree, which was cut to pieces, and even the roots of which were dug up and carried off by relic hunters, was fully a quarter of a mile from the place of meeting, and the only historic interest that could be attached to it was that General Lee rested under its shade a few minutes while waiting for the return of his flag of truce. The only tree anywhere near the place of meeting was a small locust thorn, which is still standing, about twenty yards from the spot.)

General Lee said that, when he met General Grant, they exchanged polite salutations, and he stated to him at once that he desired a conference in reference to the subject matter of their correspondence. "General Grant returned you your sword, did he not, General?" one of the company asked. The old hero, straightening himself up, replied, in most emphatic tones: "No, sir! he did not. He had no opportunity of doing so. I was determined that the sidearms of officers should be exempt by the terms of surrender, and of course I did not offer him mine. All that was said about swords was that General Grant apologized to me for not wearing his own sword, saying that it had gone off in his baggage, and he had been unable to get it in time." (This spoils a great deal of rhetoric about "Grant's magnanimity in returning Lee's sword," and renders as absurd as it is false the attempt of Northern artists to put the scene on canvas or into statuary. Even General Grant's connivance at this so-called "historic scene" will not save it when the world knows that R. E. Lee said that *nothing of the sort occurred.*) General Lee stated in this conversation that he was accompanied, when he met Grant, only by Colonel Charles Marshall, of his personal staff, who went with one of General Grant's staff to find a suitable room in which to hold the conference; that they were first shown to a vacant house, and, declining to use that, were conducted by Major McClean to his house and shown into his parlor. General Grant was accompanied by several of his staff officers, and several of his generals (among them Sheridan and Ord) entered the room and participated in the slight general conversation that occurred. The two generals went aside and sat at a table to confer together, when General Lee opened the conversation by saying: "General, I deem it due to proper candor and frankness to say at the very beginning of this interview that I am not willing even to discuss any terms of surrender inconsistent with the honor of my army, which I am determined to maintain to the last." General Grant replied: "I have no idea of proposing dishonorable terms, General, but I would be glad if you would state what you consider honorable terms." General Lee then briefly stated the terms upon which he would be willing to surrender. Grant expressed himself as satisfied with them, and Lee requested that he would formally reduce the propositions to writing.

With a common lead pencil, General Grant then wrote and handed General Lee the following paper:

"Appomattox Courthouse,
April 9, 1865.
"*General* R. E. Lee, *commanding Confederate States Army.*

"In accordance with the substance of my letter to you of the 8th inst., I propose to receive the surrender of the Army of Northern Virginia on the following terms, to wit:

"Rolls of all the officers and men to be made in duplicate, one copy to be given to an officer designated by me, the other to be retained by such officers as you may designate.

"The officers to give their individual parole not to take arms against the government of the United States until properly exchanged; and each company or regimental commander to sign a like parole for the men of their commands.

"The arms, artillery, and public property, to be parked, and stacked, and turned over to the officers appointed by me to receive them.

"This will not embrace the sidearms of the officers, nor their private horses or baggage.

"This done, each officer and man will be allowed to return to their homes, not to be disturbed by United States authority so long as they observe their parole, and the laws in force where they may reside.

"Very respectfully,
"U. S. Grant, *Lieutenant General.*"

General Lee read it carefully and without comment, except to say that most of the horses were the private property of the men riding them. General Grant replied that such horses would be exempt from surrender, and the paper was then handed to Colonel Badeau (Grant's secretary), and copies in ink made by him and Colonel Marshall. While this was being done, there were inquiries after the health of mutual acquaintances, but nothing bearing on the surrender, except that General Lee said that he had on his hands some two or three thousand prisoners, for whom he had no rations. Sheridan at once said, "I have rations for twenty-five thousand men."

General Grant having signed his note, General Lee conferred with Colonel Marshall, who wrote this brief note of acceptance of the terms of surrender offered, General Lee striking out the sentence, "I have the honor to reply to your communication," and substituting "I have received your letter of this date."

"HEADQUARTERS ARMY NORTHERN VIRGINIA,
April 9, 1865.

"GENERAL: I have received your letter of this date, containing the terms of surrender of the Army of Northern Virginia, as proposed by you. As they are substantially the same as those expressed in your letter of the 8th inst., they are accepted. I will proceed to designate the proper officers to carry the stipulations into effect.

"Very respectfully, your obedient servant,
"R. E. LEE."

This terminated the interview, and General Lee rode back to his headquarters, which were three-quarters of a mile northeast of the Courthouse.

The above is the substance, and for the most part the exact language, of General Lee's own account of the surrender.

A great deal that has been said about "Grant's magnanimity," and "Lee's warm thanks for the liberal terms accorded," originated in the imagination of the writers. We would not rob General Grant of his just meed of praise for the kind courtesy with which he received General Lee, and the delicate consideration for the feelings of the vanquished with which he conducted the details of the surrender.

But he knew perfectly well that he proposed *the only terms* which General Lee would have accepted; and he was too well acquainted with the mettle of that great captain, and the heroic remnant of the army which had so often defeated him, not to rejoice in an opportunity of covering himself with glory by accepting the surrender of Lee's army on almost any terms.

The appearance of General Lee upon this momentous occasion was thus described by a correspondent of a Northern newspaper, who was present:

"General Lee looked very much jaded and worn, but nevertheless presented the same magnificent *physique* for which he has always been noted. He was neatly dressed in gray cloth, without embroidery or any insignia of rank, except three stars worn on the turned portion of his coat collar. His cheeks were very much bronzed by exposure, but still shone ruddy underneath it all. He is growing quite bald, and wears one of the side locks of his hair thrown across the upper portion of his forehead, which is as white and fair as a woman's. He stands fully six feet one inch in height, and weighs something over two hundred pounds, without being burdened with a pound of superfluous flesh. During the whole interview he was retired and dignified to a degree bordering on taciturnity, but was free from all exhibition of temper or mortification. His demeanor was that of a thoroughly possessed gentleman who had a very disagreeable duty to perform, but was determined to get through it as well and as soon as he could."

As General Lee rode back from this interview, his sad countenance told the story to all who met him, and, when he explained it to his officers, they one by one took him by the hand, and, with deep emotion, expressed their approbation of what he had done.

The announcement was received by the troops generally with mingled emotions—satisfaction that "Marse Robert" had done right, but bitter grief that it had at last come to this.

As showing the spirit of the men who participated in the brilliant action that morning, it may be mentioned that many of them crowded around the bearer of one of the flags of truce—a widely-known and loved chaplain, who, since the capture of his regiment at Spottsylvania Courthouse, had served with great gallantry on General Gordon's staff—and eagerly asked if the enemy had sent in to surrender their force on that road, thinking that in flanking us Grant had pushed a part of his force too far. They had no dream that *they* were to be surrendered. But gradually the truth broke upon them, and great was their chagrin when these high-mettled victors in the last battle of the Army of Northern Virginia learned that they must "yield to overwhelming numbers and resources"—that, after all their marches, battles, victories, hardships, and sufferings, the cause they loved better than life itself must succumb to superior force. Many bosoms heaved with emotion, and

> *"Something on the soldier's cheeks*
> *Washed off the stain of powder."*

The next day General Lee published to the troops the following order—the last which ever emanated from this peerless soldier—which will go down the ages as a touching memento of that sad day at Appomattox Courthouse:

"HEADQUARTERS ARMY NORTHERN VIRGINIA,
April 10, 1865.

"After four years of arduous service, marked by unsurpassed courage and fortitude, the Army of Northern Virginia has been compelled to yield to overwhelming numbers and resources. I need not tell the survivors of so many hard-fought battles, who have remained steadfast to the last, that I have consented to this result from no distrust of them; but, feeling that valor and devotion could accomplish nothing that could compensate for the loss that would have attended the continuation of the contest, I have determined to avoid the useless sacrifice of those whose past services have endeared them to their countrymen. By the terms of the agreement, officers and men can return to their homes, and remain there until exchanged.

"You will take with you *the satisfaction that proceeds from the consciousness of duty faithfully performed;* and I earnestly pray that a merciful God will extend to you his blessing and protection. With an unceasing admiration of your constancy and devotion to your country, and a grateful remembrance of your kind and generous consideration of myself, I bid you an affectionate farewell.

"R. E. LEE, *General.*"

The spirit of the private soldiers may be illustrated by one of many similar incidents which occurred when the Confederate regiments were stacking their arms: A gallant color-bearer, as he delivered up the tattered remnant of his flag, burst into tears and said to the Federal soldiers who received it: "Boys, this is not the first time that you have seen that flag. I have borne it in the very forefront of the battle on many a victorious field, and I had rather die than surrender it now." "Brave fellow," said General Chamberlain, of Maine, who heard the remark, "I admire your noble spirit, and only regret that I have not the authority to bid you keep your flag and carry it home as a precious heirloom."

The calm dignity of General Lee amid these trying scenes, the deep emotion with which the men heard his noble farewell address, and crowded around to shake his hand—how they were thrilled by his simple words, "Men, we have fought through the war together; I have done my best for you; my heart is too full to say more"—Gordon's noble farewell speech—the tender parting of comrades who had been bound so closely together by common hardships, sufferings, dangers, and victories, and now by this sad blighting of cherished hopes—can only be appreciated by those who witnessed that scene which is forever daguerreotyped upon the memories and hearts of that remnant of Lee's splendid army.

And it is proper to add that the Federal soldiers deported themselves with a consideration for the feelings of the vanquished worthy of all praise.

I am fortunate in being able to add to this account of the surrender two letters from General Lee to President Davis, which have never been published, and which, while of course not entering so much into detail, fully confirm the facts given above:

"PETERSBURG, VA., 3 P.M.,
April 2, 1865.

"*His Excellency* JEFFERSON DAVIS, *Richmond, Va.*

MR. PRESIDENT: Your letter of the 1st is just received. I have been willing to detach officers to recruit negro troops, and sent in the names of many who are desirous of recruiting companies, battalions, or regiments, to the War Department. After receiving the general orders on that subject, establishing recruiting depots in the several states, I supposed that this mode of raising the troops was preferred. I will continue to submit the names of those who offer for the service, and whom I deem competent, to the War Department; but, among the numerous applications which are presented, it is difficult for me to decide who are suitable for the duty. I am glad your excellency has made an appeal to the governors of the states, and hope it will have a good effect. I have had a great desire to confer with you upon our condition, and would have been to Richmond before this, but, anticipating movements of the enemy which have occurred, I felt unwilling to be absent. I have considered our position very critical, but have hoped that the enemy might expose himself in some way that we might take advantage of and cripple him. Knowing, when Sheridan moved on our right, that our cavalry would be unable to resist successfully his advance upon our communications, I detached Pickett's division to support it. At first Pickett succeeded in driving the enemy, who fought stubbornly; and, after being reinforced by the Fifth Corps (U.S.A.), obliged Pickett to recede to the Five Forks on the Dinwiddie Courthouse and Ford's Road, where, unfortunately, he was yesterday defeated. To relieve him, I had to again draw out three brigades under General Anderson, which so weakened our front line that the enemy last night and this morning succeeded in penetrating it near the Cox Road, separating our troops around the town from those on Hatcher's Run. This has enabled him to extend to the Appomattox, thus enclosing and obliging us to contract our lines to the city. I have directed the troops from the lines on Hatcher's Run, thus severed from us, to fall back toward Amelia Courthouse, and I do not see how I can possibly help withdrawing from the city to the north side of the Appomattox tonight. There is no bridge over the Appomattox above this point nearer than Goode's and Bevil's, over which the troops above mentioned could cross to the north side and be made available to us; otherwise I might hold this position for a day or two longer, but would have to evacuate it eventually, and I think it better for us to abandon the whole line on James River tonight if practicable. I have sent preparatory orders to all the officers, and will be able to tell by night whether or not we can remain here another day; but I think every hour now adds to our difficulties. I regret to be obliged to write such a hurried letter to your excellency, but I am in the presence of the enemy, endeavoring to resist his advance. I am most respectfully and truly yours,

"R. E. LEE, *General.*"

"NEAR APPOMATTOX COURTHOUSE, VA.,
April 12, 1865.

"*His Excellency* JEFFERSON DAVIS.

"MR. PRESIDENT: It is with pain that I announce to your excellency the surrender of the Army of Northern Virginia. The operations which preceded this result will be reported in full. I will therefore only now state that, upon arriving at Amelia Courthouse on the morning of the 4th, with the advance of the army, on the retreat from the lines in front of Richmond and Petersburg, and not finding the supplies ordered to be placed there, nearly twenty-four hours were lost in endeavoring to collect in the country subsistence for men and horses. This delay was fatal, and could not be retrieved. The troops, wearied by continued fighting and marching for several days and nights, obtained neither rest nor refreshment, and on moving on the

5th, on the Richmond and Danville Railroad, I found at Jetersville the enemy's cavalry, and learned the approach of his infantry and the general advance of his army toward Burkeville. This deprived us of the use of the railroad, and rendered it impracticable to procure from Danville the supplies ordered to meet us at points of our march. Nothing could be obtained from the adjacent country. Our route to the Roanoke was therefore changed, and the march directed upon Farmville, where supplies were ordered from Lynchburg. The change of route threw the troops over the roads pursued by the artillery and wagon trains west of the railroad, which impeded our advance and embarrassed our movements. On the morning of the 6th General Longstreet's corps reached Rice's Station on the Lynchburg Railroad. It was followed by the commands of Generals R. H. Anderson, Ewell, and Gordon, with orders to close upon it as fast as the progress of the trains would permit, or as they could be directed, on roads farther west. General Anderson, commanding Pickett's and B. R. Johnson's divisions, became disconnected with Mahone's division forming the rear of Longstreet. The enemy's cavalry penetrated the line of march through the interval thus left, and attacked the wagon train moving toward Farmville. This caused serious delay in the march of the center and rear of the column, and enabled the enemy to mass upon their flank. After successive attacks, Anderson's and Ewell's corps were captured or driven from their position. The latter general, with both of his division commanders, Kershaw and Custis Lee, and his brigadiers, were taken prisoners. Gordon, who all the morning, aided by General W. F. Lee's cavalry, had checked the advance of the enemy on the road from Amelia Springs, and protected the trains, became exposed to his combined assaults, which he bravely resisted and twice repulsed; but the cavalry having been withdrawn to another part of the line of march, and the enemy massing heavily on his front and both flanks, renewed the attack about 6 P.M., and drove him from the field in much confusion. The army continued its march during the night, and every effort was made to reorganize the divisions which had been shattered by the day's operations; but, the men being depressed by fatigue and hunger, many threw away their arms, while others followed the wagon trains and embarrassed their progress. On the morning of the 7th, rations were issued to the troops as they passed Farmville, but, the safety of the trains requiring their removal upon the approach of the enemy, all could not be supplied. The army, reduced to two corps, under Longstreet and Gordon, moved steadily on the road to Appomattox Courthouse, thence its march was ordered by Campbell Courthouse, through Pittsylvania toward Danville. The roads were wretched and the progress slow. By great efforts the head of the column reached Appomattox Courthouse on the evening of the 8th, and the troops were halted for rest. The march was ordered to be resumed at one (1) A.M. on the 9th. Fitz Lee with the cavalry, supported by Gordon, was ordered to drive the enemy from his front, wheel to the left and cover the passage of the trains, while Longstreet, who from Rice's Station had formed the rear guard, should close up and hold the position. Two battalions of artillery and the ammunition wagons were directed to accompany the army; the rest of the artillery and wagons to move toward Lynchburg. In the early part of the night the enemy attacked Walker's artillery train near Appomattox Station on the Lynchburg Railroad, and were repelled. Shortly afterward their cavalry dashed toward the Courthouse, till halted by our line. During the night there were indications of a large force massing on our left and front. Fitz Lee was directed to ascertain its strength, and to suspend his advance till daylight if necessary. About five (5) A.M. on the 9th, with Gordon on his left, he moved forward and opened the way. A heavy force of the enemy was discovered opposite Gordon's right, which, moving in the direction of Appomattox Courthouse, drove back the left of the cavalry and threatened to cut off Gordon from Longstreet: his cavalry at the same time threatening to envelop his left flank. Gordon withdrew across the Appomattox River, and the cavalry advanced on the Lynchburg road and, became separated from the army. Learning the condition of affairs on the lines where I had gone, under the expectation of meeting General Grant, to learn definitely the terms he proposed in a communication received from him on the 8th, in the event of the surrender of the army, I requested a suspension of hostilities until these terms could be arranged. In the interview which occurred with General Grant, in compliance with my request, terms having been agreed on, I surrendered that portion of the Army of Northern Virginia which was on the field, with its arms, artillery, and wagon trains, the officers and men to be paroled; retaining their sidearms and private effects. I deemed this course the best under all the circumstances by which we were surrounded. On the morning of the 9th, according to the reports of the ordnance officers, there were seven thousand, eight hundred and ninety-two (7,892) organized infantry with arms, with an average of seventy-five (75) rounds of ammunition per man. The artillery, though reduced to sixty-three (63) pieces, with ninety-three (93) rounds of ammunition, was sufficient. These comprised all the supplies of ordnance that could be relied on in the state of Virginia. I have no accurate report of the cavalry, but believe it did not exceed twenty-one hundred (2,100) effective men. The enemy was more than five times our numbers. If we could have forced our way one day longer, it would have been at a great sacrifice of life, and at its end I did not see how a surrender could have been avoided. We had no subsistence for man or horse, and it could not be gathered in the country. The supplies ordered to Pamplin's Station from Lynchburg could not reach us, and the men, deprived of food and sleep for many days, were worn out and exhausted.

"With great respect, your obedient servant,

"R. E. LEE, *General.*"

I have given this detailed account of the surrender, not only to illustrate the character of General Lee, but in order to place on record (against the many incorrect versions that have been published) *the true story of Appomattox Courthouse.*

General Lee illustrated in his own noble bearing the remark he made to one of his officers at the surrender—"Human virtue should be equal to human calamity"—and gave to the world a bright example of firmness under trials such as have rarely come upon one of his sensitive nature. He bore himself with Roman firmness, until his very heartstrings burst asunder, and his pure spirit went to its rest.

Chapter IX

General Lee's affectionate regard for those under his charge and his tender solicitude for their welfare were equaled only by their admiration and love for him. Unlike some military chieftains who would sacrifice thousands of men without scruple, if their fame demanded it, he was willing at any time to allow his own reputation to suffer in order to preserve his men. His soldiers knew that he would not expose them when he could avoid it; that it was through no fault of his if their rations were scant and their hardships many; and that he regularly robbed his own poorly supplied mess table of luxuries which friends would send him, in order that they might go to his ragged, suffering boys in the hospital.

They knew that their great chieftain cared for their welfare, and did all in his power to promote it, and their admiration for his splendid genius as a soldier was even excelled by their love for him as a man. Time and again have I seen these brave men—many of them the very *élite* of Southern society, who had been raised in luxury, and never knew what want was before—ragged, barefooted, and hungry, and almost ready to break out into open revolt at the idea that their sufferings were due to the inefficiency of the quartermaster and commissary departments. But a single word from General Lee, assuring the men that the supply department was doing all that it could to relieve their wants, would act like a charm, and the magic words, "Marse Robert says so," would hush every murmur and complaint.

When he rode among his troops he was always greeted with enthusiastic cheers, or other manifestations of love and admiration. I one day saw a ragged private, whom he met on the road (while riding alone, as was his frequent custom), stand with uncovered head, as if in the presence of royalty, as he rode by. General Lee instantly took off his own hat, and treated the humble man with all possible courtesy and respect, and, as he rode on, the soldier enthusiastically said: "God bless 'Marse Robert!' I wish he was emperor of this country, and that I was his carriage-driver."

Nothing so pleases the private soldier as to see his officers willing to share his dangers; and, among our Confederate soldiers especially, the officer who did not freely go himself wherever he ordered his men, soon lost their confidence and respect. But General Lee was an exception to this rule— the soldiers could never bear to see him exposed to personal danger, and always earnestly remonstrated against it.

On the morning of May 6, 1864, in the Wilderness, as Heth's and Wilcox's divisions, of A. P. Hill's corps, were preparing to withdraw from the line of their gallant fight of the day before, to give place to Longstreet's corps, which was rapidly approaching, the enemy suddenly made upon them a furious attack with overwhelming numbers. These brave men were borne back by the advancing wave; General Lindsay Walker, with his artillery (superbly served under the immediate eye of Lee and Hill), was gallantly beating back the enemy, but they were gathering for a new attack, and it was a crisis in the battle when the head of Longstreet's corps dashed upon the field. General Lee rode to meet them, and found the old Texas Brigade, led by the gallant Gregg, in front. The men had not seen him since their return from Tennessee, and as he rode up and said, "Ah! these are my brave Texans— *I know you,* and I know that you can and will keep those people back"—they greeted him with even more than their accustomed enthusiasm as they hurried to the front. But they were soon horrified to find that their beloved chief was going with them into the thickest of the fight. The men began to shout: "Go back, General Lee! Do go back! General Lee to the rear—General Lee to the rear!" A ragged veteran stepped from the ranks and seized his reins; and at last the whole brigade halted, and exclaimed, with one voice, "We will not advance unless General Lee goes back; but, if he will not expose himself, we pledge ourselves to drive the enemy back." Just then General Lee saw Longstreet, and rode off to give him some order, and these gallant Texans rushed eagerly forward, and nobly redeemed their pledge. The rest of Longstreet's corps hurried to the front, Hill's troops rallied, the enemy was driven in confusion, and only the wounding of Longstreet at this unfortunate juncture prevented the utter rout, if not the crushing, of that wing of Grant's army.

On the 10th of May, 1864, the Confederate lines were broken near Spottsylvania Courthouse; the Federal troops poured into the opening, and a terrible disaster seemed imminent. As Early's old division, now commanded by General John B. Gordon, was being rapidly formed to recapture the works, General Lee rode to the front and took his position just in advance of the colors of the Forty-ninth Virginia Regiment. He uttered not a word—he was not the man for theatrical display—but as he quietly took off his hat, and sat his warhorse, the very personification of the genius of battle, it was evident to all that he meant to lead the charge, and a murmur of disapprobation ran down the line. Just then the gallant Gordon spurred to his side, seized the reins of his horse, and exclaimed, with deep anxiety: "General Lee, this is no place for you! Do go to the rear. These are Virginians and Georgians, sir—men who have never failed—and they will not fail now—Will you, boys? Is it necessary for General Lee to lead this charge?"

Loud cries of "No! no! General Lee to the rear!—General Lee to the rear! We always try to do just what General Gordon tells us, and we will drive them back if General Lee will only go to the rear," burst forth from the ranks.

While two soldiers led General Lee's horse to the rear, Gordon put himself in front of his division, and his clear voice rang out above the roar of the battle, "Forward! Charge! and remember your promise to General Lee!" Not Napoleon's magic words to his Old Guard—"The eyes of your emperor are upon you!"—produced a happier effect; and these brave fellows swept grandly forward, stemmed the tide, drove back five times their own numbers, retook the works, reestablished the Confederate line, and converted a threatened disaster into a brilliant victory.

A similar scene was enacted on the memorable 12th of May (when Hancock had broken the Confederate lines), just in front of the "bloody angle," where General Lee was only prevented from leading Harris's Mississippi Brigade into the thickest of that terrible fight by the positive refusal of the men to go forward unless their beloved chieftain would go to the rear.

These *three* incidents are all well authenticated. But Miss Emily Mason, in her biography, gives a correspondence between Hon. John Thomson Mason and General Lee, in which the former details the incident as it occurred with Gregg's Texas Brigade, and asks the general about it. The reply is characteristic, and is as follows:

"LEXINGTON, VA.,
December 7, 1865.

"MY DEAR SIR: I regret that my occupations are such as to prevent me from writing at present a narrative of the event which you request in your letter of the 4th inst.

"The account you give is substantially correct. General Gordon was the officer. It occurred in the battles around Spottsylvania Courthouse.

"With great respect, your friend and servant,

"R. E. LEE."

"Hon. JOHN THOMSON MASON."

These incidents will go on the page of history as among the grandest battle scenes of the war; but General Lee evidently considered the part he played in them of so little importance that he mingles two into one, and does not even allude to the third. At this time there was the deepest anxiety all through the army and throughout the country lest General Lee should be killed in battle, and President Davis wrote him a touching letter begging that he would not needlessly expose his person.

It was no uncommon sight to see badly wounded men join in the cheers which greeted the appearance of their loved chieftain among his troops.

One day he met coming to the rear a gallant Georgian whose right arm was very badly shattered. "I grieve for you, my poor fellow," said the tenderhearted chief; "can I do anything for you?" "Yes, sir!" replied the brave boy with a proud smile; "you can shake hands with me, General, if you will consent to take my *left* hand." General Lee cordially grasped the hand of the ragged hero, spoke a few kind words which he could never forget, and sent him on his way rejoicing that he had the privilege of suffering under such a leader.

One night some soldiers were overheard discussing the tenets of atheism around their campfire, when a rough, honest fellow cut short the discussion by saying: "Well, boys, the rest of us may have *developed* from monkeys; but I tell you *none less than a God could have made such a man as 'Marse Robert!'* "

We have already described the scene at Appomattox Courthouse, and the affectionate enthusiasm with which he was greeted by both officers and private soldiers. His farewell address was read amid the weeping of veterans of a hundred fields who were really more distressed on account of their loved chief than on their own. How different the feelings of the troops and of the people of the South toward him after the surrender, from those of the army and people of France toward Louis Napoleon after Sedan, or Bazaine after Metz! When General Lee reentered Richmond— the scene of his many triumphs and the reminder of his sad disaster—an immense crowd assembled to greet him with most marked expressions of admiration and love, as they escorted him to his home. And, from that day until his death, he received nothing but tokens of enthusiastic devotion from the soldiers and people whom he had led to a final overthrow of all their fondly cherished hopes.

Not long after the surrender, the general was waited upon by two ragged Confederate soldiers who had just returned from prison, and who said that they came as the representatives of "sixty other fellows around the corner, who are too ragged to come themselves," and who sent them to tender their loved chieftain a home in the mountains of Virginia. "We will give you," said the spokesman, "a comfortable house and a fine farm. We boys will work it for you, and you and your family shall never suffer want. And we hear, general, that Underwood is going to have you indicted and tried for 'treason and rebellion'; now, if you will just accept our proposition we know a mountain hollow to which you can retreat, and we will rally the boys there in force sufficient to defy the whole Federal army."

It was with difficulty that General Lee could restrain his tears sufficiently to say in reply: "Why, my poor fellows, I could not think of accepting your generous offer and being a burden to you. Besides, you would not have your general to hide in the mountains and become what his enemies would call a fugitive from justice. No! I am deeply touched at your offer, and cannot command words to express my gratitude, but I must, of course, decline it."

The noble fellows were persistent, insisting that it would not be a burden—that they had more land than they wanted—and that they would all consider it a high privilege to be permitted to work for their loved chief; and it was only after the general had given them suits of his own clothing in place of their rags that, in their eagerness to show their treasures to their comrades, he succeeded in getting rid of their importunities.

The offer of these ragged soldiers was but the outgushing of the feeling of the whole Southern people. Despite their deep poverty they would have bestowed upon Lee houses, and lands, and money, that would have made him a millionaire had he permitted it. But he preferred to set the people the example of earning his bread by his own honest toil, and steadfastly refused to accept all gratuities.

Upon another occasion he received the following letter from one of his old soldiers, which deeply touched his feelings:

"DEAR GENERAL: We have been fighting hard for four years, and now the Yankees have got us in Libby Prison. They are treating us awful bad. The boys want you to get us out if you can, but, if you can't, just ride by the Libby, and let us see you and give you a good cheer. We will all feel better after it."

It was touching to witness the tender interest which General Lee manifested in the welfare of his old soldiers. When in the autumn of 1865 I met him for the first time since the surrender, I took occasion to mention a number of facts, showing the energy with which our returned soldiers had gone to work to rebuild their ruined fortunes, and the scrupulous care with which they were observing the terms of their parole, and deporting themselves in a quiet and orderly manner, amid the strongest provocation to an opposite course. He expressed himself highly gratified, said that this was in accordance with his own observation and information, and added: "But it is just what we might have expected of them; they were a noble body of men who composed that army."

I remember telling him the following incident, which I will here give in full, as it deserves to be put on record for the use of the future historian: I was traveling one day, in the summer of 1865, in Eastern Virginia, when I saw a young man ploughing in the field, guiding the plough with one hand while an "empty sleeve" hung at his side. I know not how it may be with others, but for myself I never see the empty sleeve or halting gait of the true Confederate soldier, that I do not feel inclined to take off my hat in profound respect for the man. I never pass his vocal grave that I do not linger to cast at least one little violet upon it. I never see a vacant place of honor or emolument, that I do not instinctively look out for some Confederate soldier competent to fill it; and I hope never to see the day when I shall be unwilling to divide with his widow or orphans the last crust that God may give me! Accordingly, I stopped and determined that I would speak with this young man. As he drew near, I recognized him as one whom I had baptized in the army. Our greeting was most cordial, and I was deeply touched by his situation. I knew his history: that he had been raised in affluence, that the breaking out of the war found him at college, with a bright prospect of bearing off its highest honors, and winning for himself a high position in his chosen profession; that he had responded to the call of his native state at the first tap of the drum, had proved as gallant a soldier as ever kept step to the music of "Dixie," and had returned home to find his fortune a wreck, and a widowed mother and several helpless orphans dependent upon him for daily bread. It was sad to see him thus, and I expressed myself in terms of warm sympathy. With a proud smile the noble fellow replied: "Oh! it is all right. I thank God that I have *one* arm left, and an opportunity to use it for the support of those I love." And he went forth cheerfully to his work, guiding the plough with one hand, and singing in a clear, ringing voice a stanza of that grand old hymn, which, by-the-way, was a great favorite, with General Lee, and was sung during his burial services:

> *"In every condition—in sickness, in health,*
> *In poverty's vale, or abounding in wealth,*
> *At home and abroad, on the land, on the sea,*
> *As thy days may demand, shall thy strength ever be."*

As I told this incident of one of his old soldiers, General Lee's face flushed, and with manifest feeling he replied: "What a noble fellow! But it is just like one of our soldiers. The world has never seen nobler men than those who belonged to the Army of Northern Virginia."

He was deeply interested in many details which I was able to give him of particular officers and men whom he remembered, and manifested the liveliest satisfaction at hearing of their welfare.

But when I told him of the general revival of religion then extending through the state, and that large numbers of our returned soldiers were among the converts, tears started in his eyes, as he replied with deep emotion: "I am delighted to hear that. I wish that all of them would become Christians, for it is about all that is left the poor fellows now."

He said very little about it, but, whenever any place of honor or profit was to be filled by his voice or influence, he always gave the preference to one of his veterans, and would not unfrequently say very quietly, "He was a good soldier."

When I was starting in the spring of 1869 on a tour through several of the Southern states, General Lee said to me: "You will meet many of my old soldiers during your trip, and I wish you to tell them that I often think of them, try every day to pray for them, and am always gratified to hear of their prosperity." As this message was repeated at different points, strong men wept as they said, "God bless the old chief; he is the noblest specimen of a man that ever lived!"

One day at the White Sulphur Springs, while in the large parlor conversing with some ladies, and surrounded by the brilliant coterie accustomed to assemble at that abode of fashion, he was told that two of his old soldiers desired to see him. The men had come down from the mountains to bring some marketing, and were dressed in coarse homespun, but were so eager to take their loved chieftain by the hand that they came direct into the parlor. With that instinctive politeness which characterizes Southern society, the company made way for them, and stood silent and deeply interested spectators, while General Lee received these humble men with as genuine courtesy and cordiality, and treated them with as distinguished consideration, as if they had been scions of some royal house. Indeed, the man who could truly say, "I was a soldier of the Army of Northern Virginia, and was true to my colors to the last," had in the eyes of this great man a badge of honor which no earthly potentate could ever bestow.

His deep interest in honoring the memory of the Confederate dead was evinced upon all suitable occasions. The four following letters are specimens of many others he wrote:

"LEXINGTON, VA.,
June 23, 1866.

"*Mr.* WM. H. TRAVERS, *Charlestown, Jefferson County, Va.*

"MY DEAR SIR: I am much gratified to learn, by your letter of the 21st inst., that the citizens of Jefferson County have collected the remains of the Confederate dead in their vicinity, and have reinterred them in the cemetery at Charlestown. It would give me pleasure to accept the invitation of the ladies, through whose instrumentality this good work has been chiefly accomplished, to be present at the services to be performed on the 27th inst., but I am compelled to be here at that time to attend the commencement at Washington College. I must ask you, therefore, to present to the ladies, of whose holy office the graves which contain the ashes thus sacredly collected will be enduring monuments, the apology for my absence.

"Very respectfully, your obedient servant,
"R. E. LEE."

"LEXINGTON, VA.,
August –, 1866.

"*Miss* VIRGINIA S. KNOX, *Fredericksburg, Va.:*

"I have had the honor to receive your letter of the 3d inst., enclosing an appeal of the Ladies' Memorial Association of Fredericksburg for the protection of the graves of the dead around them. It is one which, I am sure, will touch every humane heart, and will raise up willing hands to perform the sacred labor of collecting, in one hallowed spot, the scattered remains of those who now rest far away from their homes and families.

"With my best wishes that success may attend the pious efforts of your association,

"I am, with great respect, yours truly,
"R. E. LEE."

"LEXINGTON, VA.,
May 5, 1865.

"*Mrs.* WM. COULLING, *Chairman of Committee on Lectures, etc.,* ⎫
"*Care of Messrs. Lancaster & Co., Richmond:* ⎭

"I am very much obliged to the ladies of the 'Memorial Association for Confederate Dead' for their invitation to attend the inaugural celebration of their society on the 10th inst. It would be most grateful to my feelings to unite in the celebration of a society formed for so pious an object, but it will be impossible for me to do so.

"The graves of the Confederate dead will always be green in my memory, and their deeds be hallowed in my recollection.

"With great respect, your obedient servant,
"R. E. LEE."

"LEXINGTON, VA.,
December 15, 1866.

"*My dear* FITZ:

"I have considered the subject of your letter, which has been unaccountably delayed on the journey, and, though I have no desire that my views should govern in the decision of a question in which others are equally interested, I will give them for your consideration. In the first place, I have no fears that our dead will receive disrespectful treatment at the hands of the Gettysburg Association. If they do, it will then be time, as it will also furnish the occasion, for us to apply for their transfer to our care. I am not in favor of disturbing the ashes of the dead, unless for a worthy object, and I know of no fitter resting place for a soldier than the field on which he has nobly laid down his life. If our state governments could reflect the wishes of their citizens, and each state could receive its own dead, I think it would be very appropriate to return them to their native soil for final interment, if possible, and I know it would be soothing to the feelings of their friends to have their sacred dust committed to their affectionate keeping. But, so far as I know, this cannot be done, and perhaps the attempt might prevent the very object we wished to accomplish. In the present state of affairs, I presume nothing would be permitted except individual action on the part of respective friends, and I do not know how far that would be available. After the action of the Gettysburg Association, I think it could be better determined whether any good can be accomplished.

"You must give my best love to your father, mother, and brothers. All are as usual, and would unite in my regards did they know I was writing. Your affectionate uncle,

"R. E. LEE."

"General FITZ LEE."

As the army passed through Farmville, on its retreat from Petersburg, General Lee was seen to ride up to the home of the widow of the gallant and lamented Colonel Thornton. Dismounting, and entering the house, he said, with deep emotion, "I have not time to tarry, but I could not pass by without stopping for a moment to pay my respects to the widow of my honored soldier, Colonel Thornton, and to tender her my deep sympathy in the sore bereavement which she sustained when the country was deprived of his invaluable services."

It was this tender feeling for them which made General Lee the idol of his soldiers, and gave him a place in their affections which made them seek every opportunity of expressing their enthusiastic love and admiration for him. His visit to the South, in quest of health, in the spring of 1870, was one continued ovation, notwithstanding the restraint of his known desire to avoid popular applause; and his old soldiers would come for miles to grasp his hand, and gaze once more on his noble form and benevolent countenance.

When the news of his death flashed over the wires, there was mourning in every home in the South, for all of our people felt that they had sustained a personal loss. But his old soldiers wept that a loved and loving *father* had passed from their midst.

It may be well to put on permanent record a few of the expressions of our veterans as they met to honor the memory of their grand old chieftain.

The day after his death a meeting of the officers and soldiers of the Confederate Army resident in Rockbridge assembled in Lexington. Captain A. Graham, Jr., was made chairman, and Rev. J. William Jones (a former chaplain of the Army of Northern Virginia) was made secretary. Major J. B. Dorman reported a series of resolutions, which were unanimously adopted, as follows:

"1. *Resolved,* That, as humble members of the great army of which General Robert Edward Lee was the illustrious head and chief, we mourn his death. With feelings untinged by bitter memories of a stormy past, and with no vain thought of exalting his name in the opinion of mankind, we meet to do him honor. At his open grave, passion must stand abashed, and eulogy is dumb. Striving to mount up to that clear air, wherein his own spirit dwelt, of calm wisdom and heroic patience, we seek only to render a last, simple, but just tribute to his memory. At different times, he was known to some or all of us from the day that he received the sword of Virginia at the hands of her sovereign convention, and from the seven days around Richmond, through the varying fortunes of an unequal fight, to the closing scenes at Appomattox. He has been known to us again as the beloved and venerated citizen of our own community, and the president of the noble institution of learning to which George Washington gave an endowment and a name. We have been daily witness to his quiet, unostentatious, Christian life; we have seen him prove that 'him no adversity could ever move, nor policy at any time entice to shrink from God and from his word.' Knowing him, as we thus did, in war and in peace, we pronounce him to have been, in all the elements of real greatness which may challenge cavil and defy the touch of time, the peer of the most renowned of any age or country, and the foremost American of the wondrous century in which he lived.

"He is gone from among us—'gone before the Father; far beyond the twilight judgments of this world; high above its mists and obscurities'—no more shall we look upon his noble form, meet his benignant smile, or receive his kindly greeting. But here, where he set his last great example of steadfast, unselfish devotion to duty, the memory of his greatness and his worth must ever linger; and, while we reverently bow in submission to the summons of Infinite Wisdom calling him away, we send up a solemn aspiration of thankfulness that to us was the honor and the blessing of communion with him in his last days on earth, and to our people is committed the pious office of consigning his mortal remains to the tomb. Hallowed, through all time, shall be the spot whence his spirit passed from earth to heaven!

"2. *Resolved,* That we tender to Mrs. Lee and her family the expression of our profound sympathy in an affliction which we feel full well can be but little mitigated by poor words of human consolation.

"3. *Resolved,* That the usual badges of mourning be worn for six months.

"4. *Resolved,* That the officers and soldiers of the late Confederate States resident in Rockbridge unite in an association for the erection of a suitable monument at this place; and that the chairman appoint a committee to report a plan of organization to an adjourned meeting on Saturday next."

In Baltimore there was an immense meeting at Masonic Temple, presided over by Major General I. R. Trimble, who opened the exercises with an appropriate address which he began as follows:

"*Fellow Soldiers:* We are assembled together to express our sense of the grievous loss which we have sustained in the death of a beloved commander, a man who possessed the enviable power of inspiring, beyond all comparison, more of the respect, the admiration, and the love of mankind, for his virtues, his genius, and for his kindly, generous nature than any distinguished character who has ever inscribed his name on the pages of all the histories. We have deemed it our appropriate privilege, without any desire for display, to assemble together the companions in arms of General Lee. We claim tonight to feel a peculiar sorrow for the loss of a beloved commander and friend, and no one, we hope, would deny us the mournful consolation of shedding a soldier's tear over a soldier's grave. We accord to all who love him the same sacred privilege. We could not hinder them if we would, for who shall forbid the hearts of a world from loving and mourning for General Robert E. Lee? Who shall restrain the eyes that weep and the tears which fall to swell the ocean of a nation's sorrow?"

The following telegram was read to the meeting:

"HAGERSTOWN, MD., *October* 15, 1870.
"*To Colonels* CHARLES MARSHALL, JAMES R. HERBERT, ⎫
    and others, Masonic Temple;   ⎭

"Your fellow soldiers here are stricken with sorrow like yours, and unite with you tonight in doing reverence to the memory of their great commander. The wounds we felt when Stonewall fell bleed afresh, and Virginia is made trebly sacred by the graves of Washington, Jackson, and Lee.

"HENRY K. DOUGLASS."

Colonel Charles Marshall then made the eloquent address from which the quotation in a previous chapter is taken. He began by saying:

"In presenting the resolutions of the committee, I cannot refrain from expressing the feelings inspired by the memories that crowd upon my mind, when I reflect that these resolutions are intended to express what General Lee's soldiers feel toward General Lee.

"The committee are fully aware of their inability to do justice to the sentiments that inspire your hearts. How can we portray in words the gratitude, the pride, the veneration, the grief that now fill the hearts of those who shared his victories and his reverses, his triumphs and his defeats? How can we tell the world what we can only feel ourselves? How can we give expression to the crowding memories recalled by the sad event we are met to deplore?"

He then gave the incidents we have already quoted, spoke of the confidence of the soldiers in their chief, and concluded as follows:

"Need I speak of the many exhibitions of that confidence? You all remember them, my comrades. Have you not seen a wavering line restored by the magic of his presence? Have you not seen the few forget that they were fighting against the many because he was among the few? But I pass from the contemplation of his greatness in war to look to his example under the oppressive circumstances of final failure —to look to that example to which it is most useful for us now to refer for our guidance and instruction. When the attempt to establish the Southern Confederacy had failed, and the event of the war seemed to have established the indivisibility of the Federal Union, General Lee gave his adhesion to the new order of affairs.

"His was no hollow truce, but, with that pure faith and honor that marked every act of his illustrious career, he immediately devoted himself to the restoration of peace, harmony, and concord. He entered zealously into the subject of education, believing, as he often declared, that popular education is the only sure foundation of free government. He gave his earnest support to all plans of internal improvements designed to bind more firmly together the social and commercial interests of the country, and among the last acts of his life was the effort to secure the construction of a line of railway communication of incalculable importance as a connecting link between the North and the South. He devoted all his great energies to the advancement of the welfare of his countrymen while shrinking from public notice, and sought to lay deep and strong the foundations of the new fabric of government which it was supposed would rise from the ruins of the old. But I need not repeat to you, my comrades, the history of his life since the war. You have watched it to its close, and you know how faithfully and truly he performed every duty of his position.

"Let us take to heart the lesson of his bright example. Disregarding all that malice may impute to us, with an eye single to the faithful performance of our duties as American citizens, and with the honest and sincere resolution to support with heart and hand the honor, the safety, and the true liberties of our country, let us invoke our fellow citizens to forget the animosities of the past by the side of this honored grave, and 'joining hands around this royal corpse, friends now, enemies no more,' proclaim perpetual truce to battle."

Colonel Marshall then reported the following resolutions, which were enthusiastically adopted:

"The officers, soldiers, and sailors of the Southern Confederacy, residing in Maryland, who served under General Robert E. Lee, desiring to record their grief for his death, their admiration for his exalted virtues, and their affectionate veneration for his illustrious memory:

"*Resolved,* 1. That leaving with pride the name and fame of our illustrious commander to the judgment of history, we, who followed him through the trials, dangers, and hardships of a sanguinary and protracted war, who have felt the inspiration of his genius and valor in the time of trial, who have witnessed his magnanimity and moderation in the hour of victory, and his firmness and fortitude in defeat, claim the privilege of laying the tribute of our heartfelt sorrow upon his honored grave.

"2. That the confidence and admiration which his eminent achievements deserved and received were strengthened by the noble example of his constancy in adversity, and that we honored and revered him in his retirement, as we trusted and followed him on the field of battle.

"3. That, as a token of our respect and sorrow, we will wear the customary badge of mourning for thirty days.

"4. That a copy of these resolutions and of the proceedings of this meeting be transmitted to the family of our lamented chief."

Rev. Thomas U. Dudley then made an eloquent address, from a report of which the following extract is taken:

"Mr. Dudley said he counted himself happy that, though almost a stranger in this home of his adoption, he was permitted to speak as a Confederate soldier to Confederate soldiers gathered about the effigy of their leader who is gone, because he knew that their hearts beat as his heart. He counted himself happy that, by the courtesy of the committee of arrangements, he was permitted to bring his little flower to add to the royal wreath of *immortelles* they were gathered to place on the grave of their father chieftain who was gone.

"Yes, they have buried him today, brother soldiers, in his mountain home, beneath the church he had builded. Perhaps some day a nation shall demand that his dust shall be buried near her capital. Perhaps some day the Richmond he defended will guard the precious remains. Let him be buried there––not on the hill with the presidents, but bury him where the boys lie, that when the grand reveille sounds they may behold their chieftain in their midst. For that grand reveille *will* sound, and it is of this that he would speak. He came not to speak of him as patriot—for they had been told by one who knew and loved him long, who sat at his feet as his pupil, the capacity of his great heart to take in its embrace *all* the land he served. He would not speak of him as soldier, for they had been just told of the glory which he had put upon that flag which poor, puny malice would not suffer to be lowered at half-mast in honor of him dead. He would not speak of him as soldier to men who had seen under his prescient guidance a handful chase a thousand; who had seen the marvelous circle of retreat, ever keeping the shield of his army between the foe and the city he defended. He came to speak of him, not as patriot, but as Christian patriot; not as soldier, but as Christian soldier. They were building tonight, in their breasts, a monument to the dead hero; patriot and soldier are graven there. He came to write Christian above them."

Mr. Dudley then gave a delineation of his Christian character, and concluded as follows:

"There is left to us, brother soldiers, other than the mournful privilege to tell over to our hearts, and to our children, the battles, sieges, fortunes, he had passed. There is left to us the grand example of God's faithful servant, that we may follow. He, being dead, yet speaketh, bidding you, his soldiers, to enlist under this Christian banner. This is his command. You did never fail to follow where he led; you did never flinch or falter to do his bidding. This is the command he speaks: Enlist and battle for God and Christ, so that, when our end shall come, we, too, like him, may ever wrap the drapery of our couch about us, and lay us down, not to dreams, but to the eternal realities which eye hath not seen nor ear heard, nor hath entered into the heart of man, but which God hath prepared for them that love Him—that we, too, may hear, as we trust he has heard, the greeting:

> *"Soldier of Christ, well done!*
> *Rest from thy loved employ;*
> *Thy battle's o'er, thy victory won—*
> *Enter thy Master's joy!"*

Similar meetings were held, and similar expressions of grief given, by the soldiers at Louisville, St. Louis, Memphis, New Orleans, Galveston, Mobile, Savannah, Atlanta, Charleston, Raleigh, and, indeed; in wellnigh every city, town, and village of the South; but we have space for only a brief notice of the great soldiers' meeting in Richmond, which assembled in response to the following call from General Early:

"LYNCHBURG, VA.,
October 24, 1870.
"*To the Surviving Officers and Soldiers of the Army of Northern Virginia.*

"COMRADES: The sad tidings of the death of our great commander came at a time when, by the interruption of all the ordinary modes of traveling, very many of us were debarred the privilege of participating in the funeral ceremonies attending the burial of him we loved so well, or, by concerted action, of giving expression to our feelings on the occasion. While the unburied remains of the illustrious hero were yet under the affectionate care of friends who were bowed down with a sorrow unutterable, the hoarse cry of 'treason' was croaked from certain quarters, for the vile but abortive purpose of casting a stigma upon his pure and exalted character. His fame belongs to the world and to history, and is beyond the reach of malignity; but a sacred duty devolves upon those whom, in defense of a cause he believed to be just, and to which he remained true to the latest moment of his life, he led so often to battle, and for whom he ever cherished the most affectionate regard—we owe it to our fallen comrades, to ourselves, and to posterity, by some suitable and lasting memorial, to manifest to the world, for all time to come, that we were not unworthy to be led by our immortal chief, and that we are not now ashamed of the principles for which Lee fought and Jackson died.

"Already steps have been taken by some Confederate officers and soldiers, assembled at Lexington, the place of General Lee's death and burial, to inaugurate a memorial association; and being, as I believe, the senior in rank of all officers of the Army of Northern Virginia now living in the state, I respectfully suggest and invite a conference at Richmond, on Thursday, the 3d day of November next, of all the survivors of that army, whether officers or privates, and in whatever state they may live, who can conveniently attend, for the purpose of procuring concert of action in regard to the proceeding contemplated. I would also invite to that conference the surviving officers and soldiers of all the other Confederate armies, as well as the officers, sailors, and marines of the Confederate navy.

"This call would have been made sooner, but for my absence, up to this time, in a county where there are no railroads or telegraphs, and where I was detained by imperative duties.

"Your friend and late fellow soldier,

"J. A. EARLY."

In response to this call, there was an immense gathering of Lee's veterans in a meeting which, for deep feeling and warm enthusiasm for its object, has been rarely equaled. As indicating the representative character of the meeting, we give the following names of gentlemen who served on committees:

On Permanent Organization.

General WILLIAM TERRY,	Bedford, *Chairman.*
Major ROBERT STILES,	Richmond.
S'g't J. VANLEW McCREERY,	Richmond.
Corp'l WILLIAM C. KEAN, JR.,	Louisa.
Lieutenant JOHN E. ROLLER,	Rockingham.
Lieutenant HENRY C. CARTER,	Richmond.
General GEORGE E. PICKETT,	Richmond.
General JOHN R. COOKE,	King William.
General HARRY HETH,	Baltimore.
Colonel THOMAS H. CARTER,	King William.
Colonel H. P. JONES,	Hanover.
Private W. H. EFFINGER,	Rockingham.
Capt. JAMES WILLIAM FOSTER,	Leesburg.
Colonel THOMAS L. PRESTON,	Albemarle.
General WILLIAM H. PAYNE,	Fauquier.
Colonel ROBERT S. PRESTON,	Montgomery.
Captain W. C. NICHOLAS,	Maryland.
Colonel WILLIAM ALLAN,	Lexington.
Private ABRAM WARWICK,	Richmond.
Major A. R. VENABLE,	Prince Edward.
Lieutenant SAMUEL WILSON,	Surry.
Major RO. W. HUNTER,	Winchester.
Lieutenant JAMES POLLARD,	King William.
Colonel WILLIAM NELSON,	Hanover.
Captain R. D. MINOR,	Richmond.
General JAMES H. LANE,	North Carolina.
Colonel W. W. GORDON,	New Kent.
Hon. WILLIAM WELSH,	Kent County, Md.
Captain J. L. CLARKE,	Baltimore.

On Resolutions

Colonel CHARLES S. VENABLE,	Albemarle, *Chairman.*
Hon. R. T. BANKS,	Baltimore.
Major JOHN W. DANIEL,	Lynchburg.
Lieut. RICHARD H. CHRISTIAN,	Richmond.
Major WILLIAM H. CASKIE,	Richmond.
General BENJAMIN HUGER,	Fauquier.
General WILLIAM MAHONE,	Norfolk.
General L. L. LOMAX,	Fauquier.
GEORGE H. PAGELS, Esq.,	Baltimore.
Colonel EDMUND PENDLETON,	Botetourt.
Private JOHN A. ELDER,	Richmond.
Com. MATTHEW F. MAURY,	Lexington.
General GEORGE H. STEWART,	Baltimore.
General C. W. FIELD,	Baltimore.
General W. S. WALKER,	Georgia.
Serg't LEROY S. EDWARDS,	Richmond.
Lieut. S. V. SOUTHALL,	Albemarle.
Captain J. M. HUDGINS,	Caroline.
Col. WILLIAM E. CAMERON,	Petersburg.
Colonel WILLIAM WATTS,	Roanoke.
General HARRY HETH,	Baltimore.
Gen. WILLIAM B. TALIAFERRO,	Gloucester.
General SAMUEL JONES,	Amelia.
Private JOHN B. MORDECAI,	Henrico.
Capt. J. McHENRY HOWARD,	Baltimore.
Captain E. GRISWOLD,	Baltimore.
Lieutenant R. C. JONES,	Alleghany County, Md.

Lieutenant General J. A. Early was made temporary chairman of the meeting, and, in taking the chair, made a characteristic address, from which we take the following extract:

"*Friends and Comrades:* When the information of the death of our illustrious commander was flashed over the telegraphic wires to all parts of the civilized world, good men everywhere mourned the loss of him who, in life, was the noblest exemplar of his times, of all that is good, and true, and great in human nature; and a cry of anguish was wrung from the hearts of all true Confederate soldiers, which was equaled only by that which came up from the same hearts when the fact was realized that the sword of Robert E. Lee was sheathed forever, and that the banner to which his deeds had given such luster was furled amid gloom and disaster. After the first burst of grief had subsided, the inquiry arose in the breasts of all, What can we do to manifest our esteem and veneration for him we loved so well? It was but necessary that the suggestion should be made, to elicit an expression of the general sentiment. I thought that I could take the liberty of making that suggestion to my old comrades, and I therefore made the call under which you are here assembled. Although I made that call as the former senior in rank of all the officers of the Army of Northern Virginia, now living in the state, I desire to say to you that at the tomb of General Lee all distinctions of rank cease. The private soldier who, in tattered uniform and with sore and bleeding feet, followed the banner upheld by Lee and Jackson, and did not desert his post or skulk in the hour of danger, but did his duty faithfully to the end of the war, and is now doing his duty by remaining true to the principles for which he fought, is the peer of the most renowned in fame or exalted in rank among the survivors. He has an equal share in the proud heritage left us in the memory of the glorious deeds and exalted virtues of our great chieftain. All such I greet and welcome here, as I do those of every rank, claiming them all as my friends, comrades, and brothers.

"My friends, if it is expected that I shall on this occasion deliver a eulogy on General Lee, you will be disappointed. I have not the language with which to give expression to my estimate of the greatness and goodness of his character. I will say, however, that, extended as is his fame, the world at large has not fully appreciated the transcendent abilities of General Lee, nor realized the perfection of his character. No one who has not witnessed the affectionate kindness and gentleness, and often playfulness, of his manners in private, his great self-control and dignity in dealing with important public affairs, the exhibition of his high and unyielding sense of duty on all occasions, and the majestic grandeur of his action and appearance in the shock of battle, can form more than an approximate estimate of his real character."

The following permanent officers were elected:

President
Hon. JEFFERSON DAVIS.

Vice Presidents.

Maj. Gen'l JOHN B. GORDON.

Maj. Gen'l EDWARD JOHNSON.

Maj. Gen'l J. R. TRIMBLE.

Maj. Gen'l W. B. TALLAFERRO.

Brig. Gen'l WM. N. PENDLETON.

Maj. Gen'l WILLIAM SMITH.

Brig. Gen'l J. D. IMBODEN.

Colonel CHARLES MARSHALL.

Colonel WALTER H. TAYLOR.

Colonel W. K. PERRIN.

Colonel PEYTON N. WISE.

General M. RANSOM.

Captain ROBERT PEGRAM.

General L. L. LOMAX.

Major General FITZ LEE.

Colonel HENRY PEYTON.

Colonel J. L. FRENCH.

Colonel ROBERT E. WITHERS.

Major WM. N. BERKELEY.

Colonel WILLIAM WILLIS.

Col. WM. PRESTON JOHNSON.

Captain MANN PAGE.

Corporal WILLIAM C. KEAN.

Private ROBERT MARTIN.

Private G. HOUGH.

Private G. ELDER.

Serg't W. WIRT ROBINSON.

Secretaries.

Captain E. S. GREGORY.

Sergeant GEORGE L. CHRISTIAN.

Captain C. G. LAWSON.

Sergeant JAMES P. COWARDIN.

Captain W. A. ANDERSON.

Private ABNER ANDERSON.

Captain THOS. D. HOUSTON.

Captain GEORGE WALKER.

Major WILLIAM B. MYERS.

The advance of Mr. Davis to the platform was greeted with a burst of irrepressible enthusiasm, which plainly showed that he still had a warm place in the hearts of his old soldiers. His address (from which we have quoted in a previous chapter, and now give the following extracts) thrilled every heart, and elicited the most unbounded expressions of approbation. JEFFERSON DAVIS's tribute to ROBERT E. LEE will always deserve a place on the page of history. He began by saying:

"*Soldiers and Sailors of the Confederacy, Countrymen and Friends:* Assembled on this sad occasion, with hearts oppressed with the grief that follows the loss of him who was our leader on many a bloody battlefield, there is a melancholy pleasure in the spectacle which is presented. Hitherto, in all times, men have been honored when successful; but here is the case of one who, amid disaster, went down to his grave, and those who were his companions in misfortune have assembled to honor his memory. It is as much an honor to you who give as to him who receives, for above the vulgar test of merit you show yourselves competent to discriminate between him who enjoys and him who deserves success.

"Robert E. Lee was my associate and friend in the Military Academy, and we were friends until the hour of his death. We were associates and friends when he was a soldier and I a Congressman; and associates and friends when he led the armies of the Confederacy and I held civil office, and therefore I may claim to speak as one who knew him. In the many sad scenes and perilous circumstances through which we passed together, our conferences were frequent and full, yet never was there an occasion on which there was not entire harmony of purpose and accordance as to means. If ever there was difference of opinion, it was dissipated by discussion, and harmony was the result. I repeat, *we never disagreed,* and I may add that I never in my life saw in him the slightest tendency to self-seeking. It was not his to make a record, it was not his to shift blame to other shoulders; but it was his with an eye fixed upon the welfare of his country, never faltering, to follow the line of duty to the end. His was the heart that braved every difficulty; his was the mind that wrought victory out of defeat.

"He has been charged with 'want of dash.' I wish to say that I never knew Lee to decline to attempt anything man might dare.''

He then gave the incidents quoted in a previous chapter, defended General Lee in his conduct of the Gettysburg and other campaigns, and continued as follows:

"I shall not attempt to review the military career of our deceased chieftain. Of the man, how shall I speak? He was my friend, and in that word is included all that I could say of any man. His moral qualities rose to the height of his genius. Self-denying—always intent upon the one idea of duty—self-controlled to an extent that many thought him cold—his feelings were really warm, and his heart melted readily at the sufferings of the widow and the orphan, and his eye rested with mournful tenderness upon the wounded soldier. During the war he was ever conscious of the insufficiency of the means at his control; but it was never his to complain or to utter a doubt—it was always his to do. When in the last campaign he was beleaguered at Petersburg, and painfully aware of the straits to which we were reduced, he said, 'With my army in the mountains of Virginia I could carry on this war for twenty years longer.' His army greatly diminished, his transportation deficient, he could only hope to protract the defense until the roads should become firm enough to enable him to retire. An untoward event caused him to anticipate the movement, and the Army of Northern Virginia was overwhelmed. But in the surrender he trusted to conditions that have not been fulfilled: he expected his army to be respected and his paroled soldiers to be allowed the peaceful enjoyment of civil rights and property. Whether these conditions have been fulfilled, I leave it to others to determine.

"Here he now sleeps in the land he loved so well, and that land is not Virginia only, for they do injustice to Lee who believe he fought only for Virginia. He was ready to go anywhere, on any service for the good of his country, *and his heart was as broad as the fifteen states struggling for the principles that our forefathers fought for in the Revolution of 1776.* He sleeps with the thousands who fought under the same flag—and happiest they who first offered up their lives—he sleeps in the soil to him and to them most dear. That flag was furled when there was none to bear it. Around it we are assembled, a remnant of the living, to do honor to his memory, and there is an army of skeleton sentinels to keep watch above his grave. This good citizen, this gallant soldier, this great general, this true patriot, had yet a higher praise than this or these—he was a true Christian. The Christianity which ennobled his life gives to us the consolatory belief that he is happy beyond the grave.

"But, while we mourn the loss of the great and the true, drop we also tears of sympathy with her who was a help-meet to him—the noble woman who, while her husband was in the field leading the army of the Confederacy, though an invalid herself, passed the time in knitting socks for the marching soldiers! A woman fit to be the mother of heroes, and heroes are descended from her. Mourning with her, we can only offer the consolations of the Christian. Our loss is not his, but he now enjoys the rewards of a life well spent, and a never wavering trust in a risen Savior. This day we unite our words of sorrow with those of the good and great throughout Christendom, for his fame is gone over the water—his deeds will be remembered; and, when the monument we build shall have crumbled into dust, his virtues will still live, a high model for the imitation of generations yet unborn."

Colonel Charles S. Venable, of the University of Virginia, then presented the appropriate resolutions, which were enthusiastically adopted by the meeting, and made the eloquent address from which we have quoted in a previous chapter.

General John S. Preston, of South Carolina, then made an eloquent address, from which we make the following extract:

"*Mr. President and Comrades of the Army of the Confederate States:* There was a time when, with wicked and impatient infidelity, I feared it was not a kind Providence which permitted men with gray beards to survive our war. But, having seen Robert Lee live as righteously as he fought gloriously, and that we are now spared to the holy duty of honoring his memory and perpetuating his faith, I recant the heresy, and meekly wait the way of the Lord; and am grateful for that consideration which calls me to appear in this stately procession. Yet I scarcely dare to bring my little blade of grass to lay upon a grave already glittering with tears and pearls, flowing from the eyes and hearts of a mourning world. On no occasion of my life have I been so utterly unable to tell the feelings of my heart, or the crowding thoughts which come rushing on my brain. But, comrades, we are not here to find rhetorical forms, modes, and shows of grief, not even to speak singly, but all together, as in these complete resolutions, with one tongue, one heart, in the simplest words of our language, to join our grief and our honor.

"As a Virginian, as a Confederate, as a man, as a friend, I am overwhelmed with the emotions which emanate from all these attributes of my being. Standing here before the most illustrious and the bravest living, I feel as if I were in the very presence of the greatest dead who has died in my generation—of him to whom my spirit bowed as to the anointed champion of the purest human faith I have ever cherished—of him who, by his great deeds, by his pure life, by his humble faith in the meek and lowly Jesus, has justified to the world, and is now pleading with a God of truth for, that cause which made him the most illustrious living man and the most mourned of all the dead who have died in his generation. It was the greatness of his cause, and the purity of his faith in that cause, which made Robert Lee great, for we who know him best do know that Robert Lee could never have achieved greatness in an ignoble cause, or under an impure faith. God gave him to us, to sanctify our faith, and to show us and the world that, although we might fail, his chosen servant had made that cause forever holy."

General Preston was followed by General John B. Gordon, of Georgia, who spoke as follows:

"*Mr. Chairman, Ladies, and Fellow Soldiers:* If permitted to indulge the sensibilities of my nature, I would gladly have fled the performance of this most honorable task your kindness has imposed, and in silence tonight have contemplated the virtues of the great and good man whose loss we so deplore. I loved General Lee, for it was my proud privilege to have known him well. I loved him with a profound and filial awe—a sincere and unfeigned affection. We all loved him, and it is not a matter of surprise that the sons and daughters of Virginia should contend for that sweetest of all privileges now left us—to keep special watch over his grave.

"But where his remains shall lie is not the subject we are here to consider. We are met to provide, as suggested by the resolutions, for the erection of a monument in honor of our great captain. Honor, did I say? Honor General Lee! How vain! What utter mockery do these words seem! Honor Lee! Why, my friends, his deeds have honored him. The very trump of Fame is proud to honor him. Europe and the civilized world have honored him supremely, and history itself will catch the echo and make it immortal. Honor Lee! Why, sir, the sad news of his death, as it was borne to the world, carried a pang even to the hearts of marshals and of monarchs; and I can easily fancy that, amid the din, and clash, and carnage of battle, the cannon, in transient pause at the whispered news, briefly ceased its roar around the walls of Paris.

"The brief time it would be proper for me to occupy tonight is altogether insufficient to analyze the elements which made him great. But I wish to say that it has been my fortune in life to have come in contact with some whom the world pronounced great; but of no man whom it has ever been my fortune to meet can it be so truthfully said, as of Lee, that, grand as might be your conceptions of the man before, he arose in incomparable majesty on more familiar acquaintance. This can be affirmed of few men who have ever lived or died, and of no other man whom it has been my fortune to approach. Like Niagara, the more you gazed the more its grandeur grew upon you, the more its majesty expanded and filled your spirit with a full satisfaction, that left a perfect delight without the slightest feeling of oppression. Grandly majestic and dignified in all his deportment, he was genial as the sunlight of May, and not a ray of that cordial, social intercourse but brought warmth to the heart, as it did light to the understanding."

General Gordon then gave the discussion of General Lee's military career, which is quoted in a previous chapter, and proceeded as follows:

"General Lee is known to the world only as a military man, but it is easy to divine from his history how mindful of all just authority, how observant of all constitutional restrictions would have been his career as a civilian. When, near the conclusion of the war, darkness was thickening about the falling fortunes of the Confederacy, when its very life was in the sword of Lee, it was my proud privilege to note, with special admiration, the modest demeanor, the manly decorum, and the respectful homage, which marked all his intercourse with the constituted authorities of his country. Clothed with all power, he hid its every symbol behind a genial modesty, and refused to exert it save in obedience to law. And even in his triumphant entry into the territory of the enemy, so regardful was he of civilized warfare, that the observance of his general orders as to private property and private rights left the line of his march marked and marred by no devastated fields, charred ruins, or desolated homes.

"But it is his private character, or rather, I should say his personal emotion and virtues, which his countrymen will most delight to consider and dwell upon. His magnanimity, transcending all historic precedents, seemed to form a new chapter in the book of humanity. Witness that letter to Jackson, after his wounds at Chancellorsville, in which he said, 'I am praying for you with more fervor than I ever prayed for myself'; and that other, more disinterested and pathetic, 'I could for the good of my country wish that the wounds which you have received had been inflicted upon my own body'; or that of the latter message, 'Say to General Jackson that his wounds are not so severe as mine, for he loses but his left arm, while I, in him, lose my right'; or that other expression of unequaled magnanimity in which he ascribed the glory of their joint victory to the sole credit of the dying hero. Did I say unequaled? Yes, that was an avowal of unequaled magnanimity, until it met its parallel in his own grander self-negation, in assuming the sole responsibility for the failure at Gettysburg. Ay, my countrymen, Alexander had his Arbela, Cæsar his Pharsalia, Napoleon his Austerlitz, but it was reserved for Lee to grow grander and more illustrious in defeat than ever in victory—grander, because in defeat he showed a spirit grander than victory, the heroism of battles, or all the achievements of the war—a spirit which crowns him with a chaplet far greener than ever mighty conqueror wore.

"I turn me now to that last closing scene at Appomattox, and draw thence a picture of this man as he laid aside the sword of the unrivaled soldier, to become the most exemplary of citizens.

"I can never forget the deferential homage paid this great captain by even the Federal soldiery, as with uncovered heads they contemplated in mute admiration this now captive hero, as he rode through their ranks. Impressed forever, daguerreotyped on my heart, is that last parting scene with the handful of heroes still crowding around him. Few, indeed, were the words then spoken, but the quivering lip and the tearful eye told of the love they bore him, in symphonies more eloquent than any language can describe. Can I ever forget? No, never, never, can I forget the words which fell from his lips as I rode beside him amid the dejected and weeping soldiery, when turning to me he said, 'I could wish that I were numbered among the fallen in the last battle'; and oh! as he thought of the loss of the cause—of the many dead scattered over so many fields, who sleeping neglected, with no governmental arms to gather up their remains, sleeping isolated and alone beneath the tearful stars, with naught but their soldier blankets about them; oh! as these emotions swept over his great soul, he felt that he would fain have laid him down to rest in the same grave where lies buried the common hope of his people. But Providence willed it otherwise. He rests now forever, my countrymen, his spirit in the bosom of that Father whom he so faithfully served, his body in the Valley, surrounded by the mountains of his native state—mountains the autumnal glories of whose magnificent forests now seem but habiliments of mourning—in the Valley, the pearly dewdrops on whose grass and flowers seem but tears of sadness:

'No sound shall awake him to glory again.'

"No more shall he lead his invincible lines to victory. No more shall we gaze upon him, and draw from his quiet demeanor lessons of life. But oh! it is a sweet consolation to us, who loved him, that no more shall his bright spirit be bowed down to the earth with the burden of his people's wrongs. It is sweet consolation to us that this last victory, through faith in his crucified Redeemer, is the most transcendently glorious of all his triumphs.

"It is meet that we should build to his memory a monument here; here in this devoted city; here on these classic hills—a monument as enduring as their granite foundations—here beside the river, whose banks are ever memorable, and whose waters are vocal with the glories of his triumphs.

"Here let the monument stand, as a testimonial to all peoples, and countries, and ages, of our appreciation of the man who, in all the aspects of his career, and character, and attainments—as a great captain, ranking among the first of any age; as a patriot, whose self-sacrificing devotion to his country renders him the peer of Washington; as a Christian like Havelock, recognizing his duty to his God above every other consideration; with a native modesty which refused to appropriate a glory all his own, and which surrounds with a halo of light his whole career and character; with a fidelity to principle which no misfortunes could shake; with an integrity of life and sacred reverence for truth which no man can dare to assail—must ever stand peerless among men in the estimation of Christendom."

Colonel Charles Marshall next delivered the following address, which we give in full, as beautifully illustrating the influence of General Lee over his disbanded soldiers, as well as their warm affection for him, and ardent desire to honor his memory:

"Nothing but an earnest desire to do all in my power to promote the object of our meeting tonight induces me to occupy this stand. I feel my unfitness to address those who have listened to men whose names, I may say, without flattery, are historic—whose valor and constancy deserved and enjoyed the confidence of our great leader. More especially am I unworthy to stand where just now he stood, who—amid all the cares and trials of the eventful period during which he guided the destinies of the Confederacy; amid all the dangers and difficulties that surrounded him; amid all the vicissitudes of victory and disaster—always and on all occasions, gave the aid of his eminent abilities, his unfaltering courage, and his pure patriotism, to our illustrious chief.

"But, on behalf of those who are with me tonight from Maryland, I desire to say a few words in support of the resolutions of the committee.

"These resolutions require that a monument shall be erected, and that it shall be erected in Richmond.

"In both propositions we most heartily concur.

"We are assembled, not to provide for the erection of a tombstone on which to write, 'Here lies ROBERT E. LEE,' but to rear a cloud-piercing monument which shall tell to coming generations,

'HERE LIVED ROBERT E. LEE.'

"We desire something worthy to transmit the lesson of his example, and of our undying love, to posterity; and to this end we invoke the aid not only of those who followed the flashing of his stainless sword, but of all who reverence the memory of his spotless life. We wish to concentrate all efforts upon the attainment of this great end, not that we may honor him, but that we may preserve, for the good of all mankind, the memory of his achievements, and the teaching of his example.

"And it is eminently proper that such a monument should be erected in Richmond.

"Here was the scene of his greatest labors and his greatest triumphs. In defense of this city he displayed those great qualities which have given him the lofty position assigned him by the unanimous voice of his time, and secured for him the love, the gratitude, and the affectionate veneration of the people for whose liberties he fought.

"All his campaigns, all the battles, whether among the hills of Pennsylvania and Maryland, or upon the banks of the Chickahominy and the Appomattox, had for their great object the protection of Richmond.

"Here lie buried the dead of every state from Maryland to Texas, and to this spot, to Hollywood, the hearts of wives, of mothers, and of sisters, from the banks of the Potomac to those of the Rio Grande, are ever sadly but proudly turning.

"No other place in the South unites so entirely the sympathies and affections of her people.

"To raise his monument here within sight of the fields on which he won his fame, and among the graves of those who were faithful to him undo death, seems to us, therefore, to be most appropriate. We do not propose now to say what that monument shall be, but to adopt measures which will enable us to invite the taste, the cultivation, and the genius of our age to compete in furnishing a suitable design.

"And we hope to find someone who can rise to the height of the great argument, grasping the subject, realizing the character and achievements of our leader, feeling the love, the gratitude, the veneration of our people, and, grouping all around this hallowed spot, write in one enduring word the story of General Lee, his army, and his country.

"There is one other reason why we should erect a monument, and why we should erect it here. It is that we may perpetuate for our guidance the lesson taught by his example when war was done, and all his efforts had ended in failure. In that lesson, the whole country has an immediate interest. History presents no parallel to the sudden cessation of resistance on the part of the Southern people after the surrender at Appomattox. In a few short weeks, where armies had but lately confronted each other, peace was fully restored, and not an armed Southron could be found within our borders.

'It seemed as if their mother earth
Had swallowed up her warlike birth.'

"The Federal government manifested its confidence in the pledges made by the soldiers and people of the Confederacy, by sending companies and regiments, to control those before whom corps and armies had fled. That government knew well that the handful of troops sent ostensibly to over-awe the South could repose securely upon that honor which they insulted by their presence.

"And in that confidence, shame be it said, wrongs were inflicted upon our people, which, we have the authority of unquestioned loyalty for say-ing, ought not to be meekly borne by men of English blood.

"But the Federal government knew that the Southern people looked for guidance to their leaders, and that, foremost among those leaders, they looked to General Lee. He had given the pledge of his honor, and his people regarded his honor as their own.

"Relying upon his influence with his countrymen, and knowing that his influence would be exerted to secure the most perfect compliance with the terms of his surrender, the dominant party in the North entered upon a course of systematic oppression and insult which would have justified him in renouncing the obligations of the terms made at Appomattox.

"But his word was given, and nothing could change it. The dastardly wrongs inflicted upon his people could break and did break his great heart, but could not make him swerve from his truth. He bore all in silence until he died, and his people looked upon him and gathered strength to bear.

"New outrages upon our liberties and rights, new insults to our honor, may tempt us sometimes to forget that our hands no longer hold the sabre or the rifle. To whom shall we turn for that strength which will enable us to keep faith with the faithless?

"We can no longer see the noble example which he set before us, but, that we may not err from the path in which he trod, let us here, at the place toward which the eyes and hearts of all our people turn, rear a monument, to which, when tempted to resist, we may look, and learn afresh the lesson of that sublime patience which he illustrated, and which, my fellow soldiers and countrymen, be assured, will, like the anvil, wear out many hammers."

General Henry A. Wise (ex-governor of Virginia) then made a char-acteristic address, from which we make the following extract:

"*Mr. President and Comrades of the Confederacy:* I cannot trust the fullness of my heart at the moment of this meeting to prompt my lips with the words becoming the bier of General Robert E. Lee, whose death has called together some of his surviving comrades.

"It is no occasion for any sketch of biography or history; eulogy upon his life and death is vain; his character excels all praise; his merits need not to be disclosed, and his faults had no 'dread abodes,' for they all leaned to virtue's side. Whatever faults he had, and whatever blame belonged to him, no friend or foe could point them out half as readily as his truthful ingenuousness would admit and mourn them. He was swifter than the accuser to accuse himself, and ever generous to the faults of others; he was ever foremost to acknowledge his own. If nothing is to be said of the dead but what is good, there is a superabundance of good in his life and death to compose volumes for the instruction of mankind. He is departed and gone to his Father, but it cannot be said of him that he is 'no more.' His fame is left to earth for all time—his great and good soul is in heaven for all eternity; and from his example proceed a moral power and divine force which all the arms of earth and powers of darkness cannot subdue, a wisdom and virtue which shall hover over the land he loved, and spread it with the fruits of righteousness and truth. That is enough to be said of him, and it is left for us to cherish his memory, and keep the legacies of lessons he taught.

"The first fruit of his demise is the happy result of bringing us together, for the first time since he gave up the sword, which he accepted with the pledge to devote it to the gods and the altars of his home, and to sheathe it only when his work was finished. He sheathed it not until his whole duty was discharged and his work was done. He made us honor, love, and confide in him, and taught us how to deserve the honor, love, and confidence of each other; and I pray you now to form a brotherhood in peace which shall perpetuate our comradeship in war, worthy of the armies of the Confederacy and of their illustrious chief."

The next speaker was Colonel Wm. Preston Johnston (son of General Albert Sidney Johnston), of Washington and Lee University, who opened his address as follows:

"*Mr. President and Fellow Soldiers:* A few minutes since, I was informed that I was expected to address you. This unexpected honor greatly embarrasses me, tired with two days' travel, just off the cars, and physically unfit to appear before you. It would ill become me, moreover, to follow with any elaborate attempt the golden-mouthed orator of Virginia, or to utter panegyric after him whose lightest word makes history; and who, while he stood at the head of the Confederacy, never failed to cheer his chosen captain with counsel and comfort, or to uphold his arm in the hour of battle with all the force at his command. It would ill become me here, surrounded by the soldiers who shared in the glories of Lee, and after the speeches of his trusted military friends and of his great lieutenants, who rode down with him to battle, to paint again the meridian splendor of his great campaigns. But, if you are willing to listen to some brief passages of his latter life, I will not detain you long.

"It was my fortune after the war to be called from my distant home in Kentucky by a request which, in the mouth of General Lee, was to me equivalent to a command. For four years I have watched with reverential affection the final scenes of that life, so magnificent in achievements and then so beautiful toward its end. When he had gone down through the bitter waters of Appomattox from the martial glories of the war to the quiet of civic pursuits, that life, always consecrated to duty, was rounded to a perfect close. Turning his face to the desolated land for which he had done and suffered so much, he stretched forth his hand to stanch the wounds he had been unable to avert, and that hand willingly did the work it found to do. As president of Washington College, teaching the sons of his soldiers by precept and example, he presented to the world the noble spectacle of one who could take up the several threads of a career, broken by disaster, and bind them in all their former strength and usefulness. Here in the sunset of his days shone forth his exalted worth, the wonderful tenderness of his nature, and the dignity and composure of his soul. As an illustration of some of these qualities, I may mention that the last hours of his active life were spent in a vestry meeting, where I was present, and that he there evinced great solicitude that the veteran soldier of the Cross, who served as his minister, should be secure of a decent maintenance, and that the house of God where he worshiped should be a not unworthy temple to his name. Yet, even there, he passed the few minutes preceding the meeting in smoothing away the asperities springing from differences of opinion, with playful anecdote and pleasant reminiscence of that saintly servant of God, Bishop Meade, and that noble pillar of constitutional jurisprudence, Chief Justice Marshall.

"Fifteen minutes after we parted from him he was stricken with his last illness, and during this it was sometimes my sad duty to minister to his needs. I feel that, in an assembly where every heart throbs with sorrow for our departed chieftain, I violate no confidence by adverting to a death-bed every way worthy of the life it ended. Once in the solemn watches of the night, when I handed him the prescribed nourishment, he turned upon me a look of friendly recognition, and then cast down his eyes with such a sadness in them, that I can never forget it. But he spoke not a word; and this not because he was unable, for, when he chose, he did speak brief sentences with distinct enunciation, but because, before friends or family or physicians feared the impending stroke, he saw the open portals of death and chose to wrap himself in an unbroken silence as he went down to enter them. He, against whom no man could charge, in a long life, a word that should not have been spoken, chose to leave the deeds of that life to speak for him. To me, this woeful silence, this voice-less majesty, was the grandest feature of that grand death. . . .”

The closing address was made by Colonel R. E. Withers (since lieuten-ant governor of Virginia, and United States senator-elect), and was as follows:

“*Mr. President and Comrades:* After the gorgeous offerings, which, in such rich profusion, have been laid in votive heaps on the tomb of our departed hero, it is perhaps but meet that I should appear bearing the feeble tribute of my love, and with respectful reverence place the modest chaplet on the same holy shrine; for I stand before you the representative of the mass of officers and men of his command. It was to have been expected that the companions of his earlier years, and the friends of his later manhood—that those endeared by the sweets of daily social inter-course, and, yet more, those trusted heroes who launched with red right hand the bolts of his admirable strategy upon the forefront of the enemy—that these should give utterance to feelings of high appreciation, of pro-found admiration, of reverential regard. But I can lay claim to no such enviable intimacy. My personal intercourse with General Lee was infre-quent; yet I, in common with every ragged and dust-begrimed soldier who followed his banner, loved him with deepest devotion. And why was this the predominant sentiment of his soldiery? The answer is obvious: *Be-cause he loved his men.* His military achievements may have been rivaled, possibly surpassed, by other great commanders. Alexander, Marlborough, Wellington, Napoleon, each and all excited the admiration, enjoyed the confidence, and aroused the enthusiasm of their soldiers; but none of these were loved as Lee was loved.

"*They* considered their soldiers as mere machines prepared to perform a certain part in the great drama of the battlefield. They regarded not the question of human life as a controlling element in their calculations; with unmoved eye and unquickened pulse, they hurled their solid columns against the very face of destruction, without reck or care for the destruction of life involved. But General Lee never forgot that his men were fellow beings as well as soldiers. He cared for them with parental solicitude, nor ever relaxed in his efforts to promote their comfort and protect their lives. A striking exemplification of this trait can be found in the fact that it was his constant habit to turn over to the sick and wounded soldiers in the hospital such delicate viands as the partiality of friends furnished for his personal consumption, preferring for himself the plain fare of the camp, that his sick soldiers might enjoy the unwonted luxuries. These facts were well known throughout the army; and hence his soldiery, though often ragged and emaciated, though suffering from privations, and cold, and nakedness, never faltered in their devotion, or abated one tittle of their love for him. They knew it was not *his* fault.

"Of the indignities and injuries inflicted on General Lee and his countrymen it becomes us not now to speak. I have no resentful feelings toward those who met us in manly conflict, but the atrocities perpetrated since the war upon a defenseless people arouse such a storm of passionate remembrance as neither the solemnity of the occasion nor the sanctity of the place will suffice to quell. I can only raise my eyes to Lee's God, and pray for grace to forgive as I hope to be forgiven.

"The resolutions proposed by the committee meet with my hearty approval. Monumental rewards are but the expression of a nation's gratitude for distinguished service, and reverence for the mighty dead. They are not designed to do honor to the dead, but mark the respect and love of the living; and surely no one has commanded such respect and gratitude, or excited such love, as our late commander. Whether the monument be reared in Richmond or in Lexington—whether it casts its shadows over the rushing waters of the James, or bathes its summit in the pure air of the mountains, amid which his parting spirit took its upward flight—it will cause all who gaze upon it to feel their hearts more pure, their gratitude more warm, their sense of duty more exalted, and their love of country touched by a holier flame. But neither classic bust, nor monumental marble, nor lofty cenotaph, nor stately urn, nor enduring bronze,

nor everlasting granite, can add to his glory in this land he loved so well—
for here

> 'The meanest rill, the mightiest river,
> Roll mingling with his fame forever.' "

The eloquent addresses delivered at this grand meeting were listened to by the soldiers present with rapt attention and mingled emotions. Now they would cheer to the echo some fitting tribute to their great leader, and anon the starting tear and deep emotion of these bronzed veterans of a hundred fields would attest their deep grief at his loss. It was an occasion which none present can ever forget, and well expressed the sentiments which the soldiers of Lee universally cherish for their great commander.

Chapter X

HIS DOMESTIC LIFE

It will not do to follow to their homes or trace the domestic lives of many of the world's "heroes." They shine before the public gaze, but are very unlovely in their domestic relations. Not so with this great man. Those virtues which were so admired by the public were all the more conspicuous in the home circle, and his private character was as stainless as it was unassailed by the breath of slander.

It will be pleasant to read a sketch of his family as given by himself in the following letter:

"LEXINGTON, VA.,
November 20, 1865.

"MY DEAR SIR: I received by the last mail your letter of the 13th inst., inquiring into my family history.

"I am a poor genealogist, and my family records have been destroyed or are beyond my reach. But, as you 'insist' on my furnishing the information asked for, and desire it for your 'own private use,' I will endeavor to give you a general account. I am the youngest son of Henry Lee, of the Revolutionary War, who commanded Lee's Legion under General Greene in the Southern Department of the United States, and was born at Stratford, on the Potomac, Westmoreland County, Virginia, the 19th of January, 1807.

"My mother was Anne Hill Carter, daughter of Mr. Charles Carter, of Shirley, on James River. My father was twice married, first to Miss Lee, and then to Miss Carter. 'Major Henry Lee,' of the War of 1812, of whom you inquire, was the only son of the first marriage, and consequently my half-brother. 'Charles Carter Lee,' of whom you also ask, and Sidney Smith Lee, are my full brothers. I had two sisters, Mrs. Anne R. Marshall and Mrs. C. Mildred Childe, neither of whom is living. The first left one son, Colonel Louis H. Marshall, of the United States Army, and the second a son and daughter, who reside in Europe. 'General Fitzhugh Lee' is the eldest son of my second brother, Sidney Smith Lee, who has five sons. My eldest brother Charles Carter Lee, has also six children, the oldest of whom, George, is about eighteen years old. I have three sons, Custis, William H. Fitzhugh, and Robert, and three daughters, Mary, Agnes, and Mildred. My father died in 1818, my mother in 1829. My grandfather was Henry Lee, of Stafford County, Virginia; my great-grandfather Henry Lee, son of Richard Lee, who first came from England to America, and from whom the Southern Lees are descended. Richard Henry, Arthur, and Francis Lightfoot Lee, of the Revolution, were cousins of my father. 'John Fitzgerald Lee,' whom you mention, is the grandson of Richard Henry Lee. I believe I have answered all your questions, and must now express the pleasure I feel in learning that your ancestors were fellow soldiers with mine in the great war of the Revolution. This hereditary bond of amity has caused me, at the risk of being tedious, to make to you the foregoing family narrative. I am also led by the same and other feelings to grieve with you at the death of your brave nephews who fell in the recent war. May their loss be sanctified to you and to their country!

"Very respectfully, your obedient servant,
"R. E. LEE."

An extract from a review of a recently published book from the graceful pen of the gifted author Paul H. Hayne may be appropriately inserted at this point:

"A scene witnessed by us at Fort Sumter, on a spring afternoon of 1861, comes vividly back to memory. Leaning against a great Columbiad which occupied an upper tier of the fortress, we were engaged in watching the sunset when voices and footsteps toward the right attracted our notice.

"Glancing round we saw approaching us the then commander of the fort, accompanied by several of his captains and lieutenants; and, in the middle of the group, topping the tallest by half a head, was, perhaps, the most striking figure we had ever encountered, the figure of a man seemingly about fifty-six or fifty-eight years of age, erect as a poplar, yet lithe and graceful, with broad shoulders well thrown back, a fine, justly proportioned head *posed* in unconscious dignity, clear, deep, thoughtful eyes, and the quiet, dauntless step of one every inch the gentleman and soldier.

"Had some old English cathedral crypt or monumental stone in Westminster Abbey been smitten by a magician's wand and made to yield up its knightly tenant restored to his manly vigor, with a chivalric soul beaming from every feature, some grand old crusader or 'red-cross' warrior who, believing in a sacred creed and espousing a glorious principle, looked upon mere life as nothing in the comparison, we thought that thus would he have appeared, unchanged in aught but costume and surroundings! And this superb soldier, the glamour of the antique days about him, was no other than Robert E. Lee, just commissioned by the president, after his unfortunate campaign in western Virginia, to travel southward and examine the condition of our coast fortifications and seaboard defenses in general. . . .

"Few chapters in the volume before us are more interesting than the introductory chapter upon Lee's ancestry. He was born, as everybody knows, on the 19th of January, 1807, at Stratford, in Westmoreland County, Virginia. But the splendors of his descent are not, perhaps, so universally accredited. Of pure Norman blood, the long line of the Lees may be traced back to a certain Launcelot Lee, of Louder, in France, who accompanied William the Conqueror upon his grand freebooter's expedition to England. After Harold's golden head and brave standard had sunk forever at Hastings, Launcelot was rewarded for his services by an estate in Essex. From that memorable date the name of Lee occurs continually in English annals, and 'always,' we are told, 'in honorable connection.'

"There is Lionel Lee, who fought by Cœur de Lion's side in Palestine, and who for his gallantry at Acre, and in other battles with the infidel, was, on his return home, made the first Earl of Litchfield, and presented by the king with the estate of Ditchley; subsequently held, as all the readers of Walter Scott must remember, by that indomitable old knight, Sir Henry Lee, who figures so conspicuously in 'Woodstock.'

"Then comes Richard Lee, the period of the unfortunate Surrey and his ally during that 'woeful expedition' across the Tweed, into Scotland. About the same time, two other Lees (whose Christian names are unknown) 'so distinguished themselves as to have their banners suspended in St. George's Chapel, Windsor, with the Lee coat-of-arms emblazoned thereon,' and the 'significant family motto, *Non incautus futuri!*'

"Coming down to the time of the first Charles, we find the Lees in Shropshire, all stanch cavaliers. Then it was (probably during some lull in the civil war, or when the civil war had closed) that the 'accomplished' Richard Lee 'determined to remove to the New World.' 'He was,' says Bishop Meade, 'a man of good stature, comely visage, enterprising genius, sound head, vigorous spirit, and most generous nature,' words we may apply literally to the person and character of his illustrious descendant. With this gentleman the noble stock of the Virginia Lees originated.

"Henry, his fifth son, was a direct ancestor of our general. 'He married a Miss Bland; their third son (Henry) married a Miss Grymes,' and became the father of the celebrated cavalry leader of the old Revolution, popularly known as 'Light-Horse Harry.'

"By a second wife, Anne Hill Carter—an aristocrat of the bluest Virginia blood—he was blessed with his son, Robert E. Lee, in the glory of whose renown the fame of the family line grows dim, comparatively, and feeble.

"Lee's claims to high descent having been made clear, this biography intends to narrate his experiences and portray his character, rather in private than in public life. All of us know him as the soldier, but in this little book alone do we meet the man divested, in great measure, of the trappings of office, the halo of command. We learn, for the first time, to know him intimately in his civil, social, and domestic relations—as the citizen, companion, friend, husband, father, the wise instructor of the young, and, in one comprehensive phrase, as the Christian gentleman.

"In all such relations he appears to have been perfect. We scarcely exaggerate in saying that, since the death of the last of the Evangelists, probably no mortal man has passed through life, 'walking habitually nearer to his God,' in thought, conversation, worship, sublime simplicity of faith, in action, whose watchword was duty; and devout contemplation, soothed by the spirit and promises of the Redeeming Christ!

"His virtues, like his religion, were of large, simple, antique mold. His soul, mellowed, chastened, ennobled by suffering gravely yet nobly borne, had, as it were, 'a look southward, and was open to the beneficent noon of Nature' and Deity!

"He could no more have stooped to a meanness than he could voluntarily have committed moral suicide! A broad, unsophisticated, childlike, medieval nature was his, infinitely uplifted, gloriously enlightened by modern culture, and all the graces and amenities of a true Christian discipleship. Take him all in all, and he stands, morally, alone.

"Conventional standards of comparison fail us here. We cast aside our pretty rules, our ordinary methods of inference, our poor standard measurements of everyday character, our common judgments, too small by far to embrace a majestic personality like this."

Miss Emily V. Mason, in her *Popular Life of General Lee,* gives the following account of his early life: "When he was but four years of age, his father removed to Alexandria, the better to educate his children; and there are many persons yet living in that old town who remember him at that early age. From these sources, we are assured that his childhood was as remarkable as his manhood for the modesty and thoughtfulness of his character, and for the performance of every duty which devolved upon him. The family lived on Cameron Street, near the old Christ Church, then on Orinoco Street, and afterward in the house known as the parsonage.

"At this period, General Henry Lee was absent in the West Indies, in pursuit of health, and, in one of his admirable letters written to his son Carter, then a student at Cambridge, he says: 'Robert, who was always good, will be confirmed in his happy turn of mind by his ever-watchful and affectionate mother.'

"When eleven years of age, his father died. From one of the family who knew him best, we are told that from his excellent mother he learned at this early age to 'practice self-denial and self-control, as well as the strictest economy in all financial concerns,' virtues which he retained throughout his life.

"This good mother was a great invalid; one of his sisters was delicate, and many years absent in Philadelphia, under the care of physicians. The oldest son, Carter, was at Cambridge; Sidney Smith in the navy, and the other sister too young to be of much aid in household matters. So Robert was the housekeeper, carried the keys, attended to the marketing, managed all of the outdoor business, and took care of his mother's horses.

"At the hour when the other school boys went to play, he hurried home to order his mother's drive, and would there be seen carrying her in his arms to the carriage, and arranging her cushions with the gentleness of an experienced nurse. One of his relatives, who was often the companion of these drives, still lives. She tells us of the exertions he would make on these occasions to entertain and amuse his mother, assuring her, with the gravity of an old man, that unless she was cheerful the drive would not benefit her. When she complained of cold or 'draughts,' he would pull from his pocket a great jack knife and newspapers, and make her laugh with his efforts to improvise curtains, and shut out the intrusive wind which whistled through the crevices of the old family coach.

"When he left her to go to West Point, his mother was heard to say: 'How can I live without Robert? He is both son and daughter to me.'

"Years after, when he came home from West Point, he found one of the chief actors of his childhood's drama—his mother's old coachman, Nat—ill, and threatened with consumption. He immediately took him to the milder climate of Georgia, nursed him with the tenderness of a son, and secured him the best medical advice. But the springtime saw the faithful old servant laid in the grave by the hands of his kind young master.

"General Lee used to say that he was very fond of hunting when a boy; that he would sometimes follow the hounds on foot all day. This will account for his well-developed form, and for that wonderful strength which was never known to fail him in all the fatigues and privations of his afterlife. . . .

"Only last summer, when General Lee was in Alexandria, one of the old neighbors found him gazing wistfully over the palings of the garden in which he used to play. 'I am looking,' said he, 'to see if the old snow-ball trees are still here. I should have been sorry to miss them.'

"One of his friends gives a remarkable incident to show the influence which, even at this early day, his simple dignity and high sense of right exercised upon all who came in contact with him, the old as well as the young. Being invited during a vacation to visit a friend of his family who lived in the gay, rollicking style then but too common in old Virginia, he found in his host one of the grand old gentlemen of that day, with every fascination of mind and manner, who, though not of dissipated habits, led a life which the sterner sense of the boy could not approve. The old man shrunk before the unspoken rebuke of the youthful hero. Coming to his bedside the night before his departure, he lamented the idle and useless life into which he had fallen, excusing himself upon the score of loneliness, and the sorrow which weighed upon him in the loss of those most dear. In the most impressive manner he besought his young guest to be warned by his example, prayed him to cherish the good habits he had already acquired, and promised to listen to his entreaties that he would change his own life, and thereby secure more entirely his respect and affection."

General Lee's recollections of his childhood home were always as vivid as they were tender and pleasant. To the young lady who made the sketch of his birthplace which we give, he wrote the following characteristic letter:

"LEXINGTON, VA.,
May 28, 1866.
"*Miss* MATTIE WARD, *Care of Rev. Wm. N. Ward, Warsaw Post Office, Va.*

"MY DEAR MISS WARD: I have just received from Richmond the two photographic copies of your painting of Stratford. Your picture vividly recalls scenes of my earliest recollections and happiest days. Though unseen for years, every feature of the house is familiar to me.

"I return my sincere thanks for the pleasure you have given me, and beg you to accept my earnest wishes for your future happiness.
"Your obedient servant,
"R. E. LEE."

His first teacher was Mr. W. B. Leary, an Irish gentleman, who seems to have been a fine scholar and an excellent teacher. There always existed a warm friendship between Mr. Leary and his distinguished pupil. After the close of the war he came to Lexington on a special visit to General Lee; and during his Southern tour, the spring before his death, he came a long way to see him, and they had a most pleasant interview.

Just after his visit to Lexington, the general wrote his old teacher the following letter:

"LEXINGTON, VA.,
December 15, 1866.

"*Mr.* WILLIAM B. LEARY.

"MY DEAR SIR: Your visit has recalled to me years long since passed, when I was under your tuition, and received daily your instruction. In parting from you, I beg to express the gratitude I have felt all my life for the affectionate fidelity which characterized your teaching and conduct toward me.

"I pray that the evening of your days may be blessed with peace and tranquillity, and that a merciful God may guide and protect you to the end.

"Should any of my friends, wherever your lot may be cast, desire to know your qualifications as a teacher, I hope you will refer them to me; for of them I can speak knowingly and from experience.

"Wishing you health, happiness, and prosperity,

"I am affectionately your friend,
"R. E. LEE."

Under Mr. Leary's instruction he acquired that knowledge of the classics and fondness for them which surprised some of his friends who knew only of his military education.

As soon as it was decided that he should go to West Point, he was sent to the school of Mr. Benjamin Hallowell, who was for so many years a famous teacher in Alexandria, in order to perfect himself in mathematics. This gentleman, although espousing the Federal cause during the war, always spoke in enthusiastic terms of his painstaking, successful pupil.

Entering West Point at the age of eighteen, he was always a great favorite among the cadets, although he declined to engage in their "pranks," and for a good part of the time was one of the "cadet officers," and exercised a rigid discipline over them. He was an equal favorite among the professors and officers of the Academy, and graduated *second* in an unusually brilliant class, without having ever received a single demerit.

Soon after his graduation he was summoned to the bedside of his mother, whom he nursed with the tenderest devotion—administering all of her medicine and nourishment with his own hands, and faithfully watching her waning strength—until her summons came, and he was deprived of the affectionate counsel of that one to whom he was accustomed to say he "owed everything." Much has been written of what the world owes to "Martha, the mother of Washington"; but it owes scarcely less to "Anne, the mother of Lee."

When a boy, he was accustomed to visit Arlington, the splendid estate of George Washington Parke Custis (the grandson of Mrs. Washington, and the adopted son of the Father of his Country), and there had as his playmate Mary Randolph Custis. This childish friendship ripened into love, and on June 30, 1831, he led to the altar this only daughter of that illustrious house—the marriage ceremony being performed by Rev. Dr. Keith, of the Theological Seminary near Alexandria. Rarely have two more congenial spirits united their fortunes, or walked together more lovingly the pathway of life. By this marriage Lieutenant Lee became a frequent resident at Arlington, of which Miss Mason gives the following vivid description: "This fine mansion stands on the Virginia Heights opposite Washington City, overlooking the Potomac, and was for many years an object of attraction to all visitors to Washington, on account of its historical associations, and the Washington relics collected and preserved by the patriotic father of Mrs. Lee. Here were to be seen the original portraits of General and Mrs. Washington, painted at the time of their marriage, which have been so constantly reproduced; the portrait of Mrs. Washington's first husband, Colonel Parke Custis; of many of his progenitors; and several pictures of the great Revolutionary battles, painted by Mr. Custis, whose delight it was to perpetuate upon canvas the features of the great man who had been to him a father, and to commemorate the important scenes in which he had been an actor.

"Here, also, was the *last* original portrait of General Washington, by Sharpless, a distinguished English artist, who painted in crayons. Many of the pictures, and much of the old furniture of Mount Vernon, were here: the china presented to Mrs. Washington by certain English merchants, upon which was her monogram; that given to General Washington by the Society of the Cincinnati; the tea table at which Mrs. Washington always presided; a bookcase made by General Washington's own directions; and the bed upon which he died. Arlington House was surrounded by groves of stately trees, except in front, where the hill descended to a lovely valley spreading away to the river. The view from the height showed Washington, Georgetown, and a long stretch of the Potomac, in the foreground, with wooded hills and valleys making a background of dark foliage."

This beautiful home was the happy abode of the young officer and his accomplished bride during such time as he could spare from the active duties of his profession. And as the years went on, Arlington became more attractive by the sunshine which the presence of children brings.

The present writer never enjoyed the privilege of a visit to Arlington, but, from what he knew of the model home in Lexington, is fully prepared to believe the statement of others that a happier home circle never gathered around the hearth-stone, and that it was at the same time the abode of a real "old Virginia hospitality," rarely equaled even in the "Ancient Dominion."

But, while unable to speak from personal observation of this part of General Lee's domestic life, I am indebted to the kindness of the family for some of his letters which beautifully illustrate it.

Under the date of October 16, 1837, he thus writes from St. Louis to his wife: "The improved condition of the children, which you mention, was a source of great comfort to me; and as I suppose, by this time, you have all returned to Arlington, you will be able to put them under a proper restraint, which you were probably obliged to relax while visiting among strangers, and which that indulgence will probably render more essential. Our dear little boy seems to have among his friends the reputation of being hard to manage—a distinction not at all desirable, as it indicates self-will and obstinacy. Perhaps these are qualities which he really possesses, and he may have a better right to them than I am willing to acknowledge; but it is our duty, if possible, to counteract them and assist him to bring them under his control. I have endeavored, in my intercourse with him, to require nothing but what was in my opinion necessary or proper, and to explain to him temperately its propriety, at a time when he could listen to my arguments, and not at the moment of his being vexed and his little faculties warped by passion. I have also tried to show him that I was firm in my demands, and constant in their enforcement, and that he must comply with them; and I let him see that I look to their execution, in order to relieve him as much as possible from the temptation to break them. Since my efforts have been so unsuccessful, I fear I have altogether failed in accomplishing my purpose, but I hope to be able to profit by my experience. You must assist me in my attempts, and we must endeavor to combine the mildness and forbearance of the mother with the sternness and, perhaps, unreasonableness of the father. This is a subject on which I think much, though M—— may blame me for not reading more. I am ready to acknowledge the good advice contained in the textbooks, and believe that I see the merit of their reasoning generally; but what I want to learn is to apply what I already know. I pray God to watch over and direct our efforts in guarding our dear little son, that we may bring him up in the way he should go. . . .

". . . Oh, what pleasure I lose in being separated from my children! Nothing can compensate me for that; still I must remain here, ready to perform what little service I can, and hope for the best."

While on his way to St. Louis, two years later, he wrote Mrs. Lee the following letter:

"LOUISVILLE,
June 5, 1839.

"MY DEAREST MARY: I arrived here last night, and, before going out this morning, will inform you of my well-doing thus far.

"After leaving Staunton, I got on very well, but did not reach Guyandotte till Sunday afternoon, where, before alighting from the stage, I espied a boat descending the river, in which I took passage to Cincinnati. . . . You do not know how much I have missed you and the children, my dear Mary. To be alone in a crowd is very solitary. In the woods I feel sympathy with the trees and birds, in whose company I take delight, but experience no pleasure in a strange crowd.

"I hope you are all well and will continue so, and therefore must again urge you to be very prudent and careful of those dear children. If I could only get a squeeze at that little fellow turning up his sweet mouth to 'keese baba!' You must not let him run wild in my absence, and will have to exercise firm authority over all of them. This will not require severity, or even strictness, but constant attention and an unwavering course. Mildness and forbearance, tempered by firmness and judgment, will strengthen their affection for you, while it will maintain your control over them."

The following letter, to one of his sons, well illustrates his method of gaining the affectionate confidence of his children:

"FORT HAMILTON, NEW YORK,
March 31, 1846.

"I cannot go to bed, my dear son, without writing you a few lines to thank you for your letter, which gave me great pleasure. I am glad to hear you are well, and hope you are learning to read and write, and that the next letter you will be able to write yourself. I want to see you very much, and to tell you all that has happened since you went away.

"I do not think I ever told you of a fine boy I heard of in my travels this winter. He lived in the mountains of New Hampshire. He was just thirteen years old, the age of Custis. His father was a farmer, and he used to assist him to work on the farm as much as he could. The snow there this winter was deeper than it has been for years, and one day he accompanied his father to the woods to get some wood. They went with their wood sled, and, after cutting a load and loading the sled, this little boy, whose name was Harry, drove it home while his father cut another load. He had a fine team of horses and returned very quickly, when he found his father lying prostrate on the frozen snow under the large limb of a tree he had felled during his absence, which had caught him in its fall, and thrown him to the ground. He was cold and stiff; and little Harry, finding that he was not strong enough to relieve him from his position, seized his axe and cut off the limb, and rolled it off of him. He then tried to raise him, but his father was dead and his feeble efforts were all in vain. Although he was out in the far woods by himself, and had never before seen a dead person, he was nothing daunted, but backed his sled close up to his father, and with great labor got his body on it, and, placing his head in his lap, drove home to his mother as fast as he could. The efforts of his mother to reanimate him were equally vain with his own, and the sorrowing neighbors came and dug him a grave under the cold snow, and laid him quietly to rest. His mother was greatly distressed at the loss of her husband, but she thanked God who had given her so good and brave a son.

"You and Custis must take great care of your kind mother and dear sisters when your father is dead. To do that you must learn to be good. Be true, kind, and generous, and pray earnestly to God to enable you to 'keep his commandments, and walk in the same all the days of your life.'

"Alec and Frank are well, and the former has begun to ride his pony, Jim, again. Captain Bennett has bought his little boy a donkey, and, as I came home, I met him riding him, with two large New-foundland dogs following, one one each side. The dogs were almost as large as the donkey. My horse Jerry did not know what to make of them. I go to New York, now, on horseback every day; one day I ride Jerry, and the next Tom, and I think they begin to go better under the saddle than formerly. I hope to come on soon to see that little baby you have got to show me. You must give her a kiss for me, and one to all the children, and to your mother and grandmother.

"Good-bye, my dear son.

> "Your affectionate father,
> "R. E. LEE."

A year later he wrote the following:

> "SHIP MASSACHUSETTS, OFF LOBOS,
> *February* 27, 1847.

"MY DEAR BOYS: I received your letters with the greatest pleasure, and, as I always like to talk to you both together, I will not separate you in my letters, but write one to you both. I was much gratified to hear of your progress at school, and hope that you will continue to advance, and that I shall have the happiness of finding you much improved in all your studies on my return. I shall not feel my long separation from you, if I find that my absence has been of no injury to you, and that you have both grown in goodness and knowledge, as well as stature. But, ah! how much I will suffer on my return, if the reverse has occurred! You enter all my thoughts, into all my prayers; and on you, in part, will depend whether I shall be happy or miserable, as you know how much I love you. You must do all in your power to save me pain. You will learn, by my letter to your grandmother, that I have been to Tampico. I saw many things to remind me of you, though that was not necessary to make me wish that you were with me. The river was so calm and beautiful, and the boys were playing about in boats, and swimming their ponies. Then there were troops of donkeys carrying water through the streets. They had a kind of saddle, something like a cartsaddle, though larger, that carried two ten-gallon kegs on each side, which was a load for a donkey. They had no bridles on, but would come along in strings to the river, and, as soon as their kegs were filled, start off again. They were fatter and sleeker than any donkeys I had ever seen before, and seemed to be better cared for. I saw a great many ponies, too. They were larger than those in the upper country, but did not seem so enduring. I got one to ride around the fortifications. He had a Mexican bit and saddle on, and paced delightfully, but, every time my sword struck him on the flanks, would jump and try to run off. Several of them had been broken to harness by the Americans, and I saw some teams, in wagons, driven four-in-hand, well matched and trotting well. We had a grand parade on General Scott's arrival. The troops were all drawn up on the bank of the river, and fired a salute as he passed them. He landed at the market, where lines of sentinels were placed to keep off the crowd. In front of the landing the artillery was drawn up, which received him in the center of the column, and escorted him through the streets to his lodgings. They had provided a handsome gray horse, richly caparisoned, for him, but he preferred to walk, with his staff around him, and a dragoon led the horse behind us. The windows along the streets we passed were crowded with people, and the boys and girls were in great glee, the Governor's Island band playing all the time.

"There were six thousand soldiers in Tampico. Mr. Barry was the adjutant of the escort. I think you would have enjoyed with me the oranges and sweet potatoes. Major Smith became so fond of the chocolate that I could hardly get him away from the house. We only remained there one day. I have a nice stateroom on board this ship; Joe Johnston and myself occupy it, but my poor Joe is so sick all the time I can do nothing with him. I left Jem to come on with the horses, as I was afraid they would not be properly cared for. Vessels were expressly fitted up for the horses, and parties of dragoons detailed to take care of them. I had hoped they would reach here by this time, as I wanted to see how they were fixed. I took every precaution for their comfort, provided them with bran, oats, etc., and had slings made to pass under them and attached to the coverings above, so that, if in the heavy sea they should slip, or be thrown off their feet, they could not fall. I had to sell my good old horse Jim, as I could not find room for him, or, rather, I did not want to crowd the others. I know I shall want him when I land. Creole was the admiration of every one at Brazos, and they hardly believed she had carried me so far, and looked so well. Jem says there is nothing like her in all the country, and I believe he likes her better than Tom or Jerry. The sorrel mare did not appear to be so well after I got to the Brazos. I had to put one of the men on her, whose horse had given out, and the saddle hurt her back. She had gotten well, however, before I left, and I told Jem to ride her every day. I hope they may both reach the shore again in safety, but I fear they will have a hard time. They will first have to be put aboard a steamboat and carried to the ship that lies about two miles out at sea, then hoisted in, and how we shall get them ashore again, I do not know. Probably throw them overboard, and let them swim there. I do not think we shall remain here more than one day longer. General Worth's and General Twiggs's divisions have arrived, which include the regulars, and I suppose the volunteers will be coming on every day. We shall probably go on the 1st down the coast, select a place for debarkation, and make all the arrangements preparatory to the arrival of the troops. I shall have plenty to do there, and am anxious for the time to come, and hope all may be successful. Tell Rob he must think of me very often, be a good boy, and always love papa. Take care of Speck and the colts. Mr. Sedgwick and all the officers send their love to you.

"The ship rolls so that I can scarcely write. You must write to me very often. I am always very glad to hear from you. Be sure that I am thinking of you, and that you have the prayers of your affectionate father,

"R. E. LEE."

The general related a pleasing incident of one of his boys with whom he was walking out in the snow one day, at Arlington. The little fellow lagged behind, and, looking over his shoulder, the father saw him imitating his every movement, with head and shoulders erect, and stepping exactly in his own footprints. "When I saw this," said the general, "I said to myself, 'It behooves me to walk very straight, when this fellow is already following in my tracks.' " And accordingly there was never a more circumspect father than was this great man.

After his brilliant career in Mexico, he returned to the States, and found his chief joy in the bosom of his family. His stay at West Point as its superintendent was pleasant on account of the opportunity it afforded him of seeing more of his family, and his only regret at being ordered in February, 1856, to the rough service of the frontier seems to have been the fact that he would thus be far distant from his loved ones.

Some extracts from his letters written about this period have already been given.

The following is a pleasing insight into his feelings as he thought of home in his far-off field of duty:

"FORT BROWN, TEXAS,
December, 1856.

". . . The time is approaching, dear M——, when I trust that many of you will be assembled around the family hearth of dear Arlington to celebrate another Christmas. Though absent, my heart will be in the midst of you. I shall enjoy in imagination and memory all that is going on. May nothing occur to mar or cloud the family fireside, and may all be able to look with pride and pleasure to their deeds of the past year, and with confidence and hope to that in prospect! I can do nothing but love and pray for you all."

The following is the close of a long letter dated "Fort Brown, Texas, December 27, 1856":

"I hope you all had a joyous Christmas at Arlington, and that it may be long and often repeated. I thought of you, and wished to be with you. Mine was gratefully but silently passed. I endeavored to find some presents for the children in the garrison, and succeeded better than I anticipated. The stores were very barren, but by taking them the week beforehand in my daily walks, I picked up something for all. Tell M—— I found a beautiful Dutch doll for little Emma, one of those crying babies that can open and shut their eyes; for two others, handsome French teapots to match their cups. Then with knives and books I satisfied the boys. After this, went to church, then, by previous invitation, Major Thomas and I dined with the clergyman, Mr. Passmore, on roast turkey and plum pudding. God bless you all!

"Yours,
"R. E. LEE."

The following shows that he had a heart to feel for the afflicted:

"CAMP COOPER,
June 22, 1857.

"There is little to relate. The hot weather seems to have set in permanently. The thermometer ranges above one hundred degrees, but the sickness among the men is on the decrease, though there has been another death among the children. He was as handsome a little boy as I ever saw—the son of one of our sergeants, about a year old; I was admiring his appearance the day before he was taken ill. Last Thursday his little waxen form was committed to the earth. His father came to me, the tears flowing down his cheeks, and asked me to read the funeral service over his body, which I did at the grave for the second time in my life. I hope I shall not be called on again, for, though I believe that it is far better for the child to be called by its heavenly Creator into his presence in its purity and innocence, unpolluted by sin, and uncontaminated by the vices of the world, still it so wrings a parent's heart with anguish that it is painful to see. Yet I know it was done in mercy to both—mercy to the child, mercy to the parents. The former has been saved from sin and misery here, and the latter have been given a touching appeal and powerful inducement to prepare for hereafter. May it prove effectual, and may they require no further severe admonition!

"May God guard and bless you all! Truly and affectionately yours,
"R. E. LEE."

The following was written to one of his sons soon after he joined the army:

"ARLINGTON,
May 30, 1858.

"I received yesterday in Alexandria, my dearest son, your letter of the 19th inst., from 'Camp C. F. May.' I had heard of your departure from Governor's Island, and was very glad to learn of your safe arrival at your starting point, and of your assignment to the adjutancy of Captain Heth's battalion. You are now in a position to acquire military credit, and to prepare the road for promotion and future advancement. Show your ability and worthiness of distinction, and if an opportunity offers for advancement in the staff (I do not refer to the quartermaster's or commissary department), unless that is not your fancy, take it. It may lead to something favorable, and you can always relinquish it when you choose.

"I hope you will always be distinguished for your avoidance of the 'universal balm,' *whiskey,* and every immorality. Nor need you fear to be ruled out of the society that indulges in it, for you will acquire their esteem and respect, as all venerate if they do not practice virtue. I am sorry to say that there is great proclivity for spirit in the army in the field. It seems to be considered a substitute for every luxury. The great body may not carry it to extremes, but many pursue it to their ruin. With some it is used as a means of hospitality, and your———commanding used to value it highly in this way, and perhaps partook of it in this spirit. I think it better to avoid it altogether, as you do, as its temperate use is so difficult. I hope you will make many friends, as you will be thrown with those who deserve this feeling, but indiscriminate intimacies you will find annoying and entangling, and they can be avoided by politeness and civility. You see I am following my old habit of giving advice, which I dare say you neither need nor require. But you must pardon a fault which proceeds from my great love and burning anxiety for your welfare and happiness. When I think of your youth, impulsiveness, and many temptations, your distance from me, and the ease (and even innocence) with which you might commence an erroneous course, my heart quails within me, and my whole frame and being tremble at the possible result. May Almighty God have you in His holy keeping! To His merciful providence I commit you, and will rely upon Him, and the efficacy of the prayers that will be daily and hourly offered up by those who love you."

Then follow some interesting items about army movements, family matters, etc.

The following is given in full, as a model family letter:

"ARLINGTON,
August 7, 1858.

"I was delighted, my dear son, to receive your letter of the 7th of July, and to learn that you were well, and so contented and happy in your new life. I know that, although there is much to weary and annoy in a campaign, there is much to cheer and excite, and I recognize in the expression of your feelings many of my own experiences. I am sorry that my letters are so dilatory in reaching you. They will follow you in time, and, I hope, lose no interest by the way. You must make allowances for your forward movement, as well as the distance they have to overcome. I wrote immediately on the reception of your letter from Leavenworth, and your mother has replied to those to her from the Blue and Platte Rivers. As you have heard so regularly from C———, I hope you have been compensated for the absence of other letters. But what has she been saying to you, that you talk of coming back this winter to be married? I thought that ceremony had been postponed for two years! However, if you young people so wish it, I suppose it will have to come off earlier. About that, you must determine. You will have heard, by this time, of the destination of your regiment. If it goes to Oregon, which, I think, is more than probable, will you be able to leave it on the route? I think that will be the difficulty. After reaching Oregon, and the service is accomplished for which the troops are sent there, I should think you might get a leave of absence, and take C——— back with you *en route* to China, to see the Celestials. Would that answer as a wedding tour? Of all this, you, being on the spot, and knowing all the circumstances, will be the better judge, and must determine. I can only hope and pray that all things may work together for the good and happiness of you both. I had hoped, before this, to have seen C——— at the Alum Springs, and had made my preparations to have carried your mother a fortnight since, *nolens volens,* to the *Hot.* But, two days before the day fixed for our departure, Mr. M——— was taken sick with a complicated attack from which he has not yet recovered. He is now better, but is not yet able to come out. I hope, by Tuesday next, 10th inst., we shall be off. I think your mother is very glad of the detention, and, except on her account and the benefit that I hope she will derive from the trip, I should be, too. I leave home with great inconvenience, and shall have to return, after depositing her there. Annie goes with her, and I thought I would take her over to the Alum, to see Charlotte. The other children do not incline to the *Hot*. R———, who is with us, begs that he may not suffer again, and Agnes is going on a tour of her own to Ravensworth, Chantilly, etc. M———, you know, is in B———, nursing your aunt Anne. She is well, and proposes going to the *Sulphuret Soda* with your uncle Carter, who is expected along about this time.

"Your mother, I presume, has told you of all home news. I will not, therefore, repeat. I am getting along as usual—trying to get a little work done, and to mend up some things. I succeed very badly. I am very glad, my dear son, you are progressing so well. I hope you will prove yourself a capable soldier, and win golden opinions from the whole army. I have good accounts of you from all. There is no military news, and the papers will inform you of all else. Remember me to all the officers. Take care of yourself in *all* respects, and think constantly of

"Your devoted father,
"R. E. Lee."

Under date of January 1, 1859, he writes from Arlington the following playful letter to his son:

"A happy New Year! and many returns of the same to you, my precious Roon! Ours has been gladdened by the reception of your letter of the 4th of December, from Presidio Barracks. It is the first line that has reached us since your second letter from Fort Bridger. I am sorry you have received nothing from us. I have written often, and by various routes, and other members of the family have done the same. Those that are toiling over the plains, I suppose, will never reach you. When I first learned that the Sixth was ordered to the Pacific, I sent some letters to Benicia; when your letter arrived from Fort Bridger, saying your regiment had departed from Salt Lake, and that you were called to Camp Floyd, I enclosed some letters to Major Porter's care. After seeing that the regiment was stopped at Carson's Valley, and had sent back for animals, I conjectured that you would be pushed on with your recruits, and would labor through to the Pacific, and I resumed my direction to Benicia. Surely, some of these latter should reach you. . . . But, now that you have caught Custis, I hope you are indemnified for all your privations. I am delighted at you two being together, and nothing has occurred so gratifying to me for the past year. Hold on to him as long as you can. Kiss him for me, and sleep with him every night. He must do the same to you and charge it all to my account. God grant that it could be my good fortune to be with you both! I am glad that you stood the march so well, and are so robust and bearded. I always thought and said there was stuff in you for a good soldier, and I trust you will prove it. I cannot express the gratification I felt, in meeting Colonel May in New York, at the encomiums he passed upon your soldiership, zeal, and devotion to your duty. But I was more pleased at the report of your conduct. That went nearer my heart, and was of infinite comfort to me. Hold on to your purity and virtue. They will proudly sustain you in all trials and difficulties, and cheer you in every calamity. I was sorry to see, from your letter to your mother, that you smoke occasionally. It is dangerous to meddle with. You have in store so much better employment for your mouth. Reserve it, Roon, for its legitimate pleasure. Do not poison and corrupt it with stale vapors, or tarnish your beard with their stench. . . .

"All send love.

"Very truly and affectionately, your father,
"R. E. Lee."

He thus begins a letter to his son, dated "Arlington, New Year, 1860":

"I was delighted yesterday, my dearest Fitzhugh, at receiving your letter of the 28th ult., and to my cordial congratulations at your prospects for the New Year, and sincere wishes for many and more gratifying returns, will this morning add my heartfelt gratitude at your joyous commencement of life. May you and my dear Charlotte realize your highest anticipations, and experience the happiness of a long, well-spent life, and the full satisfaction of the performance of all your duties to God and man! . . ."

Then follows exceedingly practical advice about the best methods of farming the plantation at the White House.

The following pleasant letter, on a most important family event, will be read with interest:

"RINGGOLD BARRACKS,
April 2, 1860.

"I was delighted, my dear son, at the reception of your letter of the 10th ult., announcing the birth of that anxiously expected little boy! I sincerely congratulate you and my darling daughter at his prosperous advent, and pray that his future career may give more happiness to his parents than even his present existence. You must kiss his dear mother for me, and offer her my warmest thanks for this promising scion of my scattered house, who will, I hope, resuscitate its name and fame. Tell her I have thought much of her, and long to see you both, and your little treasure, who must, I think, greatly resemble his papa. . . .

"And now the schoolhouse must be commenced, or it will not be in time. I hope both mother and child are well and increasing daily in strength, so as to enjoy the fine spring weather which must have commenced in earnest by this time. Your mamma must have rejoiced at another *baby* in the house, and have had all her former feelings brought back afresh. I never could see the infantine beauties that she did, but I will be able to appreciate him by the time I shall see him . . ."

In a letter from San Antonio, dated June 2, 1860, he says:

"In a letter to Charlotte, written since my return, I expressed the gratification I felt at the compliment paid me in your intention to call my first grandchild after me. I wish I could offer him a more worthy name and a better example. He must elevate the first, and make use of the latter to avoid the errors I have committed. I also expressed the thought that under the circumstances you might like to name him after his great-grandfather, and wish you both, 'upon mature consideration,' to follow your inclinations and judgment. I should love him all the same, and nothing could make me love you two more than I do. . . ."

In a long and eminently commonsense letter written to his son, under date of August 22, 1860, he says:

"I am glad to hear that your mechanics are all paid off, and that you have managed your funds so well as to have enough for your purposes. As you have commenced, I hope you will continue, *never to exceed your means.* It will save you much anxiety and mortification, and enable you to maintain your independence of character and feeling. It is easier to make our wishes conform to our means than to make our means conform to our wishes. In fact, we want but little. Our happiness depends upon our independence, the success of our operations, prosperity of our plans, health, contentment, and the esteem of our friends. All of which, my dear son, I hope you may enjoy to the full. . . ."

He thus begins the letter from which a quotation is made in a previous chapter:

"FORT MASON, SAN ANTONIO POST OFFICE,
January 29, 1861.

"MY DEAR SON: I have received your letter of the 6th instant, giving me the pleasing account of your quiet and happy Christmas, the presence of Rob, the visit of Mr. D———, and the christening of your boy. So he is called after his grandpapa, the dear little fellow; I would wish him a better name, and hope he may be a wiser, and more useful man than his namesake. Such as it is, however, I gladly place it in his keeping, and feel that he must be very little like his father if it is not elevated and ennobled by his bearing and course in life. You must teach him, then, to love his grandpapa, to bear with his failings, and avoid his errors, to be to you as you have been to me, and he may then enjoy the love and confidence of his father, which I feel for you, greater than which no son has ever possessed. But what is the matter with my precious Chass? I fear her house is not warm enough for her in this cold and snowy weather. She must be very careful not to take cold, but to go out every day. Tell her I want to see her very much, and love her more and more."

These family letters show that a happier home circle could not be found than that of this loving family, when the storm of war burst upon the peaceful abode of Arlington. It was a bitter trial for General Lee, as it was for each member of his family, to sunder these ties, and give up this happy home; and yet, when his loved Virginia called, he did not hesitate to lay on her altar Arlington with all its hallowed associations, and to go forth an exile forever from the dear old roof tree.

His three sons promptly followed him into the Confederate army, and his noble wife and accomplished daughters bade a sad farewell to Arlington just before the "Grand Army" crossed the Potomac, and occupied its beautiful groves as their first camping ground on the soil of Virginia.

It was, perhaps, not intended *then;* but, as the fierce struggle went on, this beautiful home was desolated, its groves were cut down, its furniture was carried off, its precious relics of Washington (the great "rebel" of 1776) were scattered all over the North, the estate seized and held by the United States government (under the form of a bogus "tax sale"), the grounds converted into a soldiers' cemetery, and the rightful heirs banished from their ancestral halls. (May the day be not far distant when this blot upon the American name shall be removed, at least so far as to pay the lawful heir who yet survives a just compensation for the property thus wrested from him!)

General Lee's family sought refuge at "the White House" on the Pamunkey, where Washington had married the "Widow Custis," and which had been bequeathed by G. W. P. Custis to the "second son" of Lieutenant Lee's marriage with his daughter.

But when General McClellan advanced up the Peninsula, in the spring of 1862, the family became refugees again.

Before leaving the last homestead which remained to her, Mrs. Lee wrote and affixed to the door of the house the following appeal:

"Northern soldiers who profess to reverence Washington, forbear to desecrate the home of his first married life, the property of his wife, now owned by her descendants.
                    "A GRANDDAUGHTER OF MRS. WASHINGTON."

One of McClellan's officers wrote beneath this: "A Northern officer has protected your property in sight of the enemy, and at the request of your overseer."

But, unfortunately, the "protection" did not last long, and, during McClellan's famous "change of base," the house was burned to the ground, and "not a blade of grass left to mark the culture of more than a hundred years."

The letters written by General Lee to his family, during the war, would of themselves form a volume of interest. I am fortunate in being able to present a number of them—regretting that want of space prevents the insertion of many more:

"SEWELL MOUNT,
October 12, 1861.

"MY DEAR FITZHUGH: I am grieving over your absence, and fear you are not comfortable. Tell me how you are. I learn that the baby is doing very well and getting quite fat. Your poor mother, who was in Charlottesville Saturday, was going to Richmond to join C——— and accompany her to the White House. I hope they will enjoy the quiet of the place, and each other's company. Annie and Agnes are in Richmond, on their way to Cedar Grove. They have been to Uncle Carter's, and are well satisfied with their visit.

"The enemy in strong force threatened us for a week. I was in hopes they would attack, but after some sharp skirmishing with their reconnoitering parties last Saturday night they retired, and by day-break next morning their rear guard was fifteen miles off. We followed the first day without provisions, and had to return at night in a drenching rain. We have only lived from day to day, and on three-fourths rations at that. It is the want of supplies that has prevented our advancing, and up to this time there is no improvement. The strength of the enemy is variously reported, by prisoners and civilians, as from seventeen to twenty-four thousand. General Floyd puts them down at eighteen thousand. I think their numbers are much overrated, but that they are much stronger than we are. I believe they have crossed the Gauley, and will not return this winter.

"God bless you, my dear son!

"Your devoted father,
"R. E. LEE."

The following was written just after the first Manassas:

"RICHMOND,
July 27, 1861.

"I have received, dear M———, your letter from E——— View and am glad your visit has been so agreeable. . . . That indeed was a glorious victory, and has lightened the pressure upon our front amazingly. Do not grieve for the brave dead. Sorrow for those they left behind, friends, relations, and families. The former are at rest, the latter must suffer. The battle will be repeated there in greater force. I hope God will again smile upon us, and strengthen our hearts and arms.

"I wished to participate in the former battle, but the president thought it more important that I should be here. I could not have done as well, but could have helped, and taken part in the struggle for my home and neighborhood. So the work is done, I care not by whom it is done. I leave tomorrow for the new army.

"I wished to go before, as I wrote you, and was all prepared, but the indications were so evident of the coming battle that, in the uncertainty of the result, the president forbade my departure. Now it is necessary, and he consents. I enclose a letter from M———. Write to her if you can, and thank her, for I have not time. Every moment is occupied, and all my thoughts and strength are given to the cause to which my life, be it long or short, will be devoted."

The following was written while he was on duty on the coast of South Carolina, and is indeed a gem worth preserving:

"COOSAWHATCHIE, S. C.,
December 25, 1861.

"MY DEAR DAUGHTER: Having distributed such poor Christmas gifts as I had to those around me, I have been looking for something for you. Trifles even are hard to get these war times, and you must not therefore expect more. I have sent you what I thought most useful in your separation from me, and hope it will be of some service. Though stigmatized as 'vile dross,' it has never been a drug with me. That you may never want for it, restrict your wants to your necessities. Yet how little will it purchase! But see how God provides for our pleasure in every way. To compensate for such 'trash,' I send you some sweet violets, that I gathered for you this morning while covered with dense white frost, whose crystals glittered in the bright sun like diamonds, and formed a brooch of rare beauty and sweetness which could not be fabricated by the expenditure of a world of money. May God guard and preserve you for me, my dear daughter! Among the calamities of war, the hardest to bear, perhaps, is the separation of families and friends. Yet all must be endured to accomplish our independence, and maintain our self-government. In my absence from you, I have thought of you very often, and regretted I could do nothing for your comfort. Your old home, if not destroyed by our enemies, has been so desecrated that I cannot bear to think of it. I should have preferred it to have been wiped from the earth, its beautiful hill sunk, and its sacred trees buried, rather than to have been degraded by the presence of those who revel in the ill they do for their own selfish purposes. You see what a poor sinner I am, and how unworthy to possess what was given me; for that reason it has been taken away. I pray for a better spirit, and that the hearts of our enemies may be changed. In your homeless condition, I hope you make yourself contented and useful. Occupy yourself in aiding those more helpless than yourself. . . . Think always of your father,

"R. E. LEE."

If any apology is needed for unveiling to the public gaze the following letter (and others addressed to the same person that will be afterward given), it may be found in the fact that the affectionate, playful nature of the great man is thus more beautifully brought out than in any other way, and a chief objection to the publication is, alas! removed in the untimely death of the accomplished woman to whom it was addressed:

"COOSAWHATCHIE, S. C.,
December 29, 1861.

"You have no occasion to inform me, you precious Chass, that you have not written to me for a long time. That I already knew, and *you* know that the letters I am obliged to write do not prevent my reading letters from you.

"If it requires fits of indignation to cause you to ventilate your paper, I will give occasion for a series of spasms, but in the present case I am innocent, as my proposition was for you to accompany your mamma to Fayetteville, and not to run off with her son to Fredericksburg. I am afraid the enemy will catch you; and, besides, there are too many young men there. I only want you to visit the old men, your grandpapa and papa. But what has got into your heads to cause you to cut off of them your hair? If you will weave some delicate fabrics for the soldiers of the family out of it, I will be content with the sacrifice; or, if it is an expression of a penitential mood that has come over you young women, I shall not complain. Poor little A———! Somebody told me that a widower had been

making sweet eyes at her through his spectacles. Perhaps she is preparing for caps. But you can tell her not to distress herself. Her papa
is not going to give her up in that way. I am, however, so glad that
you are all together that I am willing you should indulge in some
extravagances if they do not result in serious hurt, as they will afford
a variety to the grave occupation of knitting, sewing, spinning, and
weaving. You will have to get out the old wheels and looms again,
else I do not know where we poor Confederates will get clothes. I
have a plenty of old ones for the present, but how are they to be
renewed? And that is the condition of many others. I do not think
there are manufactories sufficient in the Confederacy to supply the
demand; and, as the men are all engrossed by the war, the women
will have to engage in the business. Fayetteville or Stratford would
be a fine position for a domestic manufactory. When you go to see
your grandpa, consult him about it. I am glad to hear that he is well,
and hope he will not let these disjointed times put him out of his
usual way or give him inconvenience. I would not advise him to
commence building at Broadneck until he sees whether the enemy
can be driven from the land, as they have a great fondness for destroying residences when they can do it without danger to themselves. . . . Do not let them get that precious baby, as he is so sweet
that they would be sure to eat him. . . . Kiss F ——— for me and the
baby. That is the sweetest Christmas gift I can send them. I send you
some sweet violets; I hope they may retain their fragrance till you
receive them. I have just gathered them for you. The sun has set,
and my eyes plead for relief, for they have had no rest this holy day.
But my heart with all its strength stretches toward you, and those
with you, and hushes in silence its yearnings. God bless you, my
daughter, your dear husband, and son! Give much love to your
mamma, and may every blessing attend you all, prays

"Your devoted father,
"R. E. Lee."

In a letter to one of his sons, under date of February 16, 1861, he
says:

"I am very glad to hear that you are well, and that you have
attained such a high position by your own merit. I hope you will

strive hard to show that you deserve it, and that you will go on increasing in honor and usefulness. Our country requires now every one to put forth all his ability regardless of self, and I am cheered in my downward path in life by the onward and rising course of my dear sons."

The following playful letter was written to one of his daughters on her attaining her sixteenth birthday:

"SAVANNAH,

February, 26, 1862.

"And are you really sweet sixteen? That is charming, and I want to see you more than ever. But, when that will be, my darling child, I have no idea. I hope, after the war is over, we may again all be united, and I may have some pleasant years with my dear children, that they may cheer the remnant of my days. I am very glad to hear that you are progressing so well in your studies, and that your reports are so favorable. Your mother wrote me about them. You must continue to do likewise to the end of the session, when I hope you will be able to join your mother. It has been a long time since I have seen you, and you must have grown a great deal. Rob says he is told that you are a young woman. I have grown so old, and become so changed, that you would not know me. But I love you just as much as ever, and you know how great a love that is. You must remember me to the P———s, your cousin M———, Mrs. B———, the C———s, etc., and tell them how obliged I am for their kindness to you. I hope you appreciate it, and that your manners and conduct are so well regulated as to make your presence and company agreeable to them.

"I hope you will be admired and loved by all my friends, and acquire the friendship of all the good and virtuous.

"I am glad S——— agrees with you so well. You know it is considered vulgar for young ladies to eat, which I suppose is the cause of your abstinence. But do not carry it too far, for, you know, I do not admire young women who are too thin.

"Who is so imprudent in Clarke as to get married? I did not think, in these days of serious occurrences, that anyone would engage in such trivial amusements.

"This is a serious period, indeed, and the time looks dark; but it will brighten again, and I hope a kind Providence will yet smile upon us, and give us freedom and independence.

"These reverses were necessary, to make us brace ourselves for the work before us. We were getting careless and confident, and required correction. You must do all you can for our dear country. Pray for the aid of our dear Father in heaven, for our suffering soldiers and their distressed families. I pray day and night for you. May Almighty God guide, guard, and protect you! I have but little time to write, my dear daughter. You must excuse my short and dull letters. Write me when you can, and love always your devoted father,

"R. E. LEE."

No apology is needed for the introduction of the following letters. The publication of these expressions of his warm paternal affection (which has doubtless been purified and intensified in the brighter home above) will be pardoned in view of the light thus thrown on the character of the great soldier who, amid the stern realities and pressing duties of war, found time and inclination for family letters, of which these are but a few specimens:

"RICHMOND, VA.,
April 26, 1862.

"I have just received your note of Thursday night, dearest Chass, and write to say that I *have* taken time to read it and enjoy it, too, and shall always do so as long as I live. So do not hesitate to write. I want to see you very much, and am always thinking of you. It is very hard, I think, for you to say that you did not want to come to me. I hope, at least, F——— will be able to go to you, and, if he does, you must tell him to kiss you for me, double and treble. Do not accuse your mamma; you told me yourself. You are such a little sieve, you cannot retain anything. But there is no harm, you sweet child, and I love you all the more for it, and so does F———.

"I am glad you get such delightful tidings of him. C——— left him yesterday, very indignant at some of his pickets having been captured. I hope he will get them back, and indemnify himself with many of the enemy. He is very well, but sent no particular messages. I am glad you rejoice in the good service he is doing his country.

Encourage him to continue to the end. We have received some heavy blows lately, from the effects of which, I trust, a merciful God will deliver us. I fear New Orleans has fallen, though nothing certain has yet been received. The last accounts received prepare me for its fall. Remember me to your grandpapa and all, at Hickory Hill. Kiss my grandson for me, and tell him you are mistaken. I want to do so for myself very much, but do not know when I can have that pleasure. I must confess that I desire more to kiss his mother; but I catch that from F———. Good-bye, my sweet daughter. May Heaven guard and protect you and yours, prays

> "Your affectionate father,
> "R. E. LEE."

> "NEAR RICHMOND, VA.,
> *June* 2, 1862.

"You may have heard that a battle has been fought near Richmond, my darling Chass, and be uneasy about your husband. I write, therefore, to inform you that he is well. The cavalry was not engaged, and, of course, he was not exposed . . . I am sorry to say that General Johnston was wounded Saturday evening, not seriously, I am told; but, when I left Richmond yesterday, the extent of his wound was not known. . . . I am now in the field again. The wound of General Johnston obliging him to leave it, rendered it necessary, in the opinion of the president, that I should take his place. I wish his mantle had fallen upon an abler man, or that I were able to drive our enemies back to their homes. I have no ambition and no desire but for the attainment of this object, and therefore only wish for its accomplishment by him that can do it most speedily and thoroughly. I saw F——— Friday. Was at his camp. . . . He is well, and so are *Shiloh,* Moses, etc. I told him about you, and gave him your address. He said he would write. I hear nothing of your poor mamma, or the White House. Kiss Agnes for me; also, your fine boy. I wrote to both of you some days since—but I can do nothing but think of you. God bless you both and all, and keep you for Himself, now and forever!

> "Your affectionate father,
> "R. E. LEE."

"MRS. CHARLOTTE LEE.

"Dabb's,
June 22, 1862.

"I must take a part of this holy day, my dearest Chass, to thank you for your letter of the 14th. I am very glad that my communication after the battle reached you so opportunely, and relieved your anxiety about your F———. He has, since that, made a hazardous scout, and been protected by that Divine Providence which, I trust and pray, may always smile on, as I know it will ever watch over, you and yours. I sent you some account of this expedition in a former letter, as well as the order of General Stuart on the subject. It was badly printed, but may serve to show you that he conducted himself well. The general deals in the flowery style, as you will perceive, if you ever see his report in detail; but he is a good soldier, and speaks highly of the conduct of the two Lees, who, as far as I can learn, deserve his encomiums. Your mamma is very zealous in her attentions to your sick brother. He is reported better. I think he was a few evenings since, when I saw him, and a note this morning from her states that he slowly improves. I hope he will soon be well again. He is much reduced, and looks very feeble. I suppose he will be obliged to go to the 'North Carolina White Sulphur,' to keep you young women company. How will you like that? And now I must answer your inquiries about myself. My habiliments are not as comfortable as yours, nor so suited to this hot weather; but they are the best I have. My coat is of gray, of the regulation style and pattern, and my pants of dark blue, as is also prescribed, partly hid by my long boots. I have the same handsome hat which surmounts my gray head (the latter is *not* prescribed in the regulations), and shields my ugly face, which is masked by a white beard as stiff and wiry as the teeth of a card. In fact, an uglier person you have never seen, and so unattractive is it to our enemies that they shoot at it whenever visible to them. But, though age with its snow has whitened my head, and its frosts have stiffened my limbs, my heart, you well know, is not frozen to you, and summer returns when I see you. Having now answered your questions, I have little more to say. Our enemy is quietly working within his lines, and collecting additional forces to drive us from our capital. I hope we shall be able yet to disappoint him, and drive him back to his own country. I saw F——— the other day. He was looking very well in a new suit of gray. . . .

"And now I must bid you farewell. Kiss your sweet boy for me, and love always

> "Your devoted papa,
> "R. E. LEE."

"MRS. WILLIAM H. FITZHUGH LEE."

> "JEFFERSONTON,
> *August* 26, 1862.

"I arrived at my tent last night, my dear Chass, and to my delight found your F———. It was the first time I had seen him since the battles around Richmond. He is very well, and the picture of health. He could not stay very long, as he had to return to his camp, about four miles distant. In the recent expedition to the rear of the enemy (with a view of cutting off their railroad communication), he led his regiment, during a terrible storm at night, right through the camp of the enemy to Catlett's Station, capturing several hundred prisoners and some valuable papers of General Pope. His cousin L. M——— is said to have escaped at the first onset, leaving his toddy untouched.

"I am so grateful to Almighty God for preserving, guiding, and directing him in this war! Help me pray to Him for the continuance of his signal favor. F——— left me a letter of M. L———'s to read. It is so full of sympathy, piety, and affection, that I enclose it to you. I sent you several messages in a letter to your mother yesterday. Kiss her for me. I have heard from neither of you since I left R———.

"Give much love to everybody, and believe me, my dear child,

> "Affectionately your father,
> "R. E. LEE."

After the burning of the White House in June 1862, Mrs. Lee and her daughters occupied a rented house on Franklin Street, in Richmond, which is now pointed out as an object of interest to the tourist.

It is needless to say that they bore their full share of the privations, sacrifices, and untiring devotion to the cause of the Confederacy, which so preeminently characterized the women of Richmond during those dark days. Mrs. Lee busied herself knitting socks for the soldiers, or going as an "angel of mercy" to the sick and wounded of the hospitals, and her daughters proved themselves worthy of their illustrious father and gallant brothers.

Many a humble soldier cherishes today as among his most hallowed memories acts of kindness which he received from the family of his loved chieftain.

General Lee's family letters at this period continued to be of deepest interest.

He wrote the following to a daughter within the enemy's lines:

> "CAMP NEAR FREDERICKSBURG,
> *November* 24, 1862.

> "MY DEAR DAUGHTER: I have just received your letter of the 17th, which has afforded me great gratification. I regretted not finding you in Richmond, and grieve over every opportunity of seeing you that is lost, for I fear they will become less and less frequent. I am glad, however, that you have been able to enjoy the society of those who are so well qualified to render you happy, and who are so deservedly loved and admired. The death of my dear Annie was indeed to me a bitter pang. But the Lord gave, and the Lord has taken away; blessed be the name of the Lord. In the hours of night, when there is nothing to lighten the full weight of my grief, I feel as if I should be overwhelmed. I had always counted, if God should spare me a few days of peace after this cruel war was ended, that I should have her with me. But year after year my hopes go out, and I must be resigned. I write with difficulty, and must be brief. F——— and R——— are near me and well. Nephew F——— has laid aside his crutches, and I hope will soon join me. Your mother, I presume, informs you of the rest. General Burnside's whole army is apparently opposite Fredericksburg, and stretches from the Rappahannock to the Potomac. What his intentions are he has not yet disclosed. I am sorry he is in position to oppress our friends and citizens of the 'Northern Neck.' He threatens to bombard Fredericksburg, and the noble spirit displayed by its citizens, particularly the women and children, has elicited my highest admiration. They have been abandoning their homes night and day, during all of this inclement weather, cheerfully and uncomplainingly, with only such assistance as our wagons and ambulances could afford—women, girls, and children, trudging through the mud, and bivouacking in the open field. . . .

> "Believe me always your affectionate father,
> "R. E. LEE."

The daughter, whose death is so touchingly alluded to in the above letter, was Miss Annie Carter Lee, who died at Warren White Sulphur Springs, N.C., the 20th of October, 1862. At the close of the war the citizens of the county erected over her grave a handsome monument, which was unveiled with appropriate ceremonies. In response to an invitation to be present, General Lee wrote the following characteristic letter:

"ROCKBRIDGE BATHS,
July 25, 1866.

"LADIES: I have read with deep emotion your letter of the 17th inst., inviting myself and family to witness the erection of a monument over the remains of my daughter at Warren White Sulphur Springs on the 8th of next month.

"I do not know how to express to you my thanks for your great kindness to her while living, and for your affectionate remembrance of her since dead.

"My gratitude for your attention and consideration will continue through life, and my prayers will be daily offered to the throne of the Most High for his boundless blessings upon you.

"I have always cherished the intention of visiting the tomb of her who never gave me aught but pleasure; but, to afford me the satisfaction which I crave, it must be attended with more privacy than I can hope for on the occasion you propose.

"But there are more controlling considerations which will prevent my being present. Her mother, who for years has been afflicted with a painful disease, which has reduced her to a state of helplessness, is this far on her way to the Mineral Springs, which are considered the best calculated to afford her relief. My attendance is necessary to her in her journey, and the few weeks I have now at my disposal is the only time which can be devoted to this purpose.

"Though absent in person, my heart will be with you, and my sorrow and devotions will be mingled with yours.

"I hope my eldest son and daughter may be able to be present with you, but, as they are distant from me, I cannot tell under what circumstances your invitation may find them. I feel certain, however, that nothing but necessity will prevent their attendance.

"I enclose, according to your request, the date of my daughter's birth, and the inscription proposed for the monument over her tomb. The latter are the last lines of the hymn which she asked for just before her death.

"I am, with great respect, your obedient servant,
"R. E. LEE."

"Mrs. JOSEPH S. JONES, Mrs. THOMAS CARROLL, Miss BROWNLOW, Miss M. ALSTON, Mrs. J. M. HECK, Mrs. LUCINDA JONES—COMMITTEE."

The date of the following letter gives it additional interest. The movements of Burnside were developing themselves, and the sanguinary battle of Fredericksburg was about to open; but the charger of the great captain must "wait at his tent door" while from a heart as tender as that of the gentlest woman he sends these lines of affectionate sympathy to the bereaved mother:

"CAMP FREDERICKSBURG,
December 10, 1862.

"I heard yesterday, my dear daughter, with the deepest sorrow, of the death of your infant. I was so grateful at her birth. I felt that she would be such a comfort to you, such a pleasure to my dear Fitzhugh, and would fill so full the void still aching in your hearts. But you have now two sweet angels in heaven. What joy there is in the thought! What relief to your grief! What suffering and sorrow they have escaped! I can say nothing to soften the anguish you must feel, and I know you are assured of my deep and affectionate sympathy. May God give you strength to bear the affliction He has imposed, and produce future joy out of your present misery, is my earnest prayer.

"I saw F——— yesterday. He is well, and wants much to see you. When you are strong enough, cannot you come up to Hickory Hill, or your grandpa's, on a little visit, when he can come down and see you? My horse is waiting at my tent door, but I could not refrain from sending these few lines to recall to you the thought and love of

"Your devoted father,
"R. E. LEE."

"Mrs. WM. H. FITZHUGH LEE."

"CAMP FREDERICKSBURG,

March 3, 1863.

"I received today, my darling daughter, your letter of the 28th, and it has furnished me such pleasing thoughts! I am glad you are so well and happy. Tell F——— I know you 'look very well,' and, more than that, you look beautiful, and that he must answer all your questions, and R——— must drive you out every day. You and that young bride must make fine company for each other, affording each other so much time for fruitful thought, and, when you do speak, always on the same subject, your husbands. How deluded each must appear to the other! As to F———, the Misses H——— need take no credit to themselves for perceiving his condition. It is patent to all the world, and requires no Columbus to discover it. Tell him that he must look at you as much as he can, and be with you as much as he can, for the spring is approaching, and we have a great deal before us. I am glad you have had this opportunity to be together, and hope the war with all its baneful effects will always be removed far from you. It is strange, though, that nobody writes to you now. You are both such good correspondents that I should think you would be overwhelmed with letters. Your mamma says neither of you ever writes to her. But I tell her it is the fault of the mails. Your poor mamma has been a great sufferer this winter. I have not been able to see her, and fear I shall not. She talks of coming to Hickory Hill this month, when the weather becomes more fixed. We are up to our eyes in mud, now, and have but little comfort. Mr. Hooker looms very large over the river. He has two balloons up in the day, and one at night. I hope he is gratified at what he sees. Your cousin, Fitz Lee, beat up his quarters the other day with about four hundred of his cavalry, and advanced within four miles of Falmouth, carrying off one hundred and fifty prisoners, with their horses, arms, etc. The day after he recrossed the Rappahannock, they sent all their cavalry after him, and even brought Sir Percy Wyndham and his three regiments from Chantilly down upon him; but the bird had flown. It was reported that they displayed ten thousand cavalry—I suppose half that number would be nearer the truth. I hope these young Lees will always be too smart for the enemy. Kiss F——— for me, and give much love to R———. I pray daily to our heavenly Father to guard, guide, and protect you all. Tell F——— I will not write to him this time. It is so dark I can hardly see. I am obliged to him for his letter.

"Your devoted papa,

"R. E. LEE."

The following is without date, but was evidently written about this time:

"MY DEAR FITZHUGH: . . . I wrote you a few lines the other day, and also to daughter Charlotte. Tell her she must talk quick to you. Her time is getting short, and the soldiers complain of the officers' wives visiting them when theirs cannot. I am petitioned to send them off. Your poor mother is, I fear, no better. I received yesterday a very pleasing letter from Rev. Dr. S———, complimentary of precious———. I have mailed it to your mother. Kiss Chass for me, and tell her that daughters are not prohibited from visiting their papas. It is only objected to wives visiting their husbands. But she and Mrs. R——— are not included in the prohibition. Your uncle Carter says that they had him, with a gun and sword buckled to him, guarding a ford on James River during Stoneman's last expedition. You and Fitz must not let them capture your uncle. I wish I could have seen your review; I hope Chass did.

"Affectionately your father,

"R. E. LEE."

"General WM. FITZHUGH LEE."

The two following letters were written on the occasion of the wounding of his son in the severe cavalry fight of Brandy Station:

"MY DEAR SON: I send you a dispatch received from C——— last night. I hope you are comfortable this morning. I wish I could see you, but I cannot. Take care of yourself, and make haste and get well, and return. Though I scarcely ever saw you, it was a great comfort to know that you were near and with me. I could think of you and hope to see you. May we yet meet in peace and happiness! Kiss Chass for me. Tell her she must not tease you while you are sick, and she must write and let me know how you are. God bless you both, my children!

"Truly your father,
"R. E. LEE."

"CULPEPER,
June 11, 1863.

"I am so grieved, my dear daughter, to send Fitzhugh to you wounded. But I am so grateful that his wound is of a character to give us full hope of a speedy recovery. With his youth and strength to aid him, and your tender care to nurse him, I trust he will soon be well again. I know that you will unite with me in thanks to Almighty God, who has so often shielded him in the hour of danger, for this recent deliverance, and lift up your whole heart in praise to Him for sparing a life so dear to us, while enabling him to do his duty in the station in which He had placed him. Ask him to join us in supplication, that He may always cover him with the shadow of His almighty arm, and teach him that his only refuge is in Him, the greatness of whose mercy reacheth unto the heavens, and His truth unto the clouds. As some good is always mixed with the evil in this world, you will now have him with you for a time, and I shall look to you to cure him very soon, and send him back to me; for, though I saw him seldom, I knew he was near, and always hoped to see him. I went today to thank Mrs. Hill for her attention to him and kindness to you. She desired me to give her regards to you both. I must now thank you for the letter you wrote to me while at Fredericksburg. I kept it by me till preparing for the battlefield, when, fearing it might reach the eyes of General Hooker, I destroyed it. We can carry with us only our recollections. I must leave F———— to tell you about the battle, the army, and the country. . . . Tell Cousin A———— I am rejoiced that W———— is unhurt, though pretty S———— might like to see the ambulance driving up again. I want all the husbands in the field, and their wives at home encouraging them, loving them, and praying for them. We have a great work to accomplish, which requires the cordial and united strength of all. . . . Give much love to Cousin A————, Mrs. L———— and her sweet children, Mr. W————, and my dear Uncle W————. Tell F————

he must make haste and get well—that I am sad without him. You and R——— must let me know how he gets on.

"Truly and affectionately yours,
"R. E. LEE."

While slowly recovering from this wound, the son was captured by a raiding party of the enemy and carried to prison. General Lee wrote the following letter soon after this event:

"CAMP CULPEPER,
July 26, 1863.

"I received last night, my darling daughter, your letter of the 18th from Hickory Hill. I was also glad to hear from M——— S——— that you accompanied your mother from Ashland on the 22d—I presume on your way to the Alum Springs. I hope the water and mountain air will invigorate you and make you well. You must not be sick while F——— is away, or he will be more restless under his separation. Get strong and hearty by his return, that he may the more rejoice at the sight of you. You give such an account of yourself that I scarcely recognize you. What sort of a closet is that to which you compare yourself? I see no resemblance, and will have none. I can appreciate your distress at F———'s situation. I deeply sympathize with it, and in the lone hours of the night I groan in sorrow at his captivity and separation from you. But we must all bear it, exercise all our patience, and do nothing to aggravate the evil. This, besides injuring ourselves, would rejoice our enemies, and be sinful in the eyes of God. In His own good time He will relieve us, and make all things work together for our good, if we give Him our love, and place in Him our trust. I can see no harm that will result from F———'s capture except his detention. I feel assured that he will be well attended to. He will be in the hands of old army officers and surgeons, most of whom are men of principle and humanity. His wound, I understand, has not been injured by his removal, but is doing well. Nothing would do him more harm than for him to learn that you were sick and sad. How could he get well? So cheer up, and prove your fortitude and patriotism. What, too, should I do? I cannot bear to think of you except as I have always known you— bright, joyous, and happy. You may think of F———, and love him as much as you please, but do not grieve over him or grow sad. That will not be right, you precious child! I hope I shall be able to see you on your return from the Springs, and be able to welcome F———, too. I miss him very much, and want his assistance, too. Perhaps I should have been able to have done better in Pennsylvania if he had been with me. . . . General Stuart is as dashing as ever. Colonel Chambliss commands F———'s brigade now. The cavalry has had hard service, and is somewhat pulled down. But we shall build it up now. It has lost some gallant officers, which causes me deep grief. Indeed, the loss of our gallant officers and men through-out the army causes me to weep tears of blood, and to wish that I never could hear the sound of a gun again. My only consolation is, that they are the happier, and we that are left are to be pitied.

"I am sorry for the disappointment I caused you by returning to Virginia, but under the circumstances it was the best to be done. Had not the Shenandoah been so high, I should have gone into Loudon; but, being unable to cross it, I determined to come here. You must think of me, and pray for me always, and know that I am always thinking of you. I am so sorry that the enemy treated my dear Uncle Williams so badly. I also grieve at not seeing M———. Good-bye, my dear child. May God in His great mercy guard and protect you, and your dear husband! I saw Mrs. Hill today, and she inquired very kindly after you and F———.

"Your affectionate papa,
"R. E. LEE."

The hopes expressed in the above letter were sadly blighted. The husband lingered in a wearisome captivity at Fortress Monroe, the accomplished wife died before his release, and the father was plunged into deepest grief. He wrote the following letter soon after the son's return from prison:

"CAMP ORANGE COUNTY,
April 24, 1864.

"I received last night, my dear son, your letter of the 22d. It has given me great comfort. God knows how I loved your dear, dear wife, how sweet her memory is to me, and how I mourn her loss. My grief could not be greater if you had been taken from me. You were both equally dear to me. My heart is too full to speak on this subject, nor can I write. But my grief is for ourselves, not for her. She is brighter and happier than ever—safe from all evil, and awaiting us in her heavenly abode. May God in His mercy enable us to join her in eternal praise to our Lord and Savior. Let us humbly bow ourselves before Him, and offer perpetual prayer for pardon and forgiveness. But we cannot indulge in grief, however mournfully pleasing. Our country demands all our strength, all our energies. To resist the powerful combination now forming against us will require every man at his place. If victorious, we have everything to hope for in the future. If defeated, nothing will be left us to live for. I have not heard what action has been taken by the department in reference to my recommendations concerning the organization of the cavalry. But we have no time to wait, and you had better join your brigade. This week will in all probability bring us active work, and we must strike fast and strong. My whole trust is in God, and I am ready for whatever He may ordain. May He guide, guard, and strengthen us, is my constant prayer!

> "Your devoted father,
> "R. E. LEE."

"General WILLIAM F. LEE."

The above letter, written on the eve of the great campaign of 1864, is the last I shall introduce of his family letters written during the war.

His wife and daughters continued to reside in Richmond, where he joined them after the surrender. A few weeks later he escaped the publicity of a residence in Richmond, which was at that time so annoying to him, and sought a quiet home in Cumberland County—two of his sons having gone to farm the plantations at the White House and Ronancocke. The following letter gives an inside view of his feelings and purposes at this time:

> "NEAR CARTERSVILLE, CUMBERLAND COUNTY, VA.,
> *July* 29, 1865.

"MY DEAR FITZHUGH: I was very glad to receive by the last packet from Richmond your letter of the 22d. We had all been quite anxious to hear from you, and were much gratified to learn that you were all well, and doing well. It is very cheering to me to hear of your good prospects for corn, and your cheerful prospects for the future. God grant they may be realized, which, I am sure, they will be, if you will unite sound judgment to your usual energy in your operations.

"As to the indictments, I hope you, at least, may not be prosecuted. I see no more reason for it than for prosecuting *all* who ever engaged in the war. I think, however, we may expect procrastination in measures of relief, denunciatory threats, etc. We must be patient, and let them take their course. As soon as I can ascertain their intention toward me, if not prevented, I shall endeavor to procure some humble but quiet abode for your mother and sisters, where I hope they can be happy. As I before said, I want to get in some grass country, where the natural product of the land will do much for my subsistence . . .

"Our neighbors are very kind, and do everything in the world to promote our comfort. If A———— is well enough, I propose next week to ride up to Bremo. I wish I was near enough to see you. Give much love to R————, and J————, the C————s, and B————s. All here unite in love and best wishes for you all.

"Most affectionately, your father,
"R. E. LEE."

Not long after General Lee assumed charge of Washington College, his family removed to Lexington, and occupied a house on the college *campus* until the new president's house was built.

It was my privilege to see much of his "domestic life" in Lexington, to have been the frequent inmate of his model home, and to have seen him in the pleasant intercourse of the family circle.

And, while I may not violate the confidence reposed in me, or expose to the public gaze the privacy of that home, I may say that, if one wanted to paint a model husband and father, he would search the world in vain for a brighter example than that of this great man. Whether, with affectionate playfulness, teasing his daughters, tenderly wheeling Mrs. Lee (who had become a confirmed invalid) in her chair, or providing in other ways for her comfort, or entertaining his visitors with that inimitable courtesy and grace which seemed inseparable from the man, he always won your admiration, and made you feel that he was the very embodiment of all the virtues of the domestic circle.

Of Mrs. Lee it may be truly said that she was worthy to grace the home and cheer the eventful life of this king of men. Though rendered by sickness incapable of walking, and never free from pain, she bore her sufferings with Christian cheerfulness, and always seemed contented and happy. Very domestic in her tastes and habits, and of unconquerable industry, she would paint, knit, sew, write, or entertain her friends, and was an earnest worker for all of the interests of her church, as she was a liberal contributor to every charity that presented itself. Noted for her extraordinary common sense and sound judgment—thoroughly educated and very accomplished—fond of reading, and remarkably well read in general literature—a fine conversationalist and a most genial, pleasant entertainer— in a word, *a Virginia matron of the old school*—she combined domestic virtues worthy to link together the families of Washington and Lee, was the light and joy of her home, and the recognized leader of the social circle of Lexington. The friend of the poor, she was beloved by all, and her death last year excited in the community a sorrow such as it had not experienced since General Lee died.

The feelings with which General Lee entered upon his new work, and established in this mountain town his new home, may be gathered from the following extract from a letter to his son, dated October 30, 1865:

"I was delighted to receive, by the last mail, your letter of the 17th inst. Your affection is a great comfort to me, and the prospect of your society in my declining years has always been to me a source of great pleasure. I accepted the presidency of the college in the hope that I might be of some service to the country, and the rising generation, and not from any preference of my own. I should have selected a more quiet life, and a more retired abode than Lexington, and should have preferred a small farm where I could have earned my daily bread. If I find I can accomplish no good here, I will then endeavor to pursue the course to which my inclinations point. The people have been very considerate and kind to me, and do everything to promote my comfort, and so far the classes are studying remarkably well."

The following letter to one of his old servants illustrates his kindly feeling for his domestics, which might be treated of at length. Never did servants have kinder master, or one who provided better for their comfort and happiness:

"LEXINGTON, VA.,
March 9, 1866

"AMANDA PARKS.

"AMANDA: I have received your letter of the 27th ult., and regret very much that I did not see you when I was in Washington. I heard, on returning to my room Sunday night, that you had been to see me, and I was sorry to have missed you, for I wished to learn how you were, and how all the people from Arlington were getting on in the world. My interest in them is as great now as it ever was, and I sincerely wish for their happiness and prosperity. At the period specified in Mr. Custis's will, five years from the time of his death, I caused the liberation of all the people at Arlington, as well as those at the White House and Romancocke; to be recorded in the Hustings Court at Richmond, and letters of manumission to be given to those, with whom I could communicate, who desired them. In consequence of the war which then existed, I could do nothing more for them.

"I do not know why you should ask if I am angry with you. I am not aware of your having done anything to give me offense, and hope you would not say or do what was wrong. While you lived at Arlington you behaved very well, and were attentive and faithful to your duties. I hope you will always conduct yourself in the same manner. Wishing you health, happiness, and success in life,

"I am, very truly,
"R. E. LEE."

The following throws additional light on his life and feelings:

"LEXINGTON, VA.,
February 26, 1867.

"MY DEAR SON: You must not think, because I write so seldom, that you are absent from my thoughts. I think of you constantly, and am ever revolving in my mind all that concerns you. I have an ardent desire to see you reestablished at your home, and enjoying the pleasure of prosperity around you. I know this cannot be accomplished at once, but must come from continuous labor, economy, and industry, and be the result of years of good management. We have now nothing to do but to attend to our material interests, which collectively, will advance the interests of the State, and to await events. The dominant party cannot reign forever, and truth and justice will at last prevail. I hope I can get down to see you and R——— during the next vacation. I shall then have a more correct apprehension of existing circumstances, and can follow your progress more satisfactorily. I was very much obliged to you for the nice eyeglasses you sent me Christmas, and asked your mother and the girls to thank you for them, which I hope they did; I fear they are too nice for my present circumstances. . . . We have all now to confine ourselves strictly to our necessities. . . . I wish I was nearer to you all. M——— is still in Baltimore, though she contemplates leaving there soon and going to Norfolk. She speaks also of halting at B——— on her way to Richmond. All here unite in much love. Your mother is about the same—busy with her needle and her pen, and as cheerful as ever. C——— has not been well of late, but I hope he is now better; and the girls are quite well. Your friends in town frequently inquire after you, and will be glad to see you again.

> "Affectionately, your father,
> "R. E. LEE."

A number of his letters, expressing his delight at his son's contemplated marriage, giving vivid pictures of home life at Lexington, and kindly and most sensible advice about the details of farming, etc., would be of deep interest to the reader, but may not be inserted because of their personal reference to individuals who are still, fortunately, living.

I will, however, give the following extracts from other letters. In a letter dated December 21, 1867, he thus alludes to his visit to Petersburg to attend his son's marriage:

"My visit to Petersburg was extremely pleasant. Besides the pleasure of seeing my daughter, and being with you, which was very great, I was gratified in seeing so many old friends.

"When our army was in front of Petersburg, I suffered so much in body and mind on account of the good townspeople, especially on that gloomy night when I was forced to abandon them, that I have always reverted to them in sadness and sorrow. My old feelings returned to me as I passed well-remembered spots, and recalled the ravages of hostile shot and shell. But, when I saw the cheerfulness with which the people were working to restore their fortunes, and witnessed the comforts with which they were surrounded, a cloud of sorrow which had been pressing upon me for years was lifted from my heart.

"This is bad weather for completing your house, but it will soon pass away, and your sweet helpmate will make everything go smoothly. When the spring opens, and the mockingbirds resume their song, you will have much to do, so you must prepare in time. . . ."

In a letter to the same, under date of March 30, 1868, he pleasantly says:

"I am very glad that you are so pleased with your house. I think it must be my daughter that gives it such a charm. I am sure that she will make everything look bright to me. It is a good thing that the wheat is doing so well, for I am not sure that—

> *'The flame you are so rich in*
> *Will light a fire in the kitchen,*
> *Nor the little god turn the spit, spit, spit.'*

Some material aliment is necessary to make it burn brightly, and furnish some good dishes for the table. Shad are good in their way, but they do not swim up the Pamunkey all the year."

The quotations from his family letters will be concluded with the following, written just before his trip South the spring before his death:

"LEXINGTON, VA.,
March 22, 1870.

"MY DEAR FITZHUGH: Your letter of the 17th instant has been received. Lest I should appear obstinate if not perverse, I have yielded to the kind importunity of my physicians, and of the faculty, to take a trip toward the South. In pursuance of my resolution, I expect to leave here Thursday next in the packet boat, and hope to arrive in Richmond Friday afternoon. I shall take Agnes with me as my companion (she has been my kind and uncomplaining nurse), and, if we could only get down to you that evening, we would do so, for I want to see you, my sweet daughter, and dear grandson. But as the doctors think it important that I should reach a southern climate as soon as practicable, I fear I shall have to leave my visit to you till my return. I shall go first to Warrenton Springs, North Carolina, to visit the grave of my dear Annie, where I have always promised myself to go, and I think if I am to accomplish it I have no time to lose. I wish to witness her quiet sleep, with her dear hands crossed over her breast, as it were, in mute prayer, undisturbed by her distance from us, and to feel that her pure spirit is roaming in bliss in the land of the blessed.

"From there, according to my feelings, I shall either go down to Norfolk or to Savannah, and take you, if practicable, on my return. . . . We are all as usual. Your mother still talks of visiting you, and, when I urge her to make preparations for her journey, she replies, rather disdainfully, that she has none to make, they have been made years ago. C—— and M—— are well, and M—— writes that she will be back by the 1st of April. We are having beautiful weather now, which I hope may continue. I am so tired sitting at my table that I must conclude. Love to all, from

"Your affectionate father,

"R. E. LEE."

Many other letters of similar character might be given, and much more might be written on the domestic life of this great and good man; but the above must suffice. The home circle has been, alas! sadly broken. The illustrious head of the house—the noble matron who shared his joys and sorrows—the accomplished daughters who were indeed a light and a joy in the home—come not back to their accustomed places, and there are vacant chairs, and missing forms, and silent voices, which tell of a desolated hearthstone and a broken family circle. Father, mother, and daughter, rest together beneath the college chapel at Lexington, while the noble women of the old North State guard the resting place of the other. But their pure spirits bask in the sunlight of the brighter home above, and await the day when, in one of those mansions which Jesus went to prepare, the home circle shall be reunited, and the "domestic life" be *joyous forever.*

Chapter XI

His Love for Children

No record of General Lee's character would be complete without some mention of his marked fondness for children, and the incidents illustrating this are so numerous that I am at a loss to know which to recite.

On the morning of July 4, 1861, little Henry T——— (a bright little boy of five, and an enthusiastic Confederate) went with his father to call on General Lee at his headquarters in Richmond, and to present him with a handsome copy of the Bible in four volumes.

One of the staff met them at the door and reported that the general was too busy to see them; but, when the great chieftain heard the prattle of the little boy, he called to his aide to admit them.

Receiving them with great cordiality, he accepted the gift of the Bible with evident gratification, and was fondling the little boy on his knee, when the father inconsiderately asked Henry, "What is General Lee going to do with General Scott?"

The little fellow, who had caught some of the slang of the camp, and fully entered into the confident spirit which we all had in those early days of the war, instantly replied, "He is going to *whip him out of his breeches!*"

General Lee's voice and manner instantaneously changed, and, lifting Henry down, he stood him up between his knees, and, looking him full in the face, said, with great gravity: "My dear little boy, you should not use such expressions; war is a serious matter, and General Scott is a great and good soldier. None of us can tell what the result of this contest will be."

A few days after this, General Lee rode out to pay a special visit to little Henry. He told him that he wished to make him some return for his present; that he was very much pleased at such a gift from a little boy, and that he could not have given him *anything* which he would have prized so highly as the Holy Bible, especially in so convenient a form. He then handed him a copy of Mr. Custis's *Recollections of General Wash-*

ington, edited by Mrs. Lee, in which he had written his own name and its presentation to Henry.

It is hard to say whether the boy was most delighted with the visit or the book, or with being placed by the general in his saddle on the back of Richmond, the horse he then rode.

While at Petersburg in the winter of 1864 he attended preaching one day at a crowded chapel, and noticed a little girl, dressed in faded garments, standing just inside the door and timidly looking around for a seat. "Come with me, my little lady," said the great soldier, "and you shall sit by me." And taking the little girl by the hand he secured her a comfortable seat at his side.

Rev. W. H. Platt, of Louisville, who lived in Petersburg during the war, gives the following: "One day in Richmond a number of little girls were rolling hoops on the sidewalk, when word was passed from one to another that General Lee was riding toward them. They all gathered into a still group to gaze upon one of whom they had heard so much, when, to their surprise, he threw his rein to his attending courier, dismounted, and kissed every one of them, and then, mounting, rode away, with the sunny smile of childhood in his heart and plans of great battles in his mind.

"Once in Petersburg, he called to see a child in whom he felt a special interest, and finding her sick, begged to be shown to her room. When the mother, who was at a neighbor's for a moment, came home, she found him by the bedside of her sick child, ministering to her comfort and cheering her with his words."

In calling one day in Petersburg upon the accomplished lady of the gallant and lamented General A. P. Hill, his bright little girl met him at the door and exclaimed, with that familiarity which the kind-hearted old hero had taught her: "O General Lee, here is 'Bobby Lee' (holding up a puppy); "do kiss him."

The general pretended to do so, and the little creature was delighted.

Many children all through the land were named after him, and, instead of being annoyed by it, as some men of distinction have been, he seemed to regard it as a compliment, which he always acknowledged. The following are specimens of many similar letters:

"LEXINGTON, VA.,
May 29, 1866.
"*Mr.* A. P. M———, *La Grange, Ga. (for Robert Lee M———).*

"MY DEAR YOUNG FRIEND: I have just become acquainted with you, through a letter from your father, and hasten to express the pleasure this knowledge gives me. I shall watch your future career with great interest, and pray that it may be one of great usefulness to your friends and to your country. That it may be so, listen to the teachings of your parents, obey their precepts, and from childhood to the grave pursue unswervingly the path of honor and of truth. Above all things, learn at once to worship your Creator and to do His will as revealed in His Holy Book.

"With much affection, I am your sincere friend,
"R. E. LEE."

"LEXINGTON, VA.,
August 29, 1866.
"*Mrs.* ROBERT W———, *Clark County, Ind.*

"I am much obliged to you for your letter of the 22d inst., and thank you sincerely for the kind feelings you express toward the people of the South. The compliment paid me by your brother-in-law, Mr. H———, is highly appreciated, and I pray that his little son may be guided through life by a merciful Providence, and be led into the way of everlasting happiness.

"I am, with great respect,
"R. E. LEE."

One day, on the street in Lexington, a little girl of six summers was trying in vain to induce her younger sister to go home, when, seeing General Lee approaching, she appealed to him with childlike simplicity: "O General! Fanny won't go home—please, make her!"

The kindhearted old hero could not resist this call of childhood, but with gentle persuasion induced the little girl to comply with her sister's request, and trudged back a quarter of a mile to lead the little ones by the hand, and enjoy their innocent prattle.

The superintendent of one of the Sunday schools of Lexington once offered a prize to the scholar who should bring into the school by a given time the largest number of new scholars, and the pastor of the church urged that they should not confine their efforts to the children, but should seek to bring in the old as well, since none were too wise to study God's word. A boy of five caught the spirit of the pastor's speech and went after his friend General Lee, to beg him to "go with me to our Sunday school and be my new scholar." The little fellow was greatly disappointed when told that the general attended another church, and said with a deep sigh: "I am very sorry. I wish he belonged to our church, so that he could go to our Sunday school and be my new scholar."

The general was very much amused, and kindly answered his little friend: "Ah! C———, we must all try to be *good Christians*—that is the most important thing. I can't go to your Sunday school to be your new scholar today. But I am very glad that you asked me. It shows that you are zealous in a good cause, and I hope that you will continue to be so as you grow up.

"And I do not want you to think that I consider myself too old to be a Sunday school scholar. No one ever becomes too old to study the precious truths of the Bible."

This last remark was evidently intended for several of the college students who were nearby and listening with deep interest to the colloquy between the general and the young recruiting officer of the Sunday school army.

He knew all of the children in Lexington, and along, the roads and bypaths of his daily rides, and it was pleasing to witness their delight when they met him.

He could be seen at any time stopping on the streets to kiss some bright-eyed little girl, or pass a joke with some sprightly boy.

One of these was accustomed to go to the chapel service frequently and sit by the general, who treated him so cordially and kindly as to make him feel entirely at his ease, and give him the idea that wherever he saw General Lee his place was by his side.

Accordingly, at the next college commencement, the little fellow stole away from his mother, and, before she was aware of it, was on the platform, sitting at the general's feet, gazing up into his face, utterly oblivious of the crowd, and entirely unconscious that he was out of place. After remaining in this position for some time, receiving an occasional kind word from General Lee, he went fast to sleep, resting his head on the general's knees. The great man remained in one position for a long time, and put himself to considerable inconvenience and discomfort that he might not disturb the sleeping child. A distinguished lady present remarked that "this picture of helpless innocence confidingly resting on greatness formed a subject worthy of the greatest artist."

At the Healing Springs in 1868 General Lee was one day sitting in the parlor, conversing with a number of ladies and children who had assembled to see him, when Frank S————, a bright little fellow from Richmond, ran in from a romp on the lawn. Seeing a foot conveniently crossed, and belonging to a kind-looking old gentleman, he, without further ceremony, mounted it for his horse, and began to ride in approved boy-fashion, to the no small amusement of the company and annoyance of the mother, who feared that General Lee would be displeased with so unwarrantable a liberty. But the general was delighted, and, after suffering the little fellow to ride to his heart's content, took him in his lap, and sought an introduction to the mother of his "merry little friend."

In the summer of 1867 General Lee, accompanied by one of his daughters, rode on horseback from Lexington to the Peaks of Otter. In a mountain defile, not far from a humble home, they came suddenly upon some children who were playing near the road, and who began to scamper off on his approach. General Lee called them back, and asked:

"Why are you running away? Are you afraid of me?"

"Oh, no, sir!" replied a little girl, "we are not afraid of you, but we are not dressed nice enough to see *you*."

"Why, who do you think I am?"

"You are General Lee—we knew you by your picture."

The admiration and love of the children for General Lee was not confined to those who met him. But his pictures are in every home in the South, and the children of city and mountain alike were taught to love him when living, and are now taught to cherish and revere his memory. The writer has never seen children manifest more sincere grief at the death of a near relative than that exhibited by the children of Lexington at the death of General Lee.

The schools were all closed, their usual sports were abandoned, and the children mingled their tears with those of strong men and women, as they realized that their kind, dearly loved friend had gone from among them. And all over the South the weeping little ones attested how they loved the great chieftain who always had a pleasant smile and a kind word for them.

Chapter XII

His Christian Character

But I must pass by many other points of General Lee's character, and speak of him, in conclusion, as a Christian.

In this age of hero-worship there is a tendency to exalt unduly the virtues of great men, and to magnify the religious character of one professing to be a Christian. This is so well understood that there may be with those who never came in contact with this great man a lingering doubt as to the genuineness of his piety—a fear that, with him as with so many others, his profession of religion was merely nominal. A few incidents, culled from the many that might be given, will serve to dissipate any such impression, and to show beyond all cavil that, with General Lee, vital godliness was a precious reality.

I can never forget my first interview and conversation with General Lee on religious matters. It was in 1863, while our army was resting along the Rapidan, soon after the Gettysburg campaign. Rev. B. T. Lacy and myself went, as a committee of our chaplain's association, to consult him in reference to the better observance of the Sabbath in the army, and especially to urge that something be done to prevent irreligious officers from converting Sunday into a grand gala day for inspections, reviews, etc. It was a delicate mission. We did not wish to appear as either informers or officious intermeddlers, and yet we were very anxious to do something to further the wishes of those who sent us, and to put a stop to what was then a growing evil, and, in some commands, a serious obstacle to the efficient work of the chaplain. The cordial greeting which he gave us, the marked courtesy and respect with which he listened to what we had to say, and expressed his warm sympathy with the object of our mission, soon put us at our ease. But, as we presently began to answer his questions concerning the spiritual interests of the army, and to tell of that great revival which was then extending through the camps, and bringing thousands of our noble men to Christ, we saw his eyes brighten and his whole countenance glow with pleasure; and as, in his simple, feeling words, he expressed his delight, we forgot the great warrior, and only remembered that we were communing with a humble, earnest Christian. When Mr. Lacy told him of the deep interest which the chaplains felt in his welfare, and that their most fervent prayers were offered in his behalf, tears started in his eyes, as he replied: "I sincerely thank you for that, and I can only say that I am a poor sinner, trusting in Christ alone, and that I need all the prayers you can offer for me."

The next day he issued a beautiful address, in which he referred to his previous orders enjoining the observance of the Sabbath—ordered that nothing should be done on the Lord's Day not absolutely necessary to the subsistence or safety of the army, directed that every facility should be given for religious services, and urged upon officers and men regular attendance upon such services. He always set the example himself, and never failed to attend preaching when his duties did not absolutely preclude his doing so. Nor was he a mere listless attendant. The simple truths of the Gospel had no more attentive listener than General Lee; and his eye would kindle and his face glow under the more tender doctrines of grace. He used frequently to attend preaching at Jackson's headquarters; and it was a scene which a master hand might have delighted to paint— those two great warriors, surrounded by hundreds of their officers and men, bowed in humble worship before the God and Savior in whom they trusted.

General Lee always took the deepest interest in the work of his chaplains and the spiritual welfare of his men. He was a frequent visitor at the chaplains' meetings, and a deeply interested observer of their proceedings; and the faithful chaplain who stuck to his post and did his duty could be always assured of a warm friend at headquarters.

While the Army of Northern Virginia confronted General Meade at Mine Run, near the end of November 1863, and a battle was momentarily expected, General Lee, with a number of general and staff officers, was riding down his line of battle, when, just in rear of General A. P. Hill's position, the cavalcade suddenly came upon a party of soldiers engaged in one of those prayer meetings which they so often held on the eve of battle. An attack from the enemy seemed imminent—already the sharpshooting along the skirmish line had begun—the artillery was belching forth its hoarse thunder, and the mind and heart of the great chieftain were full of the expected combat. Yet, as he saw those ragged veterans bowed in prayer, he instantly dismounted, uncovered his head, and devoutly joined in the simple worship. The rest of the party at once followed his example, and those humble privates found themselves leading the devotions of their loved and honored chieftains.

It is related that, as his army was crossing the James, in 1864, and hurrying on to the defense of Petersburg, General Lee turned aside from the road, and, kneeling in the dust, devoutly joined a minister present in earnest prayer that God would give him wisdom and grace in the new stage of the campaign upon which he was then entering.

Rev. Dr. T. V. Moore gave the following in his memorial sermon:

"About the middle of the war, when the horizon looked very dark, I spent an evening with him, at the house of a friend, and he was evidently, in spite of his habitual self-command, deeply depressed. Happening to be alone with him as we parted for the night, I endeavored to cheer him with the fact that so many Christian people were praying for him. I shall never forget the emphasis with which he grasped my hand, as, with a voice and eye that betrayed deep emotion, he assured me that it was not only his comfort, but his only comfort, and declared the simple and absolute trust that he had in God, and God alone, as his helper in that terrible struggle. Another incident impressed me still more, because it brought out a most beautiful trait in his character. No one ever rendered him a service, however humble, that was not instantly and gratefully acknowledged, however lowly the person might be. During the summer of 1864, after he had been holding at bay the tremendous forces of General Grant for long weeks, retreating step by step as he was outflanked by overwhelming numbers, until he reached the neighborhood of Cold Harbor, I had occasion to render him a slight service, so slight that, knowing at the time that he was sick, and overburdened with the great responsibilities of his arduous and continually menaced position, I never expected it to be acknowledged at all; but, to my surprise, I received a letter thanking me for this trivial service, and adding: 'I thank you especially that I have a place in your prayers. No human power can avail us with out the blessing of God, and I rejoice to know that, in this crisis of our affairs, good men everywhere are supplicating Him for His favor and protection.' He then added a postscript, which most touchingly exhibited his thoughtful and tender recollection of the troubles of others, even in that hour when all his thoughts might be supposed to be absorbed by his vast responsibilities as the leader of the Army of Northern Virginia."

Not long before the evacuation of Petersburg, a chaplain was one day distributing tracts along the trenches, when he perceived a brilliant cavalcade approaching. General Lee—accompanied by General John B. Gordon, General A. P. Hill, and other general officers, with their staffs—was inspecting our lines and reconnoitering those of the enemy. The keen eye of Gordon recognized and his cordial grasp detained the humble tract distributor, as he warmly inquired about his work. General Lee at once reined in his horse and joined in the conversation, the rest of the party gathered around, and the humble colporteur thus became the center of a group of whose notice the highest princes of the earth might well be proud. General Lee asked if he ever had calls for prayer books, and said that if he would call at his headquarters he would give him some for distribution—that "a friend in Richmond had given him a new prayer book, and, upon his saying that he would give his old one, that he had used ever since the Mexican War, to some soldier, the friend had offered him a dozen new books for the old one, and he had, of course, accepted so good an offer, and now had twelve instead of one to give away." He called at the appointed hour. The general had gone out on some important matter, but even amid his pressing duties had left the prayer books with a member of his staff, with instructions concerning them. He had written on the flyleaf of each, "Presented by R. E. Lee," and we are sure that those of the gallant men to whom they were given who survive the war now cherish them as precious legacies, and will hand them down as heirlooms to their descendants.

General Lee's orders and reports always gratefully recognized "the Lord of hosts" as the "Giver of victory," and expressed a humble dependence upon and trust in Him.

He thus began his dispatch to the president the evening of his great victory at Cold Harbor and Gaines's Mill.

"HEADQUARTERS,
June 27, 1862.

"*His Excellency President* DAVIS.

"MR. PRESIDENT: Profoundly grateful to Almighty God for the signal victory granted to us, it is my pleasing task to announce to you the success achieved by this army today."

His beautiful general order of congratulation to the troops on their series of splendid victories during the seven days' battles opened with these memorable words:

"General Order No. 75.

"HEADQUARTERS, IN THE FIELD, *July* 7, 1862.

"The commanding general, profoundly grateful to the Giver of all victory for the signal success with which He has blessed our arms, tenders his warmest thanks and congratulations to the army by whose valor such splendid results have been achieved."

His dispatch, announcing his great victory at Fredericksburg, contains the brief but significant sentence, *"Thanks be to God."*

The following extracts, from an order which he issued to the troops not long after the battle of Fredericksburg, show the same spirit:

"General Order No. 132.

"HEADQUARTERS ARMY OF NORTHERN VIRGINIA, *December* 31, 1862.

"The general commanding takes this occasion to express to the officers and soldiers of the army his high appreciation of the fortitude, valor, and devotion, displayed by them, which under the blessing of Almighty God have added the victory of Fredericksburg to the long list of their triumphs . . . That this great result was achieved with a loss small in point of numbers only augments the admiration with which the commanding general regards the prowess of the troops, and increases his gratitude to Him who hath given us the victory. . . . The signal manifestations of Divine Mercy that have distinguished the eventful and glorious campaign of the year just closing give assurance of hope that under the guidance of the same Almighty hand the coming year will be no less fruitful of events that will insure the safety, peace, and happiness of our beloved country, and add new luster to the already imperishable name of the Army of Northern Virginia.

"R. E. LEE, *General.*"

In his dispatch to President Davis, after Chancellorsville, he said: "We have again to thank Almighty God for a great victory."

And in his general orders to his troops he holds this significant language: ". . . While this glorious victory entitles you to the praise and gratitude of the nation, we are especially called upon to return our grateful thanks to the only Giver of victory for the signal deliverance. He has wrought.

"It is, therefore, earnestly recommended that the troops unite, on Sunday next, in ascribing unto the Lord of hosts the glory due unto his name."

He announced the victory at Winchester in the following characteristic dispatch:

"*June* 15, 1863.

"*To His Excellency* JEFFERSON DAVIS:

"God has again crowned the valor of our troops with success. Early's division stormed the enemy's intrenchments at Winchester, capturing their artillery, etc.

"R. E. LEE."

His order requiring the observance of the fast day appointed by President Davis in August, 1863, was as follows:

"General Order No. 83.

"HEADQUARTERS ARMY NORTHERN VIRGINIA, *August* 13, 1863.

"The president of the Confederate States has, in the name of the people, appointed the 21st day of August as a day of fasting, humiliation, and prayer. A strict observance of the day is enjoined upon the officers and soldiers of this army. All military duties, except such as are absolutely necessary, will be suspended. The commanding officers of brigades and regiments are requested to cause divine services, suitable to the occasion, to be performed in their respective commands.

"Soldiers! we have sinned against Almighty God. We have forgotten his signal mercies, and have cultivated a revengeful, haughty, and boastful spirit. We have not remembered that the defenders of a just cause should be pure in his eyes; that 'our times are in his hands'; and we have relied too much on our own arms for the achievement of our independence. God is our only refuge and our strength. Let us humble ourselves before Him. Let us confess our many sins, and beseech Him to give us a higher courage, a purer patriotism, and more determined will; that He will convert the hearts of our enemies; that He will hasten the time when war, with its sorrows and sufferings, shall cease, and that He will give us a name and place among the nations of the earth.

"R. E. LEE, General."

We can never forget the effect produced by the reading of this order at the solemn services of that memorable fast day. A precious revival was already in progress in many of the commands. The day was almost universally observed; the attendance upon preaching and other services was very large; the solemn attention and starting tear attested the deep interest felt; and the work of grace among the troops widened and deepened, and went gloriously on until there had been at least *fifteen thousand* professions of faith in Christ as a personal Saviour. How far these grand results were due to this fast day, or to the quiet influence and fervent prayers of the commanding general, eternity alone shall reveal.

When General Meade crossed the Rapidan in November 1863, the troops were stirred by the following address:

"General Order No. 102.

"HEADQUARTERS ARMY NORTHERN VIRGINIA, November 26, 1863.

"The enemy is again advancing upon our capital, and the country once more looks to this army for protection. Under the blessings of God, your valor has repelled every previous attempt, and, invoking the continuance of his favor, we cheerfully commit to Him the issue of the coming conflict.

"A cruel enemy seeks to reduce our fathers and our mothers, our wives and our children, to abject slavery; to strip them of their property, and drive them from their homes. Upon you these helpless ones rely to avert these terrible calamities, and secure them the blessing of liberty and safety. Your past history gives them the assurance that their trust will not be in vain. Let every man remember that all he holds dear depends upon the faithful discharge of his duty, and resolve to fight, and, if need be, to die, in defense of a cause so sacred, and worthy the name won by this army on so many bloody fields.

"R. E. LEE, General."

We give the following, as illustrating not only his trust in God, but also his tender solicitude for his soldiers:

"General Order No. 7.

"HEADQUARTERS ARMY NORTHERN VIRGINIA, January 22, 1864.

"The commanding general considers it due to the army to state that the temporary reduction of rations has been caused by circumstances beyond the control of those charged with its support. Its welfare and comfort are the objects of his constant and earnest solicitude; and no effort has been spared to provide for its wants. It is hoped that the exertions now being made will render the necessity of short duration; but the history of the army has shown that the country can require no sacrifice too great for its patriotic devotion.

"Soldiers! you tread, with no unequal steps, the road by which your fathers marched through suffering, privation, and blood, to independence!

"Continue to emulate in the future, as you have in the past, their valor in arms, their patient endurance of hardships, their high resolve to be free, which no trial could shake, no bribe seduce, no danger appall; and be assured that the just God, who crowned their efforts with success, will, in his own good time, send down his blessings upon yours.

"R. E. LEE, General."

The following was his order for the observance of the fast day appointed for April 1864:

"General Order No. 23.

"HEADQUARTERS ARMY NORTHERN VIRGINIA, *March* 30, 1864.

"In compliance with the recommendation of the Senate and House of Representatives, his Excellency the president has issued his proclamation calling upon the people to set apart Friday, the 8th of April, as a day of fasting, humiliation, and prayer. The commanding general invites the army to join in the observance of the day. He directs due preparations to be made in all departments, to anticipate the wants of the several commands, so that it may be strictly observed. All military duties, except those that are absolutely necessary, will be suspended. The chaplains are desired to hold services in their regiments and brigades. The officers and men are requested to attend.

"Soldiers! let us humble ourselves before the Lord our God, asking, through Christ, the forgiveness of our sins, beseeching the aid of the God of our forefathers in the defense of our homes and our liberties, thanking Him for his past blessings, and imploring their continuance upon our cause and our people.

"R. E. LEE, General."

In his dispatch announcing the result of the first day's battle in the Wilderness he says:

". . . By the blessing of God we maintained our position against every effort until night, when the contest closed . . ."

And in his dispatch concerning the advance of the enemy on the next day he says:

". . . Every advance on his part, thanks to a merciful God, has been repulsed . . ."

He closes his dispatch concerning the first day at Spottsylvania by saying, "I am most thankful to the Giver of all victory that our loss is small"; and that concerning the action of June 3, 1864, with "Our loss today has been small, and our success, under the blessing of God, all that we could expect . . ."

He closed his announcement of A. P. Hill's brilliant victory at Reams's Station, in August 1864, by saying:

". . . Our profound gratitude is due the Giver of all victory, and our thanks to the brave men and officers engaged . . ."

In his order assuming the command of all of the Confederate forces, he said:

". . . Deeply impressed with the difficulties and responsibility of the position, and humbly invoking the guidance of Almighty God, I rely for success upon the courage and fortitude of the army, sustained by the patriotism and firmness of the people, confident that their united efforts, under the blessing of Heaven, will secure peace and independence . . ."

We give the above only as specimens of his dispatches and general orders, which all recognized in the most emphatic manner his sense of dependence upon and trust in God.

With the close of the war, and the afflictions which came upon his loved land, the piety of this great man seems to have mellowed and deepened, and we could fill pages concerning his life at Lexington, and the bright evidence he gave of vital, active godliness.

He was a most regular attendant upon all of the services of his own church, his seat in the college chapel was never vacant unless he was kept away by sickness, and if there was a union prayer meeting or a service of general interest in any of the churches of Lexington, General Lee was sure to be among the most devout attendants.

His pew in his own church was immediately in front of the chancel, his seat in the chapel was the second from the pulpit, and he seemed always to prefer a seat near the preacher's stand. He always devoutly knelt during prayer, and his attitude during the entire service was that of an interested listener or a reverential participant.

He was not accustomed to indulge in carping criticisms of sermons, but was a most intelligent judge of what a sermon ought to be, and always expressed his preference for those sermons which presented most simply and earnestly the soul-saving truths of the Gospel. The writer heard him remark in reference to one of the Baccalaureate sermons preached at the college: "It was a noble sermon—one of the very best I ever heard—and the beauty of it was that the preacher gave our young men the very marrow of the Gospel, and with a simple earnestness that must have reached their hearts and done them good."

Upon another occasion a distinguished minister had addressed the Young Men's Christian Association of the college, and on the next night delivered a popular lecture. Speaking of the last, General Lee said: "It was a very fine lecture, and I enjoyed it. But I did not like it as much as I did the one before our Christian Association. *That* touched our hearts, and did us all good."

He had also a most intelligent appreciation of the adaptation of religious services to particular occasions, and of the appropriateness of prayers to the time and place in which they were offered.

He once said to one of the faculty: "I want you to go with me to call upon Mr.———, the new minister, who has just come to town. I want to pay my respects to him, and to invite him to take his turn in the conduct of our chapel exercises, and to do what he can for the spiritual interests of our young men.

"And do you think that it would be any harm for me to delicately hint to Mr.——— that we would be glad if he would make his morning prayers *a little short?* You know our friend———is accustomed to make his prayers too long. He prays for the Jews, the Turks, the heathen, the Chinese, and everybody else, and makes his prayers run into the regular hour for our college recitations. Would it be wrong for me to suggest to Mr.——— that he *confine his morning prayers to us poor sinners at the college, and pray for the Turks, the Jews, the Chinese, and the other heathen, some other time?*"

The suggestion is one which those who lead in public prayer would do well to ponder.

General Lee was emphatically a *man of prayer*. He was accustomed to pray in his family, and to have his seasons of secret prayer, which he allowed nothing else, however pressing, to interrupt. He was also a constant reader and a diligent student of the Bible, and had his regular seasons for this delightful exercise. Even amid his most active campaigns he found time to read every day some portion of God's Word.

As the writer watched alone by his body the day after his death, he picked up from the table a well-used pocket Bible, in which was written, in his characteristic chirography, "R. E. Lee, lieutenant colonel, U. S. Army." How he took this blessed book as the man of his counsel and the light of his pathway—how its precious promises cheered him amid the afflictions and trials of his eventful life—how its glorious hopes illumined for him "the dark valley and shadow of death," eternity alone will fully reveal.

And he always manifested the liveliest interest in giving to others the precious Bible. During the war he was an active promoter of Bible distribution among his soldiers, and soon after coming to Lexington he accepted the presidency of the Rockbridge Bible Society, and continued to discharge its duties up to the time of his death. We give his letter accepting this office:

"GENTLEMEN: I have delayed replying to your letter informing me of my having been elected president of the Rockbridge Bible Society, not for want of interest in the subject, but from an apprehension that I should not be able to perform the duties of the position in such manner as to advance the high object proposed. Having, however, been encouraged by your kind assurances, and being desirous of cooperating in any way I can in extending the inestimable knowledge of the priceless truths of the Bible, I accept the position assigned me.

"With many thanks to the Society for the high compliment paid me by their selection as president,

"I am, with great respect, your obedient servant,

"R. E. LEE."

"Rev. DR. PENDLETON,
Colonel J. L. T. PRESTON, } Committee."
Mr. WILLIAM WHITE,

The following paper may be appropriately introduced here:

"At the meeting of the board of managers of the Rockbridge County Bible Society, on the 12th inst., for the purpose of imparting to the organization greater efficiency, in addition to other important measures adopted, and in substance since published, the undersigned were appointed a committee to prepare and publish a minute expressing the deep sense which the managers and members of this society have of the exalted worth of their last president, the illustrious General R. E. Lee—of the blessed influence which he exerted as a Christian man, and in his official relation to this cause, and of the grievous loss to us in his removal even to celestial joy.

"The duty is to us most grateful. Worldwide and enduring as must be the renown of our honored friend, for great abilities, grandeur of character, and achievements, perhaps, in proportion to appliances never surpassed, his crowning glory was, in our view, the sublime simplicity of his Christian faith and life. To the inviolable dignity of a soul among the noblest of all history was in him thoroughly united that guileless, unpretending, gentle and yet earnest spirit of a little child so emphatically designated by our Lord as the essential characteristic of his chosen ones. These were the traits which, while they justly endeared him to children, and friends, and all the people, rendered him prompt to every—even the humblest—duty, and caused him, although burdened with weighty cares, to accept the quietly useful task of presiding over so inconspicuous a good work as that of the Rockbridge County Bible Society. Of the judicious zeal with which he undertook this service, evidence conclusive was at once given in the wisely simple yet stirring appeal which he penned and sent forth to the several ministers and congregations of the county, urging them to renewed energy in remedying Bible destitution throughout our borders. Well may the friends of this cause mourn the loss of such a leader, and record on the tablets of their hearts an example so good, as an incentive to their own efficiency for the future!

"In connection with this testimonial of the society's loving estimate of their last president, the undersigned were instructed to cause to be published the appeal above referred to, written by General Lee's own hand, of which copies were at the time sent to all the ministers and congregations of the county. The original remains a precious memento in the archives of the society. To it, as hereunto subjoined in print, we ask the attentive consideration due alike to its great author and to the important cause for which he pleads. Facts and principles bearing on the question are today very much as they were five years ago, when the mind of this great and good man was moved so impressively to put them forth in the following circular.

"Although now resting from his labors, his works do follow him. Shall they not, in this and in other forms, effectually plead with all to be alive to Christian privilege in this matter, and faithful to duty therein and in all things?

"W. N. PENDLETON, ⎫
J. L. CLARKE,   ⎬ *Committee.*"
J. W. PRATT,   ⎭

"LEXINGTON, VA.,
January 14, 1869.

"The Rockbridge County Bible Society, whose operations were interrupted and records lost during the war, was reorganized on the 5th of last October by representatives of different churches of the county, in pursuance of a notice given through the *Lexington Gazette.* A new constitution was adopted, which provided for the reorganization of a board of managers composed of the ministers of each church and one representative from each congregation appointed by them, to meet at least once a year, on the first Saturday in October; and that the officers of the society shall be a president, vice-president, secretary and treasurer, and librarian, who shall constitute the executive committee of the society.

"At the meeting mentioned the following officers were elected:

"R. E. LEE, *President;*

J. T. L. PRESTON, *Vice-President;*

WILLIAM G. WHITE, *Secretary and Treasurer;*

JOHN S. WHITE, *Librarian.*

"In compliance with a resolution of the meeting requesting the executive committee to take measures to procure a supply of Bibles and to obtain from the congregations of the county funds for the purpose, it is respectfully requested that you will make at the earliest and most suitable occasion a collection in your congregation for this object and cause, the amount to be transmitted to the treasurer, Mr. William G. White, at Lexington, and inform him at the same time, as far as practicable, how many copies of the Bible will be required to meet the wants of the congregation, as the constitution provides that each congregation shall mainly conduct the work of their distribution within their respective spheres.

"The revival of the time-honored organization of the Rockbridge Bible

Society, it is believed, will fill with pleasure the hearts of all good citizens in the county, and the executive committee earnestly appeal to the churches, their members, and all persons interested in the great work of the society, to unite cordially and promptly with them for its accomplishment. The first object is to supply every family with a copy of the Bible that is without it, and as many years have elapsed since there has been a distribution of the Holy Scriptures among us, it is feared, for reasons that are apparent, that there is at this time a great destitution among the people. The united and zealous efforts of all the denominations in the county are therefore earnestly solicited in aid of this good work.

"Respectfully submitted.

"R. E. LEE, *Pres. Rockbridge Bible Society.*

"To the MINISTERS and CHURCHES of the County of Rockbridge, Va."

General Lee was also deeply interested in the Virginia Bible Society and their noble work of giving the Word of God to the people.

He wrote as follows to the president of that society:

"LEXINGTON, VA.,

April 5, 1869.

"REVEREND AND DEAR SIR: Your letter of the 1st inst. was only received this morning.

"To reach Richmond by tomorrow evening, the anniversary of the Bible Society, I should have to ride all tonight to take the cars at Staunton tomorrow morning. I am suffering with a cold now, and fear the journey would lay me up.

"I would, however, make the trial, did I think I could be of any service to the great object of the society. If the managers could suggest any plan, in addition to the abundant distribution of the Holy Scriptures, to cause the mass of the people to meditate on their simple truths, and, in the language of Wilberforce, 'to read the Bible— read the Bible,' so as to become acquainted with the experience and realities of religion, the greatest good would be accomplished.

"Wishing the society all success, and continual advancement in its work,

"I am, with great respect, most truly yours,

"R. E. LEE."

"Rev. GEORGE WOODBRIDGE, President of the Virginia Bible Society."

The following graceful acknowledgment of a copy of the Scriptures sent him by some English ladies may be appropriately introduced at this point:

"LEXINGTON, VA.,
April 16, 1866.

"*Hon.* A. W. BERESFORD HOPE, *Bedgebury Park, Kent, England.*

"I have received within a few days your letter of November 14, 1864, and had hoped that by this time it would have been followed by the copy of the Holy Scriptures to which you refer, that I might have known the generous donors, whose names, you state, are inscribed upon its pages.

"Its failure to reach me will, I fear, deprive me of that pleasure; and I must ask the favor of you to thank them most heartily for their kindness in providing me with a book in comparison with which all others in my eyes are of minor importance, and which in all my perplexities and distresses has never failed to give me light and strength. Your assurance of the esteem in which I am held by a large portion of the British nation, as well as by those for whom you speak, is most grateful to my feelings, though I am aware that I am indebted to their generous natures, and not to my own merit, for their good opinion.

"I beg, sir, that you will accept my sincere thanks for the kind sentiments which you have expressed toward me, and my unfeigned admiration of your exalted character.

"I am, with great respect, your most obedient servant,
"R. E. LEE."

General Lee was a most active promoter of the interests of his church, and of the cause of Christ in the community, and all the pastors felt that they had in him a warm friend.

He was a most liberal contributor to his church and to other objects of benevolence. At the vestry meeting, which he attended, and over which he presided, the evening he was taken with his fatal illness, an effort was being made to raise a certain sum for an important object. General Lee had already made an exceedingly liberal contribution, but, when it was ascertained that fifty-five dollars were still lacking, he quietly said, "I will

give the balance." These were the last words he spoke in the meeting—
his contribution, his last public act. The writer happens to know that,
within the last twelve months of his life, he gave one hundred dollars to
the education of soldiers' orphans, one hundred dollars to the Young Men's
Christian Association of the college, and smaller sums to a number of
similar objects—making, in the aggregate, a most liberal contribution.
And, then, his manner of contributing was so modest and unostentatious.
In giving the writer a very handsome contribution to the Lexington Baptist
Church, he quietly said: "Will you do me the kindness to hand this to
your treasurer, and save me the trouble of hunting him up? I am getting
old now, and you young men must help me." And his whole manner was
that of one receiving instead of bestowing a favor.

General Lee was not accustomed to talk of anything that concerned
himself, and did not often speak freely of his inner religious feelings. Yet
he would, when occasion offered, speak most decidedly of his reliance for
salvation upon the merits of his personal Redeemer, and none who heard
him thus talk could doubt for a moment that his faith was built on the
"Rock of Ages."

He one day said to a friend, in speaking of the duty of laboring for the
good of others: "Ah! Mrs. P———, I find it so hard to keep one poor
sinner's heart in the right way, that it seems presumptuous to try to help
others." And yet he did, quietly and unostentatiously, speak "a word in
season," and exert influences potent for good in directing others in the
path to heaven. He was a "son of consolation" to the afflicted, and his
letter book contains some touching illustrations of this. We give the following extract from a letter written to an afflicted mother on the death,
by drowning, of her son (then a student at the college):

"Lexington, Va.,
April 6, 1868.

"My dear Madam: It grieves me to address you on a subject which
has already been announced to you in all of its woe, and which has
brought to your heart such heavy affliction.

"But I beg to be permitted to sympathize in your great sorrow,
and to express to you on the part of the faculty of the college their
deep grief at the calamity which has befallen you. It may be some
consolation in your bereavement to know that your son was highly

esteemed by the officers and students of the college, and that this whole community unite in sorrow at his untimely death. May God in his mercy support you under this grievous trial, and give you that peace which, as it passeth all understanding, so nothing in this world can diminish or destroy it."

On the death of Bishop Elliott, of Georgia, he wrote the following letter to the widow:

"LEXINGTON, VA.,
February 21, 1867.

"MY DEAR MRS. ELLIOTT: It would be in vain for me to attempt to express my grief at your great affliction. In common with the whole country I mourn the death of him whom, for more than a quarter of a century, I have admired, loved, and venerated, and whose loss to the church and society where his good offices were so important I can never expect to see supplied.

"You have my deepest sympathy, and my earnest prayers are offered to Almighty God that He may be graciously pleased to comfort you in your great sorrow, and to bring you in his own good time to rejoice with him whom, in his all-wise providence, He has called before you to heaven.

"With great respect, most truly yours,
"R. E. LEE."

The following to the widow of his cherished friend, General George W. Randolph (for a time Confederate secretary of war), will be read with mournful pleasure by the large circle of admirers and friends of this gifted and widely lamented Virginian:

"LEXINGTON, VA.,
April 11, 1867.

"*Mrs.* MARY RANDOLPH.

"MY DEAR MRS. RANDOLPH: The letter I received this morning from your niece affords me an opportunity of writing to you on a subject over which I deeply mourn. But it is the survivors of the sad event whom I commiserate, and not him whom a gracious God has called to himself, and whose tender heart and domestic virtues make the pang of parting the more bitter to those who are left behind. I deferred writing, for I knew the hopelessness of offering you consolation; and yet, for what other purpose can a righteous man be summoned into the presence of a merciful God than to receive his reward? However, then, we lament, we ought not to deplore him or wish him back from his peaceful, happy home. I had hoped to have seen him once more in this world, and had been pleasing myself with the prospect of paying him a special visit this summer. But God, in mercy to him has ordered otherwise, and I submit.

"The recollection of his esteem and friendship will always be dear to me, and his kind remembrance in his long and painful illness will be gratefully cherished. His worth and truth, his unselfish devotion to right, and exalted patriotism, will cause all good men to mourn the country's loss in his death, while his gentle, manly courtesy, dignified conduct, and Christian charity, must intensely endear him to those who knew him.

"Mrs. Lee and my daughters, while they join in unfeigned sorrow for your bereavement, unite with me in sincere regards and fervent prayers to him who can alone afford relief, for his gracious support and continued protection to you. May his abundant mercies be showered upon you, and may his almighty arm guide and uphold you!

"Please thank Miss Randolph for writing to me.

"With great respect and true affection, your most obedient servant,

"R. E. LEE."

The following expresses a great deal in brief compass:

"LEXINGTON, VA.,
February 28, 1870.
"*Mr.* SAMUEL R. GEORGE, 71 *Mt. Vernon Place, Baltimore, Md.*

"MY DEAR SIR: I have learned, with deep regret, the great sorrow that has befallen you, and sincerely sympathize in your overwhelming grief; but the great God of heaven takes us at the period when it is best for us to go, and we can only gratefully acknowledge his mercy and try to be resigned to his will. Every beat of our hearts marks our progress through life, and admonishes us of the steps we make toward the grave. We are thus every moment reminded to prepare for our summons. With my earnest sympathy for yourself and kindest regards to your children, in which Mrs. Lee and my daughters unite.

> "I am most truly yours,
> "R. E. LEE."

The friendship between General Lee and the venerable Bishop Meade, of Virginia (whose efficient labors in the cause of evangelical piety were widely known and appreciated even outside of his own communion), was touchingly beautiful, and the following letter will be read with peculiar interest:

> "LEXINGTON, VA.,
> *March 7, 1866.*

"*Rt. Rev.* JOHN JOHNS, *Bishop of Virginia, Theological Seminary, near Alexandria, Va.*

"RT. REV. AND DEAR SIR: I am very glad to learn from your note of the 27th ult. that you have consented to write a memoir of our good and beloved Bishop Meade. Of all the men I have ever known, I consider him the purest; and a history of his character and life will prove a benefit to mankind. No one can portray that character or illustrate that life better than yourself; and I rejoice that the sacred duty has devolved upon you.

"In compliance with your request, I will state as far as my recollection enables me the substance of what occurred in the short interview I had with him the evening before his death; and I do so the more readily as you were present and can correct the inaccuracies of my memory. I received a message about dark that the bishop was very ill, and desired to see me. On entering his room he recognized me at once, and, extending his hand, said that his earthly pilgrimage was nearly finished, and that before the light of another day he should have passed from this world; that he had known me in childhood, when I recited to him the church catechism, taught me by my mother before I could read; that his affection and interest began at that time, and strengthened by my marriage with his Godchild, and continued to the present. Invoking upon me the guidance and protection of Almighty God, he bade me a last farewell.

"With kindest regards to Mrs. Johns and your daughters,

"I am most truly yours,

"R. E. LEE."

A clergyman present, in describing this last interview, states that the bishop said to the great soldier: "God bless you! God bless you, Robert, and fit you for your high and responsible duties! I can't call you 'General'; I must call you 'Robert'; I have heard you your catechism too often."

General Lee was deeply affected by the interview, and, when he turned to leave the room, the bishop, much exhausted and with great emotion, took him by the hand and said: "Heaven bless you! Heaven bless you, and give you wisdom for your important and arduous duties."

On the death of Randolph Fairfax, who fell at Fredericksburg, struck down by a fragment of the same shell that mortally wounded Lieutenant Colonel Lewis Minor Coleman (the Christian soldier, accomplished scholar, and peerless gentleman) and Arthur Robinson (a grandson of William Wirt), General Lee, who highly appreciated the manly virtues of this young soldier of the cross, wrote the following letter to his bereaved father:

"CAMP FREDERICKSBURG,

December 28, 1862.

"MY DEAR DOCTOR: I have grieved most deeply at the death of your noble son. I have watched his conduct from the commencement of the war, and have pointed with pride to the patriotism, self-denial, and manliness of character he has exhibited. I had hoped that an opportunity would occur for the promotion he deserved; not that it would have elevated him, but have shown that his devotion to duty was appreciated by his country.

"Such an opportunity would undoubtedly have occurred; but he has been translated to a better world, for which his purity and piety eminently fitted him. You do not require to be told how great is his gain. It is the living for whom I sorrow. I beg you will offer to Mrs. Fairfax and your daughter my heartfelt sympathy, for I know the depth of their grief. That God may give you and them strength to bear this great affliction, is the earnest prayer of

"Your early friend,

"R. E. LEE.

"Dr. Orlando Fairfax, Richmond."

On the death of his personal friend, George Peabody, General Lee wrote the following to Mr. Peabody Russell:

"LEXINGTON, VA.,
November 10, 1869

"MY DEAR MR. RUSSELL: The announcement of the death of your uncle, Mr. George Peabody, has been received with the deepest regret wherever his name and benevolence are known; and nowhere have his generous deeds, restricted to no country, section, or sect, elicited more heartfelt admiration than at the South.

"He stands alone in history for the benevolent use and judicious distribution of his great wealth, and his memory has become justly entwined in the affections of millions of his fellow citizens in both hemispheres.

"I beg in my own behalf, and in behalf of the trustees and faculty of Washington College, Virginia, which has not been forgotten by him in his acts of generosity, to tender our unfeigned sorrow at his death.

"With great respect, your obedient servant,

"R. E. LEE."

Upon the death of Professor Frank Preston, of William and Mary College, General Lee issued the following announcement:

WASHINGTON COLLEGE,
November 23, 1869.

"The death of Professor Frank Preston, a distinguished graduate, and late Assistant Professor of Greek in this college, has caused the deepest sorrow in the hearts of the faculty and members of the institution.

"Endowed with a mind of rare capacity, which had been enriched by diligent study and careful cultivation, he stood among the first in the state in his pursuit in life.

"We who so long and so intimately possessed his acquaintance, and so fully enjoyed the privilege of his companionship, feel especially his loss, and grieve profoundly at his death; and we heartily sympathize with his parents and relatives in their great affliction, and truly participate in the deep sorrow that has befallen them.

"With a view of testifying the esteem felt for his character and the respect due to his memory, all academic exercises will be suspended for the day; and the faculty and students are requested to attend, in their respective bodies, his funeral services at the Presbyterian Church, at eleven o'clock, to pay the last sad tribute of respect to his earthly remains, while cherishing in their hearts his many virtues.

"R. E. LEE, *President.*"

The above was written, *currente calamo,* immediately on his hearing of the death of Professor Preston, whom he most highly esteemed, not only as an accomplished scholar and high-toned gentleman, but as one who had been a gallant Confederate soldier, and wore till his death a badge of honor in the "empty sleeve" that hung at his side.

We also give the following extract from a letter to Rev. Dr. Moses D. Hoge, of the Presbyterian Church, Richmond, soon after the death of his wife. After writing of a number of matters connected with the interests of the Virginia Bible Society, he concludes as follows:

"And now, my dear sir, though perhaps inappropriate to the occasion, you must allow me to refer to a subject which has caused me great distress, and concerning which I have desired to write ever since its occurrence; but, to tell the truth, I have not had the heart to do so. I knew how powerless I was to give any relief, and how utterly inadequate was any language that I could use even to mitigate your suffering.

"I could, therefore, only offer up my silent prayers to Him who alone can heal your bleeding heart; that in his infinite mercy He would be ever present with you to dry your tears and stanch your wounds; to sustain you by His grace, and support you by His strength.

"I hope you felt assured that, in this heavy calamity, you and your children had the heartfelt sympathy of Mrs. Lee and myself, and that you were daily remembered in our prayers.

"With our best wishes and sincere affection,

"I am very truly yours,

"R. E. LEE."

Extracts of the same character could be multiplied, but the above must suffice.

General Lee manifested the deepest concern for the spiritual welfare of the young men under his care. Soon after becoming president of Washington College, he said, with deep feeling, to Rev. Dr. White, then the venerable pastor of the Lexington Presbyterian Church: "I shall be disappointed, sir—I shall fail in the leading object that brought me here, unless these young men become real Christians; and I wish you, and others of your sacred profession, to do all you can to accomplish this."

Rev. Dr. Brown, editor of the *Central Presbyterian,* and one of the trustees of Washington and Lee University, says, in his paper:

"The crowning excellence of such men as Jackson and Lee was their sincere Christian piety. The remark made by General Lee to the Rev. Dr. White was made to us upon another occasion in a form even more emphatic. 'I dread,' said he, 'the thought of any student's going away from the college without becoming a sincere Christian.' "

At the beginning of each session of the college he was accustomed to address an autograph letter to the pastors of Lexington, inviting them to arrange for conducting in turn the regular chapel services of the college, asking them to induce the students to attend their several churches, Bible classes, etc., and urging them to do all in their power for the spiritual good of the students. Not content with this general request, he was accustomed to prepare lists of students who belonged themselves to, or whose families were connected with, particular churches, and to hand these to the several pastors, with the earnestly expressed wish that they would consider these young men under their especial watch-care, and give them every attention in their power; and he would frequently ask a pastor after individual students—whether they belonged to his Bible class, were regular in their attendance at church, etc.

General Lee did not believe in *enforced* religion, and never required the students, by any college law, to attend chapel or church, but he did everything in his power to influence them to do so, and with the largest success.

At the "Concert of Prayer for Colleges," in Lexington, in 1869, a pastor present made an address in which he urged that the great need of our colleges was a genuine, pervasive revival—that this could only come from God; and that, inasmuch as He has promised his Holy Spirit to those who ask him, we should make special prayer for a revival in the colleges of the country, and more particularly in Washington College and the Virginia Military Institute. At the close of the meeting, General Lee went to him and said, with more than his usual warmth: "I wish, sir, to thank you for your address; it was just what we needed. Our great want is a revival which will bring these young men to Christ."

During the great revival in the Virginia Military Institute in 1869, he said to his pastor: "That is the best news I have heard since I have been in Lexington. Would that we could have such a revival in all of our colleges!" Rev. Dr. Kirkpatrick, Professor of Moral Philosophy in Washington College, relates the following concerning a conversation he had with General Lee just a short time previous to his fatal illness: "We had been conversing for some time respecting the religious welfare of the students. General Lee's feelings then became so intense that for a time his utterance was choked; but, recovering himself, with his eyes overflowed with tears, his lips quivering with emotion, and both hands raised, he exclaimed, 'O Doctor! if I could only know that all the young men in the college were good Christians, I should have nothing more to desire.' "

General Lee was deeply interested in the Young Men's Christian Association of the college, and seemed highly gratified at its large measure of success. His letter, in reply to one making him an honorary member of the association, was as follows:

"MY DEAR SIR: I have received your letter announcing my election as an honorary member of the Young Men's Christian Association of Washington College, a society in whose prosperity I take the deepest interest, and for the welfare of whose members my prayers are daily offered. Please present my grateful thanks to your association for the honor conferred on me, and believe me,

"Very respectfully, your obedient servant,
"R. E. LEE."

"Mr. A. N. GORDON, Corresponding Secretary
"Young Men's Christian Association."

Rev. Dr. Brantly, of Baltimore, and Bishop Marvin, of Missouri, who stayed at his house during the college commencement of 1870, both speak of the warm gratification which General Lee expressed at the encouraging report of the religious interest among the students.

General Lee was a member of the Episcopal church, and was sincerely attached to the church of his choice; but his large heart took in Christians of every name; he treated ministers of all denominations with the most marked courtesy and respect; and it may be truly said of him that he had a heart and hand "ready to *every* good work." When once asked his opinion of a certain theological question, which was exciting considerable discussion, he replied: "Oh! I never trouble myself about such questions; my chief concern is to try to be a humble, earnest Christian myself."

An application of a Jewish soldier for permission to attend certain ceremonies of his synagogue in Richmond was endorsed by his captain: "Disapproved. If such applications were granted, the whole army would turn Jews or shaking Quakers." When the paper came to General Lee, he endorsed on it: "Approved, and respectfully returned to Captain——, with the advice that he should always respect the religious views and feelings of others."

The following letters, addressed to a prominent rabbi of Richmond (to whom I am indebted for copies), will serve to illustrate the broad charity of this model Christian:

"HEADQUARTERS, VALLEY MT.,
August 29, 1861.
"*Rabbi* M. J. MICHELBACHER, *Preacher Hebrew Congregation,* ⎱
House of Love, Richmond, Va. ⎰

"REV. SIR: I have just received your letter of the 23d inst., requesting that a furlough from the 2d to the 15th of September be granted to the soldiers of the Jewish persuasion in the Confederate States Army, that they may participate in the approaching holy services of the synagogue. It would give me great pleasure to comply with a request so earnestly urged by you, and which, I know, would be so highly appreciated by that class of our soldiers. But the necessities of war admit of no relaxation of the efforts requisite for its success, nor can it be known on what day the presence of every man may be required. I feel assured that neither you nor any member of the Jewish congregation would wish to jeopardize a cause you have so much at heart by the withdrawal even for a season of its defenders. I cannot, therefore, grant the general furlough you desire, but must leave it to individuals to make their own applications to their several commanders, in the hope that many will be able to enjoy the privilege you seek for them. Should any be deprived of the opportunity of offering up their prayers according to the rites of their church, I trust that their penitence may nevertheless be accepted by the Most High, and their petitions answered. That your prayers for the success and welfare of our cause may be answered by the Great Ruler of the universe, is my ardent wish.

"I have the honor to be, with high esteem, your ob't servant,

"R. E. LEE, *General commanding.*"

"HEADQUARTERS ARMY NORTHERN VIRGINIA, *April 2,* 1863.
"M. J. MICHELBACHER, *Minister of Hebrew* ⎱
    Congregation, Richmond, Va. ⎰

"SIR: It will give me pleasure to comply with the request contained in your letter of the 30th ult., as far as the public interest will permit. But I think it more than probable that the army will be engaged in active operations, when, of course, no one would wish to be absent from its ranks, nor could they in that event be spared. The reports from all quarters show that General Hooker's army is prepared to cross the Rappahannock, and only awaits favorable weather and roads.

"The sentence in the case of Isaac Arnold has been suspended, until the decision of the president shall be known. Thanking you very sincerely for your good wishes in behalf of our country, I remain, with great respect,

"Your obedient servant,
"R. E. LEE."

"HEADQUARTERS ARMY NORTHERN VIRGINIA,
September 20, 1864.
"*Rev.* M. J. MICHELBACHER, *Richmond, Va.*

"SIR: I have received your letter of the 15th inst., asking that furloughs may be granted to the Israelites in the army, from September

30th to October 11th, to enable them to repair to Richmond to observe the holy days appointed by the Jewish religion.

"It would afford me much pleasure to comply with your request
did the interests of the service permit; but it is impossible to grant
a general furlough to one class of our soldiers without recognizing
the claims of others to a like indulgence. I can only grant furloughs
on applications setting forth special grounds for them, or in accordance with the general orders on that subject applicable to all the
army alike.

"I will gladly do all in my power to facilitate the observance of
the duties of their religion by the Israelites in the army, and will
allow them every indulgence consistent with safety and discipline.
If their applications be forwarded to me in the usual way, and it
appears that they can be spared, I will be glad to approve as many
of them as circumstances will permit. Accept my thanks for your
kind wishes for myself, and believe me to be,

"With great respect, your obedient servant,

"R. E. LEE."

This characteristic was noted by all who came in contact with him, and
not a few will cordially echo the remark of the venerable Dr. White, who
said, with deep feeling, during the funeral services: "He belonged to one
branch of the church, and I to another; yet, in my intercourse with him—
an intercourse rendered far more frequent and intimate by the tender sympathy he felt in my ill health—the thought never occurred to me that we
belonged to different churches. His love for the truth, and for all that is
good and useful, was such as to render his brotherly kindness and charity
as boundless as were the wants and sorrows of his race."

It were an easy task to write pages more in illustration of the Christian
character of our great leader; but want of space forbids.

If I have ever come in contact with a sincere devout Christian—one
who, seeing himself to be a sinner, trusted alone in the merits of Christ,
who humbly tried to walk the path of duty, "looking unto Jesus" as the
author and finisher of his faith, and whose piety constantly exhibited itself
in his daily life—that man was General R. E. LEE.

Chapter XIII

SKETCH OF HIS SICKNESS, DEATH, AND FUNERAL OBSEQUIES

Although a resident of Lexington at the time, and fully acquainted with all the circumstances of the sickness, death, and funeral obsequies of General Lee, I deem myself fortunate in being able to present the following account from the graceful pen of Colonel William Preston Johnston, whose intimacy with our illustrious chief, added to the fact that he was an almost constant watcher at his dying bedside, will add a peculiar interest to the narrative which he has kindly prepared for this volume.

"DEATH OF GENERAL LEE.

"The death of General Lee was not due to any sudden cause, but was the result of agencies dating as far back as 1863. In the trying campaign of that year, he contracted a severe sore throat, that resulted in rheumatic inflammation of the sac inclosing the heart. There is no doubt that after this sickness his health was always more or less impaired; and, although he complained little, yet rapid exercise on foot or on horseback produced pain and difficulty of breathing. In October 1869, he was again attacked by inflammation of the heart sac, accompanied by muscular rheumatism of the back, right side, and arms. The action of the heart was weakened by this attack; the flush upon the face was deepened, the rheumatism increased, and he was troubled with weariness and depression.

"In March 1870, General Lee, yielding to the solicitations of friends and medical advisers, made a six weeks' visit to Georgia and Florida. He returned greatly benefited by the influence of the genial climate, the society of friends in those states, and the demonstrations of respect and affection of the people of the South; his physical condition, however, was not greatly improved. During this winter and spring he had said to his son, General Custis Lee, that his attack was mortal; and had virtually expressed the same belief to other trusted friends. And now, with that delicacy that pervaded all his actions, he seriously considered the question of resigning the presidency of Washington College, 'fearful that he might not be equal to his duties.' After listening, however, to the affectionate remonstrances of the faculty and board of trustees, who well knew the value of his wisdom in the supervision of the college, and the power of his mere presence and example upon the students, he resumed his labors with the resolution to remain at his post and carry forward the great work he had so auspiciously begun.

"During the summer he spent some weeks at the Hot Springs of Virginia, using the baths, and came home seemingly better in health and spirits. He entered upon the duties of the opening collegiate year in September with that quiet zeal and noiseless energy that marked all his actions, and an unusual elation was felt by those about him at the increased prospect that long years of usefulness and honor would yet be added to his glorious life.

"Wednesday, the 28th of September, 1870, found General Lee at the post of duty. In the morning he was fully occupied with the correspondence and other tasks incident to his office of president of Washington College, and he declined offers of assistance from members of the faculty, of whose services he sometimes availed himself. After dinner, at four o'clock, he attended a vestry meeting of Grace (Episcopal) Church. The afternoon was chilly and wet, and a steady rain had set in, which did not cease until it resulted in a great flood, the most memorable and destructive in this region for a hundred years. The church was rather cold and damp, and General Lee, during the meeting, sat in a pew with his military cape cast loosely about him. In a conversation that occupied the brief space preceding the call to order, he took part, and told, with marked cheerfulness of manner and kindliness of tone, some pleasant anecdotes of Bishop Meade and Chief Justice Marshall. The meeting was protracted until after seven o'clock, by a discussion touching the rebuilding of the church edifice and the increase of the rector's salary. General Lee acted as chairman, and, after hearing all that was said, gave his own opinion, as was his wont, briefly and without argument. He closed the meeting with a characteristic act. The amount required for the minister's salary still lacked a sum much greater than General Lee's proportion of the subscription, in view of his frequent and generous contributions to the church and other charities; but just before the adjournment, when the treasurer announced the amount of the deficit still remaining, General Lee said, in a low tone: 'I will give that sum.' He seemed tired toward the close of the meeting, and, as was afterward remarked, showed an unusual flush, but at the time no apprehensions were felt.

"General Lee returned to his house, and, finding his family waiting tea for him, took his place at the table, standing to say grace. The effort was vain, the lips could not utter the prayer of the heart. Finding himself unable to speak, he took his seat quietly and without agitation. His face seemed to some of the anxious group about him to wear a look of sublime resignation, and to evince a full knowledge that the hour had come when all the cares and anxieties of his crowded life were at an end. His physicians, Drs. H. T. Barton and R. L. Madison, arrived promptly, applied the usual remedies, and placed him upon the couch from which he was to rise no more. To him henceforth the things of this world were as nothing, and he bowed with resignation to the command of the Master he had followed so long with reverence.

"The symptoms of his attack resembled concussion of the brain, without the attendant swoon. There was marked debility, a slightly impaired consciousness, and a tendency to doze; but no paralysis of motion or sensation, and no evidence of softening or inflammation of the brain. His physicians treated the case as one of venous congestion, and with apparently favorable results. Yet, despite these propitious auguries drawn from his physical symptoms, in view of the great mental strain he had undergone, the gravest fears were felt that the attack was mortal. He took without objection the medicines and diet prescribed, and was strong enough to turn in bed without aid, and to sit up to take nourishment. During the earlier days of his illness, though inclined to doze, he was easily aroused, was quite conscious and observant, evidently understood whatever was said to him, and answered questions briefly but intelligently; he was, however, averse to much speaking, generally using monosyllables, as had always been his habit when sick. When first attacked, he said to those who were removing his clothes, pointing at the same time to his rheumatic shoulder, 'You hurt my arm.' Although he seemed to be gradually improving until October 10th, he apparently knew from the first that the appointed hour had come when he must enter those dark gates that, closing, reopen no more to earth. In the words of his physician, 'he neither expected nor desired to recover.' When General Custis Lee made some allusion to his recovery, he shook his head and pointed upward. On the Monday morning before his death, Dr. Madison, finding him looking better, tried to cheer him: 'How do you feel today, General?' General Lee replied, slowly and distinctly: 'I feel better.' The doctor then said: 'You must make haste and get well; Traveler has been standing so long in the stable that he needs exercise.' The general made no reply, but slowly shook his head and closed his eyes. Several times during his illness he put aside his medicine, saying, 'It is of no use'; but yielded patiently to the wishes of his physicians or children, as if the slackened chords of being still responded to the touch of duty or affection.

"On October 10th, during the afternoon, his pulse became feeble and rapid, and his breathing hurried, with other evidences of great exhaustion. About midnight he was seized with a shivering from extreme debility, and Dr. Barton felt obliged to announce the danger to the family. On October 11th, he was evidently sinking; his respiration was hurried, and his pulse feeble and rapid. Though less observant, he still recognized whoever approached him, but refused to take anything unless presented by his physicians. It now became certain that the case was hopeless. His decline was rapid, yet gentle; and soon after nine o'clock, on the morning of October 12th, he closed his eyes, and his soul passed peacefully from earth.

"General Lee's physicians attributed his death in great measure to moral causes. The strain of his campaigns, the bitterness of defeat aggravated by the bad faith and insolence of the victor, sympathy with the subsequent sufferings of the Southern people, and the effort at calmness under these accumulated sorrows, seemed the sufficient and real causes that slowly but steadily undermined General Lee's health and led to his death. Yet to those who saw his composure under the greater and lesser trials of life, and his justice and forbearance with the most unjust and uncharitable, it seemed scarcely credible that his serene soul was shaken by the evil that raged around him.

"General Lee's closing hours were consonant with his noble and disciplined life. Never was more beautifully displayed how a long and severe education of mind and character enables the soul to pass with equal step through this supreme ordeal; never did the habits and qualities of a lifetime, solemnly gathered into a few last sad hours, more grandly maintain themselves amid the gloom and shadow of approaching death. The reticence, the self-contained composure, the obedience to proper authority, the magnanimity, and the Christian meekness, that marked all his actions, still preserved their sway, in spite of the inroads of disease, and the creeping lethargy that weighed down his faculties.

"As the old hero lay in the darkened room, or with the lamp and hearth-fire casting shadows upon his calm, noble front, all the massive grandeur of his form, and face, and brow, remained; and death seemed to lose its terrors, and to borrow a grace and dignity in sublime keeping with the life that was ebbing away. The great mind sank to its last repose, almost with the equal poise of health. The few broken utterances that evinced at times a wandering intellect were spoken under the influence of the remedies administered; but as long as consciousness lasted, there was evidence that all the high, controlling influences of his whole life still ruled; and even when stupor was laying its cold hand on the intellectual perceptions, the moral nature, with its complete orb of duties and affections, still asserted itself. A Southern poet has celebrated in song those last significant words, 'Strike the tent'; and a thousand voices were raised to give meaning to the uncertain sound, when the dying man said, with emphasis, 'Tell Hill he *must* come up!' These sentences serve to show most touchingly through what fields the imagination was passing; but generally his words, though few, were coherent; but for the most part indeed his silence was unbroken.

"This self-contained reticence had an awful grandeur, in solemn accord with a life that needed no defense. Deeds which required no justification must speak for him. His voiceless lips, like the shut gates of some majestic temple, were closed, not for concealment, but because that within was holy. Could the eye of the mourning watcher have pierced the gloom that gathered about the recesses of that great soul, it would have perceived a presence there full of an ineffable glory. Leaning trustfully upon the all-sustaining Arm, the man whose stature, measured by mortal standards, seemed so great, passed from this world of shadows to the realities of the hereafter.

"FUNERAL.

"On the morning of Wednesday, October 12th, the church bells tolled forth the solemn announcement that General Lee was dead. A whisper had passed from lip to lip that he was sinking; and the anxious hearts of the people understood the signal of bereavement. Without concert of action, labor was suspended in Lexington; all stores, shops, and places of business, were closed; and the exercises at the college, Military Institute, and schools, ceased without formal notice. Little children wept as they went to their homes; the women shed tears as if a dear friend had gone from among them; and the rugged faces of men, inured to hardship of war, blanched as the sorrowful word was spoken. The courtesies and little kindnesses that the departed had strewed with gentle hand among all classes of the community came back; and memory recalled his stately form, not surrounded with the splendor of his fame, but in the softer light of a dear neighbor and friend who had vanished from sight forever. The sense of national calamity was lost in the tenderer distress of personal grief. General and heartfelt mourning followed, and the ordinary pursuits of business were not resumed until the next week.

"In all the Southern states the people felt that the death of General Lee was a loss to every community and to each individual. By a common impulse they met in whatever bodies they were accustomed to assemble; and in mass-meetings, corporate bodies, and voluntary societies, passed resolutions and voted addresses of respect and condolence. The pulpit, the bar, the bench, the halls of legislation, municipal authorities, benevolent associations, and all the organizations through which men perform the functions of society, spontaneously offered tributes to the memory of the illustrious dead.

"The chosen orators of the land came forward to eulogize his fame. A whole people, who at his council had borne in silence five years of accumulated sufferings, gave way to sorrow at the death of their loved leader; but it was a sorrow in which tenderness was exalted by the dignity of the dead, and the bereaved felt that they shared in the heritage of an undying name. It might seem invidious to select from testimonials so general and so honorable any even to serve as illustrations or examples of the universal sorrow; but it may be said of all that never was the sense of public calamity more completely chastened in its expression by deep and real feeling.

"The authorities of Washington College having tendered to Mrs. Lee the college chapel as a burial place for General Lee, the offer was accepted; and 1½ o'clock P.M. on the 14th of October was the time fixed on for the removal of the remains from the residence of the deceased to the chapel, where they were to lie in state until Saturday, the 15th of October, the day appointed for the burial. At the hour named, the procession to convey the body was formed under the charge of Professor J. J. White as chief marshal, aided by assistants appointed by the students. The escort of honor consisted of Confederate soldiers, marshaled by the Hon. J. K. Edmondson, late colonel of the Twenty-seventh Virginia Regiment. Following the escort came the hearse, preceded by the clergy, and attended by twelve pallbearers, representing the trustees, faculty, and students of Washington College, the authorities of the Virginia Military Institute, the soldiers of the Confederate army, and the citizens of Lexington. Just in the rear of the hearse, Traveler, the noble white warhorse of General Lee, with saddle and bridle covered with crepe, was led by two old soldiers. Then came in order the long procession composed of the college author- ities and students, the corps of cadets with their faculty, and the citizens. The body was borne to the college chapel, and laid in state on the dais; the procession passing slowly by, that each one might look upon the face of the dead. The body, attired in a simple suit of black, lay in a metallic coffin, strewed by pious hands with flowers and evergreens. The chapel, with the care of the remains, was then placed in charge of the guard of honor, appointed by the students from their own number. This guard kept watch by the coffin until the interment, and gave to all who desired it the opportunity of looking once more upon the loved and honored face.

"On Friday morning, October 14th, the college chapel was filled at nine o'clock with a solemn congregation of students and citizens, all of whom seemed deeply moved by the simple exercises. Rev. Dr. Pendleton read from Psalm xxxvii, 8–11, and 28–40, and with deep feeling applied its lessons to the audience, as illustrated in the life and death of General Lee. The speaker had for forty-five years been intimately associated with this great and good man as fellow student, comrade-in-arms, and pastor; and testified to his singular and consistent rectitude, dignity, and excellence under all the circumstances of life, and to that meekness in him that under the most trying adversity knew not envy, anger, or complaint. 'The law of God was in his heart,' therefore did 'none of his steps slide.' 'Mark the perfect man and behold the upright, for the end of that man is peace.' The minister powerfully illustrated the text of his discourse in the career of this great and good man, and urged his hearers to profit by the example of this servant of the Lord.

"The venerable Dr. White, Stonewall Jackson's pastor, and the Rev. John William Jones, of the Baptist church, who had served as chaplain in the Confederate army, and had since been intimately connected with Gen- eral Lee, followed with brief but interesting remarks on the Christian char- acter of the deceased.

"On the 14th of October, General W. H. F. Lee, Captain Robert E. Lee, and other members of the family, arrived; and on this and the following

day delegations from the legislature of Virginia and from various places
in the commonwealth reached Lexington over roads almost impassable
from the ravages of the recent great flood. The flag of Virginia, draped in
mourning, hung at half-mast above the college, badges of sorrow were
everywhere visible, and a general gloom rested on the hearts of old and
young.

"Saturday, October 15th, was the day appointed for the funeral. A
cloudless sky and a pure, bracing air made a suitable close to the splendid
and unsullied career of the man who was now to be consigned to the
tomb. It was desired to avoid all mere pageantry and display, and that all
the honors paid should accord with the simple dignity of the dead. This
spirit prevailed in all the proceedings, and gave character to the ceremonies of the day.

"It was thought proper that those who had followed his flag should lay
the honored body of their chief in its last resting place, and the escort of
honor of Confederate soldiers, much augmented in numbers, and commanded by General B. T. Johnson, assisted by Colonel Edmondson, Colonel Maury, and Major Dorman, was assigned the post of honor in the
procession.

"The following account of the ceremonies is taken from a newspaper
letter, written at the time, by Rev. J. Wm. Jones:

" 'The order of the procession was as follows:

Music.
Escort of Honor, consisting of Officers and Soldiers of the
Confederate Army.
Chaplain and other Clergy.
Hearse and Pallbearers.
General Lee's Horse.
The Attending Physicians.
Trustees and Faculty of Washington College.
Dignitaries of the State of Virginia.
Visitors and Faculty of Virginia Military Institute.
Other Representative Bodies and Distinguished Visitors.
Alumni of Washington College.
Citizens.
Cadets Virginia Military Institute.
Students Washington College as Guard of Honor.

" 'At ten o'clock precisely the procession was formed on the college grounds in front of the president's house, and moved down Washington Street, up Jefferson Street to the Franklin Hall, thence to Main Street, where it was joined, in front of the hotel, by the representatives of the state of Virginia and other representative bodies in their order, and by the organized body of the citizens in front of the courthouse.

" 'The procession then moved by the street to the Virginia Military Institute, where it was joined by the visitors, faculty, and cadets of the institute, in their respective places. The procession was closed by the students of Washington College as a guard of honor, and then moved up through the institute and college grounds to the chapel.

" 'The procession was halted in front of the chapel, when the cadets of the institute and the students of Washington College were marched through the college chapel past the remains, and were afterward drawn up in two bodies on the south side of the chapel. The remainder of the procession then proceeded into the chapel and were seated under the direction of the marshals. The gallery and side blocks were reserved for ladies.

" 'As the procession moved off, to a solemn dirge by the Institute band, the bells of the town began to toll, and the Institute battery fired minute guns, which were kept up during the whole exercises.

" 'In front of the National Hotel the procession was joined by the committee of the legislature, consisting of Colonel W. H. Taylor, Colonel E. Pendleton, W. L. Riddick, Major Kelley, Geo. Walker, Z. Turner, H. Bowen, T. O. Jackson, and Marshall Hanger; the delegation from the city of Staunton, headed by Colonel Bolivar Christian and other prominent citizens; and such other delegations as had been able to stem the torrents which the great freshet had made of even the smaller streams.

" 'It was remarked that the different classes who joined in the procession mingled into each other, and that among the boards of the college and institute, the faculties, the students and cadets, the legislative committee, the delegations, and even the clergy, were many who might with equal propriety have joined the soldier guard of honor; for they, too, had followed the standard of Lee in the days that tried men's souls.

" 'Along the streets the buildings were all appropriately draped, and crowds gathered on the corners and in the balconies to see the procession pass. Not a flag floated above the procession, and nothing was seen that looked like an attempt at display. The old soldiers wore their ordinary citizens' dress, with a simple black ribbon in the lapel of their coats; and

Traveler, led by two old soldiers, had the simple trappings of mourning on his saddle.

" 'The Virginia Military Institute was very beautifully draped, and from its turrets hung at half-mast, and draped in mourning, the flags of all of the states of the late Southern Confederacy.

" 'When the procession reached the institute, it passed the corps of cadets drawn up in line, and a guard of honor presented arms as the hearse passed. When it reached the chapel, where an immense throng had assembled, the students and cadets, about six hundred and fifty strong, marched into the left door and aisle past the remains and out by the right aisle and door to their appropriate place. The rest of the procession then filed in. The family, joined by Drs. Barton and Madison, the attending physicians, and Colonels W. H. Taylor and C. S. Venable, members of General Lee's staff during the war, occupied seats immediately in front of the pulpit; and the clergy, of whom a number were present, faculty of the college, and faculty of the institute, had places on the platform.

" 'The coffin was covered with flowers and evergreens, while the front of the drapery thrown over it was decorated with crosses of evergreen and immortelles.

" 'Rev. Dr. Pendleton, the long intimate personal friend of General Lee, his chief of artillery during the war, and his pastor the past five years, read the beautiful burial services of the Episcopal church. No sermon was preached, and nothing said besides the simple service, in accordance with the known wishes of General Lee.

" 'After the funeral services were concluded in the chapel, the body was removed to the vault prepared for its reception, and the concluding services read by the chaplain from the bank on the southern side of the chapel, in front of the vault.

" 'There was sung, in the chapel, the 124th hymn of the Episcopal collection; and, after the coffin was lowered into the vault, the congregation sang the grand old hymn,

"How firm a foundation, ye saints of the Lord."

" 'This was always a favorite hymn of General Lee's, and was, therefore, especially appropriate upon this sad occasion.

" 'The vault is constructed of brick, lined with cement. The top just reaches the floor of the library, and is double capped with white marble, on which is the simple inscription:

"ROBERT EDWARD LEE
BORN JANUARY 19, 1807;
DIED OCTOBER 12, 1870."

" 'This temporary structure is to be replaced by a beautiful sarcophagus, the design of which has been already committed to Valentine, the gifted Virginia sculptor.'

"The simple services concluded, the great assemblage, with hearts awed and saddened, defiled through the vaulted room in which was the tomb, to pay the last token of respect to the mighty dead. Thus ended the funeral of General Robert E. Lee.

"Since then has been laid by his side the noble matron, who was every way worthy to be his wife; and a little space away the dear daughter, so like them both in gentleness and dignity, and yet with added graces of her own. Tributes of rare and beautiful flowers, wreaths of laurels, and crosses of immortelles, placed by loving hands, decorate the sacred spot. A student of the university, to which his name has added an interest coextensive with the Confederate South, watches beside the grave, and gathers strength in the service for self-consecration to a life of duty and honor. Above the tomb rises the chapel—which his Christian zeal constructed, itself a noble monument to the illustrious dead—and which needs appropriate decoration only to make it worthy of the hero who sleeps beneath."

The sketch of Colonel Johnston has left the author nothing to add concerning the death and funeral obsequies of General Lee. He sleeps well in the beautiful Valley of Virginia, beneath the chapel he built, hard by the office which was the scene of his last and noblest labors, and which is preserved just as he left it the day of his fatal illness. The Blue Mountains of his loved Virginia sentinel his grave, and a daily guard of students delight to keep ward and watch at his tomb. The clear streams, as they flow along their emerald beds, seem to murmur his praises and roll on to the ocean his fame. From all parts of the land pilgrims come to visit his tomb, and loving hands bring fresh flowers, immortelles, and evergreens— fit emblems of the fadeless wreath which now decks his brow.

Valentine—Virginia's gifted young sculptor—is now putting into the life-speaking marble that splendid creation of his genius which will at the same time worthily decorate the grave of Lee, and write his own name among the world's greatest artists. The soldiers and the noble women of the South have resolved to rear, on some suitable spot in Richmond, a splendid equestrian statue, and it is hoped that the day is not far distant when the legislatures of the South, reflecting the wishes of the people, will liberally aid this effort to honor the noblest of her sons.

The Southern Historical Society is endeavoring to collect materials for the true history of Lee, of the army which he led, and of the cause for which he fought; and we proudly commit the story of his mighty deeds and spotless life to the calm judgment of the future historian.

Meantime, I bring this leaflet for the royal wreath with which the people of the whole country—North as well as South—will, in the years to come, deck the brow of Lee.

The world mourns for Robert E. Lee, because one of its noblest heroes has fallen—those whose proud privilege it was to have been in any way associated with him, weep that the courteous gentleman, the warm-hearted, thoughtful friend, the humble, earnest Christian, comes not again to his accustomed places. But we "sorrow not as those who have no hope." He lived the life of a faithful soldier of the Cross—he fell at the post of duty with the harness on—he died in the full assurance of faith in Jesus, and now wears the Christian's "crown of rejoicing"—

> *"That crown with peerless glories bright,*
> *Which shall now luster boast,*
> *When victors' wreaths and monarchs' gems*
> *Shall blend in common dust."*

APPENDIX

Selections from Eulogies on General Lee

The expressions of grief on the death of General Lee all over this country, and in Europe, would fill a volume much larger than this, and the author has hesitated to make even a few selections. But it seems fitting that the volume should be closed with several *representative* expressions of the common and universal sorrow. And, as a chapter has been devoted to the mutual love between the great leader and his soldiers, it seems appropriate to introduce the expression of the feelings of the faculty and students of his college. The *Southern Collegian,* the organ of the students of Washington College, thus announced his death:

"We stop our paper from going to press in order to make the saddest announcement which our pen ever wrote: Our honored and loved president is no more. He expired at his residence, on Wednesday, October 12th, at half-past nine o'clock A.M.

"For the past twelve months his continued ill health has been a source of great uneasiness to his friends, but we had fondly hoped that there were indications of improvement which promised long years of usefulness. Alas! that we are compelled to announce his death in our first issue for the current session. The real cause of General Lee's death is to be sought far back of his recent attack. His splendid physical development would probably have withstood much severer illness, and have spared him for many years, had there not been moral causes which wore away his life. The crushing responsibilities incident to his position at the head of the Confederate Army; his consuming anxiety as he saw his little band melt away before the countless host of their enemy; his crowning grief as he felt compelled 'to yield to overwhelming numbers and resources,' and see the flag he loved trail in the dust; his continued sorrow since, at witnessing the desolations of his loved South, and feeling unable to help her; and the opening of all his wounds afresh as his daily mails were flooded with piteous appeals from his maimed soldiers, or their widows and orphans— all these combined told with fatal effect upon him. He bore these things with calm exterior, and with a heroism surpassing any that he ever exhibited on the field of battle; but they gradually wore away the very fibers of his great heart.

"On Wednesday, the 28th of September, General Lee was more than usually occupied with his college duties, and in the afternoon presided over a meeting of the vestry of his church, at which most important matters were considered, and which was protracted for three hours. While sitting at the tea table that evening, he was taken suddenly ill, and the most serious fears were entertained concerning him. But the next day he rallied, and continued to improve until last Monday, October 10th, when he grew worse, and gradually passed away. His eminent physicians (Drs. H. T. Barton and R. L. Madison) give the following as the proximate cause of his death: 'Mental and physical fatigue, inducing venous congestion of the brain, which, however, never proceeded as far as apoplexy or paralysis, but gradually caused cerebral exhaustion and death.'

"There will be a natural anxiety to know about his last hours, and learn his last words; but of these there is nothing to write. He only spoke in answer to questions about his physical condition, although rational nearly the whole time, and left absolutely nothing for the sensational press to seize upon. He died as he lived, calmly and quietly, in the full assurance of the Christian's faith, and with the brightest evidence that, in 'passing over the river,' he has (with his great lieutenant) 'rested under the shade of the trees' of paradise."

Suitable resolutions were passed by a mass meeting of the students, and by the two literary societies.

The action of the faculty is appended, as being not only a graceful tribute to the memory of General Lee, but also an excellent epitome of his life:

"General Robert E. Lee, President of Washington College, died at his residence on the 12th day of October, 1870, at half-past 9 A.M.

"The faculty of the institution over which he has presided for five years testify that this dispensation of God has brought to them, personally, a grief as severe as the loss it has inflicted upon the college is irreparable.

"Eulogy has exhausted itself upon the virtues and genius of President Lee. It becomes friendship to be as simple in its tribute to the dead as his modesty while living would have sanctioned, and to let the glory of his now-ended life speak the praise due to its extraordinary incidents, and to its permanent influence for good upon his country and the world.

"He was born on the 19th day of January, 1807, at Stratford House, Westmoreland County, Virginia. He was the son of General Henry Lee, to whom Revolutionary fame attached the *sobriquet* of 'Light-Horse Harry.' His father was the ardent personal and political friend of Washington. Under his training his son was early taught to love Virginia as his country; for that father had said with impressive emphasis, what he confirmed on a solemn public occasion, 'No consideration on earth could induce me to act a part, however gratifying to me, which could be construed into disregard or foregetfulness of the Commonwealth.'

"At eleven years of age Robert E. Lee was fatherless. His boyhood was pure, ingenuous, and dutiful.

"As the son of Virginia, he entered West Point as a cadet in 1825, and graduated, without a demerit, at the head of his class. He was commissioned a lieutenant of engineers in 1829.

"When the Mexican War began, he was a captain in the Engineer Corps; and when victory marshaled the army of the United States in the capital of the enemy, the glory of its chief, by his own testimony and that of the country, was due, in a large degree, to the genius of Lee, whose numerous brevets were but a small tribute to his sagacity and skill as an officer, and to his courage and chivalry as a soldier.

"The war closed with the acquisition of a new empire to the Union, so rich and powerful that it remunerated the country tenfold for all its cost in effort and treasure.

"After the close of the war Colonel Lee continued to serve in the Engineer Department of the army until the year 1852, when he was appointed to the distinguished position of Superintendent of the West Point Military Academy. His administration there, which continued until 1855, was marked by signal ability and success, and to it he owed that practical experience in scholastic affairs which contributed so largely to his usefulness in his late career as president of Washington College. He next served upon the western frontier as lieutenant colonel of cavalry, in the regiment commanded by Colonel Albert Sydney Johnston. His last memorable service in the United States Army was in the suppression of the 'John Brown rebellion' at Harper's Ferry, Virginia, in October, 1859.

"Political conflict, growing out of sectional differences, and aggravated by the question of rights in the territory acquired from Mexico, reached the height of a strife in arms on the 15th day of April, 1861. To that strife President Lincoln summoned Virginia on that day, against her sister states of the South. On the 17th day of April, 1861, she rejected his summons, and cast in her lot with the Southern states.

"To Colonel Lee was thus presented the alternative of bearing the sword he had assumed, as a son of Virginia, for or against his native Commonwealth. A solemn conviction of duty, confirmed in his nature by a father's teachings, permitted no hesitancy in the decision. He came to Virginia, and, at her invitation, drew his sword in her defense and under her authority. How his calm patriotism, his consummate genius, and his heroic fortitude, bore him during the four years in which his country contended against numbers and resources vastly disproportioned to her own, history has recorded, and the world can never forget.

"On the 9th day of April, 1865, he sheathed his sword, which his distinguished adversary did not ask to be surrendered, upon his parole of honor to bear arms no longer against the victor, and to live the life of a peaceful citizen of a state of the Union.

"That parole of honor he has never tarnished by the slightest departure from its stipulations. He bore the confiscation of his property, the obloquy upon his name, the defeat and suffering of his fellow countrymen, without a murmur, and in the patient and silent consciousness of a strict and rigid adherence to duty in his past career.

"He was called to the presidency of Washington College on the 28th of September, 1865. His executive ability, his enlarged views of a liberal culture, his extraordinary powers in the government of men, his wonderful influence over the mind of the young, and his steady and earnest devotion to his duties, made the college spring, as if by the touch of magic, from its depression after the war, to its present firm condition of permanent and widespread usefulness.

"As president, in his relations to the faculty, he was gentle, courteous, and considerate—toward the students he was firm in discipline, yet forbearing, sympathetic, and encouraging—to all he was a model of an elevated Christian and an upright gentleman.

"During the last five years, in the discharge of his official duties as president of Washington College, which were entered upon under most trying circumstances, and maintained with serene patience and noble devotion to the end of his life, he has exhibited qualities not less illustrious than any which he displayed in his military career; and which, as they were necessary to complete the perfect harmony of his character, have thus connected his fame, in a peculiar sense, with the history of Washington College.

"He died, as he had lived, without fear, and with the reverence of all good men; calmly patient, in the consciousness of a virtuous life and of rectitude of purpose; and in that complete reliance upon God which had sustained him throughout all the changes of fortune.

"The faculty bear this simple testimony to the virtuous life, the simple and genuine piety, and the exalted genius of their illustrious and beloved president—and tender to his widow and children, and to his mourning countrymen, their hearts' sympathy in the common calamity of his irreparable loss.

"It is a deep satisfaction to receive his revered remains beneath the chapel he had built; and it will be to the college which he loved an unspeakable blessing that, though his presence is removed, the memory of his noble life will remain to us as an incentive to duty, and as an abiding inspiration to the youth of the country, as they gather at this last scene of his labors, to emulate his virtues and to follow his great example!

"*Be it therefore resolved,* That in the midst of the severe calamity which has befallen us, in the death of our beloved president, we, the faculty, of Washington College, experience a profound pleasure and pride in recognizing the fact that the fame of General Lee, while it belongs to the whole country, is, in an especial sense, the heritage of Washington College; and that it is our duty, as it is our privilege to provide here suitable memorials whereby this precious possession shall be acknowledged, and his name publicly held in grateful remembrance by this college, for all future time.

"*Resolved,* That a committee be appointed to confer with a like committee of the board of trustees, and report measures and plans for the erection of a suitable monument to General Lee, in the room in which his remains are to be interred; and, further, to consider and recommend such other monuments or memorials as may be deemed appropriate in the college.

"*Resolved,* That these committees be requested jointly to make arrangements for the delivery of a eulogy on the life and character of General Lee, in the college chapel, on the 19th day of January, being the next anniversary of his birthday; and we further express the wish that this anniversary, like the birthday of Washington, shall be hereafter always celebrated in this college.

"*Resolved,* That the said committees be requested also to confer and report upon the subject of so amending the present charter of Washington College that the name of this institution may hereafter express, in fit conjunction, the immortal names of WASHINGTON and LEE, whose lives were so similar in their perfect renown, and with both of whom equally, by singular good fortune, it is entitled to be associated in its future history.

"*Resolved,* That as a further expression of our deep sorrow, we will wear the badge of mourning during the remainder of the present session.

"*Resolved,* That a copy of the above minute be communicated to the widow and family of the deceased, and published in the *Southern Collegian* and the *Virginia Gazette.*"

The following report of a meeting of the faculty and students of the college is taken from the *Southern Collegian* and inserted as an appropriate expression of the feelings with which the faculty and students returned to their work after the funeral of their great president:

"MEETING OF THE FACULTY AND STUDENTS
OF WASHINGTON COLLEGE.

"A very touching meeting was held on the morning of the 17th of October, in the college chapel. It had been decided to resume the regular college exercises, and it was understood that before doing so the professors desired to meet with the students, and have a few words of quiet conference. Accordingly, the chapel was filled with a deeply solemn audience of students, the faculty, and a few citizens.

"After the usual chapel services, Rev. Dr. Kirkpatrick, Professor of Moral Philosophy, arose and said, in substance, that it had been deemed fitting that the students and the faculty should have a season of conference together before resuming the duties which had been so sadly interrupted. The faculty deeply felt that a great change had taken place, and that their responsibilities had been greatly increased. He desired, in behalf of the faculty, to thank the students for the uniform propriety of deportment which had marked the conduct of each one of them during this season of deep affliction. He had expected it to be so, and had not been disappointed. He said that the faculty and students were now bound together by the tenderest ties of a common grief, and that their duties to each other and to the college were sanctified by the memories of the past.

"Standing here in the very presence of the one they all honored and loved, the faculty pledged themselves to increased efforts to carry out his wishes, and to discharge faithfully their duties. They felt urged to so conduct the affairs of the college as to make it a fitting monument to President Lee. And he earnestly appealed to the students so to do their part, so to unite with the faculty, as to rear a monument to our great chieftain more durable than marble, and more precious and more honorable than the most costly material. The *instruction* of the college would be the same as heretofore: in its *discipline* and the general oversight they would sadly miss their honored president. But the faculty confidently hoped that the students would so deport themselves—so be a law unto themselves, and so remember the example, advice, and ardent wishes of our loved friend— as to give no occasion for the exercise of *discipline* in the ordinary acceptation of the term.

"Hon. J. Randolph Tucker next briefly addressed the students. He said that the saddest thing connected with the death of a great man was that it broke the thread of his life plans, and left them incomplete. Such was the case with General Lee. He had come to Washington College five years ago—had found it in a low state—with but four professors, with much of its apparatus destroyed by the Federal army, and had conceived a plan for raising it to the first rank among the institutions of learning in the land, and making it worthy of the father of his country.

"He has accomplished much. He has increased the corps of professors from four to nine in number in the academic and scientific departments, and had established a law school with two professors. He had other views for enlarging the teaching capacity of the institution, not yet consummated, but soon to be complete.

"Death put an end to his labors. Shall the good he did survive him, or shall his success be as fleeting as human life? It was for those who survive him—trustees, faculty, and students—to answer.

"This was the child of his declining years, left fatherless by his death. It is our duty to nurture and foster it—to guard and protect it—and promote its interests, until it shall become the noblest monument forever of his devotion to duty and his enlightened views of an enlarged cultivation for his young countrymen.

"We shall earnestly endeavor to carry out all his policy—to conduct the schools of the college as they have always been, and to make it in the present and in the future worthy of his name, and to advance it to its proper rank among the foremost institutions of the country; and we cordially invite the young men here to unite with us in preserving the integrity of the plans of the late president, and to carry them out to their highest success, according to his views and earnest hopes, so that it may be to the youth of the country a perpetual memorial of his name, and a permanent monument to his genius.

"Colonel William Preston Johnston then addressed the students as follows:

" 'MY FRIENDS: The faculty have requested me to address to you a few remarks in view of the position in which Washington College stands today. While I feel that what has been already so well said is sufficient, and that words of mine are scarcely necessary, I do not decline the duty. It is eminently fit that on occasions of interest the faculty and students should confer together, and such an occasion as this has not happened in the history of this college, and will not again in all time. You are now assembled as one of the estates of this commonwealth of letters, to listen to the voice of your elders, and, what has even a greater moral significance to you, to learn how best you are to perform your parts in the scheme of self-government. I am using no new language; I am but repeating the thoughts and the words of all the days and all the years in which we have been associated as instructors and pupils. A great part of the government of this college has been in your hands, and you have manifested in your moral conduct and intellectual progress what can be done through liberty, inspired by love and regulated by law. In all the recorded past, no epoch has excelled in luster and development the period of Pericles, when free Athens under his enlightened guidance made herself immortal. The republic whose citizens are gathered this morning within these walls has obeyed with willing hearts a leader who had the virtues of Pericles, without one blemish, one spot, one stain. In him duty disdained to yield to expediency, and Aristides himself would have owned him as a peer in virtue. It was the dying boast of Pericles that he had made no Athenian weep; but of our chief it may be said that for no act of his has any son of the South ever had cause to blush. With such a leader, with such an exemplar before our eyes, it has not been hard to do right. It would have been hard to do wrong, to go far astray, and face our consciences in that august presence. But how is it now! He has gone from among us; and whose calm prudence and serene majesty of soul will now rebuke the hasty word or precipitate act? Whose tender counsel will restrain the erring step? Whose broad charity will cover our multitudinous transgressions? How can we replace the lost? Ah! my friends, that is impossible. For, where in all the ranks of the living will be found his like? We will not make the vain attempt to supply his place, but we will seek to perpetuate his influence. If you feel as I do, the guide and guardian of the conduct and career of this college and of its faculty and students, will still be this mighty spirit of Lee. Trouble not your minds as to his successor. To the same wisdom that selected General Lee in his retirement, and secured his acceptance of this post, you may trust to provide for you an executive officer who will bring no discredit upon the college, or upon the memory of the dead.

" 'When the tremendous conflict in which for four years he upheld the fortunes of half a continent had ended, and finding success denied to him, he yielded to overwhelming numbers, he turned his face to the desolated land for which he had done and suffered so much, he stretched forth his hand to stanch the wounds he had been unable to avert. In the matchless dignity of voiceless woe that hand has done the work it found to do. His cultured intellect, his finished education, his ripe experience of men and things, his practical knowledge as an educator, his great executive ability, and all the forces of a mind vast yet exceedingly well balanced, were applied to the development of this college. He sketched the comprehensive plan and wrought out the details of the work, that in chaste and simple beauty to us is to rest like a capital upon the solid and splendid shaft of his civic and national renown; and Washington College stands as the last and crowning achievement of a useful and glorious life. His labor is finished; the weary is at rest; but the magnificent structure that he conceived and planned, and whose foundation he has laid, is left for completion to his country. We rest in an abiding faith that our country will not suffer to sink into dust and forgetfulness this last enduring mounment of his fame; and we may return to our appointed tasks and daily duties with cheerfulness and energy, knowing that therein we best carry out his wishes and perpetuate his fame.

" 'You need from me no outline of a moral code, no exhortations to special duties, for I sum up all by pointing to the memory of the man you honored and revered.

" 'General Lee's plan is to be carried out in the spirit in which it was conceived; and we trust that time will show that neither faculty nor students have relaxed in their zeal, or are weary in well-doing. But we enter on this year's work with saddened hearts under the chastening of a crushing calamity. Let us try to realize, as far as may be, the great thought of our dead leader, and make "human virtue equal to human calamity.' "

"Colonel William Allan next spoke as follows:

" 'It is not eight years since the great soldier who lies in yonder cemetery fell at the head of his troops, and in the moment of victory. In the order that General Lee issued announcing his death, he reminded the corps that had followed Jackson through so many perils, that, while a whole nation would weep at his tomb and cherish his virtues, it was their privilege to be in a peculiar manner the guardians of his honor and his memory. Those veterans felt this to be their noblest trust, and from the day that Stuart gave the order at Chancellorsville, "Charge, and remember Jackson!" to the last scene of the war, it was to them a sacred inspiration. On many a bloody field the weak arm was nerved and the dying heart consoled by the consciousness that the trust had been fitly kept; and it is a proud satisfaction to the survivors that, though the thirty thousand whom Jackson had commanded at Chancellorsville had dwindled to a few hundred at Appomattox, these had yet the honor of firing the last gun, and that the order for surrender found them in line of battle and engaged with the foe.

" 'From this day, gentlemen, a similar trust is confided to us—the authorities, the alumni, and the students of Washington College. While a mighty people bow in crushing sorrow over the tomb of Robert E. Lee, and do reverence to his ashes, the privilege and obligation rest especially with us to perpetuate the memory and influence of his virtues. His last great work, that to which he devoted the latest and in many respects the grandest years of his life, drops unfinished from his hands into ours. Let us take it up and carry it forward, feeling conscious, as we must, that this is the most pleasing and appropriate tribute that grateful affection can pay to the illustrious dead.

" 'His plans for the organization of this college were of the wisest and most complete character. They are his legacy to us. What honor so noble can we do to his name as to realize his intentions, and make this what he desired it should be, the first institution of the land? In so doing we shall but follow in his own footsteps. For the controlling motive with him in selecting this particular place as the scene of his labors was the fact that here they would constitute a tribute to the memory of Washington. And the reflection, though sad, renders the obligation resting on us all the more sacred, that, less fortunate than his great prototype, there remains but this work alone of all the labors of a lifetime to testify to future ages of a grand and noble career. Misfortune has swept away all he strove for, save this. If the memory of his virtues is to be kept green through coming time, it must be done here, gentlemen, and through the influences which go out from here.

" 'As has been already said, the trustees and faculty of Washington College recognize the high privilege and sound obligation that rest upon us all, and their most earnest and devoted efforts will be directed toward carrying out the designs of General Lee, and in this way toward rearing a fitting memorial of his character. But theirs is only a part of the work. With you rest the interests and welfare of the institution. Let the affection which you now feel and manifest for it continue with you as a cherished sentiment through life. Guard constantly, both here and elsewhere, its honor; labor for its prosperity and usefulness; remember it always as a trust committed to your keeping by the hero who watched over you with the wisdom of a sage, and the tenderness of a father.' "

The Virginia Military Institute, located in Lexington, and indeed all of the colleges of the South, gave utterance to similar sentiments. The following may be given:

"SUPERINTENDENT'S OFFICE, VIRGINIA MILITARY INSTITUTE,
LEXINGTON, VA.,
October 12, 1870.

"The Academic Board met at the call of the superintendent at 10 A.M.
"Present, all the members except General G. W. C. Lee.
"The superintendent announced to the Academic Board the death of General R. E. Lee, whereupon, on motion, the following minute was ordered to be spread upon the records of the board.
"We feel, in a degree which no words can adequately express, sorrow at the death of one who was so distinguished by position, so illustrious for his deeds, and so noble in character.
"Our whole land has suffered by the blow, and our whole land will mourn, while distant nations will not withhold the sympathy awakened by

the death of one whose life is a part of the history of the world, and whose moral excellences inspired love and admiration in the hearts of all the good.

"To us, as a faculty, however, the blow comes with peculiar force.

"We, individually, knew him as a neighbor and friend; but, as a faculty, we were bound to him by closer ties, as a fellow laborer in the same cause, and as the father of one of the professors of the Virginia Military Institute.

"We therefore feel a particular grief, and claim the privilege of special mourners.

"To Mrs. Lee and her family we offer the expression of our sympathy for his death, of our pride in the life of our hero, and of our assurance of the glorious immortality of the earnest Christian.

"To the faculty of our sister institution we beg to convey our sense of the great loss they have sustained by the death of their president, whose efforts in the cause of education have shed such luster upon Washington College.

"*Resolved,* That General Smith, Superintendent, and Commander Maury, be appointed a committee to present the above extract from our record to Mrs. Lee and the faculty of Washington College, with the tender of our cooperation as a faculty in whatever mode may be acceptable in the solemnities of the occasion.

"A true extract from the minutes of the Academic Board.

"F. H. SMITH, JR., *Secretary.*"

"General Order No. 26.

"HEADQUARTERS, VIRGINIA MILITARY INSTITUTE, *October* 12, 1870.

"The painful duty devolves upon the superintendent to announce to the professors, officers, and cadets of the Virginia Military Institute, the death of General R. E. Lee.

"He died at his residence at half-past nine o'clock this morning, after an illness of two weeks.

"Every heart in our Southern land will receive the sad tidings of the death of General Lee as a personal bereavement. All will feel it to be such, for he had secured by his heroic devotion to duty, by his unbending moral rectitude, by his elevated Christian principles, and by his tender, sympathizing regard for others, not only the admiration, but also the love of his countrymen.

"Moving among us as he did, in his earnest yet unobtrusive work as the president of our sister institution, Washington College, we have witnessed in his daily life the exhibition of those noble qualities which have made his name known and honored throughout the civilized world.

"It is meet, then, that the professors, officers, and cadets, of the Virginia Military Institute should honor the memory of Lee.

"It is therefore ordered:

"That all academic duties and drills be suspended until after his interment.

"That the battalion flag be draped in mourning for the period of six months.

"That the professors, officers, and cadets, wear the usual badge of mourning for the same period.

"That the professors, officers, and cadets, attend in a body his funeral, and unite in paying such honors to the memory of the illustrious dead as shall be consistent with the wishes of his family, and the arrangements of the authorities of Washington College.

"By command of Major General F. H. Smith,

"F. H. Smith, Jr., *Adjutant V.M.I.*"

The following is the conclusion of an address delivered at the Kentucky Military Institute, by Rev. R. A. Holland:

"I rejoice, young gentlemen, that I can find an embodiment of this sublime integrity of character in a hero— not of the past, but of the present—not of some distant realm, but of your own suffering land— not of foreign birth, but of blood brother to that which in your veins leaps with enthusiasm at the mention of his name.

"I rejoice that we possess a model of manhood worth more to our noblest attributes than all the fortunes spent in the terrible war that unveiled his grandeur to our gaze.

"Whatever may have been the errors of the South— errors for which, if they were committed, she has made sufficient atonement in costliest hecatombs—the world is indebted to her for a gift that will enrich mankind forever. That gift is the example of a man who, in civil war, when hate rages to flesh its fangs in hostile hearts, wins the admiration of his enemies; who charms envy into love and awes malice into silence; who from the smoke and carnage of battle comes forth with a brow unstained by dishonor and hands unclotted by cruelty; who, although victor in a hundred fights against such odds of troops and treasures as skill never vanquished before, allows no word of boasting to soil his pure lips and acknowledges his success only in modest ascriptions of gratitude to the Lord of hosts; who, marching forward in the perilous path of duty, refuses a moment's pause for dalliance with that fame which others must follow, but which, like one entranced, tracks his steps and courts the condescension of his kingly glance; who, as he kneels under triumphs, rises above reverses, and when the last blow is struck and genius can no longer cope with force, surrenders his sword with the same equanimity with which he had ever wielded it, and receives it back in mute testimonial that none but himself is worthy to wear a weapon whose blade blazes with a luster of purity and prowess bright as the scimitars of Eden's sentinels.

"Great in victory, greater still in defeat; great as descried through the red haze of war, greater still as contemplated through the clear air of peace; great as a general, but *greatest* as a *man*—behold in him a character which, if not perfect, conceals its faults with the effulgence of its virtues, even as the sun conceals the spots on its dazzling disk. I need not call his name; nor need History, when she carves for the highest niche in her Pantheon a statue to represent manhood apotheosized by its own glory, inscribe beneath it a name which the very *design* of the statue speaks aloud—the immortal name of Lee."

The following was the conclusion of a sermon preached in the First Presbyterian Church, Nashville, on Sunday afternoon, October 23, 1870, by Rev. Dr. T. V. Moore, the discourse being delivered at the request of a meeting of citizens, and before an immense congregation of the best people of the city:

"It was with all this heroic sense of duty that General Lee tendered his services first to his own state, and then to the Confederacy, of which she became a component part. And he knows but little of this great captain who thinks that it was with anything of a divided heart that he linked himself to the fortunes of the Southern people. His whole heart was with them to the last sad close; and I speak that which I know, when I say that he would gladly have laid him down in a soldier's grave, had such been the will of God, rather than survive the cause for which he fought. Indeed, he can scarcely be said to have survived it, for he has been slowly dying ever since. His physicians testify that there was no reason, in his splendid *physique,* why he should not have lived for many years; but those who have closely observed him since the fatal field of Appomattox, have seen that he received his death wound there; and, although his manly spirit has been hiding it the while, the heart bled on in secret, wrung by the woes and wrongs of his beloved people, by the sorrowful letters he was continually receiving from maimed veterans, impoverished widows, and suffering orphans, vainly begging for some opening to earn their bread, and by the sorrowful struggles of his people to repair their fallen fortunes, struggles so often doomed to the cruelest disappointment, and that, therefore, it is sadly true that, although for five long, weary years his mighty heart was breaking, yet at the last it did give way, and he died of a broken heart, a victim of the war, as truly as any of his heroic comrades in arms, whose heart's blood flowed more swiftly and easily on the battlefield.

"And yet with all his intensity of devotion to the Southern cause, there was mingled none of that bitterness and fierceness that a civil war is so likely to engender, and of which ours contains such mournful illustrations. Under provocations the most severe, his calm and well-poised mind never yielded to the impulse of vindictive emotion, and never allowed itself to be goaded beyond the rules of honorable warfare. When he led his armies into Pennsylvania, he issued the most stringent orders against pillaging and the wanton destruction of private property, and severely punished the slightest infraction of these orders, even to the disturbance of a fence needlessly, so that the people on his line of march acknowledged that they fared better at his hands than they did in the hands of the troops sent to oppose him, their own professed friends and protectors. It was this sublime elevation above the fierce, vindictive passions of the hour that excited, even during the war, the wonder of his enemies.

"There was, indeed, in his nature a singular vein of gentleness and tenderness, softening his sterner attributes of character. His natural purity and dignity, moulded by the etiquette of military life, gave him a certain stateliness of bearing, before which meanness and vice instinctively shrank, so that no thoroughly bad man could feel at ease in his presence, any more than could Satan in the presence of Ithuriel. But in the company of children, and especially of young girls, there was a winning gentleness and a playful familiarity that removed all reserve from them, and made him a special favorite of children. Indeed, among them he was a child again; and, had he been in that small circle within which Jesus set up a little child to teach the lesson of true greatness, there perhaps would have been no heart there which, in its warming love to the little, sweet, unconscious teacher, would have been better fitted than his to receive the deep and wise instructions of the Master. It was thus in the fine harmonious balance of head and heart, and the even development of the powers of each, without any exaggeration, that we find the beautiful and full-orbed completeness of his nature, linking him in deathless association with that peerless man whom he so much resembled, who, in the memorable words uttered by one of his own relatives, 'was first in war, first in peace, and first in the hearts of his countrymen.'

"There are many passages of grandeur in his long and honorable life, but the grandest of them all was its closing five years, when the fine gold of his nature stood the stern and fiery test of adversity. It was a wondrous spectacle to see him defending the beleaguered capital of the Confederacy with an army of half-clad, half-fed, and half-equipped men, outnumbered six to one, and so reduced at last in numbers that had they formed a line behind the long sweep of fortifications they were defending, that line would have been so attenuated that the men could scarcely have touched each other with their muskets, and yet a band of heroes, who felt no throb of anxiety or dread as long as they knew that that noble gray head, with its falcon-eye, was watching over them with more than a father's tenderness and care. But other men have been great warriors, yet only great in success. It was his to show his uttermost greatness in failure. Other men had conquered victory; it was his sublime preeminence to conquer defeat, and transform it into the grandest triumph. Other warriors have betrayed ambition, cruelty, and avarice in success, weakness, littleness, and selfishness in disaster; but he developed the unselfish nobleness of his nature when, bowing submissively to the resistless decrees of Providence, he sheathed his unsullied blade; and refusing the most tempting offers to engage in commercial and monetary enterprises; refusing the gifts that a grateful though impoverished people longed to lavish on him; refusing every attempt to bring him where public applause would so heartily have greeted him—he retired to the cloistered shades of his chosen position, without a word of repining or bitterness, and consecrated himself to the youth of his country, not to breathe into them a spirit of vindictive hate; not to train them for future political struggles merely, but to lead them to Jesus, and make them noble citizens, by making them sincere Christians. Hon. H. W. Hilliard, ex-member of the Federal Congress, made a speech in Augusta, Ga., at the meeting there held to do honor to the memory of General Lee, in which he said:

" 'An offer, originating in Georgia, and I believe in this very city, was made to him to place an immense sum of money at his disposal if he would consent to reside in the city of New York, and represent Southern commerce. Millions would have flowed to him. But he declined. He said: "No, I am grateful, but I have a self-imposed task, which I must accomplish. I have led the young men of the South in battle; I have seen many of them fall under my standard. I shall devote my life now to training young men to do their duty in life.' "

"Oh! does history present a spectacle that in grandeur can be compared with that? An English nobleman, standing beside the corpse of his dead boy, exclaimed to one who sought to comfort him, 'I had rather have my dead son than all the living sons in England.' And so, with a truer, fonder pride, may we exclaim, 'We would rather have our dead hero than all the living heroes of Christendom.'

"The closing scene of his life was calm and peaceful, as became a Christian soldier. When Stonewall Jackson lay dying, his mind was wandering over the scenes of the battlefield, leading his fiery columns through the smoke and thunder of the conflict, until his spirit seemed to emerge from these troubled scenes and catch a glimpse of the sweet fields beyond the swelling flood, when he softly whispered, 'Let us pass over the river and rest under the trees,' and he sweetly fell asleep to awake where the 'river of water of life, clear as crystal, comes forth from the throne of God and the Lamb.' Somewhat similar was the dying scene of our great captain. In the wanderings of his delirium he, too, was once more at the head of those battle-scarred columns of veterans, whom he had so often led to victory. Perhaps, again he spurred his fiery charger, as in the terrible scenes of Spottsylvania, when his dauntless men seized his bridle-rein, and refused to move a step until their beloved leader had withdrawn from danger, when, with one wild shout of fierce enthusiasm, they hurled themselves upon the serried masses of the foe. Perhaps he moved once more on the bloody heights of Gettysburg, where he nobly assumed the responsibility of disasters that were, doubtless, due mainly to others, and was greater in failure than other men in success. And it was a striking coincidence with the dying scene of Jackson, as well as a noble tribute to a gallant man, who poured out his blood in the trenches of Petersburg, that they should both have called for the brave and high-souled A. P. Hill in the wanderings of delirium. At last, as if he saw that the hour had come, when 'the earthly house of this tabernacle' was to be taken down, he exclaimed, 'Strike the tent!' and Death obeyed.

'His spirit, with a bound,
Burst its encumbering clay;
His tent at noontide on the ground,
A darkened ruin lay.'

"He passed over the river to recline under the trees, where 'the wicked cease from troubling, and the weary are at rest.'

"And now we must leave this noble life to teach its own lessons, for time will not permit their elaboration. Young men, who have idolized the name of Lee, will you not heed his deep and earnest desire that you should all be real Christians, and come to Jesus? Confederate soldiers, I have seen some of your comrades, and possibly some of you, following this great leader, ragged, hungry, tracking the snow with blood from your naked feet, and yet cheerful, because you were following him. Oh! will you not follow him now, as he followed Christ—follow him to the cross, follow him to the crown, follow him to heaven? Let his manly voice come down to you from the crystal battlements, saying, 'Come up hither!' and may you meet him there! Brethren and sisters, of every name and rank, of every section and shade of opinion, you may differ or agree with me in my estimate of this great man, but you cannot differ with me in the conclusion that it is a blessed thing, like him, to sleep in Jesus, and be at rest. And hence, by all that is precious in the death of the righteous, do I beseech you to accept that Savior whose service is compatible with the highest types of human nobleness and the grandest examples of human courage, whose grace can support you in the darkest hour of earthly sorrow, and whose strong rod and beautiful staff will sustain you in the dark valley, and bring you where you 'shall see the King in his beauty, and behold the land that is very far off.'

"During the darkest days of the Revolution, Washington exclaimed on one occasion: 'Strip me of the dejected and suffering remnant of my army; take from me all that I have left; leave me but a banner; give me but the means to plant it on the mountains of West Augusta, and I will yet draw around me the men who will lift up their bleeding country from the dust and set her free.' Beneath the shadow of these West Augusta mountains, from whose hardy sons the rich plains of Tennessee have been so largely populated, stands that college, endowed by the munificence of Washington, and called by his name, over which Lee presided until his death; and within whose chapel walls his remains are now sleeping. Within the sound of its bell is the grave of Stonewall Jackson. These grand old mountains, then, stand a fitting monument of this mighty triumvirate, a majestic mausoleum of three majestic men; and, as long as their gray summits shall catch the early rays of morning, or hold lovingly the last lingering flush of the setting day, as long as the crystal streams that gush from their rocky sides shall flow onward to the sea, so long shall every wind that wakes the moanings of the mountain pine, and every wave that stirs the echoes of the valley, continue to prolong the mighty dirge of a people's woe for these three bright, immortal names 'that were not born to die.'

> 'They fell devoted, but undying,
> The very gales their names are sighing,
> The silent pillar, cold and gray,
> Claims kindred with their sacred clay;
> Their spirits wrap the dusky mountain,
> Their memory sparkles o'er the fountain,
> The meanest rill, the mightiest river,
> Roll mingling with their fame forever.' "

The following conclusion of a sermon, preached at the Second Baptist Church, Atlanta, Ga., by the pastor, Rev. Dr. W. T. Brantly, from the text "He is a good man," may be appropriately introduced here:

"The discussion of the subject is closed; but it finds such a beautiful illustration in the character of the beloved man whose decease, within the past few days, has filled millions of hearts with unaffected grief, that this discourse would be strikingly incomplete without some exhibition of the fact. It is rare that a Christian minister can present one of earth's most illustrious sons as an example of a good man, in the sense in which the honorable attestation was borne to Barnabas. It happens but too rarely that the qualities which command the admiration of the world are found in unison with a devout life, but General Lee was as good as he was distinguished. He honored Christ, and was, in turn, honored by him.

"My subject does not require me to speak of him as a soldier, though I may be permitted to say that, in my view, he will take rank among the most sagacious of commanders of any age or of any country. None knew this better, conceded it more readily, than did the brave men against whom he fought. I said, one day, to the officer who led the United States troops on the bloody field in Pennsylvania, where such a severe disaster befell the Confederate arms, 'Do you know, General, why you beat us at Gettysburg? It was because Stonewall Jackson was not there.' 'You are mistaken, sir,' was the reply; 'I have found many Southerners who believed that Jackson was their great general, but it is not so.' 'Whom, then,' I inquired, 'did you look upon as the ablest officer of our side?' 'General Lee,' was the reply—General Lee, sir, undoubtedly. He is your greatest man.' And in harmony with this opinion has been the testimony, voluntarily tendered, of the highest military authorities of Europe, both in England and on the Continent.

"The great soldier is not unfrequently the man of irrepressible ambition, intent only on the aggrandizement of self. But, to military abilities of the highest order, Lee added a pure, self-sacrificing patriotism. He has been often censured for identifying his fortunes with the South; but, with his convictions of duty, he could not have done otherwise. He was educated in the doctrine that the Federal government was the creature of the states, and that allegiance was due it only through his native state. When, therefore, Virginia withdrew from the Union by a convention legally assembled, entertaining the ideas he did, he felt constrained to follow her fortunes.

"He had strong temptations to take a different view of his political status. He was an officer in the United States Army, and held a position in public esteem second only to that of the aged commander-in-chief of the army. Had he arrayed himself against his state, the probability is, that the triumphs achieved by others would have been his victories, and the rewards of place would have been his compensation. But, acting under the stern promptings of conscience, he turned from the most splendid prizes which ever allured the eye of man, and took his position with the feeble minority; counting it higher honor to hazard defeat and calamity with the weak than to triumph with the strong. He has been called a 'subjugated rebel'; but the candid and the intelligent who so pronounce, must concede that, in accordance with the political theory received from his fathers and held by himself, he was a patriot of the highest type.

"But if he had been no more than a soldier and a patriot, I should not have presented him as an illustration of my theme. He was a Christian man; and his piety shed a hallowed luster over qualities naturally shining, investing them with a higher beauty than secular renown can bestow. The evidence on which I rely for this fact is not that he was a professor of religion; for, alas! there is much profession in these days where it is to be feared that the power of godliness is wanting. 'His doctrine and his life coincident gave lucid proof that he was honest in the sacred cause.' If you will refer to his public papers, written during the war, you will see that he never failed, whenever opportunity offered, to call the attention of the people to the great Disposer of all human events, and to inspire them with gratitude or submission, as the circumstances might suggest. Even in a brief telegraphic dispatch, he rarely fails to make mention of the Sovereign Ruler of all. I know it may be said of public men, noted for irreligion and profanity, that they have often made pious allusions in their state papers; but those who knew General Lee in private, could not fail to remark that religion was with him something more than an empty name; that it was a power lodged in the heart and controlling his whole nature. It was my privilege, during the past two years, to be thrown into his society, at different times, so intimately that I saw and conversed with him every day and frequently several times a day. I discovered that, with him, religion was the theme on which he most delighted to dwell. He spoke to me with great interest of the efforts made by different denominations of Christian people to promote the spiritual good of the soldiers. He took pleasure in referring to the numbers who he hoped had been brought to the Savior through the instrumentality of the chaplains and visiting ministers. Speaking to me, last June, of the college under his control, he referred more than once, evidently with the greatest satisfaction, to the number of students who had been hopefully converted during the term then just closed. He also mentioned with much interest the work of the Young Men's Christian Association among the students. When a guest at his house, the first thing with which he greeted me, on coming down in the morning, was the Bible, with a request that I should lead the devotions of the family; and when, after reading God's word, we knelt down together, his prompt and cordial responses attested the earnestness with which he adopted the petitions addressed to the Throne of Grace.

"I have said that his piety pervaded his whole character. Three things particularly struck me as I observed him:

"1. His conscientiousness. He was called to fill a position where the trustees asked for but his name, willing to relieve him of any duty save that which he chose to assume. But he chose to be very laborious. Breakfasting at an early hour, he devoted his whole time to the interest of the pupils; and when it is remembered that there were three hundred and fifty young men under his supervision, it is manifest that his energies must have been seriously taxed. So deep was the interest which he took in the personal welfare of the students, that each one of this large number was known to him by name, and he was constantly carrying on an extensive correspondence with the patrons of the college in regard to their sons and wards.

"2. His humility was strikingly apparent. There was nothing in his demeanor to indicate that he considered himself anything more than an ordinary citizen. Some men of distinguished position never seem to lose sight of the fact themselves, and to exhibit to others such a demeanor that you would think they were anxious to remind their associates of their superiority; but no one would have inferred, from anything that was apparent in the bearing or conversation of General Lee, that he was in the company of a man who was admired and eulogized by millions.

"If any man in the country had reason to be proud, it was he. Descended from sires who filled conspicuous places in the early history of the republic, both in the cabinet and the field, graduating with the first honor from the highest military school in the country, the constant recipient of praise from multitudes, what a temptation to poor human nature to be puffed up and vain! But, in the midst of all the honors that were heaped upon him, he seemed wholly unconscious to any superior claims upon the consideration of his friends; and you never heard from him the remotest allusion indicating a self-complacent or proud temper.

"3. More beautiful still was his charity. The grace, which both Paul and Peter mentioned as a crowning excellence, was an obvious fruit of his piety. It is hard for men, who have been disappointed and overthrown, to suppress vindictive emotions toward the victors. Passion will occasionally rise to ebullition, and revengeful words will be spoken. But who ever heard a vindictive expression from Lee? I was with him in his own home, and conversed with him in all the freedom and familiarity of domestic intercourse, but I cannot recall a single word he ever uttered in denunciation of those against whom he fought for four years. The war closed, he seemed most desirous to heal the cruel breaches it had made. He refused to go to Gettysburg, last summer, as you remember, to participate in a service which proposed to preserve memorials of the war, declaring that all mementos of the unhappy strife should, as far as possible, be obliterated. A gentleman told me that, observing at the Springs, in Virginia, some persons from the North, who seemed to be wholly unacquainted with any of the guests, General Lee introduced himself to them, and then presented them to his friends. This little incident is an illustration of his charity. 'He that ruleth his spirit is mightier than he that taketh a city.' Some of the most illustrious conquerors of cities have been overthrown by their own passions. Tried by the divine test, he was a greater man than Cæsar or Alexander. His was the glorious sublimity of self-conquest. He wears, I doubt not, today, the crown which glittered to the eye of that Christian soldier who said, 'I have fought a good fight, I have finished my course, I have kept the faith, and now there is laid up for me a crown.' We mingle our tears over a common calamity, but the hand of Jesus has wiped the last tear from his eye. He has gone where 'the wicked cease from troubling, and the weary are at rest.'

"Young men! I hold up before you the lamented Lee for your imitation. Follow him as he followed Christ. You cannot acquire the military renown which he achieved. Few have the endowments which he possessed. None of you, probably, will ever see such an occasion of distinction as that which he knew. But you can imitate him in that which we now feel was his highest earthly glory, and which is the ground of his rejoicing in the skies. You can emulate his virtues, you can find, as did he, true greatness in true goodness. The crown which is bright for him, when all other laurels have faded, may, through a like faith, be that in which, living, *you* may exult, and, dying, *you* may glory."

A gentleman of New York has given the author several incidents confirmatory of statements made in the body of the volume which may be appropriately inserted here. During an intimate acquaintance with General Scott, this gentleman heard him speak frequently in the very highest terms of Colonel Robert E. Lee as a soldier and a Christian gentleman, but he remembers one occasion when in the course of a confidential interview he asked the direct question: "General, whom do you regard as the greatest living soldier?" Without hesitation, and with marked emphasis, General Scott replied: "*Colonel Robert E. Lee is not only the greatest soldier of America, but the greatest soldier now living in the world. This is my deliberate conviction, from a full knowledge of his extraordinary abilities, and, if the occasion ever arises, Lee will win this place in the estimation of the whole world.*" The general then went into a detailed sketch of Lee's services, and a statement of his ability as an engineer, and his capacity not only to plan campaigns, but also to command large armies in the field, and concluded by saying: "I tell you, sir, that *Robert E. Lee is the greatest soldier now living, and if he ever gets the opportunity he will prove himself the great captain of history.*"

About May 1, 1861, this same gentleman, accompanied by a Maryland Congressman, sought an interview with General Scott, for the purpose of getting a passport to Richmond to try and do something toward averting a resort to arms. In the course of this interview General Scott again passed the highest eulogy upon General Lee as a soldier and a man; stated the fact that the chief command of the United States Army had been tendered him just before he left Washington for Richmond; said that he would have given way most cheerfully if they could have persuaded Lee to accept it, and expressed himself as deeply regretting the loss to the country sustained in Lee's resignation. But, on the other hand, he felt confident that Lee would do everything in his power to avert the war, and would, if it came to a conflict of arms, conduct it on the highest principles of Christian civilization. He cheerfully granted the gentlemen a permit to go to Richmond, and said: "Yes! go and see Robert Lee. Tell him, for me, that we must have no war, but that we must avert a conflict of arms until the 'sober second thought' of *the people* can stop the mad schemes of *the politicians.*"

These gentlemen went to Richmond, and had a long interview with General Lee. He most cordially reciprocated the kindly feelings of General Scott, and expressed his ardent desire to avert war, and his willingness to do anything in his power to bring about a settlement of the difficulties.

But he expressed the fear that the passions of the people, North and South, had been too much aroused to yield to pacific measures, and that every effort at a peaceful solution would prove futile. Alluding to Mr. Seward's boast that he would conquer the South in "ninety days," and to the confident assertions of some of the Southern politicians that the war would be a very short one, General Lee said, with a good deal of feeling: "They do not know what they say. If it comes to a conflict of arms, the war will *last at least four years.* Northern politicians do not appreciate the determination and pluck of the South, and Southern politicians do not appreciate the numbers, resources, and patient perseverance of the North. Both sides forget that we are all *Americans,* and that it must be a terrible struggle if it comes to war. Tell General Scott that we must do all we can to avert war, and if it comes to the worst, we must then do everything in our power to mitigate its evils."

The lamented Colonel John B. Baldwin, of Staunton, who was one of the leaders of the Union Party in the Virginia Convention, but who (like General Early and others of his party), when the contest came, threw into the cause of

his native state his great intellect and untiring zeal, related the following incident, which may be appropriately given here: While acting as Adjutant General
of Virginia, and in the discharge of his duty to muster into the service new
recruits, Colonel Baldwin one day found in one of the companies twenty-five
or thirty youths under the prescribed age. He told them that he could not receive
them, under the regulations, and the brave boys were very much disappointed,
and clamored to see General Lee. Coming into the presence of the general, they
begged him to allow them to enlist, and promised that they would prove themselves worthy to march by the side of their fathers and elder brothers. General
Lee was very much affected by their appeal, but told them that he could not
receive them, that they must go home and take care of their mothers and sisters,
and that he would send for them when they were needed. After the young men
had left, General Lee said to Colonel Baldwin: "Those are beautiful boys, sir,
and I very much disliked to refuse them; but it will not do to allow boys to
enlist now. I fear we shall need them all before this war closes."

ADDRESS

ON THE CELEBRATION OF THE FIRST MEMORIAL ANNIVERSARY
AT WASHINGTON AND LEE UNIVERSITY, JANUARY 19, 1871
BY
JAMES P. HOLCOMBE, LL. D.,
OF VIRGINIA

INTRODUCTORY NOTE

The following Address is printed from the original manuscript of the author. When invited to furnish it for publication in the once projected MEMORIAL VOLUME, Mr. Holcombe undertook to revise and expand it for the press, but death arrested him in the midst of this labor of love. Yet the committee of publication were not willing to lose this beautiful tribute to General Lee, from one of the most accomplished orators of the South, and his family generously consented to place the unfinished manuscript at our disposal. It has been edited by careful and affectionate hands; yet it is only right to say that no printed oration can convey any idea of the fervor, the eloquence, and the charm of its delivery. The committee feel that the value of these memorials of Lee are enhanced by this touching memorial of the gifted and eloquent HOLCOMBE, whose untimely death is mourned by so many friends as a loss irreparable to the literature, the education, and the society of his native Virginia.

THE COMMITTEE OF THE FACULTY OF
WASHINGTON AND LEE UNIVERSITY.

ADDRESS

MR. PRESIDENT, AND GENTLEMAN OF THE FACULTY OF WASHINGTON AND LEE UNIVERSITY: I approach the duty which lies before me with unaffected diffidence and emotion. The living form of ROBERT E. LEE no longer graces the seat of honor in your assembly; but the inspiration of his spirit survives in this hall, which was the scene of his last labors, and the souls of a mourning people encircle, as with an ocean of love, that tomb which contains all that is left of him. No eloquence could find voice for the feelings which spring up within our bosoms on this immortal day, and upon this consecrated spot: feelings of grief at his loss, of reverence for his character, pride in his glory, gratitude for his services, thankfulness for his life, and devotion to his memory. Others will lay upon the altar of his fame those rich and abundant offerings which can alone satisfy the just measure of its requirements. Let my imperfect but willing service be supplied from the fullness of your recollections, and from the tenderness of your hearts.

A great life has closed—a life upon which the longer we linger the more we shall find to love and revere, for it was one over which virtue will scarce breathe a sigh, and to which fame could hardly add a chaplet. It was a life which, in every season, relation, and employment, was crowned with all that wins the affection and commands the homage of mankind. It was a life in which the fallen hero of a lost cause became the center of that admiring contemplation which is wont to follow the conqueror in his ovations; and in which achievements of arms as brilliant as ever blazoned a warrior's crest, or adorned a nation's story, were so ennobled by the exhibition of nobility of soul with which they were associated, that we almost lose sight of the soldier in gazing on the image of the grander MAN. It was a life which spanned the extremes of triumph and of calamity, but which was so transfigured by faith, hope, and charity, that its lines of suffering are even more lustrous than its lines of glory. If other lives have been sown more thickly with the glittering stars of human honor, or have rejoiced more abundantly in the gifts of earthly fortune, none have been more richly dowered with the love of man, or more divinely radiant with the beatitudes of God:

"There flowed from its mysterious urn a sacred stream, in whose calm
*   depths the beautiful and pure*
Alone were mirrored; which, though shapes of ill might hover round its
*   surface, rolled in light,*
And took no shadow from them."

Death, which withers the roses and flowers of kings, and lays in dust the pride and pomp of ambition, has no power over such a life but to touch it with lines of heaven, and seal it for immortality. On you, my countrymen, has descended, with a solemn emphasis of obligation, its sacred charge of fame. Accept this so gratefully, and guard it so piously, that the consolation, instruction, and blessing of this life, may reach not only the generation which it embraced, but all the generations which are to come. On our children and our children's children, on distant nations and remote ages, on that collective humanity which it has elevated and adorned, let the grand example shine. Let history inscribe it on unfading scrolls; let poetry embalm it in imperishable songs; let sculpture and painting pour round it their brightest inspiration; let eloquence on its successive anniversaries wake it, as with a trumpet of resurrection, to glory again; and on the undying echoes of tradition

"Let it roll from soul to soul,
And grow forever and forever!"

The county of Westmoreland is hallowed ground, for it contains two spots which men will tread with reverence to the end of time. The one is the birthplace of George Washington, the other of Robert E. Lee. The latter was born on the 19th of January, 1807, before the generation associated with the former in the most important labors of his life had passed away. It was the happy fortune of young Lee to be nursed on the breast of gentle manners, and to breathe from infancy the pure air of honor, patriotism, and virtue. His mother was a daughter of the family of Carter, long distinguished in the annals of our Virginia colony for the munificent application of large wealth to purposes of charity, learning, and religion. His father was a gentleman of ancient lineage, an illustrious patriot of the Revolution, an eminent soldier, and the historian of the struggle for independence in the South, the governor of this commonwealth, the lifelong personal and political friend of Washington, and the orator selected by the Congress of the United States to pronounce his eulogy. Robert, when only eleven years old, was deprived, by the death of his father, of paternal counsel and support. There is a single reference to him in the correspondence of the elder Lee, which, however trivial at the time, cannot be read now without melancholy pleasure. After some inquiries about other members of his family (for it was written while abroad), he adds: "Robert was always good, and in this happy turn of mind he will doubtless be confirmed by his ever-watchful and affectionate mother." And truly, through the diligent hand of that pious mother, did the Celestial Husbandman train the tender plant of his youthful nature, until it expanded into the full flower, and bore the golden fruitage of immortal virtue. At his mother's knee, that divinely appointed school, whose instruction no other teacher can impart, and whose lessons when faithfully given are worth all others we receive, he learned his obligations toward his Maker and his fellow man. Through her vigilant and loving care, he formed those habits of industry, economy, simplicity, punctuality, and scrupulous performance of duty, which distinguished him through life. With what devotion he repaid her tender solicitude may be imagined from her own words, when he was about leaving her for West Point: "How," she exclaimed to a friend, in an uncontrollable burst of emotion, "can I ever live without him? He has been son, daughter, protector—he has been all in all to me!" The child was father to the man; and in him, if ever, was realized the aspiration of the poet—that his days might be

"Bound each to each by natural piety."

In 1825 he received an appointment to West Point as a cadet from Virginia. The expense of his education was no bounty from the Federal government, but the payment of a debt to his native commonwealth, whose contributions to the Federal treasury entitled her to place a certain number of her sons at this public institution, and which were more than sufficient to defray every disbursement on their behalf. The golden hours of opportunity were not consumed in vicious indulgence, nor wasted in debasing sloth. So diligently was his time improved, that in one of the largest classes which had ever left the academy he graduated the first in military and the second in general standing. And so faithfully were the most exacting requirements of discipline observed that, during his term of four years, not a single demerit was attached to his name. Such was the presage of his future, as, crowned with the fairest laurels of youth, and arrayed in spotless robes, his Alma Mater presented him to his country. An early culture of the classics, prosecuted at least in the case of the Latin at intervals through life, had imparted to his mind a more liberal cast than can be communicated by the mathematical and scientific training of a purely military school; his faculties had been disciplined and strengthened, furnished with useful knowledge, and fitted for the discharge of the highest duties of his profession; his passions had been placed under the control of a purified reason, and his ambition consecrated to noble ends. Among the moral influences which were most operative in the formation of his character during this plastic period, three are conspicuous. The first was the social atmosphere in which he was born and raised. An old and settled society existed in Virginia, rich in the traditions of centuries, characterized by simplicity of manners, genial courtesy and hospitality, purity and refinement of domestic life, honor, dignity, manliness, and patriotism among public men, and a general and unaffected respect for religion, its officers and ministers. Robert E. Lee was early and deeply imbued with the tastes, sentiments, opinions, and habits of this society. Washington was not more truly its type and representative during that colonial and revolutionary period in which it still bore the shining impress of the aristocratic institutions of England, than was Lee of its later age of republican simplicity. The second was his own veneration for the character of Washington. The attachment of the elder Lee to Washington was almost idolatrous, and this mingled love and reverence descended to his children.

When Robert was very young, the family removed to Alexandria, and he became a frequent visitor at Arlington, where the memory of Washington was almost as much the genius of the place as at Mount Vernon. He grew up amid scenes which constantly recalled the Father of his Country, and in a social circle where the recollection of his virtues was yet fresh. It is not, therefore, surprising that this exalted character should have brooded as an ideal over the dreams and meditations of his youth. His modesty may have never permitted a statement which would have challenged such a comparison, but the impression was produced upon his classmates and early companions that it was the model upon which he was seeking to fashion his own character. In the simple yet manly tastes and habits, in the dignity of carriage which forbade too familiar approach, in the unequaled modesty, in the command of temper, in the noble self-restraint, in the impartial justice, in the inflexible adherence to truth, in the uniform and scrupulous discharge of duty, in the chastened ambition of young Lee, they saw reflected, as in the mirror of youth, the severe and majestic image of Washington. The last of these influences was a deep and abiding reverence for religion. He did not become a member of the church until after his return from Mexico; but his regular attendance upon its services, and the singular rectitude of his conduct, leave no doubt that he was seeking amid those temptations of ambition and pleasure, which assailed his opening manhood, to make the divine canon his supreme law, and to mold his character in accordance with that comprehensive precept of apostolic wisdom: "Whatsoever things are true, whatsoever things are honest, whatsoever things are just, whatsoever things are pure, whatsoever things are lovely, whatsoever things are of good report: if there be any virtue, if there be any praise, think on these things."

In 1832 he was married to Miss Mary Custis, the daughter of George Washington Parke Custis, who was the grandson of Mrs. Washington, the adopted son of Washington, and the last survivor of the household of Mount Vernon. He was thus brought still more closely within that gracious and hallowed influence which already like a tutelary genius overshadowed his life.

No event of historical significance marks his career until the commencement of the Mexican War. He had gradually risen to the rank of captain, discharging every duty that was assigned to him with a fidelity and distinction which were the earnest of larger fame. The Mexican War, like the Seven Years' War which preceded the Revolution, proved to be a training school of great soldiers. Captain Lee was attached to the engineer corps of the central army, and took part in that wonderful campaign from Vera Cruz to the capital of Mexico. His rank furnishes no measure either of the services which he rendered or of the confidence which was reposed in him. He was the favorite staff officer of General Scott, and the latter has been heard to say, on more than one occasion, that his success was owing in a great degree to the skill, valor, and undaunted energy of Robert E. Lee. His ability as an engineer led to the speedy reduction of Vera Cruz; a daring reconnoissance which he made for more than a mile in the rear of the enemy's lines contributed largely to the victory of Cerro Gordo;

his gallantry at Contreras in crossing at night, alone, and through the Mexican skirmishers, a lavafield almost impassable at any time, and doubly dangerous from recent floods, opened communication between the main body of the American army and an isolated command under General Smith, and thus secured the decisive triumph which followed on the morrow; and in the final struggle around the heights of Chapultepec, where he was severely wounded, his courage and endurance elicited the thanks of the commander-in-chief, and were rewarded by a third brevet of honor. Well might Scott refer to him as "Captain Lee, so constantly distinguished as well for daring as for felicitous conception and execution." It is no injustice to any of the brave men with whom he was associated to affirm that not one returned home around whose name had gathered such a halo of promise, while he was regarded in popular judgment as the noblest representative of our country's chivalry.

"From spur to plume, a star of tournament," the prescient eye of the commander-in-chief had discerned, and his generous tongue proclaimed, that "Lee was the greatest living soldier of America."

Shortly after the close of the war, Colonel Lee took upon himself the vow to fight manfully as Christ's soldier, a vow which was never forgotten nor disregarded until in the silence of a dying chamber his upward-pointing finger revealed the soul's hope and expectation of reward. Prosperous fortune had showered on him the choicest of earthly blessings, a loving family, troops of friends, large wealth, spotless fame, and a conscience void of offense toward God and man. But the horizon of his country was already darkening with the dread shadows of civil war. Opposing theories of constitutional construction and obligation, as well as of public policy, developed at the formation of the Constitution, after consuming more than half a century in fierce struggles for ascendency, were now being impelled on mighty tides of angry passion toward a bloody arbitrament. At the commencement of that awful drama in which he was to perform so great a part, Colonel Lee was with his regiment upon the Texan frontier. About the last of February 1861, he was summoned to Washington to sit on a board of officers convened to revise the regulations of the army. The signs of public excitement which he observed on his route to the capital, filled him with the liveliest fear of a hostile collision between the Confederate States and the United States. These apprehensions were expressed to General Scott at their first interview, coupled with the remark that in such an event his own position would become one of great delicacy. He was assured in reply that the government had no fears of such a result. After this conversation, his time was spent almost entirely with his family at Arlington. He had no further communication with General Scott, or any officer in the confidence of the president, as to his purposes and plans, until the commencement of hostilities, when he was informally tendered the command of the army of the United States in the field.

Virginia, although deeply moved by sympathy with her sister states of the South and by common wrongs, had clung to the Union in loyal hope, until the alternative was presented to her of taking part in the unnatural and unconstitutional war on communities sprung from her loins, or of receiving the first and deadliest shock of embattled legions upon her own unshielded bosom. In this hour of supreme peril she was faithful to principle and to honor. With a solemnity imposed by the full knowledge of her extreme danger, with a sorrow befitting the severance of so many bonds of friendship and of fame, but with the dignity of conscious rectitude, and with the fearless, grand resolve of freedom, she repealed the ordinance which had made her a member of the Federal Union, resumed her ancient independence, and summoning her children, wherever scattered, to her side, threw herself, with the shout of a king, along the path of invasion.

The voice of Virginia in distress did not fall unheeded upon the ear of Robert E. Lee. It pierced his bosom with the keenest anguish, for he loved the Union with a generous and passionate devotion. Had it been possible to close its yawning chasm by the sacrifice of his own life, no Roman Curtius could have leaped more freely into the gulf of death. But the Union around which were centered his affections and his obligations was not a consolidated Union, in which great communities, like his own mother commonwealth, were sunk to the level of petty counties, but a Federal Union between sovereign and equal states. The Union which he had sworn to serve had been dissolved by the power which brought it into existence; and its dissevered and exasperated sections were now gathering up their every energy for a deadly struggle. Bloody hands had rent in twain their fellowship of glory and communion of patriotism; and the government which yet claimed the name and flag of the Union was preparing to replace its ancient bonds of liberty and love—bonds woven by

celestial fingers, and consecrated by the holiest and tenderest recollections—with iron links of conquest forged in a fiery furnace of war. Could
any selfish or ignoble considerations have controlled Colonel Lee, he
would have remained in the Federal army. He was opposed to the policy
of secession. He had been through life a friend of emancipation. "If I
owned four million slaves," he had declared, "I would give them all for
the Union." His calm, prophetic judgment discerned that vast disparity in
resources, preparation, and all the elements of national military strength,
which imparted to the struggle from its commencement the character of
a forlorn hope. His own large property lay along the border, to become
the first spoils of Federal victory. The command of the army of the United
States, with the glittering perspective of that great prize which lies so close
to the topmost round in the ladder of an American soldier's fame, was
held up to his ambition. Colonel Lee's character did not permit him to
seek refuge from the perils and duties of the hour by occupying a position
of selfish neutrality. The great Italian poet has placed those who, during
the civil wars of Florence, sought escape from the dangers and responsibilities of citizenship by avoiding the discharge of its highest duty, in the
vestibule of his Inferno, as men who, having never truly lived, were disdained alike by Justice and by Mercy, and unworthy of even a passing
glance from mortal eye. This doom of scornful oblivion, pronounced in
undying verse, has been confirmed by the accordant sentiment of all suc-
ceeding ages. The only question which Colonel Lee considered was that
of comparative obligation; and this he weighed in heavenly balances, and
before the judgment seat of conscience. With a grief at parting from so
many cherished friends and associations, which in a nature so noble no
time could heal, but with a conviction of right so clear that the decision
never cost an after-pang of regret, and a resolution so firm that the world
could not have shaken it, he embraced the cause of his native commonwealth. "Our primal duties shine aloft like stars." There are universal and
irresistible instincts, sympathies, and principles, that bind us to the land
which is at once our birthplace and our home. As we grow in years, its
image becomes blended with all the hopes and fears, the loves and friend-
ships, the joys and sorrows of life. The heart fastens round it an allegiance
which no strain of time or of fate can part, but death alone unloose; and
if conscience had no vindictive sting, nor history any voice of enduring
reproach, with which to punish an apostate son, we might almost expect

the mute, insensate forms of Nature to burst into speech, and rebuke the degeneracy which in danger or misfortune could forsake or betray it.

I shall not pause in the house of his friends to justify this action on the part of Colonel Lee. It is pleasing to know, from one who was present when General Scott received the manly and pathetic letter which accompanied his resignation, that this great soldier, while expressing deep regret at the decision, gave emphatic utterance to his own conviction that it had been made under an imperative sense of duty. The opinions of Colonel Lee were those which had been entertained by the great body of the people of Virginia ever since the adoption of the Constitution. His own father, who was a member of the convention which ratified it, and of the party which placed on its powers the most liberal construction, had often avowed them. Doctrines far more extreme had been proclaimed by Jefferson and by Madison, yet the suffrages of the nation had afterward raised these great patriots to the highest offices within its gift. A New England President, Mr. John Quincy Adams, in referring to their opinions, had used this language before the House of Representatives: "Holding the converse with a conviction as firm as an article of religious faith, I see too clearly to admit of denial that minds of the highest order of intellect, and hearts of the purest integrity of purpose, have been brought to different conclusions."

No great question of politics or of ethics has ever agitated mankind, upon which wise and good men have not been almost equally divided. In ages of bigotry and ignorance, the triumphant party punished its adversaries with confiscation, torture, the dungeon, the axe, or the stake. A larger toleration of differences of opinion has been the surest index of advancing civilization; and the time must come when all will recognize the great truth that the moral character of individuals cannot be measured by the standards of a creed which they disown; that the highest virtue is confined to no sect or party; and that men who, under a common impulse of duty, have been led by honest yet conflicting judgments to range themselves under hostile banners, may still be united by the higher and immortal bond of equal fidelity to principle. Hampden and Falkland, although the one poured out his blood for the commonwealth, and the other for the king, are alike enshrined at this day in the love and reverence of England. The sentiment that "treason should be made odious," wise and just in its proper place, has no application, in morals or public law, to a civil strife between two great sections of a people, springing from ancient differences of opinion as to their constitutional relations. Ideas cannot be slain by the sword; and a frank and loyal acceptance of all the requirements of the situation has wrought no shadow of change in our convictions of truth and right. The language of Lee himself, about two years before his death, expresses the universal sentiment of the Southern people. "I did nothing more," he observed to General Hampton, "than my duty required of me; I could have taken no other course without dishonor; and, if all were to be done over again, I should act in precisely the same manner." The "married calm" of the state can never be restored without a fuller measure on all sides of that large-hearted charity which is able to recognize and revere the strength and purity of an adversary's principles. And every attempt to dishonor us by attaching to our representative heroes the degradation of crime, will only serve, by prolonging the worst oppressions of conquest, to perpetuate its deepest resentments. I know not how long men may be found who shall refuse reverence to the great character of Robert E. Lee, in consequence of his participation in our struggle for independence—a struggle in which, if we erred, we were misled by splendid illusions of liberty and virtue. But I do know that no calumny can darken his fame, for History has lighted up his image with her everlasting lamp; that no malice can profane his tomb, for the whole earth has become his sepulchre; and that no power can hush that funeral march which followed him to the grave, and yet fills the world with the music of sorrow, for it is beaten by the loving pulses of the stricken hearts of his countrymen.

Colonel Lee became, by the acceptance of his resignation, a private citizen of Virginia. The command of her military and naval forces was at once tendered to him, a position which he did not feel at liberty to decline. He was received by her convention, then in session, with imposing ceremony. The person and bearing of General Lee would have riveted the gaze of any circle: a form combining, in admirable proportion, strength with grace; a grave and lofty carriage; an air of mingled modesty and command; regular but expressive features; hair whose dark locks were just silvered by the first frosts of life's maturest season; a brow on which dignity and honor sat enthroned; an eye——

"The limpid mirror of a stately soul,
Sweet to encourage, steadfast to control,

From which subjected hosts might draw,
As from a double fountain, love and awe."

The president of the convention, Mr. Janney, a patriot of the old Roman stamp, in whom were fitly represented the mature wisdom and deliberate virtue of the commonwealth, welcomed him to a hall where could almost still be heard the echoes of the voices of the statesmen and soldiers of bygone days who had borne his name, and whose blood was now flowing in his veins. After some eloquent words of patriotic reminiscence, and of appropriate reference to the achievements which had pointed to him as the fit depositary of this great trust, Mr. Janney closed by saying that his mother, Virginia, had placed her sword in his hands on condition that it should be drawn only in her defense, and with the expectation that he would rather fall with it than see the object fail for which it was unsheathed. General Lee replied in a manner marked by the deepest solemnity: "Trusting in Almighty God, an approving conscience, and the aid of my fellow citizens, I devote myself to the service of my native state." How faithfully and how gloriously that pledge was redeemed let the great sentence of history, the applause with which the world rang, and the tears and benedictions of his countrymen, this day proclaim!

His services during the first year of the war were comparatively obscure and undistinguished—the organization of the Virginia troops, the direction of the coast defenses in South Carolina and Georgia, and a campaign in western Virginia, which, although it arrested the advance of General Rosecrans, was indecisive, and not commensurate with public expectation. But the period was marked by many incidents which revealed to those with whom he was brought in intimate contact the exalted patriotism and noble magnanimity of his character. No opportunity was afforded for the display of his great military genius until the beginning of June 1862, when General Johnston, his illustrious predecessor in the command of the Army of Northern Virginia, was disabled by a wound, and Lee was assigned to the vacant position. The limits of this discourse do not allow any detailed narrative of the subsequent history of that army; but a record of more heroic valor, directed by more consummate skill to the defense of a people's liberties, cannot be found in the annals of war. A trivial accident on the day of battle may sometimes defeat the wisest combinations of genius, and bestow the favors of fortune where they are least merited. But where a series of general engagements, all sanguinary and extending over different campaigns, take place between opposing armies drawn from the same martial race, one army being always superior to the other in numbers, arms, equipment, and artillery, and commanded by a succession of distinguished soldiers, and the inferior force, under a single leader, in every great conflict either inflicts ignominious defeat on its adversary, or repels attack with prodigious loss, or, where some strong position has fought against it, delivers so stunning a blow that its subsequent gage of battle is not accepted, the conclusion is inevitable that the transcendent ability of the commander, or the inspiration of a higher principle with the soldiery, or both, must have redressed the unequal balance of the war, and turned the scales of victory. And such, without any reference to its previous brilliant achievements under Beauregard and Johnston, was the history of the Army of Northern Virginia under General Lee, from June 1862, to the commencement of the winter of 1864 and 1865, when it was no longer that army, except in name. In June, 1862, after a struggle of seven days, it forced the Army of the Potomac, under McClellan, then almost in sight of the spires of Richmond, cowering back to the shelter of their gunboats at Harrison's Landing. In August, after three days of severe fighting, it hurled the Federal troops under Pope in rout and panic into the fortifications around Washington. Having crossed the Potomac in the grand but delusive hope of lifting up downtrodden Maryland, it met McClellan, in September, at Sharpsburg, possessed by accident of the inappreciable advantage of a knowledge of its own movements and position, and with a superiority of numbers greater than either Frederick the Great or Napoleon, in any extremity of their fortune, ever encountered, and maintaining intact, at every point, the integrity of its lines, it repelled his fearful and repeated attacks with immense slaughter. In December, at Fredericksburg, the mighty hosts of Burnside recoiled, shattered and demoralized, from its blows. In the following May, at Chancellorsville, it so chastised the insolence of Hooker, that he was compelled to seek safety for his beaten army by precipitate retreat, in the darkness of a stormy night, across the protecting stream of the Rappahannock. In June, advancing into Pennsylvania, it was attended by its usual current of success, until, assailing the almost impregnable heights of Cemetery Hill at Gettysburg, its inadequate force suffered a bloody repulse; but standing defiantly at bay, it challenged a renewal of the combat again and again, which its enemy was afraid to deliver. In the next spring, when Grant was called from the West "to fight the Army of the Potomac to its utmost capacity, and close the war as with a peal of thunder," its worsted but high-hearted columns received the masses of fresh troops which were hurled on them in succession from the Wilderness to Cold Harbor with such bloody welcome that, when an order was given, at the latter place, for a general advance along the entire front, not a soldier moved, and the whole immobile line presented silent but emphatic protest against further carnage.

"It will be difficult," General Lee wrote, while collecting materials for the history of these campaigns, "to make the world believe the odds against which we fought." The great victories of Marlborough were won with numbers in general about equal to those of his adversaries. In only one of Wellington's glorious Peninsular battles was the disparity between the French and English as much as two to one. At Leuthen, the relative inferiority of the Prussians more nearly approached that of the Confederates (and that has been regarded as the very masterpiece of military art)—the great Frederick executed one of those brilliant movements which the nature of the country never permitted in Virginia, and by which, with thirty thousand men, he defeated an army of eighty thousand before the latter could change the formation of its line of battle. The Federal superiority at Sharpsburg was as three to one; at Chancellorsville and Fredericksburg it was nearly the same; at Gettysburg it was more than three to two; in the campaign of the Wilderness it began with three to one; and, but for the slaughter which deprived General Grant of a third of his command, his reinforcements would have increased it to four to one. Under the cloud of misrepresentations which enveloped our character and institutions before the war, the world had begun to believe that the people of the South were degenerate from the strain of their great fathers, and that we needed

> "The influence of a Northern star
> To string our nerves, and steel our hearts to war."

Never was the manhood of a people more gloriously vindicated, nor the strength which lies in the love of liberty more grandly displayed, than in this campaign between Lee and Grant. Not in one battle, but in a series of desperate engagements from the 5th of May to the 10th of June, and along a line of seventy miles in extent, did the two armies wrestle for victory in deadly strife; Lee having forty thousand men on the first day, increased subsequently by eleven thousand, and Grant one hundred and thirty thousand on the first day, with reinforcements to the amount of sixty thousand. Lee assumed the offensive whenever his adversary appeared in the open field. Each availed himself as far as possible of the cover which was furnished by the nature of the ground, and improvised breastworks; and yet, with these tremendous odds against him, Lee disabled a larger number of his enemy's force than his own entire strength, and compelled an abandonment of the line which he had selected for his advance upon Richmond, and almost destroyed the *morale,* not only of his great army, but of the great people whose cause it represented. "So gloomy was the military outlook," writes the Federal historian, Mr. Swinton, "and to such a degree, by consequence, had the moral spring of the public mind become relaxed, that there was at this time great danger of a collapse of the war. The history of this conflict, truthfully written, will show this. Had not success elsewhere come to brighten the horizon, it would have been difficult to have raised new forces to recruit the Army of the Potomac, which, shaken in its structure, its valor quenched in blood, and thousands of its ablest officers killed and wounded, was the Army of the Potomac no more."

There is no campaign in history which more completely establishes the prowess of an army or the skill of its leader. That of Napoleon, when the allies invaded France, is one of the two on which his military fame will always securely rest. But the allies, with a superiority of numbers scarcely greater than that of Grant over Lee, and with no such advantages of transportation and military material of every form as the Federal army possessed, were able, in the course of the two months of February and March, to enter Paris in triumph. The close of the two months of May and June found Grant sitting down to the siege of Petersburg without an achievement which could add to his own fame, or reflect luster upon the mighty host of brave men whose blood had been so freely poured out in obedience to his orders.

The strength of the Army of Northern Virginia was never broken in battle. No crowning victory like that of Leipsic or Waterloo gilds the banners of its adversary. It did not achieve the independence of its country, but it fought with a fierce, avenging courage which has made the soil of Virginia from the mountains to the sea one vast monument—

"Where Death and Glory an eternal Sabbath keep."

It was not until wasted by that "process of attrition" through which overwhelming numbers and resources have in all ages at length subdued the free and brave; not until thinned and enfeebled by disease, privation, and famine; not until broken in heart by the accumulation of disasters in other quarters, for which it was not responsible, but which left it no reck of help or hope, that its long line of glory was closed; and then without a memory to awaken in its own bosom a sense of shame, or give to the tongue of its foe a boast of pride.

General Lee was the idol of his army. The sagacity, as unerring as an instinct, with which he divined the purposes of the enemy, and the fertility of resource with which he formed combinations to foil them, the cheerfulness with which he shared their privations, and the solicitude he ever manifested for the supply of their wants, inspired a confidence which no misfortune was ever able to shake, and a devotion which has never grown cold but in the grave. I have neither ability nor inclination to offer any criticism upon his military character. It is an axiom among the great masters of military science that no man has ever made war without committing mistakes. The failures of Lee, wherever they occurred, may be traced, not to any defect in his own plans, but to the inefficiency of subordinates, the want of resources, or to obstacles which no power at his disposal could have removed. It is not an uncommon opinion to attribute to him the extreme caution which fits for defensive rather than the bold and enterprising genius that delights in offensive war. But a study of his campaigns, from his first movement against McClellan to the last which preceded the evacuation of Petersburg, will disclose a strategist as daring as ever rode in the whirlwind or directed the storm of battle. It was this audacity of temper, joined to a confidence without limit in his troops, which led to the single disaster of his military life, that of Gettysburg; and, even there, had the storming column been properly sustained, the supreme hardihood of the enterprise would have been crowned with success.

Not the "Six Hundred," my countrymen, better deserve the meed of immortal renown than those brave heroes of Gettysburg; nor, in proportion to their respective numbers, did Death reap at Balaklava a ghastlier harvest than on Cemetery Hill. The Six Hundred rode, at swift cavalry-gallop, for twelve hundred yards, into the Russian batteries, with cannon to right and to left and in front of them, and sabered the men at their guns. This division of Confederate infantry marched for nearly a mile across an open field, exposed to the most destructive fire of musketry and artillery, not with the quick step of an effervescing enthusiasm, but with the measured tramp of disciplined courage; steadily, through a plunging storm of the missiles of destruction, they climbed the hill; they cleared the rifle-pits, and, leaping on the breastworks, planted with exultant shouts their glorious battle-flags; for some minutes, "like eagles with bloody plume," they stood triumphant on the crest of battle; but, alas! the covering and supporting columns were not equal to this heroic devotion, and the only fruit of their valor was a memory to their country which, through all the ages of time, will never grow dim.

Not military strategy, but the necessities of the political situation, kept General Lee and his army in the trenches around Petersburg. The proper authorities had been informed that he could not, with thirty-one thousand men, his whole strength, hold lines of thirty miles in extent; and that, without reinforcement, he would soon be unable to move from them. They had been unable to furnish this aid, or even the provisions which were necessary to keep the men in a physical condition to perform their duty. The sense of humanity, rising superior even to the love of liberty, had induced them to divide the wholly insufficient rations of our own army with the Federal prisoners whom they had proposed in vain to restore without equivalent, but who had been left by their own government, when we were known to be in a condition bordering on famine, to share the horrors of our situation. After a long and skillful concealment of this extreme weakness, the fatal blow was struck, and evacuation became unavoidable. When General Lee reached Amelia Courthouse, and found that the supplies which he had ordered to be collected at that point, the last gift of their country to his perishing troops, had been sent, through some official blunder, to Richmond, the necessary dispersion in search of food left scarcely a ray of hope that his worn and straggling columns could be concentrated again for effective service. Thousands of brave men dropped on the road through sheer exhaustion from want of rest and food; thousands more were cut off in detachments too small to present a front to the foe, until only eight thousand, completely enveloped in the toils of the hunter, remained to hold up the flag of their country at Appomattox. To those eight thousand, who, without hope, but without fear, proved faithful to the last, as ready in the agony of despair as under the exhilaration of triumph to die for liberty, that country, in her heart of hearts, will ever render unspeakable homage. Let us not deceive ourselves; let not our tender memories glide into deceitful hopes; let us bow without question or murmur to that inscrutable Providence which fills the ages with its mighty work of reconstruction, and is ever evolving, from the wrecks of old societies, the fairer forms of new; and let us labor frankly and loyally for the stability, liberty, and glory of the government which, after this great appeal of arms, we have accepted. But let us never fail to vindicate our fidelity to the Constitution which our fathers framed, or, spurning the heathen sentiment that a cause is consecrated by success, to defend the fame of the brave men who upheld the principles of that Constitution with such unfaltering constancy. We do not mourn as those who weep by dishonored graves; for the faith, courage, and devotion to liberty, of our Confederate dead have, like the beauty of Juliet, made the tomb itself

"A feasting presence, bright with light."

Their example is more precious to us by far than all the material wealth we have sacrificed in the struggle. The great race to which we belong has often kindled its hope and courage from fields of disaster, where the brave have fallen in defense of their principles with no stain upon their names. The fatal day at Roncesvalles furnished to European chivalry its noblest battle-song. The great fight at Hastings was begun by a Norman minstrel, who

> *"Chanted, lustily and loud, the strain*
> *Of Roland and of Charlemagne;*
> *And the dead who deathless all*
> *Fell at famous Roncesvalles!"*

In many lands, O Freedom! lie thy everlasting springs. But upon no spot of earth—not on the plains of Marathon nor in the unconquered Gulf of Salamis, not at Bannockburn or Morgarten, not at Bunker Hill or at Yorktown—hast thou unsealed fountains of inspiration purer or more unfailing than upon those heights of Gettysburg, where sleep our yet unsepulchred dead, and those fields of Appomattox, where gathered round Lee the unterrified remnant of our living braves. Such lives were too precious to be thrown away in unavailing sacrifice, and but one melancholy duty remained to their leader. With what agony that duty shook his soul, may be inferred from the exclamation which even his stern self-control could not suppress: "I would rather die a thousand deaths!" Indeed, the temptation seems most powerfully to have assailed his heroic spirit to ride along the lines to find a soldier's grave. "But, then," as he said to Gordon, "what will become of the women and children of the South? It is our duty to live." Yes, by a sacrifice nobler than death, live!—live, to pour into the bosoms of your countrymen a reviving tide of hope; live, to exhibit to the world the glory of magnanimous suffering; live, to illustrate, by sublime example, your own immortal sentiment, that "human virtue should be equal to human calamity." Over the mournful incidents of that closing scene, incidents which our people will never read except through dimming tears, I drop the veil. But none could have been brought in contact with him in that dark hour of the soul's crucifixion, and have beheld the majesty with which his spirit rose triumphant above the weakness of the flesh, the steadiness with which his gaze was bent through all the spectral gloom which enveloped the path of duty, and the fixed purpose which he manifested to follow it

"Through the long gorge to the far light,"

without feeling the truth of the almost inspired lines of the poet, that

"Virtue could see to do what Virtue would,
By her own radiant light, though sun and moon
Were in the flat sea sunk."

Whither now, O world-renowned hero! will you direct your footsteps? Will you carry to foreign courts that sword which in any service can command dignity and affluence? Will you seek in the excitement of a fresh career amid new scenes to forget the sorrows of the past, and to fill other lands with the fame of illustrious deeds?

No; you have never lived for pleasure, for ambition, or for self; you have no thought nor feeling which is not turned to your country. Come what may, be it poverty and reproach, be it confiscation and disfranchisement, be it the dungeon or the gibbet, to the edge of doom you will share the fortunes of your people! The benignant skies which bent above your boyhood shall arch your grave; and, if no other record attests your virtues, your enemies themselves must inscribe upon your tomb the Christian patriot's most fitting epitaph:

"True to the kindred points of heaven and home."

General Lee, after mature deliberation as to his future course, accepted the presidency of Washington College. He could have obtained a more lucrative position, but none so congenial to his taste, or in which he thought he could render more service to his country. And in what sphere could the highest wisdom and virtue be more worthily employed? He applied himself with characteristic energy to the mastery and discharge of his new duties. It was not long before every teacher and every pupil felt the quickening influence of his presence. The discipline of the college was invigorated, and made that of a Christian family; its schools were increased, its course of studies enlarged; its facilities for instruction multiplied; new and admirable provisions introduced in its organization, designed to avoid alike the mischiefs of the close curriculum and the abuses incident to a purely elective system; and a spirit of energy, fidelity, and liberal ambition, infused into its whole administration. Suns seem larger at their setting, and no chapter in General Lee's life has appeared to me grander than its close. Cheerfully, patiently, laboriously, with no regret at being withdrawn from the world's eye, with no ambition foreign to his work, but with a devotion as single as if on this alone he was to build his fame, did he dedicate himself to the youth of his country. Most fortunate they who heard the lessons of honor, patriotism, and piety, from his lips! May the precepts be as fruitful as the example is immortal! And may the College of Washington, now doubly hallowed as the university of Lee, never fail the patriotic hope and expectation which gave it birth, and now have raised it to the skies, but ever remain a generous nursery of learning and virtue, and an increasing benefaction to the world through the years to come! But our indebtedness to General Lee for his services since the war is not to be measured by the extent of his influence as the president of Washington College. The cheerfulness with which he endured the privations, and the silent dignity with which he submitted to the mortifications of adverse fortune, the resolution with which he laid aside the depressing memories of the past, and the energy with which he applied himself to the duties of the present hour, were of inappreciable value in reviving the almost extinguished spirit of the country. The rapidity with which France recovered from the desolating civil wars of the sixteenth century was ascribed, by Burke, to the fact that a noble pride and a generous ambition still survived in the people. In the fellowship and communion of Lee's great example we have learned to feel that misfortune involves no loss of self-respect, that men cannot be dishonored unless they dishonor themselves, that no conqueror can impose fetters upon the soul, and that, cherishing every lofty aspiration, practicing every manly faculty, and grasping every opening opportunity, we should shield ourselves with hope, bear nobly whatever Providence may ordain, and drink strength from the cup of calamity itself. The poet, moralizing upon the fall of other republics, and the brevity of the period in which a state may be destroyed as compared with that in which it can be formed, asks the question, as if it admitted of no reply,

> *"Can man its shattered splendor renovate,*
> *Recall its glories back, and vanquish time and fate!"*

Prussia after Jena, France after the triumphant invasion of 1813, and Sardinia after the Revolution of 1848, have shown us that nations may find in the very depths of their fall the elements of their recovery. It is more through the influence of General Lee than of any other human agency that we expect to furnish another example of a community rising the stronger from those storms of fate which laid it prostrate for a time. In that dawn of hope which breaks around us, we hail the approaching day. This old commonwealth, which, after filling the horizon of history so long with its meshes of golden light, had sunk into the womb of darkness, shall

> *". . . anon repair its drooping head*
> *And trick its beams, and with new-spangled ore*
> *Flame in the forehead of the morning sky."*

But a mighty sorrow was wearing away the springs of life. Grief over the lost cause, sympathy with the sufferings of his old soldiers and their families, solicitude for the future of our people, were fast breaking down a constitution which Nature and temperate habits had destined for robust old age. Kossuth, on visiting the tomb of Washington, is said to have burst into tears. "He saved *his* country," exclaimed the Hungarian patriot; "I could not save *mine!*" A similar anguish brought Lee to the grave. For nearly two years premonitions of declining health had saddened our hearts, but no warning could prepare us for the shock of his death. When the tidings flashed along the wires that Lee too had crossed over the river, and was resting with Jackson under the shade of the trees, there went up from earth the wailing voice of millions, who mourned the loss of father, friend, examplar, guide. But, upon the ear of Christian faith, there broke another strain, the jubilant anthem of everlasting peace, in sounding welcome from choral seraphim: "Blessed are the dead which die in the Lord . . . they rest from their labors, and their works do follow them."